MW00857247

THE PRODUCT OF OUR SOULS

THE PRODUCT OF OUR SOULS

*Ragtime, Race, and the Birth
of the Manhattan Musical Marketplace*

DAVID GILBERT

The University of North Carolina Press   Chapel Hill

© 2015 The University of North Carolina Press
All rights reserved
Set in Miller by codeMantra, Inc.
Manufactured in the United States of America
The paper in this book meets the guidelines for permanence and durability
of the Committee on Production Guidelines for Book Longevity of the Council on
Library Resources. The University of North Carolina Press has been a member
of the Green Press Initiative since 2003.

Jacket illustration: James Reese Europe's Society Orchestra. Photographs and
Prints Division, Schomburg Center for Research in Black Culture, New York Public
Library, Astor, Lenox, and Tilden Foundations.

Library of Congress Cataloging-in-Publication Data
Gilbert, David W. (David Walker), 1975– author.
The product of our souls : ragtime, race, and the birth of the
Manhattan musical marketplace / David Gilbert.
pages cm
Includes bibliographical references and index.
ISBN 978-1-4696-2269-9 (cloth : alk. paper) —
ISBN 978-1-4696-2270-5 (ebook)
1. African Americans—New York (State)—New York—Music—
History and criticism. 2. Ragtime music—New York (State)—New York—
History and criticism. 3. Ragtime music—Social aspects—New York (State)—
New York—History—20th century. 4. Music and race—New York (State)—
New York—History—20th century. 5. African American musicians—
New York (State)—New York. I. Title.
ML3479.G55 2015
780.89'9607307471—dc23
2014030758

For

My parents, Kathy and Jess,

And my sisters, Katie and Lizzy

Contents

Map and Figures

Acknowledgments

A historian's work takes place at innumerable desktops, both literal and metaphorical, and I have had an abundance of opportunities to work at the desks of many brilliant and generous scholars. This work, a communal effort in every way, is truly the product of many souls. David Schmitz, Tom Davis, and Dave Glenn introduced me to historical analysis, critical theory, and jazz harmony as an undergrad at Whitman College. For many years, I've been building on the skills they taught me and the interests they helped me develop, even if they most likely did not imagine I would continue in their footsteps. In this way, too, I entered graduate school before I knew it, sitting at the desks of Tim Tyson, Craig Werner, and Steve Kantrowitz for brief and casual chats. Yet at the University of Wisconsin–Madison, Tim made me into a historian. He showed me how to research, and he tried to teach me how to write. Most of all, Tim taught me how much fun a historian's life could be and how much work it took to enjoy it. Craig teaches by example. Rigorous and kind, helpful and prodding, he improves the community around him simply by being a part of it. Recently, a new addition to my extended family told me that, in college in the 1970s, Craig's father—a liberal arts professor of economics—taught her "how to be." Remarkably, this trait must have rubbed off on Dr. Werner's kin because that is exactly what Craig offers his friends and students—lessons in being. As I transitioned out of the Afro-American Studies Department and into history, Steve took me in as a roughly hewn form and continued to chisel away, hoping to find a historian underneath the craggy stone. In the process, he sculpted my historical curiosity more than he knows, and I remain deeply indebted for his attention and his aid.

Nan Enstad shaped and reshaped every idea I've ever had regarding this project. Always in my corner, Nan's queries and criticisms resound on every page, and I would never have written this work without her patience and her insight. My many visits to her coffee-table desks always filled me with encouragement, even when it took me years to understand the depth of her suggestions. Ron Radano's desk, too, has been open to me for years. Ron first introduced me to James Reese Europe's music in my second semester of graduate school, and I've been working on that term paper ever since. How lucky I have been to meet at the crosshairs of Nan's and Ron's research interests, one in history, the other in music—both aiming straight down the middle of the most pressing tensions in U.S. history and culture. I arrived to Will Jones's desk late, but I am certainly glad I did. His suggestions and deep reading—right up until the end—challenged every aspect of my research, and he propelled me into new directions that I would not have conceived but for his help. These scholars have worked with me years after I officially left their tutelage. Their desks remain open to me, and I have continued to work by the light of their lamps.

By far the most frequent desks I visited while working on this project belonged to my friends and community in Madison. In and out of class, Zoë Van Orsdol, Kori Graves, Holly McGee, Jerome Dotson, Heather Stur, Michelle Gordon, Story Matkin-Rawn, Adam Malka, Mark Goldberg, Matt Blanton, Joe Fronczak, Dave LaCroix, Marc Hertzman, Wayne (& Wax) Marshall, and Todd Courtenay shaped my intellectual development in more ways than they could imagine. Together, as we often were in our moments of leisure, this cohort of historians and cultural theorists ignited my curiosity and taught me countless new ways to understand the world. As I began to finalize the manuscript, some friends from Madison made extreme efforts to stay in touch with my work, even though we no longer shared a zip code. Tyina Steptoe, Brenna Greer, and Ryan Quintana read multiple chapters, often grasping on to little allusions of mine and transforming them into outright arguments. Charles Hughes read and reread many pages of the work at various stages along the way, and some of the best phrases in the manuscript are his. I also thank the music students in Ron Radano's graduate seminars who critiqued and improved this project over the years: Matt Sumera, Scott Carter, Griff Rollefson, Katie Graber, and Fritz Schenker.

Along the way, I have had the good fortune to work at the desks of some of the most notable institutions in the country. A fellowship at the Smithsonian Institution's National Museum of American History (NMAH) not only granted me access to archival collections and phonograph recordings but also sustained me during important months of writing. Even more important, however, was the friendship I cultivated with Pete Daniel. Weekly meetings with Pete impressed on me the need to have confidence in what we write and to ensure that our message means something beyond academia. Pete also has a beautiful writing desk, and some of my best pages took their form during the weeks I got to house-sit for him. At the NMAH, I also worked with John Hasse, Deborra Richardson, and Stacey Kluck, who pushed me to expand my research into new areas and helped me secure important sources for the manuscript. Joellen ElBashir, at Howard University's Moorland-Spingarn Research Center, also helped me find a number of sources that I otherwise would not have located. I must also thank the librarians at the New York Public Library for the Performing Arts and the Schomburg Center for Research in Black Culture. Paul Friedman, especially, helped me every time I saw him, and his interest in my project continues to this day. Thanks as well to the University of Wisconsin for a dissertation fellowship that helped me complete my research, and to Lenoir-Rhyne University, whose Lineberger Multicultural Studies Scholar-in-Residence position helped me complete my revisions and introduced me to a terrific group of students. Special thanks to Veronica McComb and Rand Brandes, whose desks at LR were always open to me as well.

This book would have never developed without help from UNC Press. Mark Simpson-Vos saw promise in my early drafts, and his recommendations dramatically shaped the scope of the book. I had two anonymous readers who pushed me to expand my focus and tighten the arguments. I am deeply indebted to these two scholars, and I thank them for helping me better conceptualize my own arguments. Karl Miller also read pages during the editing process, and I thank him for reinforcing that I was on the right track.

My lifelong friend, Kyle Sanna, offered his writing desk to me on many occasions. Having a nice place to write in New York City is no easy convenience, and many times, over many years, Kyle's desk was my favorite place to work. Kyle and I met the first day of seventh-grade geography class, and we started playing guitar together the next semester. My entire life I have looked up to him as a musician and philosopher. To enter his world in our thirties, to take part in his richly creative life, to become friends with his community of downtown musicians, and to play music together again, was a joy unparalleled. For Kyle and his various bandmates—Mathias Künzli, Ben Campbell, John Hadfield, Uri and Maya Sharlin, Raimundo Penaforte, Aaron Brown, Matt Kanelos—I have deep respect and gratitude. Other folks in New York that sustained me during this project include Blue Minor Young, Anna Truxes, and Stefan Ebaugh, with whom I was able to reconnect after years—and in Stefan's case, decades—of distance. Finally, I want to thank Claude Coleman Jr. and his band, Amandla, who took me around the country a few times in a funky van and helped subsidize my New York rent with gig money.

Additional thanks needs to go to a group of local Madison musicians, all of whom I have known since I was a kid. Their knowledge and interest, combined with their daily experiences as masters of American popular music, compelled me to tell a story that reflected their understandings of music and life. Roger Brotherhood taught me everything I know about listening and improvisation, and my education continued years after all the guitar lessons. Steve Morgan taught me barre chords and showed me how to make the enjoyment of music a lifelong endeavor. Bruce Ayers introduced me to sophisticated music and cultural criticism alongside obscure blues, jazz, and punk artists. Catfish Stephenson's lived experience as a master of the country blues impressed on me that what I was learning from the (right) history books was reflective of a world that made sense outside of the academy. Brad Pregeant and Lynnea Godfriaux, two New Orleans musicians transplanted to the Rocky Mountains via Madison, have helped me understand the sound, form, and art of ragtime music, while reminding me it's just one of many styles that we should all play. My bandmates over the years, in and out of Wisconsin: Jud Sojourn, Dan O'Brien, Matt Nafranowicz, Ben Wolf, Matt Weber, Jim Marshall, Max Waldner, C Scott, Danny Tetrault, Brian Grasso, Jon Lauterer, and Mikes Murf, Becker, and Sule. The music you have all helped me create has been an immensely necessary outlet—I never would have completed this book without the constant reminders of how important music is. Tony Martinelli, though not a musician, offered his desk to me on numerous occasions, and I composed some of my favorite pages there in Seattle.

My parents, Kathy and Jess Gilbert, have been exceptionally helpful every step of the way. My dad nearly single-handedly molded me into the type of person who would enjoy meeting Tim, Craig, and Steve in those years before grad school. At the same time, my mother generated all the support, goodwill, and love that motivated me to work through the writing process. I am writing the words now at the desk of her father. My sisters, Katie and Liz, and their wonderful families have been terrifically encouraging, and I look forward to them reading this book. I am also fortunate to have two historians in my extended family. My father's sister, Barbara, taught me the importance of a good story; and my mother's brother, Tom, taught me how to critically engage all that we hear, read, and assume. This book is the product of my family, which has supported me in every way all my life.

My greatest thanks goes to Maia Surdam for all she has inspired and given to me. A righteous scholar herself, she has brought light into my life in ways I never imagined possible. From near and far, Maia has often directed me, and this book only slightly reflects all she has enabled me to do through her caring, intensity, and historical mind. I feel so extremely fortunate to have shared her writing desk and her love of music and adventure these many years.

THE PRODUCT OF OUR SOULS

Midtown Manhattan, ca. 1910

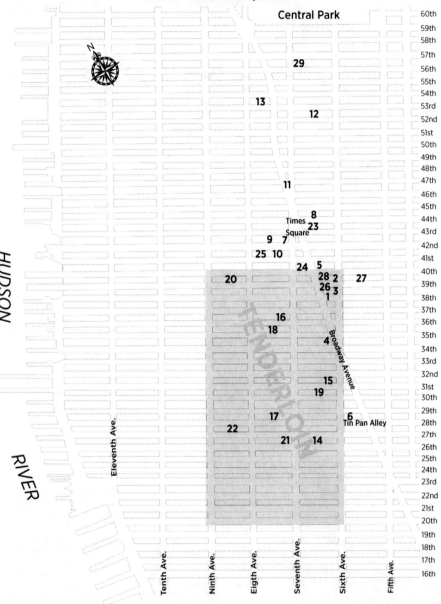

1. The Casino Theatre
2. The Maxine Eliot Theatre
3. The Knickerbocker Theatre
4. Koster and Bial's Music Hall
5. Empire Theatre
6. Proctor's Theatre
7. Hammerstein's Victoria Theatre
8. The Belasco Theatre
9. The Republic Theatre
10. The New Amsterdam Theatre
11. Palace Theatre
12. The Hotel Marshall
13. The Hotel Maceo
14. Ike Hines's Professional Club
15. Johnson and Davis's Club
16. Williams Banks's Club
17. Edmund's Café
18. Barron D. Wilkins's Little Savoy
19. The Douglass Club
20. Walter Herbert's Club
21. Sam Moore's Club
22. Dan Williams's Club
23. Rector's
24. The Café de l'Opera
25. Murray's Roman Gardens
26. Bustanoby's
27. Café des Beaux Arts
28. Churchill's
29. Carnegie Hall

INTRODUCTION

A Kind of Symphony Music That . . . Lends Itself to the

Playing of the Peculiar Compositions of Our Race

At 8:00 P.M. on May 2, 1912, an African American musician named James Reese Europe hurried along Manhattan sidewalks on his way to Carnegie Hall. His tuxedo tails trailing behind, Europe's circular, wire-rimmed eyeglasses slid down his nose as he broke a sweat. The conductor of the Clef Club Symphony Orchestra, Europe was late for the biggest production of his life: the first African American concert at Carnegie, one of the nation's premier performance spaces and an icon of a burgeoning U.S. culture of the arts. The concert was to be a political act of desegregation, a cultural intervention into the sound and meaning of American music, and—potentially—a symbol of the United States' pluralistic democratic promise. Yet fifteen minutes before showtime, Europe was still two blocks away.[1]

As he rounded the corner of Seventh Avenue and Fifty-fourth Street, Europe ran into a swarm of people blocking the sidewalks. Unaware of why they were in his way, Europe began pushing through the throng, only to realize there was nowhere to go: this interracial crowd was his audience, slowly packing Carnegie to overflow. Just the day before, less than half the concert tickets had sold. But now the show was a hit!—if only James Europe could get inside. With increasing anxiety, he approached a police officer, "one of the hundreds of reserves," Clef Club member Noble Sissle recalled, "that had rushed to Carnegie Hall to handle the tremendous crowd."

"Officer, I've got to get through," Europe declared.

"What do you mean, you gotta get through?" sneered the policeman, a man who, Sissle noted, was a "full-sized wielder of those much feared 'night sticks'" and whose "tone" indicated that his conversation with the

African American musician was immediately "beginning to tell on his nerves." The white authority treated Europe with a racial disrespect fitted to the Jim Crow era—until, that is, Europe enlisted the crowd's help to convince the officer of his identity. Only then was he able to enter the concert hall. By the time Europe reached the curtainless stage, the entire Clef Club Symphony Orchestra was standing with their instruments, already presented to the audience and awaiting their conductor's cue.[2]

Europe desegregated the august Carnegie stage with an orchestra of 125 black musicians, performing for a racially integrated audience made up of some of the most influential cultural arbiters in the United States, black and white. Augmenting traditional symphonic orchestration, Europe included dozens of "folk" instruments, ranging from banjos and guitars to mandolins and double-necked harp-guitars, alongside his violins, violas, cellos, and basses. He also included five drum kits, timpani, brass horns, and fourteen upright pianos set back to back, "saloon style," along the back of the stage, where thirty pianists jockeyed for position on any given number. Performing a diverse program of "light classical" music, popular ballads, a march, dance hits, and slave spirituals, Europe's orchestra emphasized the distinctive sounds of syncopated strumming and intensified rhythm that had made ragtime music so popular in recent years.[3]

Strikingly, given the orchestral instrumentation and concert setting, Europe began the performance with his own "Clef Club March," a composition very much in the vein of America's "March King," John Philip Sousa. The song climaxed as the 125 symphonic instrumentalists came in singing a refrain on the last strain, surprising the audience with the sheer power of voice. As the march concluded, the audience sprang to its feet and cheered. "New York woke up to the fact that it had something new in music," folklorist Natalie Curtis-Burlin wrote years later. "Music-loving Manhattan felt a thrill down its spine such as only the greatest performances can inspire when . . . that entire Negro orchestra of over a hundred men burst out singing as they played!"[4]

The Clef Club concert was memorable because it disrupted so many basic assumptions that Americans had about the pressing issues of race, culture, modernity, and nation in the early years of the twentieth century. It transcended the commonly accepted distinctions between art and entertainment, folk and modern, African American identity and American national character. James Europe's ensemble called attention to these opposing poles of cultural value, seeming to identify them as social constructs even as he undermined them. He conducted "classical" music with a European-style orchestra, yet he wove the popular strains of ragtime into his program. Europe embraced recently formed markers of black "folk" music by performing slave spirituals and including banjos in the orchestra, while the group's stylistic hybridity clearly denoted a "modern" black ensemble. He championed his orchestra as a "Negro" ensemble, but he also presented a uniquely American musical experience—one designed to place African Americans at the center of flourishing debates about the shape, sound, and meaning of American national culture. Finally, all the styles the Clef Club performed constituted viable commercial culture products; Europe featured an eclectic mix of everything he could imagine selling in the Manhattan musical marketplace.

James Reese Europe's concert at Carnegie Hall displayed the three central historical processes that this book explores. First, I examine how African Americans entered New York City's burgeoning commercial culture markets and highlighted their status as skilled professionals at a time when blacks had few such opportunities. Thus, many black entertainers self-consciously presented their artistic abilities as evidence of a broader African American capacity to engage as full and equal citizens in American society. Second, I show that black performers played central roles in establishing New York City as the center of America's culture industries and, to a degree, shaped U.S. mass culture in their own image. Third, African Americans' roles in the marketplace indicate the challenges they faced in navigating popular cultureways during the early years of Jim Crow, an era that witnessed the reorganization of a white supremacist social order in the wake of emancipation and Reconstruction. Historians have recognized that these watershed transformations in American life occurred simultaneously, between 1896 and 1919. But few have researched the connections between the rise of professional African American entertainment, mass culture markets, and a new racial status quo.

As African Americans crafted inventive cultural products and popularized new performance practices, they defined New York as a cosmopolitan symbol of American modernity. Tin Pan Alley song publishers, Broadway theaters, vaudeville circuits, dance halls, and the early recording industry began not only to include African Americans but to center on blacks' cultural innovations. Black artists walked a thin line, however, due to the increasing investment that millions of white citizens and policy makers made in white supremacist ideologies and their necessary ancillaries, ideas about black inferiority, after Reconstruction. Even when blacks successfully intervened in U.S. culture markets, they faced a long arc of American history that taught of inherent and essential differences between the races. For entertainers like James Europe, negotiating the color line often meant reinscribing the idea of natural and innate differences between blacks and whites, even as they resisted racist notions of superiority and inferiority.

The Product of Our Souls develops new interpretations of major themes in African American history. The politics of racial uplift and representation, for example, take on new meanings when viewed through the lens of popular entertainment. Many of the African Americans who transformed New York culture industries grew up in professional-class households and had unusual access to education and formal music training. These musicians may have internalized the "uplift ideology" they learned from their families and communities—many inherited the ideal that well-educated African Americans had a responsibility to uplift the less fortunate and to enact new representations of black modernity and citizenship.[5] Yet they chose to reinterpret, and sometimes critique, the elitism and internalized Eurocentrism of their elders, even as they understood themselves as modern symbols of black political and cultural advancement.

When black artists intervened in U.S. culture industries, in fact, they negotiated black and white Americans' contrasting considerations of American modernity in surprising and understudied ways. Even when African American culture workers deliberately exemplified black modernity through their ragtime performances, white consumers most often heard what they deemed black "primitivism," a distinction whites seemed to need to understand their own budding sense of themselves as moderns. These contrasting notions of modernity reveal the conundrums black entertainers faced as they entered U.S. culture markets, just as they emphasize the racial complexities that swirl throughout the history of black musical production.[6]

Finally, this excavation of ragtime culture seeks to expand standard histories of jazz and blues that emphasize the artistic agency of "great men" (and, less often, of "great women") seemingly removed from historical contexts. By historicizing "black music," this study offers alternative frameworks for understanding the Harlem Renaissance and the New Negro Movement of the 1920s, while establishing new ways to evaluate African Americans' unparalleled roles in fashioning American popular music—from jazz to hip-hop—during the twentieth century.

BLACK MUSICAL VALUE AT THE TURN OF THE TWENTIETH CENTURY

James Reese Europe's Carnegie Hall concert gave unprecedented legitimacy to African Americans' music. Concertgoers that May night did not make up just any cohort of music lovers—they represented a cultural and economic elite whose judgments shaped aesthetic trends and cultured tastes in the city and, increasingly, throughout America. Carnegie Hall boosters helped determine the value of the music they enjoyed, just as the Carnegie stage itself bestowed social prestige and encouraged financial success. Europe's arrival at Carnegie signaled a reevaluation in both elite and popular understandings of black music. The Clef Club's overwhelming success and annual invitations back announced the arrival of African American culture in ways that blacks' accomplishments in commercial music and theater could not.

This was no accident. James Europe and his community of black entertainers endeavored to reshape the cultural, social, and political meaning of their crafts. African American musicians in New York actively debated the best ways to present black culture in both formal and popular settings. They strategized about how to become professional entertainers as much as they dreamed of symbolizing a vanguard of African American citizenship. As they did so, many reaped the financial rewards of commercial success. To elucidate black entertainers' gains in Manhattan entertainment markets, I distinguish between their *professional* value and their *cultural* value. Professional value speaks to the concrete changes blacks brought to their professions as actors, singers, dancers, songwriters, and musicians, be they high wages, access to performance spaces and publishing houses (most predominantly Broadway Avenue theaters and Tin Pan Alley song publishers), or fixed expectations about musicians' work (delineations that Europe solidified with his Clef Club labor union between 1910 and 1913). Cultural value suggests more ephemeral processes, and has to do with the changing discursive and ideological meanings of African Americans as a people, vaudeville and ragtime as racialized forms of entertainment, and the role of commercial culture in an industrializing United States.[7] As Europe maneuvered between the often contradictory mandates of his audiences, he transformed black performance from a marginalized and largely stereotypical form of entertainment into a symbol of modern American culture.

The professional and cultural values of black music were intricately connected, but distinguishing between the two helps draw out the ways they mutually constituted one another. As black ragtime musicians garnered higher wages, they reshaped their own cultural value. Likewise, as African American entertainers fashioned new types of racial representations, they generated both higher wages and more professional opportunities. Black musicians' transformation of their cultural value flowed, in part, from a desire to change their professional value, which in turn led to a transformation in their cultural value yet again. Black performers, therefore, ended up advancing facets of their political agendas alongside their profits. Like two entwined snakes chasing after one another's tails, professional value and cultural value worked reciprocally, each propelling and following the other in a circle of transforming racial and representational values, a spinning dialectic of African American empowerment and cultural authority. Yet black entertainers had a tall mountain to climb—at the turn of the century, the starting place for a reevaluation of black musical value was blackface minstrelsy.

The roots of minstrelsy are as old as the North American city. Throughout the seventeenth and eighteenth centuries, Africans labored and leisured alongside Spanish, English, and French workers in marketplaces along the Atlantic coast and the commercial waterways that united coastal communities with the hinterland. In these spaces, some workers found they could earn money by performing a bit of song and dance, transforming their leisure time into a different type of work time.[8] Among a host of diverse performers, people of African descent danced out new identities as freemen, Atlantic cosmopolitans, talented entertainers, racially exotic blacks, and, perhaps, even as Americans. They also, W. T. Lhamon writes, "danced out the identities of their publics," instigating new relationships between race, identity, performance, and commerce in the British Americas.[9] In the 1830s, as the white minstrel performer T. D. "Daddy" Rice began singing and dancing "Jump Jim Crow," his blackface act inaugurated the most popular form of entertainment in the United States from the 1840s until the end of the century.[10] Grounded in white fictions about blacks, minstrelsy introduced enduring caricatures of African Americans that persisted far beyond the performance stage. Blackface images, primarily "Mammies" and "Sambos," plastered nineteenth-century consumer products; everything from soap and cigars to pancake mix and popsicles advertised racial stereotypes across America.

Yet minstrelsy set the stage for African Americans' entrance into modern commercial culture markets. Writing in 1930, James Weldon Johnson noted that minstrel companies "did provide stage training and theatrical experience for a large number of coloured men . . . [which] could not have been acquired from any other source."[11] By seizing on the popularity of minstrelsy, Johnson suggested, black entertainers refashioned the contours of popular music and vaudeville, articulating their own aesthetic and political agendas as best they could within limiting confines. Critically, as minstrelsy traded on racial fictions, it sold them as racial truths, thus establishing a premium on the notion of black "authenticity." Performative presentations of black authenticity influenced the rise of vaudeville in the 1880s. As a new form of variety theater, vaudeville retained many features of the minstrel show—from its combinations of music, dance, and comedy to its reliance on racial stereotype and blackface—even as it expanded opportunities for black entertainers.[12]

As African Americans mounted the vaudeville stage, they distinguished themselves from whites in blackface by promoting themselves as the unencumbered real deal.[13] Since the 1840s, minstrel actors had sold themselves as experts in black culture: minstrels were rarified whites who through painstaking study and practice, they claimed, had mastered the exotic performance practices of black slaves.[14] When African Americans entered minstrel markets, first in small numbers in the 1860s and then in growing ones during the following three decades, they undermined white minstrels' contentions and highlighted the humbug only barely concealed beneath the layers of burnt cork. Blacks appealed to a new sense of racial authenticity, trading on the "real" instead of the counterfeit, the "true" act versus the put on.

Black performers fashioned new promotional strategies aimed at demonstrating their authentic performances over whites' inauthentic blackface. The early vaudeville star George Walker recalled that he succeeded because he "could entertain in that way as no white boy could." Nothing in minstrels' "actions was natural, and therefore nothing was as interesting as if black performers had been dancing and singing their own songs in their own way."[15] Soon after Walker met his partner, Bert Williams, in San Francisco around 1893, the duo began touring the country as the "Two Real Coons," attempting to capitalize on their racial distinction in vaudeville markets, where novelty sold alongside exoticism. Staking a claim of racial birthright onto vaudeville performance, black entertainers fashioned new styles of music, dance, and comedy, both marking and marketing their seeming authenticity. Rather than grounded in a biological reality, the idea of racial authenticity was forged in the domain of consumer capitalism, where African Americans developed new performance practices and promotional strategies to sell their black bodies as authentic sites of American entertainment.[16]

When Walker and Europe promoted their inventive cultural commodities as expressions of black authenticity, they capitalized on the allure of racial difference, selling race in entertainment markets that would seem to undermine the idea of an unmediated black authenticity. Instead, markets propelled the idea. Both Walker and Europe worked and leisured at

the black-owned Hotel Marshall, home to a whole community of successful black entertainers in Manhattan. While Walker made contributions in
blackface vaudeville and Broadway musical theater, Europe oversaw the
rise of social dancing and ragtime culture's transition from the theater
stage to the concert hall.[17] Although they never worked together directly,
many of their partners did, and their efforts to transform the professional
and cultural values of black entertainment complemented one another.

RAGGING UPLIFT WITH MODERN NEGRO MUSIC

Even as the Clef Club orchestra capitalized on the demand for black
authenticity, it also presented itself as a deliberately modern black music
ensemble. By 1912, most Americans agreed that African Americans as a
race were excellent musicians, and, as many whites commented, in some
ways surpassed the natural musicality of white Americans.[18] This thinking
had its origins in long histories of racial difference and white supremacy.
Throughout three centuries of slavery, Africans and African Americans
demonstrated recognizably distinct approaches to music making—they
sang, danced, and played instruments such as drums and banjos (an
instrument of African origin) in ways quite different from Europeans.[19]
Throughout the nineteenth century, even as African cultural practices
intermixed with Native American, Anglo, Spanish, French, and Celtic
ones, black slaves in the United States continued to perform music in
ways that whites understood as different from their own.

When black slaves interpreted Christian hymns in the 1830s, whites
within earshot (usually slave owners sharing plantation land and aural
spaces with their slaves) emphasized the distinctive features of black
singing, rather than noting their many similarities with white musical
worship.[20] By the 1870s, African American college students—many of
them former slaves or children of slaves—began to popularize a body of
songs they called the "spirituals" as they toured the country raising money
for Fisk University. Performing in a style similar to European choral music,
the Fisk Jubilee Singers accentuated their unique qualities of voice, tim-
bre, and harmony, cementing, for a time, African Americans' voice as the
defining characteristic of black music in the minds of many Americans. Yet
by the mid-1890s, as black and white popular song composers introduced
ragtime music into commercial culture markets, rhythm began to sup-
plant the voice as the essential ingredient of African Americans' music.[21]

The Clef Club Symphony Orchestra presented rhythmic music at
a moment in which rhythm was taking on a variety of contradictory

associations, having not yet calcified into the single defining characteristic of black music. Ragtime was the most popular music in America during the first two decades of the twentieth century, and rhythmic syncopation its most prominent feature. To many, ragtime rhythms reverberated as the modern sound of African American ingenuity, cultural advance, and professionalism—attributes otherwise rarely accessible to black Americans during the early years of Jim Crow. Yet ragtime rhythms also represented the folk origins of African American music, and, to some, they resounded as the vulgar and lowdown music of the working-class juke joints and bordellos of the rural South and urbanizing Midwest. To many black elites, for instance, ragtime presented a threat.

As ragtime rhythms became a dominant characteristic of black music, and as ragtime performers like James Europe became leading authorities of black cultural authenticity, ragtime complicated ideas of who could represent black America. Since emancipation, a small population of African Americans with access to education and professional careers as preachers, teachers, and cultural critics had sought to break free from both the shackles of their slave past and white Americans' racial stereotypes. They crafted positive racial representations of African Americans as modern citizens and promoted blacks' advance into "civilization," a term that reflected European and Anglo-American ideals of societal development and progress.[22] The scholar and activist W. E. B. Du Bois, for example, called on the "best equipped teachers and leaders" in black communities—who he famously named the "Talented Tenth"—to educate and professionalize themselves, "so that all their energies may be bent toward a cheerful striving and co-operation with their white neighbors toward a larger, juster, and fuller future."[23] Black political thought of the era promoted hierarchical thinking in black communities and established what the historian Kevin Gaines has called "uplift ideology": middle-class blacks' response to the supposed "problem" that uneducated, impoverished, and migrating black masses presented to the Talented Tenth's strategic racial representations.[24]

In the minds of race leaders and many middle-class African Americans, church activities and social clubs uplifted black youth, whereas pool halls, gambling circles, and saloons were where the Devil played. For the members of Du Bois's Talented Tenth (probably closer to 0.1 percent of American blacks), ragtime culture accompanied only the latter. During the early years of Jim Crow, the Talented Tenth seized on blacks' modes of self-comportment, behavior, and leisure in their struggles against the ideologies of white supremacy and black inferiority. Public presentations of blackness mattered to middle-class blacks because of the responsibility they felt they shouldered in transforming the way white Americans perceived their fellow black citizens.

Black community leaders counseled public displays of self-restraint, temperance, and thrift to indicate that African Americans held the intellectual and moral capacity to become hardworking members of American industrial society—an approach to uplift that scholars have termed the "politics of representation" and "the politics of respectability."[25] On an individual level, respectability demanded expressions of refined manners and genteel behaviors in public; impeccably clean, modest, and functional clothing; chivalry toward women and self-restraining female morality, especially for girls and young women who, their elders imagined, needed to somehow embody the very character of feminine integrity through their everyday movements and social interactions. There were also social aspects to respectable representation, and these hinged on the types of amusements one attended and how one spent one's leisure time. The fact that ragtime—and the working-class leisure spaces where it gestated—presented affronts to the Talented Tenth's directives only made it more powerful for the black producers and consumers who embraced it.

At the very moment black elites were putting so much stock in modern racial representations and public performances of respectability, black popular entertainers and some of their black audiences shifted away from uplift ideology. Through a series of related historical processes I call "ragging uplift," performers like James Europe arrived in Manhattan intent on changing popular representations of black people and black culture. Aiming to uplift the race in the minds of consuming audiences black and white, music publishers, promoters, theater managers, cultural critics, and many black performers themselves, musicians like Europe fashioned new cultural expressions to combat the ubiquitous specter of blackface minstrelsy, as well as the recent body of state and federal legislation making blacks second-class citizens throughout much of the country. Yet Europe and his community did not advance black uplift as historians have defined it.[26]

In significant ways, black ragtime entertainers rejected conventional uplift ideology's central tenets, thereby expanding scholars' understanding of African American culture, politics, and identity. They revealed dimensions of the internalized white supremacy that uplifters harbored by shining a light on the Eurocentrism of American (and elite African American) aesthetic values.[27] Ragtime performers could reject uplift all together, or they could recognize aspects of its pragmatic uses, incorporating them into a different political approach of proving blacks' fitness for citizenship. Reflecting the slanting, deviating "angularity" that the folklorist Zora Neale Hurston ascribed to black cultural expression, black ragtimers put their own spin not only on standardizing American cultural forms but on middle-class black ones too.[28]

Ragtime music and performance disrupted uplift ideology by offering new ways to represent and experience blackness through the burgeoning avenues of commercial culture. On stage, in print, and in impromptu performance, ragtime rhythms instigated alternative racial representations in an era dominated by debates between race leaders like Booker T. Washington and Du Bois. No longer offering only stage types—Zip Coon or Jim Crow, Sambo or Mammy—the extension of black cultural expression exploded the one-dimensional nature of black characters in American society. White culture producers and audiences may have glossed over these shifts in artistic potential and black humanity. But for African American consumers of black culture—especially urban ones, and especially New Yorkers who participated in blacks' imaginative interventions along Broadway and Tin Pan Alley—ragtime offered new sounds, professional channels, commercial strategies, and different kinds of black identities to internalize and publicly represent.

James Europe's Clef Club reflected the uplift he had absorbed during his childhood in the black middle-class neighborhoods of Washington, D.C. (where he had access to a high school education and formal music training). Yet by emphasizing ragtime rhythms and including banjos, guitars, and drum kits in his orchestra, Europe also upended many African Americans' expectations of his music, and even subverted uplift ideology. The Clef Club offered black Americans an alternative to the dichotomies their race leaders constructed. Europe's music was neither highbrow nor lowdown, neither wholly formally trained nor illiterate. It constituted a performative, sonic expression of a transformation in black culture.

But Europe did not concoct new cultural representations of black America in a vacuum. He formed part of a community living and working out of the Hotel Marshall, a black-owned commercial space in a neighborhood known as Black Bohemia. At the turn of the century, the Hotel Marshall was a primary site for heated debates about the appropriate public presentations of "Negro music," where, as James Weldon Johnson recalled, "the main question talked and wrangled over being always that of the manner and means of raising the status of the Negro as a writer, composer, and performer in the New York theater and world of music."[29] For many at the Marshall, the concept of a single black musical style made no sense. Negro music did not demarcate an essential cultural expression of the race, but, rather, myriad historical and international influences. Yet for others, the Negro music of the early 1900s represented a coherent concept of "the race"; some black entertainers saw ragtime both as a reflection and a constitutive facet of urban and modern black identities, the musical expression of what Booker T. Washington called "A New Negro for a New Century."[30]

WHITE MODERNITY AND BLACK RHYTHM

Even as James Reese Europe's Clef Club Symphony Orchestra raised the value of black music on the Carnegie stage, Europe's mixed-race audience reminded everyone there of Jim Crow society. It was, after all, the first time that large numbers of blacks had been allowed into Carnegie Hall, as either performers or patrons. And even though the members of the orchestra and the audience alike occupied various identity positions as native-born Americans, naturalized citizens, or immigrants, everyone there was either black or white—there was no in-between in a country where the one-drop rule dominated. No matter how deliberately black musicians presented themselves as modern artists and U.S. citizens, white audiences rarely heard blacks' self-representations as intended.

At the turn of the twentieth century, white Americans' assessment of their own modernity did not recognize that of African Americans. It relied, in fact, on whites' denial of black modernity. To understand themselves as modern, whites needed a foil, a premodern sensibility with which to contrast their own. Far from reverberating as the modern and commercially driven popular entertainment that blacks intended, to white ears, ragtime rhythms reflected the primitivist culture of a folk people—a group of Americans seemingly excised from the project of U.S. modernity altogether. White Americans' rejection of black modernity became a constitutive cornerstone of white modernism. Simultaneously, blacks' ragtime culture became a powerful marker of racial difference during the very era in which white policy makers, capitalists, and mass consumers searched for new ways to reconstruct a white supremacist racial order. Like the ways T. D. Rice's "Jump Jim Crow" gave a name to American segregation laws and daily practices that lasted more than a hundred years, African American culture sometimes reinforced white Americans' assumptions about blacks' natural, inherent difference from whites.

With good reason did the historian Rayford Logan name the period between the end of Reconstruction in 1877 and 1901 the "nadir of the

Negro's status in American society."[31] During this era, white political and economic elites struggled to first maintain, and then recreate, a U.S. social order based on race, gender, and class inequality. Decades before the Civil War, as the westward expansion of slavery dovetailed with a growing abolition movement, Americans had begun a series of racial readjustments, changes to the status quo that did not end with the war, Reconstruction, or the end of the nineteenth century. In fact, before the 1830s, America's racial order was less fixed than it would become after emancipation. Conceptions of race and racial difference were commonly held as signs of different nationalities, ethnicities, or cultural traditions—"environmental" factors, rather than biological ones, and thus susceptible to change and adaptation. Black slaves' social standing was imputed through legal means rather than by nature or biology.[32]

After emancipation, Americans began to recognize the degree that slavery had ordered their society. As Saidiya Hartman sums up, the master-and-slave relationships of the 1830s and after not only fixed the idea of race and racial difference in American life; they "determined the meaning of white identity, the character of citizenship, and the scope of rights and entitlements" throughout the U.S.[33] After the Civil War, white supremacy—so long dependent on the institution of slavery—was not a foregone conclusion. White Americans had to find new forms, expressions, coercions, and rationales to maintain their racial order in post-slavery America. American legal, political, and economic structures moved to simplify diverse populations of African Americans into the "black race," a category whites had to redefine as innately inferior to themselves to keep white supremacy alive. Music, and especially African Americans' sonic innovations, helped realign this new racial order throughout the country.

During the years African American music became one of the most popular cultural commodities in New York City (as well as in much of the United States), black and white Americans alike understood ragtime as a symbol of American urbanity and cosmopolitan U.S. modernity. An early popular commodity wrought through the fires of industrial capitalism, ragtime sheet music helped announce the arrival of a mass consumer society in the United States. The growing popularity of sheet music in the 1890s represented advances in technology, distribution, and advertising.[34] By 1896, as African Americans introduced ragtime rhythms to song publishers, they transformed the industry, creating new sounds and performative practices, as well as a matrix of representations that white songwriters could mimic—and that white consumers could purchase. Alongside the industrial advances that made ragtime so popular appeared its racial resonances: the fast, frenetic, exiting, exotic, titillating, and dangerous associations of African Americans' music. Yet where black ragtime musicians heard the sound of American modernity, white audiences heard a black primitivism that only became modern once they had bought and enjoyed it.[35]

Rhythm, and specifically syncopation, came to mark the commodity "black music"—a cultural product that would resonate as a consistent racial-aesthetic category even as blacks' musical innovations changed drastically during the course of the twentieth century. As Europe's Clef Club orchestra indicates, African American music was quite diverse in 1912. Yet even though blacks' music was varied, ragtime's rhythms were nearly infinite, and ragtime song hits were mass-produced by a motley group of Jewish Americans, Anglos, and black Americans (through industrialized production techniques designed to signal blackness), ragtime syncopation took on a seemingly essential and timeless racial character of the black "folk." Black music became an embodiment of the black race, as though skin color alone determined musical aptitude. It is a hallmark of the process of commodification that complex and heterogeneous items transform into simplified and homogenous products, just as businesses consolidate both the means of production and the social meanings of their commodities.[36] In some ways, it is nothing shocking to assert that as African Americans commodified their song, dance, and comedic theater, their assorted artistic endeavors became simplified into essential racial categories. Yet to understand the development of early twentieth-century black music as only, or even primarily, a process of economic commodification obscures the historical context both granting African Americans a place in the developing marketplace and determining the meanings of racial art in a racist society.

That black entertainers reinforced the logic of Jim Crow when they sold their innovations in U.S. marketplaces demonstrates the peculiar binds that restrained James Europe and the Hotel Marshall community. Notions of black cultural and biological difference were not new in 1900. But the tropes black entertainers presented, often with a knowing wink to their fiction, became naturalized, nearly common sense, through performances and promotions of what Gayatri Spivak has called "strategic essentialism."[37] During a Jim Crow era defined by whites' fixation on codifying race and legislating racial difference, indications of black distinction became so apparent, so noticeably clear, for many Americans because African Americans appeared to sing and dance differently—"blacker" than whites. Describing the relationship between the rise of Jim Crow and mass consumer culture, Grace Elizabeth Hale argues that segregation "became the founding metaphor as well as policy of modern American life." Hale emphasizes the visual nature of commercial culture, the reliance of U.S. policy makers and citizens on seeing racial difference, and on the "authority of the eye—the spectacle."[38] *The Product of Our Souls* demonstrates that aural culture, and the sound of race, played an increasingly powerful role in demarcating racial difference, setting a precedent that would continue throughout a twentieth century of growing African American influence on American culture and politics through popular music.

In the chapters that follow, I chart how blacks' myriad musical innovations during a remarkably generative period became "black music," which in turn promoted a series of contradictory, though influential, signs of cultural transformation, white supremacy, and African American artistry in the United States. In 1900, "ragtime" did not designate a singular, fixed musical genre. There was neither a consistent nor coherent notion of "Negro music." There was no single or essential idea of "black culture." Yet by the time James Europe arrived home after fighting in World War I, he returned to a country deeply ensconced in the idea that black people made black music, a form of cultural expression as distinct as the color of their skin. Black music by 1919 may have received various genre names— ragtime, blues, and jazz most conspicuously. But music products (sheet music, phonographs, and stage performance) and musical sounds (rhythm, "swing," the black voice, and instrumental practices) increasingly seemed to demarcate an essentially homogenous black experience. I chart this shift to tell a story about the African Americans whose racialized commercial strategies turned into a commonsense promotion of Jim Crow–era racial assumptions, even as they expanded blacks' professional opportunities, the value of their art, and the sound of American culture. It is a story about what happened to a diverse set of sounds, aspirations, and political imperatives among a varied group when it faced the codifying and simplifying powers of industrial capitalism and Americans' narrow and essentializing notions of race and racial difference.

A NEW MUSICAL RHYTHM WAS
GIVEN TO THE PEOPLE

Ragtime and Representation in Black Manhattan

At fifteen minutes before midnight on July 5, 1898, Will Marion Cook began conducting an orchestra of white musicians as his African American chorus pranced onto the rooftop stage above New York's Casino Theatre, singing the jaunty introductory bars of Cook's ragtime operetta *Clorindy; or, The Origin of the Cakewalk.* Born in 1869, just six years after Abraham Lincoln delivered the Emancipation Proclamation, Cook was one of only a few African Americans of his generation trained in both an American music conservatory and a German one. He inaugurated the first theater performance by African Americans on Broadway Avenue, a street just becoming synonymous with the American stage.

As the show began, Cook recalled, there were "only about fifty" people in the rooftop garden. But before his troupe had completed their first piece, the Casino Theatre's main stage downstairs let out, and the "big audience heard those heavenly Negro voices and took to the elevators" to see what was happening upstairs. The rooftop theater became "packed to suffocation," and as Cook concluded his ragtime-inflected overture, the applause and cheers grew "so tumultuous," he wrote, "that I simply stood there transfixed, my hand in the air, unable to move."[1]

Evidently, Cook really did freeze. *Clorindy*'s lead actor, Ernest Hogan, a seasoned African American blackface vaudevillian and accomplished Tin Pan Alley songwriter, had to walk across the stage, step over the lights, and peer into the orchestra pit to ask, "What's the matter, son? Let's go!" Startled, Cook counted off, and Hogan began his syncopated opening number, "Hottes' Coon," with such comedic grace that he captured the crowd for the entire forty-five-minute production.[2] Cook and Hogan's ragtime music enthralled the audience with its rhythmic ingenuity. When the operetta finished, the Casino audience cried for encores. They would not let Hogan leave the stage before repeating Cook's sprightly "Who Dat Say Chicken in Dis Crowd?" ten times. Performing a pitch-perfect blend of the black "dialect" that dominated American popular song in the late 1890s and the practiced enunciation that allowed his voice to carry out of doors, Hogan swooned and shuffled across the stage as he sang:

Who Dat Say Chicken in Dis Crowd?
Speak de word agin' and speak it loud
What's de use of all dis talkin'
Let me hyeah a hen a squakin'
Who Dat Say Chicken in Dis Crowd?[3]

Years later, Cook recalled: "My chorus sang like Russians, dancing mean-while like angels, black angels! When the last note was sounded, the audience stood and cheered for at least ten minutes. . . . It was pandemonium, but never was pandemonium dearer to my heart."[4]

By the end of the night, Cook was ecstatic. Thinking that someone had handed him champagne, Cook got "gloriously drunk" off cold water and enjoyed the rest of the night high on adrenaline. Fifty years later, he still championed *Clorindy*, ending his short, unpublished memoir by highlighting its role in transforming American musical theater. "Negroes were at last on Broadway, and there to stay. Gone was the uff-dah of the minstrel! Gone the Massa Linkum stuff! We were artists and we were going a long, long way. . . . Nothing could stop us and nothing did for a decade."[5]

Cook's excitement about his success seems endearing, but it also proves disconcerting. How could a formally trained musician like Cook wind up performing blackface on Broadway, and why was he so thrilled about it? And how, in any stretch of the imagination, could singing "Who Dat Say Chicken in Dis Crowd?" be considered a departure from the "uff-dah of the minstrel"? How, indeed, could an African American musician imagine that *Clorindy* ended the "Massa Linkum stuff" that defined late-nineteenth-century black stage performance? In *Clorindy*, caricatured African Americans sang about their unquenchable desires and danced the racially marked cakewalk—a slave innovation from the antebellum era—on Broadway for a white audience. So why did Cook believe he had ushered in a transformation in American culture? If *Clorindy* marks a milestone because of African Americans' introduction to Broadway, it seems a severely compromised one.

Cook's rarefied middle-class upbringing in Washington, D.C., his Oberlin College education, his violin and composition training in Germany, and his tutelage with the Czech master Antonín Dvořák prepared him to create symphonies and large-scale musicals. He could have written his libretto in German or Italian, but he chose black dialect. In 1890s America, Cook's most promising professional opportunities depended on commercial music and performance stylings that owed more to blackface minstrelsy than European opera. Because few performance stages commensurate with Cook's race and background existed, he had to choose between the formal styles of the concert hall and informal arts of popular vaudeville. In *Clorindy*, African Americans arrived on Broadway only by enacting lively embodiments of black stereotypes that Cook and Hogan hoped to transcend. Even as *Clorindy* symbolizes black performers' early interventions into American commercial culture markets, it calls attention to the circumscribed nature of black performance and the limits American society foisted on African Americans.

At the end of the nineteenth century, black musicians, educators, and intellectuals debated the best ways to represent African Americans as U.S. citizens. Many agreed that advancing blacks' development of "culture"—a term that in the late nineteenth century implied aristocratic breeding and manners as much as the arts—presented a key strategy.[6] Black critics' evaluations of "Negro music," however, seemed in constant flux, so that ideas of "folk," "formal," "concert," and "modern" black music rarely cohered; these categories often seemed to imply class distinctions rather than aesthetic ones. Regardless of the adjectives they used, most black commentators agreed on a strict difference between "high" and "low." But while high, cultured, or "only the purest and best in music" (as one black music critic wrote in 1902) meant classically trained and formalized along the lines of European art music, low could mean anything from barely remembered slave music, refined slave spirituals, or any variation of popular music: from minstrel songs to vaudeville tunes, "coon songs" to ragtime.[7] For musicians like Will Cook, family expectations and community obligations often took the form of a racial "politics of representation," wherein black art and cultural development were tethered to the political aims of racial uplift and African American citizenship.[8]

Cook and Hogan's collaboration on *Clorindy* dramatizes a moment when a generation of young African Americans began to cultivate alternative representations of themselves as popular entertainers and modern

U.S. citizens. Musicians like Hogan and Cook were sharply attuned to the ways black intellectuals and music educators of the post-Reconstruction era fashioned uplifting representations of middle-class blacks as "respectable," "civilized," and "cultured" to prove their fitness for American citizenship. Even as Cook and Hogan broke with the elitism of the Talented Tenth, the Broadway entertainers understood their goals, and largely agreed with them. Yet rather than upholding Eurocentric notions of respectable culture and formal music, both men imagined that wider, more pluralistic notions of black culture would help African Americans become accepted as full-fledged Americans.

Many of the debates encircling Hogan and Cook dealt with conflicting ways to present African Americans as modern U.S. citizens. To embody modernity, some black culture workers and critics imagined a premodern past—something from which to distinguish themselves. For many, the music of the black slaves, and the spirituals especially, came to represent the primitive artistry of a folk people. The formal development of African American music through classical training and a studied mastery of the European art music canon, many elite African Americans hoped, would embody both their modernity and place in American society. While debates about black modernity and public representation most often took place between the diametric poles of folk and formal music, entertainers like Hogan and Cook increasingly demonstrated the power of a third path: popular music.

At the turn of twentieth century, the Manhattan musical marketplace shimmered up electricity-lighted Broadway, sang along Tin Pan Alley, and triggered the arrival of Times Square. It also crossed over into spaces of black leisure. More than just a site of economic transactions, New York City's cultural marketplace was a space where ideas about race, class, and modernity took form, where native-born Americans negotiated the meaning of U.S. citizenship with immigrants, and the engines of industrial capitalism manufactured new distinctions among elite, folk, and mass culture. Cook, Hogan, and an entire host of driven, talented, and savvy African American entertainers used the opportunities New York City offered to enter into the United States' most thriving and inventive marketplace. They began a cultural revolution that would outlast the twentieth century.

Two contradictory political and aesthetic currents gave rise to these entertainers' desegregation of Broadway Avenue. First, new cultural expressions of ragtime song, dance, and comedy became Hogan's vehicles into the Manhattan musical marketplace. The ways he embedded himself into American popular culture industries demonstrate both the

unprecedented professional opportunities and pernicious racial stereotypes African Americans encountered as they intervened in mainstream
American society. Second, raised by college-educated African Americans,
Cook had studied art music in Europe and learned the attitudes and
responsibilities of uplift ideology at a young age. Instead of growing into
an artist in the classical mold, however, Cook's education and formal training actually undermined the directives of the professional-class blacks of
his parents' generation and pushed him to revaluate the music of the black
"masses," both in the antebellum past and in the modern moment of the
preset. Hogan and Cook met on New York's Casino Garden Theatre stage
and, together, began a revolution in American culture and society.

WALKING THE MANHATTAN MUSICAL MARKETPLACE

Will Marion Cook, worldly, educated, and no bumpkin, must have walked
up Broadway Avenue in awe of Manhattan's electric lights, brash noise,
and immense architecture—hallmarks of American modernity at the
turn of the twentieth century.[9] In 1900, Broadway's theater district ran
from about Twenty-third Street to Forty-second, not yet stretching too
far past the intersection that would be known as Times Square when the
New York Times opened its new headquarters on New Year's Eve 1904.
Day and night, tall, soft-roofed automobiles competed with horse car-
riages for rights-of-way in the street, and pedestrians packed Broadway
sidewalks. Although only a few yet sprinkled Manhattan, the skyscrapers along Broadway seemed to rise high enough to live up to their names.
Completed in 1895, the three hundred-foot American Surety Building at
Broadway and Forty-third Street initiated the trend in tall buildings.

Even more shocking than skyscrapers must have been the thousands of
glass windows full of color and light. The vibrant electric lights on nearly
every first floor of every building seemed to battle for sidewalk strollers'
attention. They called out, demanded notice, and enticed commuters and
tourists alike to stop a moment and, perhaps, make a purchase. At the
turn of the century, Manhattan boasted more electric lights and window
displays than any other place in the world, turning its commercial districts
into what one ad executive admiringly referred to as "the phantasmago-
ria of the lights and electric signs."[10] Even as Midtown Manhattan glowed
long into the night, nothing boasted electric lights like Broadway theaters.

At night, the Casino Theatre where Cook produced *Clorindy* glim-
mered, its twenty-foot sign in large bulbs adding to the electric allure that
gave Broadway its recent nickname, "The Great White Way."[11] "Broadway

was one long can[y]on of light," wrote Robert Hughes in 1904. "Even the shops that were closed displayed brilliantly illuminated windows. In some of them all the trickeries of electricity were employed and rhapsodies of color glittered in every device or revolved in kaleidoscopes of fire."[12] Completed in 1892, the Casino sported an eight-story red brick turret with a wide, circular roof made from concave red clay shingles, making the southeastern corner of Broadway and Thirty-ninth Street look like a medieval castle in daylight. One of the largest and most popular theaters in New York, it was surrounded by vaudeville houses like Koster and Bial's on West Thirty-fourth Street and the Empire Theatre up Broadway on Fortieth, rendering the corner one of the brightest in the district. Although Broadway became the most conspicuous site of the revolution in American advertising and technological innovation, it merely reflected wider trends happening in New York and other American cities at the turn of the twentieth century.

Advertising made tremendous advances at the end of the nineteenth century. Propelled by new developments in print and visual media, New York City in the 1890s saw some of the earliest picture advertisements, lithograph-screened color posters, painted billboards, electric signs, and glass shop windows. As recently as the late 1880s, arresting visual advertising seemed crude and materialistic to most Americans; the historian William Leach has shown that ads were "looked down on as linked to circuses and P. T. Barnum hokum."[13] A cursory glance at American newspapers before the mid-1890s confirms this: they were all black and white and covered in tiny typeface. The rise of color advertising around 1900 paralleled the creation of mass-market magazines and national newspapers, many of them produced in New York. But by 1900, American media and advertising firms had embraced the spectacular, eye-catching commercial notice. "The successful advertisement," according to a leading ad broker of the era, "is obtrusive. It continually forces itself upon the attention." Using the same active verb, adman O. J. Gude celebrated electric sings because they "literally forced their announcements on the vision of the uninterested as well as the interested passerby."[14] As New York advertising agencies multiplied and advertisements cropped up anywhere there was free space—on the side of buildings, inside and outside public transportation, and within print media—Manhattan became the testing ground for a new type of consumer culture, and city spaces turned into high-profile studies in color, light, and electricity.

Yet New York City modernity manifested in more than spectacular visuals. When Will Cook explored Broadway Avenue, the sonic reverberations pouring out of Midtown leisure spaces must have intrigued him most. Alongside the tall buildings and their glittering facades, Cook would notice the strange amalgamations of music emerging from the scores of restaurants and hotel dining rooms. He would hear small string trios and quartets of Eastern Europeans, Italians, and Jews performing classical music, many specializing in what New Yorkers termed "Gypsy music"—those exotic minor strains accented in strange time signatures.[15] Although less conspicuous in white-owned dining rooms in 1900, Cook almost certainly also heard a few black musicians performing ragtime, both "ragging" the classics by adding unusual rhythmic syncopations to well-known compositions by Mozart and Handel, and performing original music in an exciting, seemingly frenetic but highly controlled style similar to the one made popular by the Missourian Scott Joplin.[16] Due to ragtime's growing popularity on New York vaudeville stages, both approaches to ragtime were just becoming legitimate in the eyes of Manhattan restaurant managers and patrons, a legitimacy that would grow quickly in the coming decade. But even in 1900, ragtime seemed to sparkle with ingenuity, freshness, and that intangible thing so many New Yorkers wanted to evoke: modernity.

At the turn of the century, ragtime reverberated to consumers and critics alike as the sound of Manhattan modernity, especially as African Americans and the non-immigrant Anglo–New Yorkers of a certain generation and elite social status understood it. Dreaming of distancing themselves from their parents who lived and leisured almost exclusively along Fifth Avenue, young and privileged white Manhattanites began flocking to dining rooms and other types of commercial leisure spaces on and around Broadway to participate in the newest "new thing." Gliding off vaudeville stages and sliding off music publishing presses, ragtime infiltrated New York City. Ragtime melodies came in with the whistles of young men stopping for a drink at a saloon; they entered in the singing of a merry couple having a late-night lobster dinner after a Broadway show. Ragtime floated in simply as street noise from passersby, and sometimes it slipped in through the boisterous song-pluggers who made it their job to stand on street corners, walk into department stores, or even penetrate theater houses from the audience seats to sing their song and circulate its melody. Like electric signs and colorful posters, pluggers forced their product into the marketplace.[17] Ragtime tunes were the memes of their day, and like Internet jokes and homemade viral videos, they circulated throughout the country with unprecedented quickness, drawing many Americans closer together through their increasingly shared consumption of commercial culture. Yet like many producers of mass consumer goods, even as they

hoped to nationalize their commodities' reach, music publishers cultivated their businesses in New York City.

If Cook began walking southeast along Broadway from the Casino Theatre, in eleven city blocks he would hit the production center of American popular music. The two short blocks of West Twenty-eighth Street
between Fifth and Sixth Avenues (bifurcated by the diagonally flowing
Broadway) were home to New York's leading music publishers. Tin Pan
Alley was born in the mid-1880s, when a few established firms moved
their publishing houses north of Union Square to Twenty-eighth Street,
and dozens of new publishers followed their example.[18] The rise of black
comedy and music performance on American vaudeville stages in the
1890s coincided with African Americans' entrance into music publishing. While music publishers were sprouting up in Chicago, St. Louis,
and Kansas City, New York became the industry's center. Traveling black
vaudevillians from throughout the United States made sure to stop by Tin
Pan Alley when visiting the city, hoping to drop off a recent composition
and try their luck at a "hit." When visitors and native New Yorkers alike
strolled along Sixth Avenue from Tin Pan Alley, they would have noticed
that they were walking the proverbial "tracks" separating New York's commercial amusement center from Manhattan's central black neighborhood,
the Tenderloin.

New York's Tenderloin, stretching roughly between Twentieth and
Fortieth Streets and Sixth and Ninth Avenues, was outlined on its east
side by the aura of Broadway. Tin Pan Alley ran right into the Tenderloin's
eastern border, stopping abruptly before crossing over into black streets.
When new theaters, hotels, and restaurants edged up Broadway to
Forty-second Street between 1900 and 1905, they rested at the northeast
corner of the Tenderloin, just a stone's throw from black tenements. Split-
ting the working-class district up the middle was Seventh Avenue, known
as "African Broadway." Lined with five-and-dimes, grocers, butchers, and
a few black-owned businesses, Seventh Avenue constituted the commercial shopping center of Black Manhattan.[19] The central sites of New York's
song publishing and musical theater industries along the perimeter of the
Tenderloin did not have a monopoly on New York culture. If anything,
these firms tried to muster just a bit of the excitement and energy generating in the Tenderloin.

One of many red-light districts in New York, the Tenderloin housed
many of New York's leading cabarets and nightclubs. While its brothels
and gambling clubs did not mark it particularly distinct from Five Points
and the Bowery, the Tenderloin's other leisure spaces did. As ragtime

poured out of black nightclubs, they drew increasingly diverse clientele to the Tenderloin, augmenting an already culturally rich neighborhood. Full of newly arrived migrants (mostly rural and southern), immigrants, and longtime locals, Tenderloin nightlife offered a heady mélange of African American and black Caribbean culture. In the early twentieth century, the district was home to nonblack immigrants too: Irish, Italians, Russians, and Greeks lived there, though most ethnic groups stayed on their own blocks. Nonetheless, due to their racy appeal, Tenderloin nightclubs offered some of the few racially integrated spaces in New York City.[20]

Like all New York theaters and vaudeville stages, Broadway houses segregated their audiences by race, reserving most tickets for white customers and leaving balcony seats for African Americans—if they allowed blacks at all. While Manhattan vaudeville stages along Fourteenth Street and around Union Square had presented black acts throughout the 1890s (always separate from whites ones), Broadway was indeed a "white way" until Cook's Clorindy came to town. Cook arrived on Broadway due to a combination of audacious perseverance and a little sleight of hand—it was no easy task to get a black show onto one of America's leading stages. After waiting in line every day for a month without acknowledgment, Cook overheard the Casino Theatre's booking agent, Ed Rice, set an appointment with another act. The following Monday, Cook arrived at the Casino with his twenty-six-person choir and quickly introduced himself to the theater's conductor, John Braham, saying he had "studied violin under Joachim, a bit of composition under Dvořák, harmony and mighty little counterpoint under John White," before explaining that he had written a "Negro operetta." Braham looked at Cook and turned to his orchestra, saying, "Gentlemen, a new composer!" As Braham reached for Cook's score, Cook asked if he might conduct, to which Braham turned again, replying, "Gentlemen, a new composer and conductor!" As Cook struck up his choir, Rice ran out of his office and down the theater aisle, shouting, "No nigger can conduct my orchestra on Broadway!" But before Rice made it to the stage, Braham snapped, "Ed, go back to your little cubby-hole and keep quiet! That boy's a genius and has something great!"[21] After Cook auditioned his operetta, Braham booked Clorindy, putting African Americans on Broadway and knocking Jim Crow off the stages of the Great White Way.

"COON SONGS" ON TIN PAN ALLEY

Throughout most of the nineteenth century, song publishing did not make for a lucrative business in the United States. Prior to the 1880s, song sheets were mostly published locally and accounted for just one facet of a publishers' livelihood—publishers often owned music stores or taught lessons, performed and arranged music semiprofessionally, or worked as engravers or skilled artisans. Stephen C. Foster, America's first professional songwriter, sold hundreds of thousands of copies of his famous songs "My Old Kentucky Home" (1851) and "Camptown Races" (1850) during his lifetime. But he died a pauper, barely eking out a living from his dozens of immensely popular songs. Before the 1880s, a song that sold five hundred copies was considered a success. All this changed when New York City firms began implementing the technological and bureaucratic techniques of industrialized mass production.[22]

Beginning in the mid-1880s, about a decade before the earliest ragtime songs came out, Manhattan music publishers made their industry one of the most lucrative in the budding entertainment marketplace. M. Witmark and Sons, Joseph M. Sterns, Harry Von Tilzer, and Leo Feist turned songwriting into big business by breaking down song production into discrete divisions of labor. The art of songwriting, for example, became the domain of composers, lyricists, and arrangers; by the mid-1890s, most hit songs came from a songwriting team rather than an individual. Song manuscripts began featuring four-color covers thanks to the introduction of chromolithographic color printing into the music publishing houses, and New York publishers generated sales nationally by offering better wholesale discounts on the newest releases throughout the nation's five-and-dimes, Woolworth's, and elephantine department stores like Wanamakers and Marshall Fields. Additionally, publishers no longer waited for consuming audiences to happen on their product. Instead, they aggressively promoted new songs. The most successful application of this process came from plugging, wherein publishers paid young singers to perform new songs in all manner of leisure spaces, from street corners to vaudeville theaters, from department stores to nickelodeon houses—anywhere a song could catch an ear. Like the ubiquitous use of satellite radio today, song-pluggers put the sound of popular tunes into the airwaves of urban America. As song firms established new methods of production, distribution, and promotion, they turned local business into mass culture throughout the nation.[23] Isidore Witmark, a leading New York publisher, recalled that, the mid-1890s marked the "indubitable beginnings of Tin Pan Alley as a national industry."[24]

Tin Pan Alley turned sentimental ballads, novelty numbers, marching band music, and patriotic hymns into best sellers. Yet the introduction of the jaunty, syncopated ragtime styles truly sparked the nation's music business. Scholars have debated the origins of ragtime for generations. Some rely on Scott Joplin's early professional career in and around St. Louis to suggest that ragtime originated there; others, often citing Jelly Roll Morton's foundational claims, focus on the early brass bands in New Orleans as a central location of ragtime rhythms.[25] The pianist Eubie Blake, on the other hand, made a case throughout his long life that ragtime had no single original locale. The first place Blake heard ragtime growing up in Baltimore "was in the churches." "I heard musicians playing it," he recalled, "coming back from funerals, playing marches by Verdi, Chopin, syncopating the music." Blake asserted that "everybody thinks funeral marches were played only in New Orleans but that isn't so."[26] By the late nineteenth century, African American brass bands, and their sophisticated approaches to group improvisation, performed in many black communities throughout the country. Even Joplin famously recognized in 1913 that "there has been ragtime music in America ever since the Negro race has been here, but the white people took no notice of it until about twenty years ago."[27] Joplin's suggestion for a long historical arc in describing the black origins of ragtime rhythms is nearly as telling as his appraisal that eventually white folks took notice. Segregation may have kept blacks' ragtime culture a secret from whites, but by the 1890s, American markets had begun to cross over the color line.

Since at least the 1880s, black musicians along the Mississippi River, from the upper Midwest to the South, had performed highly syncopated dance music for mostly black audiences, and as Blake's Baltimore memory demonstrates, these styles flowed throughout America's waterways. The initial ragtime performers may have been itinerant black piano "doctors" and "professors" who combined quick, often jarring, right-hand melodies against thumping straight, or "even," time in the left-handed bass register. Then as now, the contrast between steady rhythmic beats and sharp, eccentric ones created the syncopation. As ragtime became codified, syncopation most often signaled the practice of sporadically emphasizing the upbeats of a bar in contrast to the solid downbeats— the "1, 2, 3, 4" one might use to count off a song or tap one's foot. The contrasting interplay between the regular and irregular musical accents made ragtime melodies seem to rush, sometimes drag, and then rush again—often in the same line. Ragtime musicians could perform any style of music in a "ragged" way, and many gained acclaim for ragging popular European classics. But early ragtime musicians also played assortments of string instruments: banjos, mandolins, guitars, fiddles, mouth harps, harmonicas, and all manner of hand percussion. Originally, ragtime denoted a performance approach or technical practice of playing, rather than a specific musical style or genre—to "rag" a piece of music meant to enliven it with unexpected syncopated rhythms. By the early 1890s, musicians, both black and white, who toured vaudeville and minstrel circuits would have been familiar with ragtime approaches to string band and piano music.

When ragtime performance practices entered song publishing and vaudeville circuits, the sounds of syncopation quickly became codified musical styles and commodities. As the music historian Jeffrey Magee writes, "There is a sense in which ragtime did not really exist until it was named and marketed as such."[28] In contrast to Joplin's long history of the style, the abrupt rise of ragtime in American music and theater industries suggests that it emerged as a cultural commodity once it was sold as sheet music and advertised through vaudeville skits and new forms of media. One of the first published songs to feature ragtime syncopations was written by the black actor from Kentucky who Will Marion Cook landed to star in *Clorindy*.

Ernest Hogan came up through vaudeville. Born Reuben Crowdus in Bowling Green, Kentucky, on April 17, 1865, he began his professional life as a child bootblack in Kansas City and started playing on the stage at the age of twelve. He performed in various readings of *Uncle Tom's Cabin* and toured the South and Midwest as a child actor—called a "pickaninny" in black vaudeville—in what he considered the "first 'pick' act."[29] In the early 1890s, Hogan formed his own touring company and produced an unsuccessful show called *In Old Tennessee*. When he sold the publishing rights for his first song, "La Pas Ma La," to the song publisher J. R. Bell in Kansas City in 1895, he made $25 and thought he had gotten the better side of the bargain. One of the first published songs in the United States to feature heavy syncopation in the melody, "La Pas Ma La" is an early example of ragtime caught on sheet music, and it earned Hogan the title "Father of Ragtime"—a delineation much disputed later in the twentieth century, and one Hogan never used himself. Besides being an early ragtime sheet, "La Pas Ma La" was also one of the first dance-instruction songs in American popular music, anticipating later rock-and-roll, soul, and hip-hop hits with lyrics explaining a popular dance style:

Hand upon yo' head, let your mind roll
Back, back, back and look at the stars
Stand up rightly, dance it brightly,
That's the Pas Ma La.[30]

Ernest Hogan. Photographs and Prints Division, Schomburg Center for Research in Black Culture, New York Public Library, Astor, Lenox, and Tilden Foundations.

The song proved one of the most lucrative hits of the nineteenth century, earning more than $100,000 during its first year of publication. One year later, having learned how to better negotiate a contract, Hogan sold his tune, "All Coons Look Alike to Me," on a royalty basis to M. Witmark and Sons, one of the recent firms to crop up along Tin Pan Alley. After three months, he had earned $26,000 and, during the following three years, as the song kept selling in the United States and England, Hogan earned $100,000 from this single tune.[31] "All Coons Look Alike to Me" also made for the first published song to advertise a "ragtime arrangement" on its cover.[32] It became, therefore, an early ragtime commodity, circulating the name of an exciting new musical style just emerging from black neighborhoods and spreading across the country. Through Hogan's musical innovations and commercial success, an aspect of working-class black musical culture infiltrated mainstream American culture industries.

The same year Hogan published "All Coons Look Alike to Me," the United States Supreme Court ruled on a landmark case brought by Homer Plessy, a New Orleans man so light-skinned as to appear white, but whose African ancestry denied him the privileges of whiteness in Louisiana. Provoked by an 1890 state law requiring racial segregation on public transit, an interracial group helped Plessy bring a test-case suit in 1892, in hopes of shining a national spotlight on southern segregation. In 1896, federal justices decided in favor of the State of Louisiana, legalizing racial segregation and setting a standard of "separate but equal," which meant that segregation did not violate the Fourteenth Amendment's stipulation that all U.S. citizens be treated equally under the law. By and large, only southern states systematically instituted public segregation practices, but the *Plessy* decision allowed local communities and municipalities throughout the country to discriminate at will, laying the foundation for living, working, and leisuring separation between the races that continues to this day.[33] *Plessy v. Ferguson*, and the system of American apartheid known as Jim Crow that it codified, enveloped Hogan's song. And like the 1830s minstrel song, "Jump Jim Crow," which became the namesake of southern segregation, "All Coons Look Alike to Me" took on a life of its own not only as a best-selling hit but as a representation of how American popular culture helped institutionalize white supremacy.

Ironically, perhaps, Hogan claimed that "All Coons Look Alike to Me" was not an expressly derogatory song, even as he acknowledged mixed feelings about it. The song, Hogan asserted, concerned a young black woman who could not choose among her suitors who, to her, all looked the same. Hogan maintained that he had initially written the song with a chorus of "All Pimps Look Alike to Me," and then changed the word "pimp" to "coon" to be less offensive. "We have been called every name under the sun, so I added another," Hogan told the vaudevillian Tom Fletcher, "The coon is a very smart animal, so I gave the song the title."[34] Regardless of Hogan's claim, the song's social resonance took flight through the transactional avenues of mass consumer culture, and so flew far away from Hogan's authorial intentions. But his recollection conceals the ways he played to market demands to make a hit. Hogan may have thought that "coon" was a less harmful word than "pimp," but both terms point to his intent of selling his song within a publishing industry thriving on stereotypical racial imagery.

The derisively titled song's success may have come as a surprise to Hogan. But even more shocking to him was the way it spawned a new genre of American popular music: the "coon song."[35] Popularized mostly

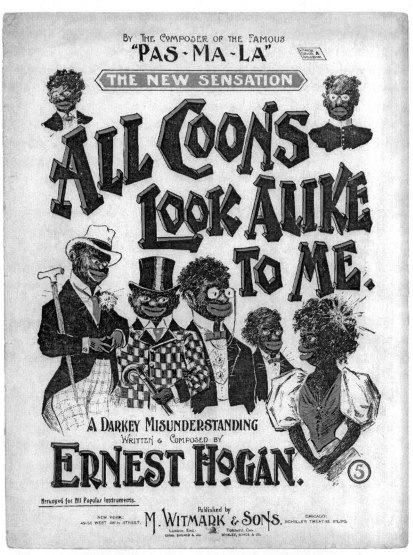

"All Coons Look Alike to Me" (1896). Courtesy of the Smithsonian Institution, National Museum of American History.

by white women on the Broadway stage, among them May Irwin, Sophie Tucker, and Anna Held, the "coon song craze" of the late 1890s resulted from updated versions of blackface minstrel caricatures meeting an expanding music publishing business. Where minstrel stereotypes had traded in antebellum notions of blacks as unintelligent and hapless— yet joking and jovial—objects of ridicule, coon songs played to whites' post-Reconstruction concerns about black northern migration, urbanity, and citizenship. Coon songs presented African American men as razor-wielding thieves, indisposed to the hard labor that urban and industrial economies in the North demanded. Lazy and criminal black men, according to America's most popular music genre, gambled away what money they had and preyed on oversexed black women to support them.

Racist parodies of men and women emphasized black sexuality, calling attention to both their uncivilized and immoral natures and to one of the most pressing concerns for Jim Crow America: interracial sex and the so-called miscegenation of the races. In the age of southern racial terrorism and lynching culture, male coons lusted not only after black women but white women too; and black women worked to seduce white men.[36] "All Coons Look Alike to Me" was not the first published song to incorporate the racially pejorative term "coon," nor was it the first to feature heavily syncopated rhythms. But as it combined racist lyrics in "black dialect" with the new, syncopated sounds of ragtime into a single commodity, the popularity of Hogan's song instigated *two* new commercial music genres simultaneously: ragtime and the coon song.[37]

In the mid-1890s, ragtime and coon songs entered American entertainment markets at nearly the same moment. As genre labels, the two were often used synonymously.[38] In most cases, ragtime songs with lyrics sold in much higher numbers than instrumental ragtime tunes. Thus by 1900, some scholars suggest, coon songs most often denoted popular ragtime ditties with lyrics, while the marker "ragtime" implied instrumental music—most often scored for solo piano. The latter style became best represented by Scott Joplin's complex and sonorous piano pieces like the "Maple Leaf Rag" (1899), which critics still call "classic ragtime."[39] But at the height of Tin Pan Alley production, little distinction existed between the use of ragtime and coon song as genre labels. Ernest Hogan himself referred to all syncopated popular music styles as coon songs, and the black Tin Pan Alley songwriter J. Rosamond Johnson called various iterations of syncopated hits ragtime.[40]

Once ragtime styles arrived in New York, they instigated a boom on Tin Pan Alley, effectively transforming American song publishing by introducing commodified versions of black musical culture, most often composed by white songwriters. Manhattan publishers capitalized on consumers' demands for exciting, propulsive ragtime rhythms, as well as the racialized stereotypes of African Americans that saturated coon songs from lyrics to cover art. Rather than having to wait for a touring show to come to town to see some "coon comedy," as black vaudeville became known,

Americans throughout the nation could buy their own sheet music of a new hit song from their local five-and-dimes, most often featuring wide-eyed black caricatures on their four-color covers. After "All Coons Look Alike to Me," music publishers in New York jumped on the coon song bandwagon. More popular than any single performer, the coon song genre became a national music fad. Hundreds of songwriters, singers, and musical producers—black and white—began to incorporate images of African Americans as idle, lusty, and violent into their products. By 1900, coon songs had become a mainstay on the Broadway stage, and more than six hundred published coon songs circulated, some selling over three million copies, with the vast majority engineered by whites and Tin Pan Alley production lines.[41] David Suisman has shown that ragtime music—implying lyrical coon songs, which always sold better—was Tin Pan Alley's "leading commercial product" during an "explosion in songwriting [taking] place around the turn of the century."[42] As such, the coon song constituted the first nationally popular music genre of the twentieth century.

Yet even as coon songs disseminated popular representations of African Americans as violent slaves to their appetites, the music's promotion of syncopated rhythms yielded a subtler effect on the listening public. By introducing syncopated rhythms to music-buying Americans, coon songs instigated the popularity of black musicians' music. Ernest Hogan died of tuberculosis as a young man in 1908, and he took the conundrums surrounding "All Coons Look Alike to Me" to his grave. As he told Tom Fletcher, the tune "caused a lot of trouble in and out of show business, but it was also good for show business. . . . With the publication of that song, a new musical rhythm was given to the people."[43] Since the popularization of jazz in the 1920s, American music fans and critics often assume direct connections between African American rhythmic inventiveness and African cultural retentions. Indeed, since the 1960s, when R & B, soul, and funk musicians joined jazz players in celebrating their connections to African liberation movements and African diasporic cultureways, black musicians have claimed their African roots to powerful artistic and political effects. But in 1900, Hogan understood ragtime rhythm as a recent innovation, something forged in the cultural imagination of African Americans to be sure, but also something that signaled modern, up-to-date African Americans rather than an ahistorical, transcontinental legacy. Unlike Joplin, Hogan heard in ragtime neither antebellum slaves nor precolonial Africans. Ragtime syncopation resonated as the sound of modern black America, and Hogan hoped that it might become an important development in American show business, by and for "the people."[44]

His partner in *Clorindy* hoped to cultivate the popular demand and social resonance of ragtime too.

In 1883, an unusually self-assured young man named Will Marion Cook left his family home in Washington, D.C., to follow his parents' footsteps to the dormitories of Oberlin College. Since 1835, Oberlin had supported the abolition of slavery and preached a progressive stance on racial equality.[45] Cook's parents, Isabel and John Hartwell Cook, had met at Oberlin, and both graduated. Born in 1869, their son demonstrated remarkable musical skill at an early age, and his parents sent him to study at Oberlin's conservatory at the age of thirteen. Graduating three years later, Cook enrolled in the Berlin Hochschule für Musik, where he studied violin with Josef Joachim, a close friend of Johannes Brahms.[46] (Cook's parents were friends with the former slave and statesman Frederick Douglass, and Douglass helped raise money to send Cook to Germany.) On his return to the states in 1889, Cook met a baritone singer named Harry T. Burleigh, who was studying under the renowned Czech composer Antonín Dvořák, the acting headmaster at the National Conservatory in New York. Burleigh, in fact, famously introduced African American slave spirituals to the Bohemian composer, having learned them firsthand from his own grandfather who had bought his freedom in 1832 and retained the melodies and lyrics to dozens of spirituals throughout his life. Cook's meeting with Dvořák spurred the younger man toward competing impulses. On the one hand, he developed a sophisticated analysis of black history, culture, and American racial oppression; on the other hand, even as he continued to cultivate his rare musical skills, he spurned European-based formal training as a form of internalized white supremacy and chose instead to compose and develop commercial styles of ragtime song and musical theater.

Cook had come of age in a black Washington community intent on proving African American fitness for U.S. citizenship. Even as the District of Columbia itself became less hospitable to African Americans—the nation's capital predated the *Plessy* decision by thirteen years, passing stringent segregation laws in 1883 that ghettoized blacks in strict neighborhoods in Georgetown and along Seventh Avenue—the city was home to a denser distribution of professional blacks than any other American urban center.[47] With educational institutions like Howard University and M Street High (renamed Dunbar High in 1916), black Washington created the conditions for expanding education and professional success among

African Americans. In the aftermath of a failed Reconstruction, music and musical education seemed a particularly appropriate vehicle toward citizenship for a small group of elite African Americans. Through their mastery of European music practices, black instructors in Washington hoped to prove the lie of black inferiority, as exemplified by an elite group of young, formally trained musicians—a Talented Tenth of would-be virtuosos. This cultural uplift agenda drew strict distinctions between art music and African American popular forms, suturing those with access to institutional training from those without.[48] Yet educators like James Monroe Trotter cared little about being perceived as elitist. In the years and decades after emancipation, as so many vied to represent the ex-slave through the American imagination—for good, for ill, and for commercial gain—members of the Talented Tenth were deeply invested in creating a model for the modern African American citizen in their own image.

In the years following the Civil War and Reconstruction, Trotter left his native Boston for the nation's capital, where he hoped to use music and musical education to combat the resurgence of white supremacy then occurring throughout America. His strategy was rooted in a politics of respectable representation. In his reliance on music education in the name of racial uplift, Trotter embodied his generation of black educators' emphasis on "civilization" and learned culture. By the 1870s, African American leaders, reformers, and spokespersons generally agreed with most middle- and upper-class whites: culture implied the behaviors, dispositions, and art of an educated, well-to-do elite minority. To be cultured in late nineteenth-century America meant belonging to a certain class that not only privileged the cultivation of intellect and talent but also had the money and leisure time to pursue them. Black and white elites understood culture as evincing from the soul; properly internalized, culture reflected an individual's or community's spiritual nature and announced a society's advancement into civilization. It was a Eurocentric consideration, one that educators like Trotter hoped might unite learned African Americans with their white counterparts—if only they imbibed the civilizing forces of European culture.[49]

Intent on proving black intellectual capacities and fitness for full and equal citizenship in the United States, black civilizationists like Trotter sought to undermine postbellum justifications for the systemic racism of American academics, policy makers, and producers of consumer culture—specifically ideas about blacks' inherent, biological inferiority to whites. Trotter hoped to raise the status of African Americans in his country by nourishing what he understood to be the civilizing tendencies of the learned arts, education, and religion in ways that demonstrated blacks' abilities to adapt to post-emancipation life in and out of the South. Trotter used the tools at his command to demonstrate the fallacy of white supremacy. Music and music education were his weapons.

In his 1878 *Music and Some Highly Skilled Musical People*, one of the first books on black music written by an African American, Trotter emphasized the importance of "scientific" training and "refined public performance" for young black musicians, skills that would demonstrate their capacity to master European pedagogical and performative approaches to music making. He insisted that blacks study theory, master sight-reading, learn to interpret difficult music, perform in public, and teach these skills to the next generation of African Americans. Trotter's book laid out his agenda for respectable musical racial representation. Part music history, part collective biography of contemporary black musicians, and part instruction manual, Trotter's book celebrated the power of music throughout human history while emphasizing African Americans' contributions. In this way, he zeroed in on black Americans' music both as a key presentation of the race to white America and as a tool of cultural uplift among blacks.[50] In his preface, Trotter noted the "haze of complexional prejudice" among white Americans that created "erroneous and unfavorable estimates of the art-capabilities of the colored race." By "contributing to the formation of a more just opinion" among whites and "aiding to establish between both race relations . . . mutual respect and good feeling," Trotter hoped to "inspir[e] the [black] people most concerned . . . with a greater pride of their own achievements."[51]

Recognizing that the emancipation of 4 million black slaves would vastly transform American society, Trotter hoped that music—and its clear appeal to Americans of all races—would help establish a "new order" in the United States, one based on equality and shared access to the rights, privileges, and protections that American citizenship promised. In Trotter's estimation, music was both unifying and universal; it offered "a language all its own . . . bearing with it ever an exquisitely touching pathos and sweetness that all mankind may feel."[52] Despite the sweeping rhetoric, though, there is no mistaking Trotter's fundamental claim: African Americans had contributed significantly to American musical culture, and they would continue to do so in larger numbers, gaining increasing respect across the nation as thousands more gained access to education and professionalization. Yet unlike the black intellectuals of the early 1900s who championed spirituals as indications of blacks influence on American music, Trotter only celebrated black musicians who had mastered

European classical styles. Antebellum artists like the opera singer Elizabeth Taylor Greenfield (known as the "Black Swan") and the Luca Family demonstrated blacks' abilities to develop a "scientific musical culture" and won Trotter's approval. These artists were quite removed from the sounds and expressions that African American slaves had created before the Civil War.[53]

Although Trotter respected the slave spirituals, he did not think they should become the primary sonic representation of African American culture. For Trotter, the spirituals relied more on emotional power and natural expression than intellectual and scientific mastery, a quality he feared might reinforce common racial stereotypes of blacks as passionate and corporal, and not cerebral and self-disciplining. Even more problematic, the spirituals reflected all too starkly the dark centuries of slavery and embodied a "former life of enforced degradation," rather than looking forward to a time when blacks would gain the skills to compose new art pieces using established European forms. Reviewing his first encounter with the Fisk Jubilee Singers, Trotter wrote that it "must be sadly remembered that these Jubilee songs . . . reminded the hearer of the unfortunate state [of slavery]; and to the cultured, sensitive members of the race . . . these reminders were always of the most painful nature." Hoping to shed completely the legacies of the past, Trotter thought it better to transcend four hundred years of slavery and cultural innovation rather than build from them. His criticism of the Fisk Singers specifically, and his appraisal of the spirituals generally, revealed his Eurocentric educational agenda and belied his investment in the notion of progress. Had the Fisk Singers established "a model for the present and the future?" he asked. "In some respects they have; in others they have not."[54]

Ultimately, Trotter hoped black composers and musicians would strive toward a "higher aim" than formal recitations of slave spirituals. He dreamt of a black musical development that would announce African Americans' aesthetic arrival into U.S. citizenship. As African Americans exhibited a mastery of European forms, performed in concert venues, and developed educational models for the future, he anticipated that black spirituals would "in a short while give place to such music as befits the new order of things."[55] Writing in the 1870s, as most Americans debated about a "new order of things" in an American society ruptured by civil war and emancipation, Trotter dared to dream. Yet just as he could not foresee the rise of a new order of white supremacy in the shape of Jim Crow segregation and discrimination, neither could he accurately anticipate the development of African Americans' musical inventiveness.

Between the 1870s—when Trotter wrote his book and the Fisk Jubilee Singers began to popularize the spirituals—and the early 1900s, African American leaders and educators started reassessing the value of slaves' vocal stylings. Around the time Will Cook made his debut on Broadway, two important critics weighed in on debates about the significance of black slave music.[56] The first was a leading European composer famous for creating critically acclaimed, large-scale pieces of formal music based on the folk melodies of his Bohemian compatriots; the second was one of America's leading African American intellectuals—a man with his own profound investment in the "black folk" and their social advancement in their American homeland.

Inspired by his student Harry T. Burleigh's singing of the spirituals, Dvořák, in 1893, famously asserted in the *New York Herald* that African American and Native American musical traditions might lay the foundation for the development of a "great and noble school of music" in the United States, adding European legitimacy to an idea that some Americans had considered for years. Dvořák's pronouncement concretized the idea that slave spirituals provided the foundational material for the formal development of American music into an expressive style of music in the European classical tradition in ways that would reverberate for generations. (In 1925 and 1936, Alain Locke would still be articulating a similar vision of black musical progress, even as he claimed to speak for a "New Negro" of the post–World War I era.) Like the German, Italian, Slavic, and Bohemian folk cultural movements that European intellectuals of the time saw as the "natural" expressions of their races, Dvořák asserted that the slave spiritual "suits itself to any mood or purpose. There is nothing in the whole range of composition that cannot be supplied with themes from this source." But the music of an uncultured folk was not enough. Trained musicians and composers must take the musical material and develop it, civilizing the folk melodies, meters, and rhythms, just as a country's leaders must reconstruct their peoples into modern citizens and proper representations of the nation. "Take those simple themes," Dvořák recommended, "and weave them into splendid and harmonious forms."[57] Formally trained African American musicians and other members of the Talented Tenth embraced the "Dvořák Statement," as it became known, as well as its wider implications, drawing the inspiration to compose new types of art music from the soul of their perceived folk inheritances.[58]

Yet more than Dvořák's statement or any other single work, W. E. B. Du Bois's celebration of the spirituals, which he called the "Sorrow Songs," in *The Souls of Black Folk* of 1903 set the terms for African American recognition of a black musical past and the spirituals' potential influence on the future. Calling the spirituals the "most beautiful expression of human experience born this side of the seas," Du Bois emphasized their unique musical and spiritual properties and famously heralded their potential to heal the wound of race in America. "Through all the sorrow of the Sorrow Songs," he determined, "there breathes a hope—a faith in the ultimate justice of things, that sometime, somewhere, men will judge men by their souls and not by their skins."[59] It was not the unlearned sonic legacies of the past, however, that called toward African America's future. Du Bois anticipated that, using the spirituals as base material, black musicians would develop new forms of African American—and American—expression. To his ears too, the Sorrow Songs recalled a folk art, one that required formal training and artistic refinement before it could resonate as the music of a nation.

Du Bois understood black music primarily as an expression of an oppressed people struggling for citizenship. He was less interested in a people's artful sounds than in the ways those sounds represented a people.[60] For Du Bois, the spirituals' transformation from primitive folk art into concert music—with their promise of further developing into sophisticated symphonic and choral forms—paralleled the plight of 4 million African Americans as they transitioned from slave to citizen. The Sorrow Songs, like the people who created them, were roughly hewn but brimming with immense potential. Much like Du Bois counseled education and entrepreneurship for a Talented Tenth of black Americans who would uplift the black masses into civilization, so would the formally trained musical elite take the basic melodies and rhythms of the spirituals and transform them into high art, ultimately making blacks a "co-worker in the kingdom of culture."[61]

Like Trotter—and most Americans, black or white, of his era—Du Bois could only hear slave spirituals as a primitive folk music of the past. Even as Du Bois broke from many of his class and generation in venerating, rather than attempting to forget, the Sorrow Songs, he still considered them folk inventions of an unlearned and impoverished people. They did not resound as the music of modern black America, an identity that Du Bois and his Talented Tenth hoped to exemplify. A sense of modernity, with its connotations of change and progress, undergirded *The Souls of Black Folk*; the text reads like a primer to both black and white Americans about the future of the African American citizen. Du Bois saw himself as a modern American—a new personality with unprecedented access to the promises of U.S. democracy and industry—and, too, as a modern African American, "a New Negro for a New Century" who would learn the lessons of his enslaved forefathers and struggle to transcend the contours of America's racial apartheid.

Like all who trafficked in the discourse of modernity, of course, Du Bois drew distinctions between himself and those who came before.[62] As he helped concretize notions of modern black concert music—the music of the spirituals and the formal music that would develop from them— he glossed over the many complexities of both, assigning a single black folk music and situating its production in the past. In 1900, the black masses, to whom elite black and white critics alike ascribed black folk culture, were a multitude. They lived in the present, not the past. And they did not create, enjoy, sell, and consume any single type of music. The musical expressions of the black masses, in fact, proved as myriad as the people themselves. Blacks lived in every state in the Union, and most danced to their own local beats.

By the early 1900s, a generation after James Trotter's heyday, black music educators' central anxiety no longer concerned debates over the spirituals but, instead, the growing interest in commercial culture across America as exemplified by entertainers like Ernest Hogan and Will Marion Cook. African American consumers were not unique in their embrace of popular culture, nor were black sounds the only commodity transforming U.S. culture. But because black vaudeville performers and ragtime songwriters played leading roles in promoting American mass culture in the mid-1890s, black leaders, educators, and social reformers fretted considerably. Their strategies to forge new public representations of black people and black culture seemed undermined by increased visual and aural representations of African Americans as minstrel caricatures and racist stereotypes.

That some blacks helped promote these images and sounds seemed doubly problematic. Trotter had worried about the commercial influence on black music and racial representation back in the 1870s. Emphasizing music's religious nature, he asserted that true art stood in contrast to commercial interest. Even student groups working to raise funds for black universities, in Trotter's assessment encouraged the commodification of black musical performance. To have the proper spiritual bearing (and political agenda), Trotter alleged, black music must be performed not for money but to illustrate a technical virtuosity that would impress the most refined white supporters of culture and the arts.[63] J. Hillary Taylor, the editor of the deliberately highbrow *Negro Music Journal*, which he published in 1902 and 1903 in Washington, D.C., may have disagreed with Trotter's assessment of the spirituals. But he dedicated much of his publication to distinguishing "the purest and best" music from the "low, trivial, popular music."[64] Contributors to the journal, who included one of America's leading African American violinists, Clarence C. White, and Harriet Gibbs Marshall, the founder of the Washington Conservatory of Music in 1903, regularly denounced "low" and "popular" ragtime, seeing in its unprecedented popularity much cause for concern.

To combat the spread of ragtime, black music critics increasingly invoked the notion of black authenticity, most often measuring mass-produced ragtime tunes against the spirituals—those "unpolished gems of Negro musical talent," as one *Negro Music Journal* contributor called them.[65] Even though, by 1902, the spirituals in question were now decades removed from slavery, contemporary performances of them still seemed to resonate with an unencumbered racial authenticity, especially when contrasted with ragtime. As the *Negro Music Journal* presented it, ragtime was merely an artificial, commercial contrivance of older and more authentic black folk forms. The spirituals, one critic proclaimed, were "as far from the vulgar [ragtime] as the electric light is from the candle."[66] Distributed through the marketplace rather than the concert hall, ragtime constituted but an inauthentic approximation of "real Negro singing." "The average 'coon song' of the present day," an unnamed commenter asserted, "bears not the least relation to these *real* Negro melodies."[67] Another critic put it this way, drawing a stark line between his readers and the black masses: "One thing is certain: the voice of the people is not the voice of culture and art."[68] Will Marion Cook disagreed.

Cook, called "a native genius of surpassing brilliance" in the *Negro Music Journal* and cited favorably five times in fifteen issues, did not consider the spirituals any more authentic than African Americans' new variations of commercial music.[69] He rejected the idea that folk music must be formalized before it could properly represent modern African Americans (or the United States, for that matter). Staking a claim in an idea that would not become popular among black leaders for decades to come, Cook chose popular music and its commercial sphere of influence as the proper form of "real Negro melodies" and "modern Negro music."[70] A few years after meeting Harry Burleigh in 1889, Cook enrolled in the National Conservatory to study with Dvořák, who initially impressed Cook because of his interest in black spirituals. Cook worked with the composer only a short time, however, before spurning his lessons and dropping out. Soon afterward, in 1894, Cook met a black vaudevillian named Bob Cole, and the duo put together a small string orchestra for Worth's Museum in

Greenwich Village.[71] Shortly afterward, Cook returned home to Washington, but he had decided to use his formal training in the service of popular music.

INVENTING MODERN NEGRO MUSIC

To the consternation of his parents, Cook dedicated the rest of his life to composing and conducting variations of ragtime musicals on commercial theater stages, opening up previously closed spaces to black entertainers and beginning a radical reevaluation of the cultural and professional values of black music. Sometime in 1894, Cook came up with an idea for an operetta, one that might allow him to showcase his studied approach to operatic music, which combined the complexity and dynamism of the European stage, with his interpretation of what he called "real Negro melodies." He asked the established young poet Paul Laurence Dunbar to help write a musical about "how the cakewalk [dance] came about in Louisiana in the early Eighteen Eighties," a show that reflected southern black culture as he had known it in Tennessee during summers with his grandfather.[72] Hoping to combine ragtime rhythms with African American slave melodies, as well as European counterpoint and harmony, Cook imagined one of the first American fusions of the arts—and anticipated an entire twentieth century of American music making.

On a humid summer night in Washington, Cook and Dunbar holed up in Cook's brother's basement apartment with two dozen bottles of beer, a quart of whiskey, and a raw porterhouse steak with red peppers and onion—but no piano. Cook recalled that the duo composed the entire storyline and libretto, all of the songs, and "all but a few bars of the ensembles" for *Clorindy*. The following morning, back at his parent's house, Cook was trying out his "most Negroid song," "Who Dat Say Chicken in Dis Crowd?" on the family parlor piano when his mother burst in with tears in her eyes. She cried "Oh Will! Will! I've sent you all over the world to study and become a great musician, and you return such a *nigger*!"[73] Her dismay derived from his choice to compose ragtime over classical music. Cook claimed that, even though his parents "loved the Dunbar lyrics," it was the ragtime syncopation that made his song too transgressive. Considering the words both Cook and his mother used to describe the sound of the song, syncopated rhythms made the song black, either appropriately so ("most Negroid") or too much so ("nigger"). Isabel Cook had not sent her son to three renowned conservatories to learn ragtime.

Will Marion Cook. Music Division, New York Public Library for the Performing Arts, Astor, Lenox, and Tilden Foundations.

But to Cook, ragtime was merely an adaptation on the black spiritual tradition. A new and distinct iteration of an earlier form, ragtime had its sound and soul rooted directly in slave culture. He considered slave spirituals "the natural growth of a race" and the foundation of all subsequent styles of African American music. Cook's reading of black musical history was far more expansive than either Trotter's or Du Bois's. He included minstrel songs, even though he noted they were "less true of real Negro aspirations and inspiration," and he considered the jubilee singing of the 1870s an "artistic triumph," one that rekindled the memory of his forebears. Yet between 1875 and 1888, the years in which educators like Trotter established their pedagogies, Cook asserted that there was no "further development in Negro music." The cause, in Cook's estimation:

> Afro-Americans had been so thoroughly taught by the white man that his color, condition, and accomplishment were inferior, that the younger generation at once threw aside all tradition. Any reference to the past became a disgrace . . . the glorious old slave hymns and spirituals frowned upon as "reminding us of a past full of shame and misery." (This is quoted from the protest of a prominent music teacher twenty years ago in the city of Washington.) . . . Result, milk and water imitations of inferior white musicians.[74]

Although the quotation Cook referenced may not have been from Trotter, Cook's attack was clear: he despised late nineteenth-century attempts to uplift black people by disregarding centuries of slave culture in favor of European art music. Formally trained himself, Cook renounced the Eurocentrism implicit in African American educators' aesthetic values. "My mother," Cook once wrote, "thought that a Negro composer should write just like a white man."[75] A percolating black nationalist, Cook rejected what he considered the internalized white supremacy of his black instructors as much as he fought the externalized racism of his white ones.

Cook regularly, and willfully, pointed out the engrained white supremacy of African Americans whenever he discerned it. When Cook met his future wife at an audition for *Clorindy*, she was just thirteen years old. Abbie Mitchell impressed Cook immediately with her excellent singing voice, one she had honed on her aunt's West Thirty-third Street fire escape in the heart of New York City's Tenderloin district. When she walked into Cook's audition, she met Dunbar and Burleigh. Sitting at a piano, Cook asked Mitchell if she knew any "Negro songs." "No," she replied, "I'm a nice girl. I only sing classics." As she remembered years later, Cook "laughed and pulled his hat further down over his eyes." Burleigh, an accomplished baritone, walked quickly over and asked her to sing him a few scales. They then began singing "Ave Maria" together before Cook interrupted them, telling the teenager that she had a "glorious voice, plenty of fire, but you can't sing a damn thing!" Before Mitchell could respond, Cook turned to the piano and played his most recent ragtime composition. "That's the kind of music you should sing," he told her; "that's Negro music and you're ashamed of it!"[76] It was the beginning of a fecund, though stormy, relationship, not unlike Cook's relations with most of the people he met or with whom he worked. In the words of a contemporary, Cook advocated the ideal of a "genuine Negro" artist, who should "eschew 'white' patterns, and not employ his efforts in doing what 'the white artist could always do as well, generally better.'"[77]

Embracing slave spirituals as the foundation of the Negro music he hoped to develop, Cook sought to translate their sonic power and racial character into forms more readily accessible to American audiences of all races in the twentieth century. He did not disdain popular music, nor did he reject commercial opportunities. Instead, Cook recognized early that America's burgeoning cultural marketplace offered unprecedented opportunities for black professionalism and unparalleled avenues within which to transform popular representations of African American people and culture. In this way, he was far ahead of the Talented Tenth. Still, like Du Bois and many others who urged black musicians to develop their talents and sonic innovations, Cook too aimed to innovate for the future while building from the roots of African American musical traditions. Like Hogan, who talked about the "new musical rhythm" his coon songs helped popularize, Cook too hoped to craft modern versions of "real Negro melodies," new styles of Negro music for a new Negro people, yet one rooted in African Americans' rich, though obscured, cultural legacies.

Ragtime, Cook believed, offered a chance to break from previous generations' rejection of black musical history. The new music marked both black musicians' embrace of their racial heritage and a true iteration of "modern Negro music." Ragtime was so popular, he suggested, because it "offered unique rhythms, curious groupings of words, and melodies that gave the zest of unexpectedness."[78] Ragtime songs with lyrics—the coon song that dominated American music markets—utilized interesting expressions of black language, often best represented through dialect verse, a style that songwriters and poets like Dunbar appropriated from the minstrel stage. Ragtime's melodies seemed to jump from line to line, spurred on by the inventive harmonies as well as the tunes' pulsing rhythms. As the name of the genre makes clear, syncopation was ragtime's dominant characteristic and the element that most distinguished Negro music from other types. Cook called it a "rhythm and swing unique as compared with the music of other races."[79] Rhythm made ragtime fresh, surprising, and immensely popular. By the time Cook began composing his own interpretations of modern Negro music in the Manhattan musical marketplace, ragtime rhythms pointed toward a future of black musical development unashamed of its roots, yet developing from them and retaining what Cook understood as its essential racial characteristics.

Cook hoped to play a role in the future development of Negro music. "What the Afro-American has thus far accomplished is only a promise—an expectation," he suggested, "the realization belongs to the future." "A school must, and will be, established," Cook proposed, "perhaps at Washington, D.C.," where "an eminent European composer and teacher (preferably a Russian) who, unhindered by prejudice, will understand, appreciate, and foster the peculiar genius of the Afro-American child."[80] Like Trotter and Du Bois, Cook felt the pull of European musical traditions as a path to legitimizing African American expression. Even as he denied Trotter's directive to abjure slave music, Cook believed in training young musicians, in incorporating European approaches to formal music education, and in mastering classical harmony alongside rhythmic dexterity. It would take this pluralistic approach to construct and cultivate new forms of black musical expression for a new century. It became Cook's lifelong goal to compose and popularize what he thought of as authentic iterations of Negro music, and he saw no contradiction in using the marketplace—or even the limitations that racialized markets imposed on him—as a vehicle for doing so.

Ragtime composers of Cook's generation understood the profundity and power of slave spirituals and saw themselves as natural heirs to slave musicians' creations. As Cook helped popularize ragtime and made black musical styles increasingly ubiquitous throughout Manhattan and U.S. entertainment markets, he understood himself as a translator of earlier forms of black music, a mediator of a transitional period for the development of black music, and an instigator for its further development. As he embraced the limitations of commercial markets and popular racial stereotypes, Cook also challenged white supremacist assumptions about black culture and opened up unprecedented opportunities for thousands of black entertainers. And although he, like all black ragtime composers and performers, would trade in racist representation to sell his hit songs, Cook did not see his ragtime commodities as any less authentic than the nineteenth-century slave spirituals he venerated. Choosing a third alternative to the dichotomous conception of black music as either folk or formal promulgated by Du Bois and Trotter, Cook imagined ripe possibilities for his music as both a powerful new representation of black culture and a commercial product in America's burgeoning mass entertainment marketplace.

COOK AND HOGAN'S PRODUCTION of *Clorindy* on a Broadway rooftop marked African Americans' arrival to the near pinnacle of American commercial culture industries in the last years of the nineteenth century. The next step would be performing inside Broadway theaters and garnering critical praise and commercial success, a step Cook would attain as the musical director for Bert Williams and George Walker's immensely popular musical theater troupe between 1902 and 1908. While the expansion of black touring shows, as well as blacks' emergence as popular songwriters, had been developing throughout the 1880s and 1890s, it was only at the dawn of the twentieth century that black entertainers found lucrative professional opportunities and avenues for social respect.

As black entertainers entered vaudeville, musical theater, and song publishing industries, they transformed them, but not in their own image, and not on their own terms. Like all popular entertainment producers and consumers, black performers fashioned a place for themselves in mass culture markets in ways subject to the desires and ideologies of U.S. society. Forced to respond to, and regularly reinscribe, the legacy of blackface minstrelsy through coon songs and coon comedy, African Americans approached the Manhattan musical marketplace as the landscape where commercial products vied for cultural value and economic worth. Besides navigating American culture producers' and consumers' racialized imperatives, black New Yorkers also had to maneuver among a wide host of directives not commonly associated with cultural marketplace demands: uplift ideology, the politics of representation and respectability, and new conceptions of folk and formal black music.

Cook and Hogan inaugurated new considerations of Negro music. They disrupted many of the rigid distinctions African American intellectuals held between folk/formal and high/low (and many others). Most significantly, the duo called attention to a historical process that turned the folk music of the American slave into the sound of modern America. Throughout most of the nineteenth century, "Negro music" connoted the vocal music of a supposedly natural and expressive, primitive and premodern folk. But in the first and second decades of the twentieth century, Negro music resounded as a rhythmic dance music representing not only African American modernity, but U.S. modernity more broadly. The changing social resonances of black music took place over time and maintained a variety of contradictions. The following chapters will explore how ragtime rhythms came to symbolize American modernity for many culture producers and consumers, black and white, while also revealing how white folks' conception of their own modernity relied both on white perceptions of black primitivism and blacks' exclusions from modern leisure spaces. A "new musical rhythm" laid the sound track for American modernity.

CHAPTER TWO

DO ALL WE COULD TO GET
WHAT WE FELT BELONGED TO US
BY THE LAWS OF NATURE

Selling Real Negro Melodies and Marketing

Authentic Black Rhythms

When the narrator in James Weldon Johnson's anonymously published novel, *The Autobiography of an Ex-Coloured Man,* first entered the New York City neighborhood known as Black Bohemia, he was immediately struck by the sound of ragtime. "The barbaric harmonies, the audacious resolutions . . . the intricate rhythms in which the accents fell in the most unexpected places, but in which the beat was never lost, produced a most curious effect," he exclaimed. "It was a music of a kind I had never heard before. It was a music that demanded physical response, patting of the feet, drumming of the fingers, or nodding of the head in time with the beat."[1] Ragtime rhythms reverberated throughout Black Bohemia, a reality Johnson knew firsthand.

Early in the summer of 1901, Johnson and his brother, J. Rosamond, rode a train from their home in Jacksonville, Florida, to New York. Having studied at the New England Conservatory in Boston for six years before touring with black vaudeville shows, Rosamond was more familiar with the rapidly urbanizing Northeast than his older brother. But the Johnsons had spent the two previous summers boarding at 260 West Fifty-third Street, just northwest of the theater district along Broadway Avenue and directly north of the Tenderloin. On their return to Black Bohemia on this third summer, the Johnson brothers found "some marked changes had taken place."[2]

James Weldon Johnson recollected that the two black-owned hotels and restaurants, the Marshall and the Maceo, were "running at full blast." In contrast to the dozens of black-owned saloons and nightclubs in the Tenderloin, these establishments offered rare upscale dining experiences that "made possible a fashionable sort of life that hitherto had not existed" for African Americans in the city. Johnson remembered that the "sight offered at these hotels, of crowds of well-dressed colored men and women lounging and chatting in the parlors, loitering over their coffee and cigarettes while they talked or listened to the music, was unprecedented."[3] As the Johnson brothers discovered, the quick propulsive sounds of ragtime piano, often accompanied by small string bands, singing voices, and rhythmic dancers, marked the neighborhood—and Hotel Marshall especially—as a generative space for African American artistry and commercial leisure. The brothers moved immediately into the hotel, where they entered a cyclone of black cultural creativity. Years before James Weldon Johnson became a leading player in the Harlem Renaissance of the 1920s, before he worked as a field secretary for the National Association for the Advancement of Colored People in 1916, and even before he became President Theodore Roosevelt's consul to Puerto Cabello, Venezuela, and Corinto, Nicaragua, between 1906 and 1912, Johnson lived in the Hotel Marshall, where he and his brother helped build a diverse community of African American performers and musicians into self-conscious symbols of black modernity.

Like the black intellectuals and formally trained musicians who made up the Talented Tenth, Hotel Marshall entertainers debated about the best ways to present new forms of black culture and how to represent African Americans as modern U.S. citizens. The Marshall community indicated a plurality of black expressions; the entertainers living, working, and leisuring out of the hotel came from diverse backgrounds with disparate access to education and social status. Nonetheless, dozens of these performers worked together on various projects, often influencing one another. The excitement Marshall musicians generated grew out of their myriad degrees of artistry, their chosen performance mediums, and their various personal and collective desires for the race. Yet even given the heterogeneity of personal style and artistic visions, Marshall musicians increasingly used their race as a defining category for their music. They developed ever-deepening conceptions of a singular, essential, and "authentic" conception of "Negro music."

James Weldon Johnson recalled that Will Marion Cook and Bob Cole most often disagreed about Negro music's stylistic development, as well as its powers of racial representation. (The duo had a long and stormy relationship ever since Cole had first introduced Cook to vaudeville, taking the Berlin-trained violinist away from Dvořák's tutelage and signing him up as a conductor in Greenwich Village in 1894.) Cook imagined producing and perfecting "genuine Negro" music, one that would "eschew 'white' patterns," while Cole hoped to master the techniques that white theater producers had established on Broadway to demonstrate African Americans' ability to innovate along established lines and thus open the "Great White Way" to black writers and producers.[4] Cook and Cole's disagreements reflected not only aesthetic differences but also variations in commercial strategy.

Theirs was not simply an argument about how to define black culture—they wanted to define it as a product they could sell in the Manhattan musical marketplace. While Cole would soon partner up with the Johnson brothers to write songs behind the scenes for white Broadway shows and Tin Pan Alley song publishers, Cook became the music director for the first African American theater troupe to make a sensation in Broadway theaters. Whereas Cole and Johnson tunes rarely announced the author's race, the musicals and hit songs of Cook, Bert Williams, and George Walker (regularly cocomposed by half a dozen other Hotel Marshall regulars) most often featured Williams and Walker on their song sheet covers, sometimes in blackface costume, other times in formal evening dress.[5] As Cook and Cole debated the best presentations, artistic innovations, and commercial strategies with which to promote black music, they frequently disagreed about the best way to establish an in for Negro music styles.

Yet no one at the Hotel Marshall questioned that African American entertainers needed to construct new cultural representations of black advancement and artistry. Most at the Marshall thought that the commercial fields of music and theater constituted worthy avenues for their transformation of American racial values. And to varying degrees, Hotel Marshall musicians invented new commercial strategies aimed at undermining the pernicious influence of blackface minstrelsy—black entertainers concocted new ways to understand black authenticity as a constitutive feature of black commodity production in the commercial culture marketplace. Black authenticity was not buried in an imagined folk past; it was something that modern African Americans could cultivate, and even sell. Among a variety of multimedia artistic interventions into various burgeoning culture industries, ragtime's syncopated rhythms increasingly came to resonate as the authentic sound of modern blackness.

In turn-of-the-twentieth century New York, black entertainers fashioned a new notion of black authenticity as a strategy to intervene into commercial markets already trading in the racist imagery of blackface.[6] Understood this way, racial authenticity emerged not as biological truth, but as a marketing tactic distributed by mass consumer capitalism. There were numerous historical precedents for ascribing notions of authenticity to black bodies and black culture, many dating to antebellum slavery. But the growth of popular music and vaudeville markets in the late nineteenth century created the conditions for black entertainers to capitalize on a product cloaked in the purported realness and racial truth of their own bodies. Black musicians in New York traded on preexisting ideas of inherent racial differences as they commodified their performances into a recognizable product to sell in popular entertainment markets. The process whereby African Americans fashioned and sold their racial status as a form of cultural value instigated a transformation in popular entertainment industries. The commodification of black cultural expression enabled black performers to claim new powers within commercial markets and to sell the idea that African Americans' race made them exceptionally talented entertainers.

Marshall musicians made ragtime culture ubiquitous in the Manhattan musical marketplace. Through a combination of talent and determination, they entered into New York's central culture industries, musical theater (as exemplified by Broadway) and song publishing (as dominated by Tin Pan Alley). In some ways, they played to racist expectations—in most cases, there was no alternative to the legacies of blackface minstrelsy, still in 1900 America's most popular form of entertainment. Ragtime music, cakewalk dancing, and blackface comedy set the aesthetic contours of New York stages and publishing firms, as they did in culture industries across America. At the same time, black entertainers in New York made concerted efforts to transform the cultural and professional values of their entertainment; more money and more respect generated more opportunities for the Marshall musicians, and for thousands more African American entertainers besides.

Yet Marshall musicians also took seriously their roles in representing black America. They hoped their new forms of entertainment would uplift popular conceptions of African Americans, both in the ways white people and institutions understood blacks, and in the way black audiences understood their cultural inventions.[7] In that regard, they relied on many of the same impulses as did the Talented Tenth, so vehemently rejected by Cook. While the next chapter puts the Marshall entertainers in direct dialogue with the Talented Tenth, the present one focuses on how black musicians created new conceptions of black authenticity to concretize a race-based approach to art making and entertainment advertising. When Hotel Marshall musicians' creative innovations made ragtime's rhythms the sonic signifier of black authenticity, they created new values of black music.

A DIVERSITY OF BLACK CULTURAL EXPRESSION

The Hotel Marshall furnished a shared social space for the leading black performers in New York, and in the two decades before the city's "Jazz Age," it became Manhattan's single most important site for the formation and circulation of new types of black cultural expressions. Between 1896 and 1912, the Hotel Marshall's rarified leisure space for black artists and interracial audiences reinforced a sense of racial and professional solidarity and generated a fertile environment wherein new ideas and contested opinions could gestate among a cohort of friendly yet often competitive African American musicians. The Marshall helped members of different theater companies compare notes and form lasting partnerships, and it provided a space for the city's most established professional performers to relax together and enjoy the rewards of their hard-earned labors. It was here under dim lights that new syncopated melodies for a Broadway show were tried out for the first time, perhaps applauded or dismissed, edited or rearranged. In the basement of the Marshall, couples invented new dances with the encouragement of small audiences and large doses of alcohol, and grandiose ideas of future black operas weaved within the tapestries of vaudeville skits. James Weldon Johnson remembered that the Marshall was "more than a 'sight.' Its importance as the radiant point of the force that cleared the way for the Negro on the New York stage cannot be overestimated."[8]

Williams and Walker's move into the Hotel Marshall in 1896 helped make it the central space for black performers in New York. A native of Nassau, Bahamas, Williams met his partner, born in Lawrence, Kansas, in San Francisco around 1893, and the duo began developing a vaudeville routine rooted in physical comedy and racialized humor. Both men sang and danced with unusual style, so as to be at once exquisitely graceful and awkwardly comedic. Billing themselves the "Two Real Coons," to distinguish themselves from white minstrels and to assert their claim on a racial authenticity, Williams and Walker toured the West together for a time before being promised work in New York by the producer George Lederer. Lederer's pledge to have the two star in *The Gold Bug* fell through on their arrival, but the performers chose to stay in the city and moved into Jim Marshall's brownstone on West Fifty-third Street. There they reconnected with a former stage employer, Ernest Hogan, who that year was making inroads into song publishing with his hit, "All Coons Look Alike to Me." Hogan had also recently arrived in New York hoping to translate his success at selling coon songs into work in vaudeville. He too began capitalizing on the color of his skin, calling himself the "Unbleached American" on stage billboards and song sheet covers throughout America.[9] At the Marshall, Williams and Walker also met the multitalented Bob Cole, who was just finishing his first full-scale stage show, *A Trip to Coontown*, and an entire community of black performers intent on breaking down racial barriers along the Great White Way. Walker remembered that by the time the comedic duo arrived in New York, they had "discovered an important fact, viz: the one hope of the colored performer must be in making a radical departure from the old 'darky' style of singing and dancing," and they began "thinking along new lines." Williams and Walker started looking for like-minded performers to help transform the look and sound of black entertainment in the nation's capital of vaudeville and popular song production.

The duo opened the doors of their Marshall flat to "all colored men who possessed theatrical and musical ability and ambition," and it quickly became the headquarters of "all artistic young men of our race who were stage struck." By "having these men around us," Walker recalled, "we had an opportunity to study the musical and theatrical ability of the most talented members of our race."[10] Hogan's partners in *Clorindy; or, The Origin of the Cakewalk*, Will Marion Cook and the poet Paul Laurence Dunbar, began showing up at the Marshall, as did the Tin Pan Alley songwriters R. C. McPherson and J. T. Brymn. By the time James Weldon Johnson and his brother Rosamond moved in and started composing ragtime hits with Cole, dozens of other singers, actors, writers, and musicians were calling the Marshall home. Rosamond Johnson ran into Jesse Shipp, a friend from his vaudeville days, who began writing scenes and songs for Williams and Walker. Theodore Drury, the city's leading black opera singer who, in 1904, would create New York's first all-black opera company, came to rub elbows with Jack Nail, a saloonkeeper and future real estate mogul of Harlem, as did countless working musicians, vaudevillians, and playwrights looking to meet talent and discuss the future of Negro music.[11]

Even as they discussed Negro music as a single, racially essential form of cultural expression, the Hotel Marshall community generated heterogeneous and multimedia cultural commodities that symbolized the diversity of black creativity, rather than any static formula. Once Williams and Walker hired Cook as their musical director around 1901, for example, the trio began to experiment with vaudeville theater and ragtime music in ways that sparked a revolution on Broadway between 1902 and 1908. Ragtime song and dance was nothing new on Broadway—white acts had been interpolating coon song hits (by both black and white composers) since Hogan's "All Coons Look Alike to Me" caught fire in 1896. But African Americans had not performed on Broadway since Hogan and Cook's *Clorindy* played on a rooftop garden in 1898, and Hotel Marshall musicians were eager to conquer America's biggest stages. Williams, Walker, and Cook juxtaposed established theatrical techniques with creative reinventions of set design, plot, humor, music, and dance, all of which the Williams and Walker Company designed to resonate as modern forms of black music and theater.[12] The Williams and Walker Company produced three large-scale musicals on Broadway between 1902 and 1908: *In Dahomey*, *Abyssinia*, and *Bandanna Land*. *Abyssinia* (1906), especially, set new standards for Broadway spectacle. With the inclusion of dozens of live animals, massive set scenery, dramatic lighting techniques, intricate costumes, and even an onstage waterfall, the musical introduced new standards for Broadway productions, influencing white shows for years to come.[13]

As they built on public interest in ragtime rhythms and coon song stereotypes, Williams and Walker made the cakewalk a sensation on the vaudeville stage in the late 1890s. But in 1902 they translated their success to the New York Theatre with their musical *In Dahomey* (1902), becoming the first black troupe to open in the main theater of a Broadway playhouse. Popularly associated with antebellum southern blacks who mimicked the formality of eighteenth-century white slave owners, the cakewalk developed over time into a slow, controlled, and straight-backed couples walk. But in late-nineteenth-century black vaudeville, the cakewalk became a ragtime dance, often the curtain closer of the show. The vaudevillian Tom Fletcher remembered that "all the big colored shows featured the Cakewalk."[14] In Williams and Walker's iterations, the cakewalk could be an exaggerated and comedic, high-kneed and spaghetti-legged walk complete with false slips and near collapses. Yet George Walker and Aida Overton Walker's interpretations of the dance demonstrated how beautiful and sensual it could be. *In Dahomey* featured a cast of one hundred actors and dancers, and the show closed with fifty couples strutting their stylized versions of the cakewalk up and down the Broadway stage to the animated applause of interracial—though segregated—Manhattan audiences before touring the United States and the United Kingdom. *In Dahomey's* success made the cakewalk a fad in many American cities.

Williams and Walker Company, cakewalk from In Dahomey.
From left: Hattie McIntosh, George Walker, Aida Overton Walker, Bert Williams,
and Lottie Williams. Billy Rose Theater Division, New York Public Library for
the Performing Arts, Astor, Lenox, and Tilden Foundations.

"At one time, in 1902 and 1903," George Walker recalled, "we had all New York and London doing the Cakewalk."[15] The principle choreographer of the company, Aida Overton Walker, won renown as an especially gifted and "graceful" cakewalk instructor to many of New York's wealthiest families.[16] Williams and Walker made the antebellum style into a modern American dance, one that symbolized black ingenuity as much as it reflected modern American performance culture.

Williams and Walker's next production, *Abyssinia*, was Cook's first opportunity to score an entire musical since *Clorindy*. Whereas *In Dahomey* had been a pastiche of prior Williams and Walker productions (including songs, jokes, and plot points from nearly a dozen Hotel Marshall musicians), *Abyssinia* offered Cook unprecedented freedom to develop his studied yet idiosyncratically ragtime-inflected musical accompaniment. He composed music for the entire show, creating a sonic consistency never before found in black musical theater. Cook worked with Williams and the Marshall regular Alex Rogers on the ragtime numbers of the show, but most striking to many observers was the complexity

"Good Morning, Carrie" (1901; by McPherson, Smith, and Bowman),
featuring Bert Williams and George Walker on the cover. Music Division, New York
Public Library for the Performing Arts, Astor, Lenox, and Tilden Foundations.

of his interludes and choral arrangements.[17] Cook's orchestration and conducting struck one critic as "exceptionally high class," while another noted that the "play depends on its musical features," where the "chorus singing is mighty good and would be worth going to hear if the rest of the show were nothing."[18] Echoing the Dvořák Statement, the *Indianapolis Freeman* reported, "'Abyssinia' is indeed a Negro play to be proud of, and the grand and diversified score of music composed and arranged by Prof. Will Marion Cooke . . . [is] to be credited with the final accomplishment of founding and substantiating a new school of American comedy and also music."[19] Yet alongside their musical ingenuity and theatrical creativity, productions by Williams and Walker retained many characteristics of minstrelsy, filling the stage with stereotypical characters, plots, and themes.

The legacy of blackface minstrelsy, and African Americans' use of its tropes, made for thorny discussions among the Hotel Marshall community. Whereas Cole and the Johnson brothers sought to bypass most minstrel conventions by working behind the scenes as songwriters for Broadway plays, the Williams and Walker act underlined the artificiality of minstrelsy, not by distancing itself, but by embracing its limits—racist stereotypes and all—and selling it back to the white culture industries that spawned minstrelsy in the first place.[20] Williams and Walker musicals usually centered on downtrodden and hapless, though humorous, characters. Williams became one of America's most popular comedians because he was so good at playing what he called the "Jonah Man," a character that wrung humor from tragic bad luck:

> My luck started when I was born, leas' so the old folks say.
> Dat same hard luck's been by bes' friend to dis very day.
> When I was young, Mama's friends—tho find a name they tried,
> They named me after Poppa—and de same day Poppa died.[21]

While Williams's Jonah Man character offered a creative update to the slow-witted "Sambo" figure from the minstrel stage, Williams and Walker shows regularly portrayed the star actors gambling, scheming, squandering their earnings, and enacting black stereotypes through jokes about chicken, watermelons, razors, fistfights, and black women. In significant respects, Williams and Walker did little to distance their act from the racialized caricatures that had undergirded American comedy since the earliest days of minstrelsy. Their iterations of blackface comedy and coon-song humor helped Williams and Walker attain new heights on New York's leading stages. But their act also threatened to undermine their goal of transcending the racial limitations they faced.

George Walker acknowledged the charade while noting the few avenues open to black performers. "Our poets," he told a white newspaper, "must stick to negro dialect to make themselves heard, or to sell their wares, and our composers must write ragtime for the same reason, until the white man's serious consideration has been earned."[22] Quite aware of the dangers they faced in negotiating the imperatives of white audiences and Broadway theater managers, Williams and Walker regularly discussed the dilemma in the white and black press, claiming to seek the slippery middle ground in producing black art while appealing to white desires. "There is something about the darkey character that appeals with peculiar force to pleasure loving people," Williams told a reporter, "and by the same token the attempt of a colored player to go out of his native line is rebuffed."[23] Writing in *Variety* magazine, Walker described the difficulties he encountered performing for whites who "only want to see him portray the antebellum 'darky.'"[24]

When Williams and Walker stepped too far from caricature, white critics thought their musicals "too white." *Abyssinia*, one critic remarked, "is a product from beginning to end of Afro-American enterprise and ability, but unfortunately for the piece the inspiration was largely Caucasian."[25] As Walker explained, the "colored man's love affairs are like his ragtime music and his dialect poems. No matter how carefully written, they must not be otherwise than amusing."[26] Alongside the cakewalk and blackface comedy tropes, the Marshall musicians' universal reliance on dialect offers a good example of a minstrel convention that became a central characteristic of African Americans' own sense of black performance of the era.

As Hotel Marshall songwriters concocted strategies to reclaim black representations from white minstrels, coon-song writers, and Broadway producers, dialect English became a central hallmark of black music and theatrical performance. Because coon songs represented blackness not only through the sound of the music but also through the very language of the lyrics—the way blacks were shown to speak—black song- and scriptwriters increasingly used dialect in creative and musical ways, emphasizing black Americans' figures of speech and rhythmic cadences. Hotel Marshall musicians, for instance, all used dialect verse to define their ragtime tunes as Negro music—a quality as essential as syncopated rhythm. Yet blackface minstrelsy had relied on dialect for decades, so African Americans' use of it proved a challenge, because it called to mind the minstrel stereotypes they sought to undermine. Writing in his autobiography years later, James Weldon Johnson described his realization of the "artificiality of conventionalized Negro dialect poetry . . . of its limitation as an instrument of expression to but two emotions, pathos and humor," a discovery that forced him to question blacks' reliance on the trope: "I could see that the poet writing in the conventionalized dialect . . . was dominated by his [white] audience . . . that when he wrote he was expressing what often bore little relation, sometimes no relation at all, to actual Negro life; that he was really expressing only certain conceptions about Negro life that his audience was willing to accept and ready to enjoy."[27] Johnson's realization grew from his conversations with Paul Laurence Dunbar, the celebrated poet who had written *Clorindy* with Will Marion Cook.

For Johnson, African Americans' use of dialect reflected the conundrums blacks faced when trying to sell cultural products to white audiences. Near the end of his short life, Dunbar confided to Johnson that he "didn't start as a dialect poet," but by "doing so, I could gain a hearing." "I gained the hearing," he lamented, "and now they don't want me to write anything but dialect."[28] Dunbar's analysis of his predicament resembles the limitations black musicians confronted when they sought to "gain a hearing" in Manhattan music markets. Will Cook understood the problem well, once telling the *London Tattler* that "the terrible difficulty that composers of my race have to deal with is the refusal of American people to accept serious things from us."[29] As we will see, Johnson and his partners would negotiate the limits and possibilities of black dialect, but most of the Hotel Marshall musicians attempted to utilize its racial connotations to their advantage. Dialect was one way to claim racial ownership over their new styles of cultural expression. Problematic as it was, dialect illustrated blackness on the stage and in music; it was a tool African Americans could wield to intervene in the Manhattan musical marketplace.[30]

SELLING BLACK AUTHENTICITY

From early on in their partnership, Williams and Walker capitalized on the color of their skin and traded on the idea of racial authenticity. They were not only some of the earliest black performers to differentiate themselves from whites in blackface by promoting their blackness; they were some of the most successful at it too. Beginning with naming themselves the "Two Real Coons," the duo replicated Jim Crow–era notions of racial difference, hoping to use racial distinction to their advantage in markets dominated by white men though mysteriously grounded in blackness. Recalling how, early in his career, he had recognized a "great demand for black faces on the stage," Walker decided that he and his partner would "do all we could to get what we felt belonged to us by the laws of nature."

In their interviews and promotional materials, Williams and Walker played to common conceptions of "nature" and the seemingly unchangeable differences between the races to sell themselves in entertainment markets. This not only played to post-1830 conceptions of inherent, biological racial difference but also doubled down on the supposed primitive and folk nature of black entertainment that the Talented Tenth aimed to transcend. Walker discussed his awakening to the fact that his race—and what he understood as the "natural" performance skills of African Americans—allowed him a leg up in competing against white minstrels' approximations of black song and dance. Because nothing in white minstrels' "actions was natural," Walker wrote in 1906, the acts were not "as interesting as if black performers had been dancing and singing their own songs in their own way."[31] Williams asserted similar points, especially to the white press. The "American Negro is a natural minstrel," he told a white reporter, "he is one in whom humor is native, often unconscious, but nevertheless keen and laugh-compelling. He dances from the cradle, almost, for his feet have been educated prenatally, it would seem. . . . There is a soul in the Negro music: There is simplicity and an entire lack of artificiality."[32]

Early twentieth-century American theater audiences loved watching performances that seemed to lack artificiality—the fact that they were paying ticket prices to watch a performance mattered little. While this might be the case for most audiences in the twentieth century, Americans, who felt themselves in the thrall of modernity, especially looked for cultural approximations of the "natural," the "real," and the "true." And a majority of white Americans had for a long time seen blackness as the most authentic form of cultural expression. Much of this had to do with the long history of minstrelsy and its lasting influences on American entertainment. At the same time, self-described moderns also yearned for a simpler and slower time—a conceit as textured by nostalgia and false memory as many whites' racial imagination. While white culture consumers' investment in performed authenticity certainly reflected wider social trends of urbanization, technological innovation, and industrial capitalism, black entertainers' promotions of black authenticity invigorated white desire for what the historian David Krasner has called "the real thing."[33] Although they did not begin the trend, black musicians of Williams's and Walker's generation increased the cultural value of black authenticity, capitalizing on it in their professional livelihoods and concretizing American audiences' desire to watch, listen, and purchase black authenticity wherever it was for sale.

By claiming a racial ownership over ragtime song, dance, and theater, Williams and Walker helped initiate a new marketing strategy based on selling black authenticity. Their pitch had two steps. First, the duo claimed the racial authority to perform in a "black style." By grounding authentic black performance in black bodies, they captured a cultural agency to own, perform, and trade in blackness in ways white minstrels could not. Second, by donning blackface themselves, singing dialect-laden coon songs of their own imagination, and dancing the most absurd cakewalk imaginable, Williams and Walker called attention to minstrelsy's artificiality and exposed the falsity of whites in blackface. The lack of realism in minstrel conventions—which the "Two Real Coons" broadcast through their performance even as they trafficked in authenticity—created a critique of the minstrel humbug, and of white supremacy more generally. In Williams and Walker's hands, racism was part of the joke. Williams and Walker sought to put a new face on black entertainment. But, once on, the burnt cork of racial essentialism proved difficult to rub off. Although Walker stopped performing in blackface after 1902, Williams continued to until his death in 1922.

When African Americans "blacked up" and performed like white actors pretending to be black, they engaged in a process commodifying a racial fiction. Minstrelsy's romantic mythos maligned African Americans and disseminated the racial animosities of the Jim Crow era through ethereal consumer culture markets. Yet minstrelsy also opened doors for African American entertainers and, already peddling the idea of racial authenticity, helped shape black performers' new commercial strategy: they took ownership of minstrelsy's racial representations, performing its purported ethnographical certainty as their own. The musicians living and working out of the Hotel Marshall were not the only ones to do so; in fact, black vaudevillians throughout the country gained entry into theater markets by claiming their status as "real Negro" performers, deliberately building on—and absconding with—minstrelsy's depictions of racial difference. Between 1895 and 1905, when African American vaudeville companies proliferated, black performers throughout America (but mainly based in New York City in the off-season) explicitly promoted themselves as raced entertainers. Traveling vaudeville troupes with names like the Colored Sports Company, the Old Sunny South Colored Company, the Black Diamond Quartet, the Lady Africa Company, Coontown 400 Company, the Hottest Coon in Dixie Company, and John Isham's Octoroons began to crisscross the nation. Besides the "Two Real Coons," Bert Williams and George Walker employed other racialized names, promoting new shows as the Kings of Colored Comedians and the Tabasco Senegambians.[34] Titles of the shows, many of which came to name the producing company, also reflect the rise of race-based branding: *Black America, A Trip to Coontown, The Black 400s Ball, The Cannibal King,* and Williams and Walker's double entendre, *The Sons of Ham,* which poked fun both at white supremacists' attempts to locate black inferiority in the Old Testament and at the pair's own "hammy" comedy styles.[35] The quick growth in race-marking names happened in half a decade—the same years in which white supremacy became recodified throughout the United States by the Supreme Court's *Plessy* decision, making Jim Crow segregation the law of the land. As black performers promoted themselves as the authentic delineators of black culture, they reified the idea of an essential black culture even as they capitalized on it.

As they traded on racial authenticity, Williams and Walker fought to wrestle the cultural value and symbolic capital of black culture away from white minstrels and coon-song shouters. In some ways they succeeded. By 1906, as Williams, Walker, and Cook staged *Abyssinia,* one white critic bemoaned the "passing of the minstrel," suggesting that "those who recall the halcyon days of the negro minstrel . . . regret this gradual extinction of a delightful form of entertainment."[36] Even as Williams and Walker undermined the value of minstrelsy, however, their increasing reliance on the idea of black authenticity reinforced the racial logic of both the antebellum slave and the Jim Crow eras: blacks differed inherently from whites, and one needed to look no further than to the stark differences between their performative cultures. Black entertainers' claims to an essential racial authenticity not only circumscribed notions of the possibilities of black culture but also led to the creation of material that would circulate in American commercial culture markets and, in crucial ways, legitimate the reformation of white supremacy during the early years of Jim Crow. While they ultimately only changed black culture workers' cultural value in slight ways, Williams and Walker had better luck raising the professional value of black entertainers.

When the "Two Real Coons" arrived on Broadway, they initiated a transformation in black entertainers' wages in New York. The duo started out earning eight dollars a week, a slightly lower-than-average wage for black vaudevillians in the early 1890s (though most likely commensurate with the youngsters' experience), and one comparable to that of black menial laborers in the urban North who received $1.25–2.25 per day at car plants and coal mines.[37] Ernest Hogan recalled paying Williams and Walker "$16 a week and refuses to go on record as to whether they even got that princely sum regularly" for a western tour years before they had arrived in Manhattan.[38] By 1906, however, as Williams and Walker began touring the country with *Abyssinia*, Hogan was "elated over the prospects of his brothers in vaudeville when he recalls that the two great colored comedians, Williams and Walker, were paid $1,750 a week." Lester Walton, the culture editor for the *New York Age*, understood the dialectical relationship between professional and cultural value well, noting Williams and Walker's interventions in both: "There are two results usually sought after by the performer—the artistic and the financial. Usually if a performer gains artistic success the other follows . . . Williams and Walker . . . not only take pride in the success they are making in vaudeville from an artistic standpoint, but they feel proud of being able to state they are receiving the largest salary ever paid to colored vaudeville performers." Between runs of their third (and last) full-scale musical, *Bandanna Land*, Walton noted that the duo made $2,000 per week in New York vaudeville.[39] Increasing their professional value by impressive figures, the pair shared the wealth with their company and expanded the earning potential of many others.

Walker also understood the direct relationship between professional value and cultural value. "Our payroll is about $2,300 a week," he told the *Age*; "Do you know what that means? Take your pencils and figure out how many families could be supported comfortably on that. Then look at the talent, the many-sided talent, we are employing and encouraging. Add to this what we contribute to maintain the standing of the race in the estimation of the lighter majority. Now do you see us as a racial institution?"[40] Walker noted the fiscal support their company gave back to the black community, comparing their theater group to more standard—and "respectable"—institutions. In 1908, Walton reported that "Colored performers are getting more money in vaudeville to-day than ever before. Cole and Johnson are receiving a large weekly salary for their act. Ernest Hogan has the record for big money for a colored individual vaudeville star. . . . When you take into consideration that years ago Williams and Walker were making a big hit in vaudeville and were receiving $100 a week, there is none who can not readily see that the Negro has made rapid, yes, very rapid, strides in vaudeville."[41] After Walker's death in 1911, Walton pronounced his unmatched role in changing the economic value of black entertainment in New York as one of the entertainer's primary legacies. "There are several colored performers to-day who possibly could fill Mr. Walker's shows as a straight man," Walton asserted, "but there is not one who could . . . bring about conditions providing positions for colored writers, composers, and performers—positions paying large salaries."[42]

Beginning work in Manhattan song publishing in 1899, Bob Cole and the Johnson brothers set out with similar aims.

Before partnering with the brothers Johnson at the Hotel Marshall, Cole had toured with one of the leading vaudeville shows of the 1890s, Black Patti's Troubadours. Born Robert Allen Cole Jr. in 1868 to former slaves in Athens, Georgia, Cole worked as a singing bellboy and performed on both cello and guitar before using his skills as a performer and writer in black vaudeville.[43] On the road with the Troubadours in 1896, he wore many hats. Sylvester Russell, the former vaudevillian and "dean of black entertainment critics," asserted that Cole had "no equal as a producer, no superior as an actor, coon song singer, coon song writer or Negro comedy writer."[44] In 1897, Cole left the Troubadours to produce the first black musical that contained a continuous plot, reoccurring characters, and songs written to convey overall thematic coherence. Historians often cite Cole and Billy Johnson's *A Trip to Coontown* as the "first full-length black musical comedy."[45] The production included numbers penned by Cole like "I Wonder What Is That Coon's Game" and "Hoola Boola," which utilized both rhythmic syncopation and black dialect to signal the blackness of its singers. The loosely knit plot may have involved a cast of reoccurring characters, but they came directly off the vaudeville stage—as evidenced by contortionist dancers, cakewalk dancers, and coon songs.[46]

A Trip to Coontown poked fun at the racist conventions of coon songs and "coon comedy." Cole's song "In Dahomey" played off Ernest Hogan's "All Coon's Look Alike to Me," suggesting that "Coontown" was the "only place on earth where all coons look alike." "No Coons Allowed" ridiculed segregation laws that kept African Americans out of various public spaces, including many theater houses in the North and South. Cole also mocked the long history of blackface by "whiting up" in white makeup to portray a white hobo named Willie Wayside. *Coontown* became a hit in New York and toured the Northeast and Midwest for three years playing to mostly white audiences.[47] During his early years as a stage performer and songwriter, Cole recognized the opportunities that his race opened up in vaudeville. Like George Walker's realization that he could "entertain in that way as no white boy could," Cole began to trade on blackness as an authentic performance quality, compared to the cross-racial practices of blackface minstrelsy and vaudeville. As early as 1896, just a few years after Walker and Williams began calling themselves the "Two Real Coons," Cole promoted his sheet music as "Genuine Negro songs by a genuine Negro minstrel." In 1898, less than two months after Cook and Hogan introduced *Clorindy* on the rooftop of the Casino Theatre, Cole and is partner, Billy Johnson, performed on the rooftop garden of one of New York's largest vaudeville houses, Koster and Bial's. They billed themselves the Kings of Koondom.[48] As his shows became successful, Cole hoped to challenge popular representations of blacks from within the confines of vaudeville. The critic I. McCorker thought Cole was on his way to transforming the presentation of blackness onstage. "If comedy is ever to be 'elevated' by colored men," he pronounced, "its elevation must come through such representatives as Bob Cole."[49] Once Cole met the Johnson brothers, the trio quickly began to lessen the disparaging aspects of coon song lyrics, even as they created new approaches to syncopated ragtime rhythms.

Soon after they met at the Hotel Marshall in 1899, Cole and the Johnsons set out to write popular songs. Knowing that most Tin Pan Alley song hits caught the public ear through nightly interpolations on Broadway stages, they sought out the white women who had popularized coon songs. One of their first sales went to May Irwin, the singer best known for making "All Coons Look Alike to Me" a hit on Broadway. Cole and the Johnsons offered Irwin less racially caricatured tunes while retaining the dialect and syncopated melodies that marked them as ragtime numbers. They hoped to take the "coon" out of the coon song while keeping what they understood as the racial characteristics of the genre. Irwin's first show to feature Cole and Johnson music was *The Belle of Bridgeport* (1900), and their partnership continued for nearly a decade (until 1909). After writing songs for *Champagne Charlie* (1901) and *The Supper Club* (1901), a stage director for Klaw and Erlanger, "the most powerful factor in the whole theatrical business," Johnson recalled, hired Cole and the Johnsons to compose tunes for an upcoming performance of *The Sleeping Beauty and the Beast*. They wrote only three songs—"Tell Me, Dusky Maiden," "Come Out, Dinah, on the Green," and "Nobody's Lookin' But the Owl and the Moon"—scoring immediate hits in one of New York's largest theaters, the Broadway. The show with Klaw and Erlanger, Johnson recollected, established the writing trio as "'top-notchers' among the writers of musical comedy" in the capital of American theater.[50]

Only months afterward, Cole and the Johnson brothers made such a hit with their song "The Maiden with the Dreamy Eyes" that they initiated new economic bargaining powers for African Americans along Tin Pan Alley. After the white Broadway star Anna Held sang the song in *The Little Duchess*, the songwriting trio secured spots for fifteen new songs in all-white

From left: Bob Cole, James Weldon Johnson, and J. Rosamond Johnson.
*Photographs and Prints Division, Schomburg Center for Research in Black Culture,
New York Public Library, Astor, Lenox, and Tilden Foundations.*

Broadway productions and signed a three-year exclusive contract with Jos. Sterns and Co., one of Tin Pan Alley's largest publishers. Cole and the Johnsons bargained for a contract that stipulated monthly cash, guaranteed to be deducted from their semiannual royalties. Most black songwriters of the era sold their songs for a onetime fee, as with Hogan's "La Pas Ma La." Hogan commanded remarkable influence, in fact, to get a percentage of the publisher's sales for "All Coons Look Alike to Me." In his autobiography, James Weldon Johnson emphasized how unique it was that the trio worked exclusively for the best companies in Manhattan, drawing explicit attention to their unusual bargaining power. Their contract, he wrote, was the "first of its kind ever executed," and they enjoyed unprecedented popularity. Johnson recalled that he and his partners "became, in measure, Broadway personalities" and that in "the fullness of our vogue," Cole and Johnson songs "were being sung in three or four current" Broadway productions.[51] In 1905, a Boston-based magazine noted that the trio had earned $28,000 in royalties the previous year.[52] Once established with Jos. Sterns and Co., Cole and the Johnsons turned to combating the insipid racism of American popular song—they shifted from transforming the professional value of their labor to raising the cultural value of their musical commodities.

As they entered into song publishing, Bob Cole and the Johnson brothers worked to transcend the derogatory racial caricatures populating coon songs by promoting more realistic, human portrayals of African Americans, while still retaining most ragtime songs' comedic appeal. Cole emphasized the marked differences between his songs and the standard. "We try to write in our songs the finer feelings of the colored race. . . . Most of the 'so-called' coon songs are rough, coarse, and often vulgar." Rather than trading on racial stereotypes, Cole presented blacks as human beings, highlighting the humor and emotions they shared with white Americans—a radical step in a northern industry thriving on coon songs and a southern culture dependent on segregation and racial violence. Songs like "Sugar Babe" and "The Congo Love Song" expressed romantic love between African Americans as a serious topic, not a joke to be lampooned during an era when songs featuring romance between blacks were rare.[53] In 1906, Hogan commended Cole and Johnson for their accomplishments in the popular magazine, *Variety*, complimenting the duo for "introducing in vaudeville new lyrics and an artistic element that had not been shown by the colored man until their debut."[54] Even one of the most august black publications in America, the *Colored American Magazine*, agreed. Cole and Johnson songs were "not 'coon song' in the common acceptance of that term," an editor suggested; "they are interpretations of the soul music of the Negro people." Another noted that Cole and Johnson's "musical compositions have been progressive" and "have invariably builded something new, something surpassing, something worthy."[55]

Cole and the Johnsons' successes for Manhattan's most established music publishers convinced theater managers, producers, and actors that tunes penned by African American could enhance their shows. Their partnership with Broadway producers and, especially, the performers who requested their numbers, opened up opportunities for other black composers at the Hotel Marshall. As Cole and the Johnsons infiltrated Tin Pan Alley, and as Williams and Walker initiated a transformation of Broadway musical theater, songs by African Americans became increasingly common in Broadway programs. The *New York Sun* took note, reporting the "negro composer has now almost a monopoly on ragtime and is reaching out into more classical work, and there has hardly been a musical play in the last two or three years which hasn't contained one or more song by negroes." Contrasting popular conceptions of black musicians as untrained and natural ragtime musicians, the *Sun* praised "most of these men" as "musicians of education and high musical ideas." The reporter also recognized the commercial imperatives limiting black composers' opportunities, echoing Williams and Walker's account of the conundrums African Americans encountered in Manhattan entertainment markets. "If pinned down," the *Sun* reported, "they admit that they write ragtime not so much for love of the thing as because it pays."[56] Although white songwriters and publishers continued to dominate the music industry by selling coon songs, Cole and the Johnson brothers began a transformation along Tin Pan Alley in three ways: they modified the lyrical content—and, to a degree, racial connotations—of ragtime music products; they further ensconced black music producers into the Manhattan musical marketplace; and they raised both the professional and cultural values of black songwriters.

The trio's unprecedented position in Tin Pan Alley and Broadway theaters reveals their unusual strategies for translating the Talented Tenth's politics of uplift and representation onto unlikely battlefields. When James Weldon Johnson traveled to New York in 1901 for his third summer in a row, he was a public school principal. Born in Jacksonville, Florida, to a headwaiter from New York and a Nassau-born schoolteacher in 1871, Johnson graduated Atlanta University and worked as a teacher at his own alma mater in Jacksonville, Edwin M. Stanton School, before becoming its principal.[57] Johnson embodied the Talented Tenth of W. E. B. Du Bois's imagination: his upbringing, education, self-assurance, and investment in representing the race all indicated the makings of a race leader, lifting as he climbed. Rosamond Johnson, too, was trained to stand out and to succeed. Besides Will Marion Cook, Rosamond Johnson was the best-trained musician at the Hotel Marshall. Like Cook, he saw little contradiction in aspiring to shape popular ragtime in his own image; unlike Cook, the Johnson brothers had accepted much of the Talented Tenth's doctrines of racial representation and respectability. And, perhaps surprisingly, Rosamond Johnson had so internalized his formal music education at the New England Conservatory that he had not yet come to value the slave spirituals he would champion in the 1920s.

Even as he became a professional songwriter in 1902, Johnson considered spirituals a folk music so lowbrow as to not warrant uplift through formal artistic explorations—or even commercial interpretations. On one occasion, as the songwriters felt the pressure of a deadline, Cole suggested Rosamond use part of the slave spiritual, "Nobody Knows the Trouble I've Seen," as a starting point for a new song. Johnson refused, citing the still prevalent distinctions between respectable and illegitimate art that he had picked up from the New England Conservatory, if not actual shame. In contrast to Will Marion Cook, who embraced the spirituals and considered his own compositions updates of their sonic power and racial representation, Johnson thought the black folk tradition beneath him, even though by 1902 increasing numbers of black composers had seen themselves emboldened by the Dvořák Statement, as well as the Bohemian composer's inclusion of "Swing Low, Sweet Chariot" in his *From the New World* (No. 9 in E minor) of 1893.[58] When Johnson resisted, Cole reputedly teased his partner asking, "What kind of musician are you anyway? Been to the Boston Conservatory and can't change a little old tune around."[59] Cole eventually prevailed, and the main melody from "Nobody Knows the Trouble I've Seen" transformed into "Under a Bamboo Tree," one of Cole and the Johnsons' best-selling hits—with more than 400,000 copies sold—and easily their longest remembered. (Its melody became the Yale University's football team's chant from 1904 through the 1960s, and its refrain was so well known that T. S. Eliot included it in his "Fragment of Agon.")[60] Still, Johnson left his name off the published sheet music of "Under a Bamboo Tree," refusing accountability for interpreting a spiritual. Years later, in an autographed copy of the manuscript to Carl Van Vechten, the white Harlem Renaissance patron and writer, Johnson made fun of himself, recalling it had been "below the dignity of a student of Music at the Conservatory" to incorporate slave music into his tune.[61] Rosamond Johnson spent the 1920s and 1930s arranging, promoting, and celebrating slave spirituals. That he was so reluctant to admit their influence in 1902 illustrates the powerful hold of a formal music education in the United States, one that had not yet learned to value African American slaves' vocal compositions and singing styles.

As Bob Cole, the Johnson brothers, Will Marion Cook, and most who worked out of the Hotel Marshall knew well, African American voice had been the central characteristic of black music during the nineteenth century: expressive singing styles, blacks' seemingly sublime and "natural" expressions of religiosity, and black harmony (which included notes known as "blue notes" by the early 1920s). African American musical practices sprang from black slaves' embrace of Christianity and its cultural rituals, a process that began in earnest in the 1830s. Slave music from the 1830s though emancipation had been primarily vocal, and, to white witnesses, seemed to flow out of black bodies so easily, that black singing increasingly came to embody African Americans' inherent spiritual connection to God.[62] White accounts of black religious singing supported a host of slave owners' racial assumptions, then undergoing an array of disruptive changes due to the rise of King Cotton, the westward expansion of slavery (into the modern-day Deep South), and a growing abolition movement in the North. In response to these ruptures, slave owners rationalized their livelihood in new ways, appealing to a paternalistic sense of duty to their slaves: unlike the racial stereotypes of the Revolutionary period—when white British and Americans openly struggled with their enslavement of fellow humans—after the 1830s, slaves were considered childlike, only partially developed people who needed guidance and protection from well-meaning, paternalistic owners.[63] The 1830s also saw the rise of blackface minstrelsy and the intensified circulation of common conceptions of blacks as naturally gifted performers and especially expressive singers.

By the 1880s, as African American vocal quartets proliferated in America's black neighborhoods, black voices resonated as the essential sound of nineteenth-century black music. While the Fisk Jubilee Singers and other student groups played an important role in popularizing both the sound of the black voice and its seeming reflections of authentic black performance after emancipation, black quartets also cropped up in every black community in America in the two decades after the Civil War. As the music scholar Lynn Abbott suggests, black quartets were "nothing less than a black national pastime," an evaluation supported by the vaudevillian Billy McClain, who recalled that in Kansas City in the 1880s, "about every four dark faces you met was a quartet."[64] Quartets performed spirituals alongside a variety of popular ballads, vaudeville tunes, "work songs," and minstrel numbers like those by Stephen Foster—confirming that vocal expression constituted the essential characteristic of nineteenth-century black music.

Yet by the time the Johnson brothers teamed up with Bob Cole in 1899, syncopated rhythms had become an increasingly recognizable feature of African Americans' music. Even as songs about black life and black characters (and blackfaced caricatures), new dances like the modern approach to the cakewalk, race-based promotional strategies, and dialect verse all helped Hotel Marshall entertainers intervene into the Manhattan musical marketplace, few questioned that rhythmic syncopation was the defining characteristic of Negro music, even though such an identifying relation between rhythm and race was relatively recently conceived.[65] As Tin Pan Alley publishers mass-produced syncopated popular songs in the mid-1890s, ragtime rhythms came to represent a new approach to black music making, confirming Ernest Hogan's hope that "a new musical rhythm was given to the people" through his "All Coons Look Alike to Me."[66] As the music historian Jeffery Magee writes, "published examples of syncopation abound before the advent of ragtime . . . but the frequency, concentration, and audacity of syncopated rhythms in ragtime made the music sound so unique as to constitute a new style."[67]

At the turn of the twentieth century, however, as Americans black and white just began to understand syncopation as the essential sound of blackness, they associated exciting rhythms with an entire world of exotic music. Even black musicians understood that they were not the only ones to emphasize musical offbeats. "The songs we are writing today have many Spanish characteristics," Bob Cole told the *New York Sun*; "the syncopation is the same."[68] Anticipating Jelly Roll Morton's famous quip that jazz music had to have a "Spanish tinge," Cole connected his musical background with that of Latin America and the Caribbean.[69] The music critic A. J. Goodrich made a similar connection when he distinguished between Spanish and "negro" syncopation, even as he argued that both examples had "obvious roots in Hungarian folk styles."[70] Yet Cole not only understood African American and "Spanish" rhythms to be "the same"; he thought that Latin-influenced dance music such as the tango or the Brazilian maxixe would become the most popular styles of music in the United States, surpassing U.S. blacks' innovations. "It will not be a great while," Cole predicted, "before all the syncopated or so-called 'ragtime' music will be swallowed up by Spanish music."[71] Black musicians' approach to syncopation, according to Cole, represented only a facet of the new styles of music coming to, and being created within, the United States. He saw himself as a part of a network of international influences on American popular music. Even as syncopation was beginning to embody blackness in U.S. music, African American musicians recognized the transnational circuits of cultural borrowing.[72]

Nonetheless, as black entertainers increasingly relied on racial authenticity as a commercial strategy, they claimed a racial ownership over the syncopated sounds of ragtime. "We try," Cole told the *New York Sun*, "to retain the racial traits, not only in the syncopated time of the music, but in the lyrics as well."[73] Cole acknowledged the importance of lyrics, but he took syncopation for granted. Like Hogan and Cook, Cole understood rhythm as an essential ingredient of black music—the authentic sound of newly forming and self-consciously modern blackness. Hotel Marshall musicians sold their ideas of racial representation as thoroughly as they invented new sounds—it was a twin attack on the sonic and ideological terrain of the American marketplace, though one shaped by the contours of the marketplace itself as much as by the vanguard of African American artists. Musical ingenuity and race-based claims about the ownership of the "new musical rhythm" alone would not necessarily have made ragtime reverberate as black. Marshall musicians entered into American culture industries that already had deep roots in racialized thinking. The Manhattan musical marketplace had formed the contours of what could be "black" or "white" (or "Spanish") cultural commodities during the early years of Jim Crow. Ragtime musicians' drive to concoct new types of racial representations through their new styles of music fit neatly into already determined market-based conscriptions, like a black hand in a white glove.

As ragtime's quick, sprightly rhythms became central markers of African American cultural expression, they also captured the musical imaginations of American culture consumers of all races. Alongside black rhythmic ingenuity, the Manhattan musical marketplace pushed professional songwriters to innovate new types of syncopation and to incorporate them into their Tin Pan Alley hits. The marketplace fueled musicians' artistic freedom to explore new worlds of syncopation because black rhythm sold. For Cole and the Johnsons to write a hit for Broadway, for example, they had to mirror aspects of the most popular tunes already succeeding. As the songwriting trio composed new iterations of ragtime tunes, they further embedded black syncopations within the marketplace, both becoming successful and influential songwriters and deepening the connections between black rhythm and the Tin Pan Alley commodity. While less vocal about the need to solidify a single authentic style of black music than Will Marion Cook and George Walker (at least publicly), Cole and the Johnsons reinforced what they understood as the basic connection between black music and ragtime rhythms by composing syncopated hits and considering them reflections of their race. And they were surprised when the connections between race and rhythm turned out to be more tenuous than they imagined.

The emergence of Cole and the Johnson brothers as popular songwriters highlights the paradoxical nature of establishing "real Negro" sounds and black musical authenticity in the Manhattan musical marketplace. Because the trio most often wrote songs for white Broadway shows, their race was not always readily apparent. Most of their song sheets featured the white "star" performers who interpreted their hits on the stage. In 1905, Edward Bok, the editor of the *Ladies Home Journal*, asked the trio to contribute a series of songs to the magazine. Rosamond wanted to write in four distinct styles, portraying the historical development of African American music. Beginning with a song in the style of a slave spiritual, they moved through minstrelsy, banjo tunes, and ragtime.[74] After the songs' publication, James Weldon Johnson met with Bok, who was excited to read him some fan mail. Months had passed since Bok had published Johnson's work, but he had recently promoted an upcoming song from a "young Negro composer in Georgia," which caused a "white woman in a little town also in Georgia" to protest. No "Negro," she declared, "had the musical skill or the artistic taste to interpret even his own race, much less the ability to do anything worthy of going into the pages of *The Ladies Home Journal.*" Unable to hold his laughter, Bok read the woman's final sentence, which implored him to "give us some more of those little Negro classics by Cole and the Johnson Brothers." Johnson recollected: "I laughed too; but my laughter was tempered by the thought that there was anybody in the country, notwithstanding the locality being Georgia, who, knowing anything at all about them, did not know that Cole and the Johnson Brothers were Negroes."[75] In the mind of the Georgian letter writer, ragtime rhythms represented the distinct attributes of African Americans, but ragtime only displayed artful coherence once mastered by whites. It served as a stark reminder not only of the racism of an average white ragtime consumer but also of the slippery connections between race and music. Even as Hotel Marshall musicians self-consciously worked to change Americans' racial assumptions, and to elevate African American citizenship, few direct avenues existed in the world of popular culture. And black musicians could never control the flow of traffic.

BY EMBRACING AND SELLING racial difference, black musicians became leading cultural innovators, symbols of modern black representation, and central players in the formation of modern American culture. This emerging racial formation was not built on an essential or homogenous blackness. Rather, the diversity of African Americans' innovations, styles, and strategies in fact made them such strong competitors in Manhattan's marketplace. The popularity of ragtime empowered African American musicians to intervene in the city's local—but nationalizing—commercial culture industries with new and inventive musical commodities that, in turn, further propelled black innovators to the top of Manhattan markets. This reflexive, mutually propelling circuit promoted the increase of black artistry alongside the expansion of New York culture industries like song publishing, musical theater, and vaudeville. It reinforced the idea that African American entertainers were some of the best in New York City and, increasingly, throughout America.

Paradoxically, black advancement in the Manhattan musical marketplace also circulated a sense of racial essentialism through U.S. mass culture. Due in large part to the Hotel Marshall musicians' deliberate claims to own ragtime rhythms as a racial right, syncopation increasingly became the authentic sound of modern Negro music. This process did not happen immediately, nor did it reflect only the work of a small community—many more musicians besides, both in New York and across America, helped codify the sound of black rhythm and commodify its racial resonance. Most of the rest of this book charts the continuing ideological and artistic development of ragtime rhythms, with special attention to the ways in which rhythm increasingly reverberated as the sound of blackness. Before following ragtime into the black-owned leisure spaces and ragtime saloons that defined nightlife in the Tenderloin district (in chapter 4), I remain with the Hotel Marshall community to explore how they used their status as professional entertainers and, especially, their rhythmic innovations to reinterpret the Talented Tenth's politics of respectable representation.

CHAPTER THREE

APPRECIATE THE NOBLE AND THE

BEAUTIFUL WITHIN US

Ragging Uplift with Rhythmic Transgressions

Two years after Will Marion Cook's success with *Clorindy; or, The Origin of the Cakewalk* in 1898, just as he was beginning to solidify working relationships with Bert Williams, George Walker, and others at the Hotel Marshall, Cook produced his second black operetta on a New York stage. Another collaboration with Paul Laurence Dunbar, *Jes Lak White Fo'ks* presented an unusually critical view of uplift ideology and the black professionals W. E. B. Du Bois called the Talented Tenth. Anticipating by generations scholarly critiques of middle-class paternalism and classist segregation among blacks, Dunbar's lyrics and libretto parodied the African American character Pompous Johnson and his attempts to uplift "Africans" through civilization and inculcations of Victorian-era genteel morality.

The title of the play said it all: the emulation of white middle-class values reinforced the white supremacy the Talented Tenth claimed to denounce, and it did so at the expense of poor and working-class African Americans from whom professional blacks distanced themselves even as they claimed to engage in uplift. Through Pompous Johnson's pretensions to get his daughter a "family tree" by marrying her to a European prince, Cook and Dunbar elucidated a sharp critique of the politics of uplift and respectability, as well as of blacks who claimed, rather dubiously, to descend from African royalty and of those who passed for white.[1]

The musical did not do well commercially. It played only a few times at the New York Winter Garden. The same year, Cook worked with Bob Cole and the Johnson brothers at the Hotel Marshall to revise the musical in hopes of creating a better product. *The Cannibal King*, as their effort was called when it opened the following summer, featured a star-studded cast from the Marshall: Ernest Hogan, Bob Cole, Rosamond Johnson, Aida Overton Walker, and Cook's wife, Abbie Mitchell. Cook and Dunbar's musical captured in text and song many of the most querulous contests taking place in black communities throughout America, especially in those urban neighborhoods witnessing an influx of rural and uneducated blacks. *The Cannibal King* used ragtime to critique the Talented Tenth's directives, while also claiming it as a positive cultural resource, in contrast to black critics of ragtime song, dance, and theater.

New York's leading black performers were "ragging uplift" and strategizing about how best to raise the professional and cultural values of black entertainment. Hotel Marshall musicians hoped to represent the race, and they took seriously their attempts to reshape popular representations of blackness in their own image. When popular entertainers invoked black authenticity—as both a racial birthright and a commercial strategy—their racial essentialism challenged Talented Tenth notions of racial identity, as well as their political strategies to represent a "respectable" black America. Ragtime increasingly symbolized precisely what the Talented Tenth attempted to uplift and denounce. Originating in disreputable black leisure spaces with practitioners of common, uneducated, and "uncivilized" stock, ragtime—and its rise to prominence in American consumer markets— seemed to threaten the Talented Tenth's goals of advancing the politics of racial respectability and black citizenship.[2] Ragtime was commercial and mass-produced, a far cry from both the soul-stirring and seemingly truth-laden slave spirituals and the European tradition of formal musical training. Ragtime culture also reinforced the most egregious racial stereotypes through coon-song lyrics and vaudeville comedy. Because of these associations, the sound of ragtime itself—the quick, intricate, and rhythmic notes—leveled a sonic critique at the Talented Tenth's uplift ideology.

Through ragtime's sounds and connotations, the Marshall community fashioned its own politics of representation, one that hinged on a different sort of black modernity. Rather than classical training and an acceptance of European (and white American) standards of middle-class respectability and highbrow aesthetic values, musicians signaled blackness through ragtime rhythms born and circulated in the mass cultural marketplace. To Cook, ragtime culture appeared more authentic than that of the conservatory because it celebrated its roots in the black masses. No longer debating a question of folk or formal, Marshall musicians used commercial music—and its far wider avenues of distribution—to circulate their conception of a modern American artist citizen.

Even as they imagined breaking from the Talented Tenth, the Marshall community remained influenced by its politics of representation and the notion that a few could represent the many. They too saw themselves as uplifters of the race. Yet rather than working to change the behaviors and cultures of the black masses, Marshall musicians aimed to change the public representations of the culture they already had—it was an uplift agenda aimed at legitimizing blacks' culture, rather than denying it. Even as they recognized that popular entertainment went against many of the Talented Tenth's strategies, performers like Aida Overton Walker and Rosamond Johnson demonstrated that they had more access to white audiences than most members of the black professional elite, and that they therefore wielded a greater influence on the ways white Americans understood black people and culture. Many Marshall musicians also believed, however, that blacks' music would continue to "develop," a subtle indication of the ways they absorbed European and Anglo-American aesthetic evaluations (alongside correlating notions of "civilization" and progress). Hotel Marshal entertainers took their roles as examples for the race seriously, even as they sought to subvert the Talented Tenth's reliance on social hierarchies and elitist aesthetic evaluations.

The Talented Tenth's agenda ultimately helped entertainers like Williams, the Walkers, Cook, and the Johnson brothers fashion their own conceptions of Negro music and black musical theater, as well as their diverse cultural meanings and social resonances. Ragtime culture opened avenues between various strains of black intellectual thought: it intersected aspects of black nationalism and back-to-Africa orthodoxy with less institutional conceptions of black pride and African American culture. Influenced by the instruction of Booker T. Washington and W. E. B. Du Bois, as well as by the thinking of men like Alexander Crummell and Hubert Harrison (and later, Marcus Garvey and A. Philip Randolph), Hotel Marshall musicians believed in the importance of racial solidarity and sought to raise American consciousness about blacks' struggles for full American citizenship. To these ends, ragtime rhythms offered young blacks a voice—or, more accurately, an entire system of symbols, connotations, and racial identities—to represent alternative approaches to black social, economic, political, and cultural advancement in the age of Jim Crow apartheid. Ragtime revolted against not only white supremacy but also black leaders' own ideals, whether wrought in resistance to or in concert with American notions of social hierarchy and power imbalances. Using ragtime song, dance, and theater as their ideal racial representations, black musicians in New York interpreted and critiqued uplift ideology, and they fashioned their own aesthetic and political categories. They ragged uplift.

RAGTIME IN THE AGE OF UPLIFT

In the early years of Jim Crow, it was the white custodians of American culture—and not the Talented Tenth—who most vocally criticized ragtime. "Let us take a stand against the *Ragtime Evil*," decried one music critic as he compared American popular music to "bad literature, the horrors of war or intemperance and other socially destructive evils."[3] Such a view was common during the early 1900s, as a wide swath of cultural critics and social reformers expressed anxiety about industrializing America, urbanization, the rise of mass culture, and the northward migrations of millions of southern blacks. Popular culture—its reliance on technology, its mass distribution, and of course its social meanings—seemed to shape the contours of a changing nation, though many saw cultural developments like ragtime as a cause for sweeping changes, rather than as a symptom. Writing a letter to the *New York Herald*, one Walter Winston Kenilworth asserted that ragtime "is threatening the morals and the very life of America."[4] Many concurred, usually by objecting to ragtime's most pronounced musical characteristic, rhythmic syncopation.

Although musicians and critics often noted that the unusual or unexpected accents of syncopated notes were a standard of all European music styles, the emphasis and exaggeration of syncopation appeared to upset music standard-bearers.[5] When warning of the evils of ragtime, critics most often decried the "excessive," "hot," "vulgar," and "mad" qualities of the style's syncopated rhythms. "Syncopation," one West Virginia music teacher wrote in a popular magazine, "by its stimulating effect, is pleasant when administered in a well-regulated form. It is spice. But when taken to excess it overstimulates; it irritates."[6] Writing in the *Musician* in 1902, W. F. Gates agreed on the importance of musical nutrition, arguing that ragtime "creates in the minds of the young a distaste for that which is more staid and solid, more dignified and useful. It is an appetite for spices rather than for nutritious foods."[7] Nearly all of ragtime's critics argued that the music was overly syncopated and that the rhythms themselves led to a wide array of problems: social, psychological, sexual, and aesthetic.[8]

What most critics actually worried about, however, was of course blackness. Kenilworth was explicit in his catalogue of problems with American life. Alongside "relaxative morality" and the "disparagement of the marital tie," he listed racial "amalgamation" and the corrupting influence of the "collective soul of the negro." Race, racial culture, and interracial sex stoked Kenilworth's anxiety. The music historian Ronald Radano has shown that white distress about black migration at the turn of the century paralleled the spread of black ragtime culture, and that racial anxiety shaped white responses to both phenomena. The idea of "black rhythm," Radano argues, did not simply develop from a recognition of African and African American music practices, but from a new sense of U.S. race relations resulting from larger historical transitions.[9] African Americans played rhythmic music before the 1890s—as histories of slave songs, dance, ring shouts, and patting practices evidence—but during early Jim Crow, a "shift in public perception" occurred that "reinvented black music as rhythm music."[10] For its critics, ragtime proved that black culture was inherently evil, pernicious, sick, and dangerous. Just like, they supposed, black people.

It was this mentality that so unnerved the Talented Tenth, and it indicates why they too feared the spread of ragtime. The realm of black culture had become contested ground, and not only among music educators like James Monroe Trotter or the editors of the *Negro Music Journal*. African American educators, clergy, and reformers deemed ragtime a poor representation of the race because it became popular precisely at the moment when they were mounting a challenge to white supremacy through a politics of representation. Black elites imagined that they might transcend American racism by publicly demonstrating their education, decorum, and culture. The growing popularity of ragtime threatened to undermine their strategy, and blacks with access to print media struck back. Echoing white critics, one writer warned that "dancing cake-walks, indulging in rag-time, and other such devilry" would eventually lead to one "going to hell." An *Indianapolis Freeman* editorial insisted that "the cakewalk is beneath the dignity of the better class of 'the race' . . . and should be frowned down by the better class of colored people."[11] Observers frequently expressed concern about ragtime dance's sexual suggestiveness; as the Atlanta reformer John Hope wrote to his wife, the cakewalk was "sensuous, alluring, and degrading." One pamphlet writer included ragtime and the cakewalk, alongside cologne and chewing gum, among a variety of evils enticing young black urbanites.[12] The cakewalk dismayed some not only because of its impropriety but also because of its roots in slavery. As another *Freeman* editor put it: the "good people of this country have nothing in common with cake walks . . . the great crime attached to cake walks is the resurrection of supposed obsolete manners."[13] The compromises entertainers like Bert Williams and Will Marion Cook had to make to gain a hearing on American stages—the coon songs, the cakewalk, the blackface comedy—meant that many members of the Talented Tenth saw ragtime culture as a direct affront to their strategies of uplifting the race through public presentations of respectability.

Perhaps surprisingly, the specter of blackface minstrelsy actually wielded remarkable influence over black elites' conception of racial uplift. Because the most popular and profitable nineteenth-century entertainment in the United States had so successfully established the basic stereotypes of African Americans in the minds of white America, the Talented Tenth focused on disputing and overturning minstrelsy's portrayals of blackness. Minstrelsy caricatured blacks as, on the one hand (in antebellum times), childlike and happy slaves in need of a firm patriarchal hand, and, on the other (after emancipation), as lazy, dangerous, and hopelessly ill-suited to industrial labor, thrift, and self-restraint. In response, black leaders aspired to shape the modes of dress, manners, behaviors, and overall public presentation of the black "masses" in ways that distanced them from the minstrel stereotypes. Minstrelsy issued racist images of blacks as unassimilating Americans and a fundamental problem for the American experiment in egalitarian democracy. Black elites countered by attempting to curtail the black masses' modes of public presentation to demonstrate that African Americans, given the correct leadership, could cultivate the necessary attributes of proper American citizens.[14]

As black leaders worked to cultivate respectable culture among nonelite African Americans, they discovered that the black masses already had culture. They had lots of it and were eager to share, especially if they could trade it for coin. Working-class black culture was as exciting and diverse as the black neighborhoods that dotted the United States during the early years of Jim Crow. From the Mississippi Delta up river to St. Louis, from the Florida Panhandle to the nation's capital, from the urban Northeast to the rural Atlantic regions, African Americans sang and danced their cultural past as they innovated and improvised their spontaneous present. Ragtime was becoming mainstream American culture in ways that indicated a black role in the production of the nation. But ragtime song and dance offered alternatives to the Talented Tenth's notions of racial uplift too. As Will Cook discovered while playing "Who Dat Say Chicken in Dis Crowd?" for his mother, the very sounds of syncopation expressed a rejection of black elites' Eurocentric musical and aesthetic values. From the Talented Tenth's point of view, ragtime rhythm threatened their entire uplift agenda, and even their own political and social identities.

The quick notes, quirky syncopated rhythms, and unresolved har-monies that became the hallmark of ragtime music seemed to embody the unordered chaos of the migrating black masses. The rhythmic notes themselves, of course, did not symbolize working-class black power and social chaos—music, or any art for that matter, has no essential, unmed-iated meaning outside its social context. It was the way American elites (black and white) talked about ragtime that gave it such representational power. Critics of ragtime concretized the style's social resonance when they expressed their anxieties about the new forms of American popu-lar entertainment. Before the critics put pen to paper, ragtime was just a series of melodic notes flying though the air, music as ephemeral as a songbird's tune. But if elite blacks and whites made such a fuss about rag-time, black musicians and their black consumers likely thought, it must be powerful stuff.

Writing in the *Colored American Magazine*, a leading outlet for Boston's Talented Tenth, one member of the Hotel Marshall community argued that popular theater could be a vehicle for the dissemination of respecta-ble and uplifting representations of African Americans. "The stage," Lester Walton suggested, "will be one of the principal factors in ultimately placing the negro before the public in his true and proper light," noting "the negro of the stage to be of material benefit in the future upbuilding of the race and in the effacement of race prejudice." Even if musical theater struck some as the antithesis of uplift, the Marshall community did not differ that much from the Talented Tenth: as "colored performers of high moral char-acter and ability assuming character roles in wholesome plays . . . [they] will serve an iconoclastic purpose in the dissipation of false impressions regarding the negro race as a whole."[15] Walton's voice in one of the most elite black monthlies in America marked a transition away from traditional evaluations of black popular culture like those found in the *Negro Music Journal*. By the time Ernest Hogan published "All Coons Look Alike to Me" and May Irwin introduced it on Broadway in 1896, the cultural expres-sions of sharecropping, wage laboring, and working-class black America—the culture of the black masses—were poised to become the culture of the American masses.

THE WILLIAMS AND WALKER COMPANY
ON THE TALENTED TENTH

As Williams and Walker became the most successful black entertain-ers in the United States, they shouldered heavy responsibilities to black

America. Like Bob Cole and Rosamond and James Weldon Johnson, Williams and Walker regularly expressed their intent to be race leaders in ways that reflected facets of the Talented Tenth's politics of racial representation. "We want our folks, the negroes, to like us," Walker wrote in the *New York Age*. "Because we feel that, in a degree, we represent the race, and every hair's breath of achievement we make is to its credit."[16] In 1902, as Williams and Walker organized their troupe for *In Dahomey*, they understood that the Talented Tenth's politics of representation put a unique onus of accountability on them because of their rare position as black entertainers succeeding in white America. They handed a pamphlet to every member of their company outlining their expectations for proper conduct offstage, making it clear that the members of the troupe represented Williams and Walker and that the Williams and Walker Company represented black America:

> We do not by any means wish to make you inmates of an asylum, nor do we wish at this time to seem to attack your deportment or behavior, but, knowing, that the bond of prejudice is drawn so tightly around us, and that the eye that sees everything we colored folks do is eve[r] ready to magnify and multiply many times over the value of the most innocent deed committed by us, we write you this letter to warn you to so conduct yourself that your manner and mode of life will disarm all criticism and place you above reproach.[17]

It was a direct appeal to embrace the politics of representation. Offstage, Williams and Walker set a standard for black professionalism that reshaped black vaudeville for the twentieth century. In 1909, a white interviewer wrote of her "surprise" when Williams claimed that he "didn't know any funny stories" and instead wanted to discuss "the uplifting of his race through the inestimable teaching qualities of dramatic productions." Williams used the opportunity to describe how he hoped for a time when "negroes on the stage will take themselves more seriously and be taken more seriously" and the "negro actor will take rank with the negro teacher." "Booker T. Washington," Williams asserted, "will have strong allies in his work of elevating the social standard of the black man."[18] By this point in his career, Williams had met with Washington on many occasions, and he knew that the Wizard of Tuskegee thought Williams and Walker important and legitimate ambassadors of the race. But the duo did not aim to change only the attitudes of the black leadership.

Williams and Walker critiqued the Talented Tenth's uplift ideology and promoted alternative visions of black culture and racial representation.

The same year Dunbar and Cook produced *Jes Lak White Fo'ks,* Williams and Walker produced *The Sons of Ham* (1900), using as many Marshall songwriters as they could. The musical's second iteration in 1901 included a song by Cole and the Johnson brothers that became one of their biggest hits, "My Castle on the River Nile." The song poked fun at African Americans who used their genealogy to prove their high breeding. "Dere ain't no use in tryin' to rise up in de social scale 'less you can trace yo' name back to de flood," sang Williams's character just before discovering that he, in fact, belonged to ancient African royalty. After discovering his heritage, Williams sang:

> In my Castle on the Nile
> I am gwinter live in elegant style
> Inlaid diamond on de flo'
> A Baboon butler at my do'
> When I wed dat princess Anna Mazoo
> Den my blood will change from red to blue
> Entertaining royalty all the while
> In my Castle on the Nile[19]

In another song from the musical, Aida Overton Walker reflected on migrating southern blacks and their reception in the urban North. "Up from the land of the fragrant pine, / Came a dusky maiden to the Northern clime," Walker sang. "She told all her friends, / Ah's gwine to see, / The difference in the sassiety," cleverly leveling the critique at a sassy black "society." She continued, borrowing from Dunbar, "Ah's heard so much 'bout their high-toned ways, / 'Bout dem actin' more like white folks ev'ry day," before announcing in the chorus: "My name's Miss Hannah from Savannah, / Ahm some blueblood ob de land-ah!"[20] Walker's appraisal of the Talent Tenth extended beyond a single ragtime ditty.

In 1905, she published an article in the *Colored American Magazine,* punctuating the class bias she felt as a member of Manhattan's black community and one of America's most successful stage performers. Born Ada Wilmore Overton in 1880 and raised in the black area of Greenwich Village, she first started performing at the age of sixteen in Black Patti's Troubadour's at the same time Bob Cole was stage-directing and acting in the troupe.[21] By 1905, however, Walker had presented a command performance for King Edward VII at Buckingham Palace and created a sensation by leading the entire royal family on a cakewalk through the royal gardens. (English nobility soon engaged George and Aida Overton Walker to "give private lessons in the Cake Walk dance," making the couple the "best draw in London."[22]) In her article, Walker offered a treatise on the politics of black theater and a refutation of "our so-called society people" who were ashamed of black stage performance. Seeming sincerely empathetic, Walker did not reprimand *Colored American* readers for not respecting black vaudeville, but suggested they were "ignorant as to what is really being done in their behalf by members of their race on the Stage." She reminded her readers that in "this age we are all fighting the one problem—that is the color problem!" Walker listed the variety of elite and royal white people for whom she and the Williams and Walker Company had performed throughout the past year in America and England. She illustrated how black performers worked as symbols of racial uplift and leading tastemakers in U.S. society.[23]

Raised in the working-class Tenderloin district, Walker had imbibed the Talented Tenth's notions of uplift through respectability. So well, in fact, did Walker understand the strategy that she was aptly prepared to critique Talented Tenth elitism. Noting black elites' consternation with white America for refusing to distinguish between educated, professional members of the race and the black masses, Walker called out black society for lumping together all stage performers. "When white people refuse to classify, in dealing with us," she cautioned, "we get highly indignant and say we should not all be judged alike, and yet we often fail to classify and make distinctions when judging ourselves." "Consistency is still a jewel!" she admonished. If black society put so much emphasis on how blacks appeared to whites, the "fact of the matter is," she pointed out, "we come into contact with more white people in a week than other professional colored people meet in a year and more than some meet in a whole decade. We entertain thousands of people in the course of a Season." Walker ended her essay by identifying herself, and her fellow actors, as uplifters—members of a cultural Talented Tenth—greatly expanding the parameters of Du Bois's term: "We must work together for the uplift of all and the progress of all that is good and noble in life."[24]

But Walker did not only slightly adjust black society's understanding of uplift and respectability. She also infused a more radical element into her argument, invoking a racial pride more akin to that of Will Marion Cook. Walker wanted to accept and praise black culture along its own lines. "As individuals," she wrote, "we must strive all we can to show that we are as capable as white people. . . . We must produce good and great actors and actresses to demonstrate that our people move along with the progress of the times and improve as they move." Walker saw black mimicry of white plays as a problem to be overcome by black creativity, and by black pride. She cautioned young black performers that "too many of our people wish to master Shakespeare." Considering this foolish, she asked blacks to "study our own graces" to "appreciate the noble and the beautiful within us, just as other peoples have discovered the graces and beauty in themselves." Anticipating Garveyism by a decade but sounding more like Aretha Franklin in the 1960s, Walker demanded that blacks throw off the shackles of engrained white supremacy and learn to love themselves: "Unless we learn the lesson of self appreciation and practice it, we shall spend our lives imitating other people and depreciating ourselves."[25] Walker illustrated the ways the Williams and Walker Company offered alternatives to political leadership from above. Cultural work from below—from the very streets of Black Manhattan—fashioned its own set of standards by which African Americans might understand and represent themselves. This type of ragging uplift was an idea the musical director of the Williams and Walker Company understood well.

Will Marion Cook's sense of black pride was not only cultural—he ardently promoted political equality and racial solidarity. He was actually born Will Mercer Cook. John Hartwell Cook, Will's father and the future dean of the Howard University Law School, named him after John Mercer Langstrom, a stand-out black Oberlin alum and U.S. diplomat, no doubt expecting his son to follow Langstrom's rarified footsteps into professional success. But after Cook returned from his sojourn in Berlin in 1889, he heard Langstrom give a talk that made him want "to vomit!" "There he was," Cook wrote to his mother, "my father's friend, the great race leader, my namesake, publicly boasting that he got his lovely hair, his tiny feet and hands from his white ancestors!" That night, Cook renounced his middle name and chose his mother's instead. "You named me after the wrong man, Ma," he declared. "From now on I'm Will Marion. If Marion's good enough to be your middle name, it suits me to a 'T.'"[26] Musicians who knew Cook recount an apocryphal story about why Cook stopped performing as a violinist.[27] At some point, most likely in 1893 or 1895, Cook performed with a white symphony orchestra, inspiring a critic to proclaim Cook the "world's greatest Negro violinist." Duke Ellington remembered that Cook became enraged. He visited the reviewer and told him, "I am not the world's greatest Negro violinist . . . I am the greatest violinist in the world!" before smashing his violin across the desk of the insulting music critic.[28] As Tom Fletcher remembered, Cook "laid his violin down and swore to never play it again in an orchestra."[29]

At an early age, Cook exhibited this strong sense of race consciousness. During World War I, Cook's stance on race may have been called "black nationalism"—a sensibility that counseled racial pride, institutional and cultural autonomy, economic self-sufficiency, and transnational conceptions of the African diaspora and universal black brotherhood. But among the Hotel Marshall community around 1900, it was commonplace for black entertainers to support racial solidarity without demanding a separate black nation, just as musicians like Cook, Cole, and the Walkers might appreciate calls for black economic self-sufficiency while aiming not for separatist but for equal access to Manhattan's music markets.

All the ingredients for black nationalism lay on the table in the basement of the Marshall. But professional entertainers were not tied to any specific ideological position—they were not looking for a political label.[30] Like Marshall musicians' self-conscious selecting among the attributes of the Talented Tenth, their investment in promoting the cultural power and modernity of black New Yorkers allowed them to pick and choose among various racial positions without boxing them into an ideological predisposition like black nationalism or racial uplift. In the aftermath of Reconstruction, Cook's race consciousness struck his mother as potentially problematic. So she sent him to live with her own tough-nailed father in Chattanooga, Tennessee. Cook only spent half a year there before his grandfather gave up on curtailing Cook's seemingly inexhaustive willpower and sent him back. Before Cook left Tennessee, however, he heard rural African American singing. Cook dedicated the rest of his life to translating the "real Negro melodies" he heard into facets of American popular music.[31]

Like the music educators and cultural critics he denounced, Cook hoped to uplift the image of African Americans through music. Yet unlike many of the Talented Tenth, Cook was less concerned with African Americans' image among whites than among blacks. According to him, and to many who knew him, Cook rarely met African Americans as vehemently opposed to the subtle internalization of white supremacy as himself—an attitude that developed at an early age. Years before he renounced his namesake, Cook had relations with a thirteen-year-old Tennessee girl who, he recalled, "considered herself a blue-blood—like some of those Negroes in Washington who boasted that they were descendants of our First President—and who looked down on Negroes generally." Cook remembered liking her enough until she asked him, "Do you have any trouble with the niggers in Washington, William?" to which Cook yelled, "What are you anyway, a damned fool?"[32] Cook's anger toward blacks' imbibed notion of white supremacy was not merely a cultural issue. Like Aida Overton Walker, Cook aimed at creating the conditions for black equality, professionalism, and American citizenship, and his race con-sciousness surely influenced Williams and Walker Company productions, especially as the troupe tackled overtly black nationalist themes such as African emigration, Pan-Africanism, and transnational black culture.

The second collaboration between Williams, Walker, and Cook, *Abyssinia*, overtly promoted nationalist ideas about the African continent as they were developing throughout black America. The musical indicated the Williams and Walker Company's support for political and social agen-das quite distinct from those of the Talented Tenth. *Abyssinia* centered on a group of African American tourists traveling not to West Africa and the hallowed ground of the North American slave trade, but to Ethiopia in northeastern Africa—the mythic land of the ancient Egyptians and the only African nation in 1900 controlled by Africans rather than European colonizers. Since the Ethiopian emperor Menelik II had banished Italian forces in 1896, the small nation had become a symbol of civilization and modernity among many black Americans, a country resilient in the face of imperialism and symbol of black nationalist aspirations. (Italy's defeat also caused a minor uproar among European and American racial the-orists; the fact that Africans had defeated a European army made some American leaders attempt to "redefine Ethiopians as nonblacks," and led one U.S. consul to circulate a "rumor that Menelik had insisted that he was Caucasian.") Rather than bringing civilization to Africa—a theme debated in *In Dahomey*—George Walker's character in *Abyssinia* wanted to visit Ethiopia to learn astronomy "on the Continent where the first authoritative school of astronomy had its birth," an African nation rich in intellectual and cultural traditions.[33]

Besides championing the past and present of an African nation, the Williams and Walker musical broached numerous topics impor-tant to black communities and leadership. It elucidated points of view that expanded African American debates about culture and citizenship and sharpened criticism of both American apartheid and the Talented Tenth. The historian Karen Sotiropoulos has charted the central themes of Williams and Walker's first two Broadway musicals: black emigra-tion and the back-to-Africa movement; European and, after 1898, U.S. imperialism and the developing notion of a "white man's burden"; black uplift ideology's reliance on Anglo evaluations of civilization; Talented Tenth politics of respectability and representation; and the changing nature of African American identity, both at home and abroad. Soti-ropoulos shows that the two men's productions "challenged the mono-lithic presumptions of Africa as primitive and savage during a moment when European colonialism and American empire building depended on such racial ideology," and that the entertainers spoke to key concerns of African and African American identity formation.[34] By presenting contemporary national, racial, and political issues with their well-rehearsed troupe on popular American and British stages, Williams and Walker appropriated the Talented Tenth's strategies of racial presentation. They put themselves—and their critiques—squarely at the center of African American debates about black culture, racial uplift, and the contours of American citizenship. Yet their interest in Africa seemed to derive from other, related concerns too—theirs was not wholly a nationalist connection to African diasporic culture.

Stage representations of "Africa," and the duo's regular discussion of the continent in the press, bolstered Williams and Walker's promotion of the idea of black cultural authenticity. When asked about their creative influences, the two broke from Ernest Hogan's presentist account of the rise of popular ragtime after his hit in 1896, and even from Will Marion Cook's sensibility that the roots of modern African American music grew from American soil. In contrast to most at the Hotel Marshall, Williams and Walker frequently noted their incorporation of what they called "African" elements into their act. "I have no hesitation," Walker asserted, "in stating that the departure from what was popularly known as the American 'darky' ragtime limitations to native African characteristics has helped greatly to increase the value of the black performer on the American stage." More than simply affirming a kind of transhistorical racial retention of African musical culture, Walker appealed to his own connections to Africa (even though he had never visited and had only minimal contact with a troupe of Dahomian entertainers in San Francisco in 1893). "Many of the themes from which some of our best lyrics have been written are purely African. We were the first to introduce the Americanized African songs: for instance, 'My Zulu Babe,' 'My Castle on the Nile,' 'My Dahomian Queen.'' Surely part of Walker's reasoning reflected his own investment in promoting the authenticity of his music. But his invocations of African influence differed quite markedly from presenting himself as one-half of the "Two Real Coons."

The two men's insistence on their own Africanness reflected overlapping agendas. Just as mid-nineteenth-century minstrels had sold their own performances as authentic, "ethnographic" observations of slave practices, Walker asserted the racial authority to align himself with Africans in a way that excluded whites. He at once updated white minstrels' promotional strategies and trumped them by claiming an insider expertise that whites in blackface no longer had. In this context, Walker's assertion that he "could entertain in that way as no white boy could" took on new resonance.[35] Even as black and white minstrels engaged in what Walker knew to be racialized fantasy, he claimed that the color of his skin also allowed him rarified access to African culture. Williams and Walker's positions as seemingly direct conduits between Africa and African America bolstered their claims of racial authenticity. At the same time, Williams and Walker seemed sincerely interested in African history and culture, and they emphasized connections between their artistry and that of their African forebears. In 1906, Walker told the *Indianapolis Freeman* that, in Africa, "the natives have always attracted travelers through that country by their tribal dances," which he linked to the "racial melodies, banjo playing and fantastic dancing of colored people" in the antebellum American South.[36]

As Williams and Walker promoted their racial authenticity, they danced along the Jim Crow color line, capitalizing on American audiences' racial essentialism and their desire for cultural exoticism. Yet as they staked a claim in their own connections to Africa, Williams and Walker translated black nationalist concerns onto the American popular stage in ways that challenged American white supremacy and confronted aspects of the Talented Tenth's leadership, making issues like dress, deportment, and presentation seem parochial and elitist indeed. The Williams and Walker Company, like many Hotel Marshall entertainers, established alternatives to Talented Tenth representations of blackness. As they did so, they lifted popular representations of blackness as they rose into the ranks of leading American professional entertainers.

BLACK MUSICAL DEVELOPMENT AND THE
FROGS IN THE HOTEL MARSHALL

The Marshall community's stance on black musical and cultural development reveals how Eurocentric aesthetic values influenced even the most self-consciously black nationalist (and anti-elitist) entertainers of the era. This complicates the group's relationship to uplift ideology. Cook, the most nationalist of the group, looked forward to further developments in blacks' music. "Developed Negro music has just begun in America," Cook told the *Chicago Defender;* "the Afro-American is finding himself. He has thrown aside puerile imitation of the white man." Yet in a rare admission, Cook acknowledged the influence of European music and African Americans' education in it. Black composers, Cook noted, have "learned that a thorough study of the masters drives the knowledge of what is good and how to create." But more than the technical mastery of European form, counterpoint, or harmony, Cook argued that Europeans' greatest gift to African Americans was the celebration of one's own folk culture—something that may not have happened in the United States without the influence of Europeans and European art. "From the Russian," Cook theorized, the black composer has "learned to get his inspiration from within: that his inexhaustible wealth of folklore legends and songs furnish him with material for compositions that will establish a great school of music and enrich musical literature."[37]

Even as Williams, Walker, and Cook complicated the Talented Tenth's politics of representation, Marshall musicians believed that African Americans had to develop their cultural expressions to demonstrate blacks' fitness for American citizenship. Put another way, although Marshall musicians critiqued and rejected aspects of the Talented Tenth's agenda, they ultimately agreed that cultural advancement would usher in political rights and social equality. As Du Bois proffered in *The Souls of Black Folk*, black musical development held the key to black equality and full participation in democracy. In 1902, Bob Cole and Rosamond Johnson took their first steps into stage performance, walking out from behind the Broadway curtain and aiming quite deliberately at uplifting black representation on the stage.

Early that year, after having made a handful of song hits in white musical theaters as offstage songwriters, Cole and Johnson had begun to book steady engagements in the best vaudeville theater houses in New York. James Weldon Johnson had left the city the previous fall to return to his teaching in Jacksonville, so he was surprised on his return to New York that summer to see his partners' names on the placard at Keith's Fourteenth Street Theater, "one of the principal vaudeville houses in the country." Cole and Johnson's act, Johnson remembered, "was unlike anything ever done by Negro performers." Cole and Johnson offered interracial—though segregated—New York audiences a show noteworthy for its distinction from blackface vaudeville. Recognizing that the Talented Tenth did not consider the vaudeville stage a location of racial uplift, the duo dressed to the nines, trading in the burnt cork of vaudeville for tuxedo tails and white gloves. The performance was, James Weldon Johnson remembered, "quiet, finished, and artistic to the minutest detail."[38]

Cole and Johnson combined their hit ragtime tunes with European art music, illustrating another way that ragtime could work to uplift racial representations. As Cook had contended, for a well-trained musician, no necessary chasm existed between popular music and classical approaches.

Rosamond Johnson (left) and Bob Cole. Billy Rose Theater Division, New York Public Library for the Performing Arts, Astor, Lenox, and Tilden Foundations.

In the right hands, all music held the potential for technical mastery and creative interpretation. The duo fashioned the show around a fictional rehearsal, with the two men acting as though they were planning and practicing for a performance yet to come. As they walked on stage, the dapper duo began with casual patter about an upcoming gig at a private party, discussing onstage how best to perform at the imaginary event. Johnson sat behind the piano and suggested that they begin with Ignacy Jan Paderewski's Minuet in G, playing the piece by way of example. After he had finished, and the audience responded with loud applause, Johnson continued, this time offering a bit of "Still wie die Nacht" (in German), before Cole interrupted him to reject it. Cole allowed his partner to finish the tune, then announced that he thought partygoers—in this case, the audience itself—would not want to hear classical music all night. So he sang the Cole and Johnson hit "Mandy" as an example of some popular ragtime for the gathering. From that point of the night on, the show consisted of original music in the ragtime vein, but played with subtle flourishes and tepid tempos. The piano/vocal duo enabled Johnson to offer counterpoint to Cole's vocal melodies, emphasizing his own musical sophistication. During choruses, he would often bring the piano's volume down so low that Cole could gracefully do a "soft shoe" dance and yet be heard.[39]

Cole and Johnson utilized syncopated rhythms and dialect verse, but presented both markers of black ragtime in a refined manner that white audiences loved. So did some of the Talented Tenth. In 1905, the *Colored American Magazine* heard the act and Cole and Johnson's music as "new"—an artistic development out of lowly ragtime and coon songs to be celebrated. "These men have made a new thing out of Negro music," one editor applauded, "and such that the Afro-American people are not ashamed of! A new music was demanded, and it is gratifying that the race had within it the men to write it."[40] Using the language of uplift, another *Colored American* contributor suggested that Cole and Johnson have "pulled up as they have mounted," demonstrating "both the persevering ability of the colored actor and the shallow crust of American prejudice."[41] Even though Cole and Johnson knew they would not convince everyone, recognition by the *Colored American* suggested their strategy of ragging uplift had opened some minds to the potential of black popular music. Still, like Cook, Rosamond Johnson imagined higher plateaus for black musicians and their music.

A conservatory-trained composer, Rosamond Johnson believed that African Americans' music had only begun its development. For Johnson, both ragtime and the slave spirituals represented steps along a musical evolution that were as significant for American national culture as they were for African Americans as a race. "If composers want themes for American symphony, or American grand opera," he implored, "let them study the sad strains of the Negro plantation songs and they will find food and inspiration for great works."[42] In a different article, Johnson explained that his artistic goal was "to evolve a type of music that will have all that is distinctive in the old Negro music and yet be sophisticated enough to appeal to the cultured musician."[43] Johnson's aspirations indicate his interest in shaping artful expressions of African American culture, modern iterations of black music that called attention to its roots in a rich musical tradition while pointing the way forward. Yet Marshall musicians also manifested in subtle ways their desires to attain highly valued artistic expressions, and the influence in their work of both Eurocentric and Anglo-American ideals about art. These goals do not mean that these self-conscious artists and deliberate spokespersons for the race necessarily harbored internalized white supremacy. Rather, Marshall musicians' aesthetic evaluations reflect the values of the Talented Tenth and that group's focus on education, respectable representation, and uplift—values less mired in internalized conceptions of black inferiority than the Tenth's political, economic, and social imperatives to demonstrate the intellectual capacities of African Americans. For Rosamond Johnson, musical development buttressed racial uplift, and both goals aimed directly at African American citizenship and equal rights.

To these ends, Johnson imagined that spirituals would also play a role in the further development of "American" music. In 1908, Johnson drew direct connections between slave spirituals and ragtime. In Johnson's appraisal, the former indicated blacks' "more serious music," while ragtime simply named the "happy expressions of the Negro." Both styles reflected a "distinctly American music" and "the only music that the musical centers of the world . . . recognize as American music." " 'Negro music,' 'American syncopation,' 'ragtime,' or 'Raggioso,' just whatever you choose to call it, is here, and it is here to stay, for it has already caught the ear of the people the world over." [44] The power of the marketplace was rendering African American popular music, whether crafted by formally trained musicians or unlettered songwriters, a symbol of U.S. culture. Johnson's stance echoed the hope expressed by Dvořák and Du Bois that African American cultural achievement would lead to black political and social equality in the United States. Like Cook, Rosamond Johnson imagined unparalleled opportunities for African Americans if they could place themselves at the center of debates about the sound of U.S. national culture, an agenda that he and his brother would take up for the rest of their artistic and literary careers.

In his own way, George Walker made the connection between the development of black art and U.S. citizenship plain. The "black man's future," he told a white newspaper, "lies in the development of his facilities—physical and mental—as a negro." Walker did not shy away from acknowledging the damage centuries of slavery had done to African Americans: "Our civilization is very little beyond its infancy, when you think of it. Why, a few hundred years ago we were savages." But this did not mean that blacks could not learn or would not develop. "There can not be any dispute about our musical ability. This, too, is undeveloped. Ragtime is just part of the chaos out of which real genius will some day be evolved. We shall have great negro masters in the generations to come."[45]

Even as Walker made concessions for what he saw as black backwardness, he did not see blacks' condition as inherent or natural. It was a cultural condition derived from slavery and systemic racism, something to be overcome as blacks developed their faculties and whites their ability to transcend bigotry and discrimination. "We must admit," Walker told *Variety*, "the progress, achievements and possibilities thus far allotted to the Negro in his work is still in its infancy, but growing very rapidly." Reminding readers that only a few years ago "Negro performers were engaged in 'cake-walking,' buck dancing, and 'slap-stick' comicalities," Walker reiterated that the reason for this was the need to "please the non-sympathetic, biased and prejudiced white man."[46] As he interpreted the Talented Tenth's politics of representation, Walker pointed not only to working-class blacks as needing reform and development, but white racists too—the originators of black stereotypes and caricatures. Thus Walker turned the Talented Tenth's critique of black culture and behavior into a challenge to white America: blacks would develop their minds, bodies, and art, but whites must join blacks in advancing their own thought, prejudices, and social structures.

Walker's goals for black cultural development overlapped with his wider goals for racial advance, aims he knew were tied to social, economic, and political institutions that curtailed access as much as they fostered discrimination. Walker sought to change the playing field on a national level. "My greatest ambition," Walker confided in 1905, "is to get enough money together to build a theatre—if possible one in New York, one in Philadelphia, one in Boston, and one in Chicago—theatres where negro boys and girls can be taught to respect themselves, their qualities and their abilities." Discussing the ways in which white supremacy seeped into blacks' minds and devalued their sense of self, Walker spoke of the internal and external struggles young boys and girls met as they grew up black in the United States. "You can't get the best out of a boy by telling him that his hair should be straight instead of kinky, that his nose should be classic instead of flat," Walker asserted, "Nor can you expect a colored girl to realize the best there is in her if you can make her believe that a black skin cannot be beautiful." Walker hoped to "erect a theatre in which we can train negroes to realize that a colored person has parts worthy of serious notice by himself and by others. There is no reason why we should be forced to [do] these old-time 'nigger' acts. . . . [T]his slap-stick, bandanna handkerchief, bladder, and flour-in-the-face act with which all negro acting is associated ought to die, and I like to think Williams and Walker have helped kill it."[47] Although Walker's theaters never materialized, he still held onto his plans near the end of his life. According to one of the Majestic Theater's last articles on Williams and Walker's *Bandanna Land* of 1908, the two were working on building their own theater, "where annually the new productions of this novel organization will be made."[48] While the theater never happened, in their last full year together, Williams and Walker organized a fraternal society for New York's most elite black performers—something like a Talented Tenth of ragtimers.

Besides a black-owned theater, Walker had long imagined a greater potential for black entertainers if they could organize themselves and cut down on intraracial competition. He hoped to organize black performers into a working body that could ensure fair industry standards and alleviate racial discrimination. As early as 1900, while living at the Marshall, he wanted to proclaim the arrival of professional black musicians to New York.[49] In January 1906, Walker wrote an open letter to the *Morning Telegraph*, inviting performing African Americans to join an actors' society. As the paper wrote, Walker "has taken the initiative, and in a public appeal he calls upon the 4,000 colored entertainers of the United States to come forward and give a hand."[50] In 1908, Walker achieved this goal, spearheading a new organization called the Frogs and becoming its first president.[51]

Bob Cole, too, had worked to establish a professional organization for black performers. As early as 1897, Cole had quit his high-profile position as stage manager, writer, and performer for Black Patti's Troubadours over disagreements with the company's white managers and hoped to better organize black vaudevillians. That year, Cole wrote a "Colored Actor's Declaration of Independence" as he announced the first all-black

*The Frogs. Photographs and Prints Division, Schomburg Center
for Research in Black Culture, New York Public Library, Astor, Lenox,
and Tilden Foundations.*

vaudeville company in the United States, one based on his show *A Trip to Coontown*. "We are going to have our own shows," Cole asserted. "We are going to write them ourselves, we are going to have our own stage manager, our own orchestra leader and our own manager out front to count up. No divided houses—our race must be seated from the boxes back."[52] In early July, Cole and Walker's aspirations became a reality through their community at the Hotel Marshall.

The Frogs was an incorporated performers' club that included only eleven men, but its roster reads like a who's who of the New York black musical theater scene in 1908. Rosamond Johnson, Bob Cole, and Cole's old partner Sam Corker joined, as did Lester Walton, the former vaudevillian, culture editor at the *New York Age*, and contributor to the *Colored American Magazine*. Williams and Walker's offstage creative partners since their earliest vaudeville shows seven years before, Jesse Shipp, Alex Rogers, and R. C. McPherson, signed the incorporation papers along with Bert Williams. And rounding out the group were two young up-and-comers on the black stage, Tom Brown and James Reese Europe. In 1906, Walker had intended his actors' society to be open to all black performers, but the Frogs began as a smaller affair. The best surviving picture of the group is a group portrait of eleven men sharply dressed in black, tailed tuxedos. Although they all look sturdy and proud in their dignified clothing, most of them are smiling, while their president, seated in the middle hunched over, grins mischievously into the camera.[53]

The Frogs' official statement of incorporation emphasized their commitment to racial uplift. Taking their name from the Aristophanes comedy, the Frogs announced that they hoped to "aid in raising the standard of the theatrical profession . . . [and] to elevate the race generally." They proposed to create a "library relating especially to the history of the Negro, and the record of all worthy achievements . . . in which the Negro has participated."[54] In an advertisement in the *Age*, the Frogs explained that their archive aimed to be a "suitable place for the Preservation of Works of Art" to ensure a record of "a priceless heritage of the best things of the race." "It is the desire of the Society," the ad continued, "to foster artistic efforts among our people . . . whose worth may make the world think."[55] Though initially quite exclusive, the club hoped to expand its ranks by including members from beyond musical theater. It sought to promote "social intercourse" between black theater performers and those connected "directly or indirectly with art, literature, music, scientific and liberal professions, and the patrons of the arts."[56] The Frogs organized annual balls, called the "Frolic of the Frogs," uptown on 155th Street at the Manhattan Casino to raise funds, and they lent their corporate name to dozens of performances during the coming few years, constituting an early staple in the changing neighborhood of Harlem. The Frogs' performances were highlights of the year for thousands of black New Yorkers and helped establish the area between 125th and 155th Streets as one of the most exciting cultural spheres in the country by 1910.[57]

HOTEL MARSHALL MUSICIANS ADVANCED new approaches to racial politics and representations. Their visions of blackness saw beauty in the vernacular of the masses. Instead of trying to change the masses, they attempted to change the perception of black vernacular expression. This created quite a different approach to the Talented Tenth's notions of racial uplift, as well as to scholarly accounts of it. Yet Marshall entertainers remained indebted to uplift. Many of their own conceptions of culture, racial solidarity, and the political nature of racial representation floated down to them from the books they read, the conversations they had, and the individual race leaders they admired. But because the Talented Tenth most often rejected ragtime music and culture, the Marshall community ultimately forged new paths. They took the elite's teachings and ideals for racial uplift and transfigured them. They boldly proclaimed ownership over an authentic black culture and staked their livelihoods on a conception of black expression that stepped outside the lines of normative—and often policed—expectations of behavior and social interaction. The Marshall community embraced ragtime's transgressive rhythms, using them to create an entire world of sound—using them, in fact, to create the foundation of American popular music and culture. As they did so, musicians like Williams and the Walkers, Cole and Cook, and the Johnson brothers rejected the condemnation of the Talented Tenth. They critiqued narrowly judgmental accounts of popular leisure and commercial entertainment and demonstrated the folly of prescribing to worldviews bifurcated in stark categories like high/low, elite/masses, and folk/formal.

Marshall musicians' strategies for increasing the professional and cultural value of black commercial culture presented a different approach to racial uplift. Centering on professionalizing African American performers and expanding the number of blacks who could become full-time professionals, Marshall entertainers expanded the social respect, cultural authority, and weekly wages of hundreds of blacks, not only in New York but throughout America, where musicals like those by Williams and Walker, Ernest Hogan's Smart Set, and Cole and Johnson garnered significant cultural capital (even when they sometimes did not earn much money). Yet as Marshall entertainers raised the professional and cultural values of hundreds, many thousands more gained but slightly. Williams and Walker did not revolutionize black vaudeville nationwide. In fact, New York players did little to change the underlying racial essentialism that separated black performers from white, nor did they successfully overturn the foundational white supremacist connotations of minstrelsy and coon songs. In some ways, in fact, later scholars' critiques of the elitism and paternalism of the Talented Tenth could be levied against the Hotel Marshall crowd as well. These entertainers became an elite class in Black Manhattan. Even as they took seriously their power to represent the race and to share their successes with as many fellow performers as they could, they could not lift everyone up to their level of professional success. The Frogs reflect, to an extent, Hotel Marshall musicians' elitism and their attempts to distinguish themselves from other black performers.

Nonetheless, as the Marshall community engaged in ragging uplift, it set new standards for the black musicians, nightclub owners, and cultural consumers in New York. While not everyone in Manhattan could attain the heights that Marshall musicians did, ragtime performers and their black audiences gained significantly because of the Marshall crowd's work. The next chapter leaves behind the hotel, turning instead to the working-class neighborhood known as the Tenderloin—the district that butted up against Tin Pan Alley, Broadway Avenue, and Times Square. Here, in basement cabarets, late-night juke joints, and black-owned nightclubs, African Americans produced and consumed ragtime music in ways both similar and distinct from the vaudeville stages and music publishers that the Marshall musicians knew. In the Tenderloin, new iterations of African American identities—"ragtime identities"— flourished in new and exciting ways, laying the groundwork and setting the scene for the emergence of both Harlem nightlife and the arrival of the "New Negro" in the 1920s.

CHAPTER FOUR

THE PIANO MAN WAS IT!

THE MAN IN CHARGE

Black Nightclubs and Ragtime Identities

in New York's Tenderloin

Eubie Blake first came to New York City in 1901 from Baltimore as a teenaged member of a traveling medicine show. Already a remarkably seasoned pianist, Blake was immediately struck by the style and dress of black New Yorkers, especially that of the ragtime musicians and "classic pimps." "I'd look at all of these fine people and I'd know that somewhere people had those diamonds and those high-class clothes, and I wanted some day to be like that. I'm not saying I wanted to be a pimp or nothin' like that, but I wanted to be somebody who could *live* like that."[1] In Blake's eyes, these "fine people" attained "high-class" status through their fashionable attire, promoting a style and social standing that he hoped to one day emulate. After his tour, Blake returned home to play ragtime piano in "hookshops" and other black leisure spots. By 1905, he began summering in Atlantic City, where he immersed himself in a ragtime scene dominated by the leading piano players of the day: "One Leg" Willie Joseph, "Slew Foot" Nelson, Richard "Abba Labba" McLean, Jack "the Bear" Wilson, and Charles "Luckey" Roberts. These and other Atlantic City musicians traveled to and from New York looking for gigs and, because steady work was hard to find, they frequently competed with one another for jobs.[2]

At the turn of the twentieth century, New York City's Tenderloin district, located around modern-day Chelsea and the Garment District, was home to the majority of black New Yorkers, black nightclubs, and African American ragtime culture. Duke Ellington, remembered the way musicians set the tone of a nightclub during the ragtime era. Even before the young

Ellington met the pianist Willie "the Lion" Smith, he felt an "impression" of "the Lion" as his music reverberated up a nightclub staircase. The sensation grew as Ellington walked down the stairs and entered the club: he was amazed to find that "everything and everybody seemed to be doing whatever they were doing in the tempo the Lion's group was lying down. . . . The waiters served in that tempo; everybody who had to walk in or out, or around the place, walked with a beat." Even the "walls and furniture seemed to lean understandably," giving Ellington "one of the strangest and greatest sensations I ever had."[3]

This strange feeling no doubt partly reflected the intense rhythms of Smith's ragtime. Outside of black churches, honky-tonks, and ragtime-inflected vaudeville and musical theater, the alarmingly visceral sound of ragtime syncopations still struck audiences in the prewar years as jarring and fresh. No stranger to black musical styles, even a young Ellington was amazed. Yet he also witnessed something else: a shared cultural space where black bartenders and servers, performers and audiences, professionals and patrons lived out their nights together.

As they worked and leisured, consumed and communed together, black New Yorkers enacted new cultural identities in Tenderloin nightclubs. That they seemed to do so all at the same tempo reinforces the potent role ragtime music played in this process of forming self-identities and communal ones. But their experiences reflect too the changing contours of Manhattan nightlife, New York City popular entertainment, and American modernity. Located both physically and ideologically in the center of the Manhattan musical marketplace, Tenderloin nightclubs created the spatial conditions for ragtime musicians, as well as for nightclub owners and their patrons, to fashion self-consciously modern forms of black identities: "ragtime identities" for a ragtime era.

This chapter explores some of the social and cultural influences that shaped new forms of black identity in New York during the first decade and a half of the twentieth century. Ragtime identities call attention to the ways Tenderloin residents participated in the formation of Manhattan commercial leisure, and how they shaped their entertainments through their pocketbooks and personal tastes as much as popular entertainments fueled their own sense of themselves as modern New Yorkers. When Tenderloin residents spent their nights out, they financed the development of black-owned nightclubs, cafés, saloons, and cabarets—new commercial spaces that provided the terrain for the cultural innovation and social interactions that led to black New Yorkers' crafting of new senses of self. As consumers, black New Yorkers participated in one of the largest commercial marketplaces in the United States, helping New York City become the capital of American popular culture; their participation in urban American life was a far cry from the stereotype of blacks as a rural folk, more fitted to sharecropping in cotton fields than financing New York modernity. And as culture producers, African Americans in the Tenderloin undermined the ideologies of America's re-forming white supremacist social order; black ragtime entertainers honed the sound of popular music in the United States and became leading artists in the nation's burgeoning commercial culture markets.

While entertainers ragged uplift and debated the proper presentation of black modernity at the Hotel Marshall in Black Bohemia (but a dozen blocks northwest along Broadway Avenue), thousands of African Americans living, working, and leisuring in the Tenderloin also expressed their intentions to represent new types of black identity. As in the Marshall, ragtime song and dance provided the sound track for a historical process transforming a diverse array of migrants and immigrants, working-class and middle-class people, commercial culture producers and consumers into black New Yorkers. But Tenderloin residents had their eye less on racial representation as it circulated throughout the Manhattan musical marketplace via Broadway Avenue and Tin Pan Alley than on how they themselves perceived black modernity. The daily lives of most African Americans in the early Jim Crow America—where 90 percent of blacks lived in the South, and three-quarters of black southerners worked as sharecroppers on white-owned plantations—demonstrated the need for black New Yorkers to concoct new images of themselves and their race.[4] They fashioned heterogeneous senses of self that found their forms in the same commercial spaces in which ragtime song and dance circulated.

Through their production of ragtime culture, and through their consumption of it in black-owned leisure spaces, Tenderloin residents also advanced their approach to the politics of representation, putting their own spin on public behaviors, fashion, and what Willie "the Lion" Smith called "attitude." Central to the Talented Tenth's conception of proper racial representation was their distinction from the black masses. Yet the masses were not monolithic, and black communities throughout America represented diverse groups of people. African Americans living in New York's Tenderloin district indicated that the so-called working-class masses varied greatly, coming from different regions and countries, raised with heterogeneous backgrounds, and holding an array of jobs. Rather than making assumptions about black New Yorkers' "class," a category that often reifies what it intends to describe, a study of the Tenderloin indicates that social status derived from a series of negotiations—which included changing conceptions of black professionalism, gender relations, and popular culture. Focusing primarily on male musicians, this chapter uses spatial analysis, class, and masculinity to elucidate some of the influences that shaped New Yorkers' ragtime identities. Always interconnected, space, class, and gender offer analytical lenses with which to document the rise of new formations of African American identities.[5] In this formulation, New Yorkers' ragtime identities become important yet understudied precursors to the development of various types of "New Negroes" during World War I and the Harlem Renaissance, and therefore change the ways historians might theorize later forms of black identity, culture, and politics in the twentieth century.[6]

NEW YORK'S TENDERLOIN

At the turn of the twentieth century, the Tenderloin was New York's preeminent black neighborhood. Located only blocks away from burgeoning Times Square, roughly between Sixth and Ninth Avenues and West Twentieth through Fortieth Streets, the Tenderloin harbored a majority of the city's African Americans. In many ways, it did not differ from dozens of other "tenderloins" across the country. Home to a predominantly poor and working-class population, it was also one of the city's "red-light" districts. Black and white preachers alike referred to the "Terrible Tenderloin," and Progressive social reformers condemned the vice, poverty, and crime there even more than they did the goings-on in the notorious Lower East Side and Five Points neighborhoods.[7] But because New York was fast becoming home to thousands of new migrants and millions of immigrants from around the world, Manhattan's Tenderloin also had a distinctive mix of Irish, German, Jewish, Slavic, and Italian immigrants, with each ethnic block harboring its own saloons, gamblers, and prostitutes. Even as the Tenderloin was segregated from other New York neighborhoods, most Tenderloin blocks and commercial spaces were also segregated by ethnicity. But the black sections of the Tenderloin surpassed the others in revelry and allure. As African Americans' new expressions of ragtime culture became the sound of New York City, the black commercial spaces in the Tenderloin seemed especially thrilling, exotic, and sensuous.

By the early twentieth century, black-owned leisure spaces like Ike Hines's Professional Club and Barron D. Wilkins's Little Savoy created a sense in the Tenderloin that black New Yorkers stood on the cusp of something new. The ragtime song and dance that poured from the doors of

Tenderloin nightclubs confirmed to many that new forms of black cultural expression played a role in marking New York City modernity. Working peoples' leisure time was often spent in public and commercial spaces; they tapped their feet to the pulsing bass of the ragtime pianists' left hands as they spoke to the bartender in the syncopated rhythms of the pianists' right-hand melodies. When Eubie Blake or Willie "the Lion" Smith performed piano rags for the crowds, the crowds themselves performed new identities: individual styles of speech, dress, dance, and actions; small flirtations among young women and men; grand gestures by gregarious boxers hoping to make an impression. Since the 1880s, black nightclubs had proliferated in the neighborhood, and by 1900, many had followed the migrating trend of black districts up the west side of Manhattan. Drawing a diverse group of blacks from the Deep South and the "West Indies," the Tenderloin gave rise to heterogeneous and cosmopolitan black communities and, with them, inventive new cultural practices.

Black Manhattan came alive as African Americans surged to break the constraints of American white supremacy and the racial segregation so prevalent throughout New York and the nation. Black-owned leisure spaces aided this process. But they did not do so by wholly removing African Americans from white institutions and power structures—racial segregation is never so total. Black nightclubs created new environments for black New Yorkers in relation to the city's white spaces and white-dominated marketplaces. As African Americans engaged in the production of new types of commercial arenas, they not only transformed the black neighborhoods in midtown Manhattan but also established key sites of culture and activity for New York City as a whole.[8] Tenderloin clubs became both an environment for, and active influences on, black cultural creativity, which in turn propelled black New Yorkers' participation in one of America's most bustling market economies. This communal transformation took place publicly, out in the open. Through their nightly transactions in Tenderloin spaces, African Americans bought, sold, and circulated new ideas about racial identity, New York City, and American modernity. In the two decades before Harlem became New York's principle black neighborhood, black musicians, dancers, singers, nightclub owners, servers, bartenders, bouncers, and various types of patrons set new standards for Manhattan nightlife and popular entertainment.[9] The neighborhood, and its ragtime leisure spaces in particular, provided an excellent environment for the cultivation of the greatest piano players of the era, including Eubie Blake.

The man was born John Hubie Blake on February 7, 1883, near Belair Market in one of Baltimore's central African American neighborhoods. His mother, Emily, washed laundry for her neighbors, and his father worked as a stevedore on the Baltimore docks, earning nine dollars a week when it did not rain. As a slave on a large Virginia plantation, John Blake Sr. had been used as a stud, siring twenty-seven children of which he knew. But since marrying immediately after emancipation, he and Emily had had little luck making a family. The Blakes had ten children before Eubie, but they had all died as infants. Eubie himself was born frail, and few who saw him as a baby would have imagined he would live to be a hundred.[10]

Blake began playing piano at the age of four or five and claimed to have first heard ragtime at his mother's church, even though she would not have considered it that way. "My mother, she carried Jesus around in her vest pocket," Blake recalled fondly—she did not approve of ragtime.[11] Even though Blake's mother considered ragtime unrespectable, when he was four or five years old, she bought Little Hubie (as she called him) a small, seventy-five dollar pump organ, paying a quarter a week until it was paid off.[12] A decade later, when Aggie Shelton, one of Baltimore's premier madams, offered Blake a job playing ragtime piano, he took it. Still wearing "short pants," Blake crawled out of his bedroom window every night for his nine o'clock shift, making sure to have time to rent full-length pants from a nearby pool hall for twenty-five cents a night. He was soon making fifteen to eighteen dollars a night playing syncopated music in a high-class "five-dollar" bawdy house, a term Blake misunderstood as "body house" for years.[13] (Musicians made good money in Baltimore during an era in which southern farm workers collected only seventy-five cents a day for long hours of back-straining labor.)[14] Blake also played at his mother's church, and it did not take long before a few of the sisters began to recognize his style.

One day, after Blake had been playing at Shelton's for a few weeks, a friend of his mother told her she had "heard somebody playing the piano at Aggie Shelton's. Sounded just like Little Hubie." Blake's mother did not know who Aggie Shelton was and asked, "What time?" "About one o'clock in the morning," came the reply." "Oh no, that boy goes to bed about nine. How you all know it was him?" Blake's mother asked. "Nobody wobbles the bass like him," the informant exclaimed; "ain't nobody plays like him."[15] Blake was in trouble, but he had to wait until his father arrived home from work to receive his punishment. When Blake Sr. arrived, Eubie told him the truth: he had been sneaking out at night. "What have you been doing with the money?" his father asked. Eubie pulled back the oilcloth floor covering in his bedroom where he securely stashed "fives, tens, twenties—maybe more money than the elder Blake had ever seen." "Mind if I take one of these?" the father asked the son, before walking downstairs and telling Emily, "Now Em, this boy is doing nothing wrong. He's gonna have to work, and this is good work with good pay. You just better leave him alone to do his work as he sees it."[16] The Blake family's standard of living increased that night, and Eubie Blake continued on a path toward a profession he would never give up. Playing ragtime was "good work" indeed for a young African American, but becoming a successful professional required hard work too. The players who made it dedicated their entire lives to being full-time musicians, and young musicians like Blake spent as much time on the road as setting down roots. New York City, as Blake would soon discover, was already a competitive marketplace for young ragtime players.

During the 1890s, as Blake came of age, black migration to New York grew rapidly. As southern states instituted systematic segregation, violence, and disenfranchisement in the wake of *Plessy v. Ferguson*, thousands of African Americans fled the cotton fields of the South in favor of the urban North. Between 1890 and 1910, the black population of New York City nearly tripled to 92,000, and it leapt to 152,407 by 1920.[17] Many of the new arrivals were foreign born, mostly from Puerto Rico and the West Indies. By 1900, for the first time in New York history, more than half the black population—53 percent—was born outside the state.[18] Eubie Blake's move, first to Atlantic City and then to New York in 1905, paralleled the migrations northward of thousands of other African Americans. But whereas Blake's proficiency as a pianist allowed him to move back and forth between northern cities, most black arrivals to New York became residents of the Tenderloin.

The neighborhood featured rows and rows of tenement buildings, narrow brick structures five and six stories high that leaned into one another and shared connecting rooftops. The compact design allowed for windows only in the front and back of the tenements, with little ventilation along the sides of the buildings. Rooms with more than one window were rare, and many had none. As a result, apartments lacked sunlight and fresh air. Tenements usually had a single airshaft in the center of the building, but because tenants frequently used them as dumping places for refuse, landlords often nailed shut the windows opening onto the shaft in an effort to block the putrid smells of rotting garbage. Humidity and heat in the summertime intensified the feeling of suffocation and made tenements dangerous places to live. Tenderloin tenements often housed twenty or more families, and rarely did a family occupy more than a two-bedroom apartment. As many as three thousand people could live on a single Tenderloin block, a circumstance that caused one reporter to note that "the present housing conditions of the vast majority of colored families in New York can only be characterized as disgraceful."[19]

Even given these conditions, African Americans had difficulty finding housing in New York. While not legally segregated, custom dictated that blacks were the last renters landlords wanted in their tenements. A graduate student at Columbia University in 1900 noted that blacks occupied the "worst houses in the Tenderloin . . . and that they paid up to five dollars more than whites did."[20] In 1901, W. E. B. Du Bois found the discrepancy slightly less, writing that blacks paid one to two dollars more per month than white renters. Originally settling in Greenwich Village in the 1860s, African Americans migrated north and, by 1900, stretched along the west side of Manhattan, from the Hudson River to Sixth Avenue, between Twentieth Street and Sixty-fourth. Besides the Tenderloin, blacks clustered in Black Bohemia in the mid-Fifties, and in San Juan Hill between West Sixtieth and Sixty-fourth Streets. The most northern West Side black district, and the last to become a black neighborhood before the migration to Harlem, San Juan Hill got its name from the famous Spanish-American War battle, due to the frequent racial violence between black and immigrant residents.[21] Most blacks in the Tenderloin constituted the working poor, and they labored as waiters, coachmen, bootblacks, and domestics. A select few, however, found other opportunities.

New York City had been cultivating a professional class since the late nineteenth century. In 1901, Du Bois estimated that 5.5 percent of black New Yorkers owned their own business, and that African Americans had a total of $1.5 million invested in real estate, catering, undertaking, hotels, and restaurants. The sixty-nine leading black establishments alone garnered $800,000 in total investments. The wealthiest blacks in the city lived in high brownstone buildings in Brooklyn and largely remained separate from the activities in the Tenderloin. The Society of the Sons of New York, an exclusive social organization founded in the 1880s, drew its membership from the wealthiest "Four Hundred" of black society and admitted only men born in the state of New York. Another such organization was the Brooklyn-based Carthaginian Lodge No. 47 of the Prince Hall Freemasons.[22] Members of black fraternal societies rarely visited the Tenderloin and generally disapproved of the various social and cultural interactions making the district infamous.

Unknown to New York's members of the Talented Tenth, however, music and even ragtime culture was working to lift more African Americans out of poverty than almost any other profession in the city. According to the census of 1900, 329 black New Yorkers identified as professional actors or showmen, while an additional 268 were musicians or music teachers. Considering too that hundreds of black wageworkers augmented their incomes by playing music in their off hours, professional entertainment offered unprecedented prospects for many black New Yorkers. In a city with only 42 black doctors and 26 lawyers, music allowed a relatively high number of African Americans to work their way out of poverty.[23] Because African Americans had little opportunity to perform European styles of classical music, only popular music held professional possibilities for blacks. And nothing was more popular in New York than ragtime.

TENDERLOIN SPACES AND THE FLUIDITY OF SOCIAL STATUS

The city's segregated blocks meant that most black New Yorkers had little choice but to live, work, and leisure in the same spaces, creating frequent cross-class interactions, what the historian Victoria Wolcott has called "'circularity' between dominant and subordinate classes."[24] Wageworking African Americans in the Tenderloin spent time in many of the same spaces of leisure as professional black sportsmen and the established "stars" of the Broadway stage who regularly frequented Tenderloin nightclubs and generated a special buzz when they showed up after a big performance. Black workers shared bar counters with entertainers like Bert Williams and George Walker. They rubbed elbows with the boxers Joe Gans and Joe Wolcott, and, if luck struck, even took part in the party when Jack Johnson, the heavyweight champion of the world (after 1908), rolled into town. Tenderloin nightclubs offered spaces that, though not removed from the dynamics of class, prompted African Americans of disparate incomes to commune.

Most inhabitants of Tenderloin leisure spaces shared the same "class," as scholars most often use the term; they worked for wages, struggled to afford food and rent, and had little contact with members of New York's Talented Tenth.[25] Yet Tenderloin residents occupied various positions along a spectrum of social status, background, employment, and income. Because class did not mean only, or even primarily, financial worth, class distinctions indicate a series of social relations in the Tenderloin, rather than a distinct social position or salary. Entrepreneurial cabaret owners and professional musicians, for example, attained levels of social status among black New Yorkers that bartenders, servers, and most customers did not, even if they took home comparable pay at the end of the night. At the same time, some patrons enjoyed a prestige in the neighborhood that surpassed that of the most established bar owners and piano ticklers—indeed, some like George Walker and Jack Johnson garnered unprecedented renown as nationally recognized entertainers. When Walker or Johnson entered a Tenderloin nightclub, they did so as "stars," receiving the adulation of many in the community, and of most in the saloon. Yet both men came from humble beginnings, and without their talent and good fortune, they too would be living in all-black, predominantly "working-class" neighborhoods with little chance to move elsewhere. On the other hand, musicians like Will Marion Cook and Rosamond Johnson came of age with rare opportunities for college educations and musical training. Yet they not only frequented Tenderloin nightclubs regularly but chose to perform popular music and theater styles, ragging uplift by transgressing established lines between "high" and "low" entertainments set out by their communities (as well as their parents). In the Tenderloin, a working black waiter might find himself at the piano bench and establish himself as a newly professional "doctor" of ragtime. It did not happen all the time, nor did it happen to everyone, but the cross-pollination of black identities, social status, and professional opportunities poured throughout the Tenderloin as richly as beer from the tap.

Black-owned commercial spaces like ragtime nightclubs created opportunities for people to enact new forms of African American identities. During the early years of Jim Crow, African Americans' sense of themselves as active consumers in New York markets undermined normative standards of blacks as preindustrial agrarian workers, standards that reflected both a legacy of slavery and contemporary white southerners' justifications for a sharecropping system that kept millions of African Americans yoked to debt peonage. In New York, blacks could be leading culture producers; they could participate in the rise of mass consumption, and some could even have their own businesses. These opportunities arose not simply from New York City, the place, but from Tenderloin leisure spaces: important sites of economic and ideological negotiation where some African Americans became central players as cultural innovators, entrepreneurial nightclub owners, and marketplace consumers. Most conspicuously in Tenderloin nightclubs, ragtime laid the sound track for African American nightlife, instigating the historical process transforming black New Yorkers' sense of themselves years before the notion of the New Negro became popular in African American political and cultural discourse.

Ragtime's syncopated rhythms saturated the air of black hot spots in the Tenderloin, putting musicians—and especially piano players—at the top of the local social hierarchy. In the nightclubs, social capital in the shape of a popular profession or "star status" could mean more than income. Ragtime musicians were, in the pianist James P. Johnson's assessment, "popular fellows, real celebrities" in the Tenderloin.[26] Club owners usually hired pianists to put a band together or, in many cases, play solo for ten to twelve hours at a time, and musicians took their roles as entertainers seriously. Piano players also worked as central organizers and MCs for the nightclubs. Willie "the Lion" Smith remembered what it meant for pianists to "take charge" of the nightclub space. "Back in those days, 'takin' charge' meant the pianist had duties and responsibilities. He played solo piano, accompanied the singers, directed whatever band was on hand, and watched the kitty to be sure no one cheated on tips. . . . The piano man was it! The man in charge." Club owners generally hired a piano player to be the "all-around showman" and the "host at the party."[27]

To poor and newly arrived black migrants, entertainers seemed like confident and accomplished professionals, community members to be proud of and to, perhaps, take after. Although they may not have been wealthy, Tenderloin musicians did not work for an hourly wage. They made their living, instead, through their intellectual and artistic labors—a rare option for African Americans in the early twentieth century. Ragtimers' professionalism and their intellectual skills challenged American white supremacy, which sought to limit African Americans' economic mobility and job opportunities in the wake of emancipation. But commercial musicians' labors and social status in black communities also undermined the Talented Tenth ideals of racial representation and proper forms of labor, especially among black men.

While competition made it difficult for men to become professional musicians, it proved even harder for female entertainers to find full-time employment. African American women performed as singers in Tenderloin nightclubs, but there is so little record of their activities that it seems they rarely led bands or garnered the social prestige the pianists did.[28] Women did, however, populate Tenderloin spaces. They were present as workers and consumers, cocktail servers and sex workers, and, to a limited degree, as entertainers. Although ragtime nightclubs were predominantly male-dominated spaces, black women helped create the conditions of black New Yorkers' ragtime identities. They also influenced men's portrayal of themselves, a fact borne out in men's frequent recollections of their interest in impressing women in the audience (even as they vastly under-recollect female musicians). Due to the work of both women and men, ragtime identities promoted empowering portrayals of black masculinity during an era in which black men rarely controlled their own public images.

Willie "the Lion" Smith seemed to revel in his ability to present himself as an aggressive and stylish professional musician in Tenderloin nightclubs. While best remembered as a leading "stride" piano progenitor in 1920s Harlem cabarets, Smith spent his early years picking up piano runs in Newark's and New York's black districts, where his musical ingenuity and competitive spirit helped symbolize ragtime identities. Although accounts of his actual birth date vary, Smith was born in late November 1897 in Groshen, New Jersey. His father, Frank Bertholoff, was light-skinned and mostly absent; his mother, Ida Oliver, had "Spanish and Negro blood, in addition to her Mohawk Indian" and, having been born with a birth caul, had "unusual insight into spiritual matters," as her son put it. On her son's birth, Ida Oliver named him William Henry Joseph Bonaparte Bertholoff Smith "to represent all the important things in [his] heritage."[29] Oliver washed and ironed laundry for white, mostly Jewish, families in the neighborhood, and at a young age, Smith became enchanted with the Hebrew lessons one of his mother's employer's gave to her children. Allowed to sit in on Mrs. Rothschild's instructions, he impressed her and the family's rabbi with his precocity and quick learning. Taken under the rabbi's wing, Smith celebrated a bar mitzvah at the age of thirteen and remained a lifelong subscriber to the Jewish faith. He even served as a cantor at a Harlem synagogue later in his life.[30] As a teenager, though, Smith had an immediate love for music of all kinds.

He first began playing organ at the age of six, learning spirituals and hymns from his mother. Even at a young age, Smith had more interest in "beautifying" song melodies than in playing them as written. He must have had a terrific ear for music because, within a few years, Smith regularly upset his mother by "ragging" and "beautifying" her religious music in their front parlor. Although Smith's family could not afford a piano, Smith won a brand-new one by studiously calculating the "number of dots in a circle" printed in a music store advertisement. His mother subscribed to uplift ideology to such an extent that she initially considered her son's ragging "sinful." "Yeah," Smith recalls early in his autobiography, "in the front parlor, where the neighbors could hear your playing, you had to sing the proper religious words and keep that lilting tempo down!"

By 1911, Smith was making the rounds in black juke joints in Newark. He met ragtime musicians and learned their musical approaches (as well as ragtime dance steps like the One-Legged Buck and Wing). He also recognized the ways urban African Americans developed stark class distinctions among themselves. At the age of fourteen, Smith started giving some of his earnings to his mother, which, while it may not necessarily have changed her perception of ragtime, made her appreciate her son's chosen vocation. Unlike Eubie Blake's and Will Marion Cook's mothers, whose sons' ragtime aspirations seemed to always threaten their sense of respectability, Ida Oliver began to defend her son when members of her church asked, "Why do you let Willie go into those saloons and play ragtime?" "He's only playing what he feels, and he isn't doing any harm," Oliver told them. "He gives me whatever money he makes. Seldom does he do anything wrong."[31] Smith's ability to supplement his single mother's income helped alleviate her concerns about ragtime culture's seeming lack of respectability.

As a young man, Smith understood racial uplift and the politics of respectability as the ideological constructs of a more affluent African American class than his own. "People don't understand the folks in the underworld," he surmised. "There are as many of God's children in the saloons and cabarets as can be found in the churches. When you come right down to it, those who frequent the pleasure spots are religious souls who are singing to release their pent-up feelings." A quick study of human psychology and social relations, Smith understood well how members of his community raised themselves up as they denounced others; and he could tell that these class distinctions often backfired, creating distress and distinction among a black community already on the margins. "The so-called righteous people who are evermore screaming, 'Down with the saloons!' or 'People should stay out of those places!' are doing more harm than good by causing rebellion in others." "The do-gooders are really jealous of those who are able to let their emotions out," Smith concluded, "Many of the churchgoers are always tearing things down."[32] Smith—a metaphysical thinker, religious moralist, mixed-race American, and musical innovator—lived his entire life according to his mother's advice: "Willie, you've got a real truth to tell the people and you've got a God-given right to scream it at them. But you must remember—that sometimes the screaming won't do any good."[33] Smith rarely had to scream to gain attention. When he moved to Manhattan as a teenager, he entered a commercial world owned and operated by African Americans.

A favorite nightclub among ragtime musicians was Ike Hines's Professional Club on West Twenty-seventh Street, a leading example of black entrepreneurial impulses and a model for black leisure sites throughout the city. Outside the front stoop of the inauspicious brownstone, Hines placed an iron gate and a red lantern that hung overhead. He covered his first- and second-floor windows with fabric or a dark paint, causing first-time visitors to notice the Chinese restaurant beneath the steps before recognizing Hines's club. Experienced Hines patrons walked up the steps and rang the bell to let the doorman know of their arrival. Inside the front door was a small vestibule opening into a long hallway leading to a tastefully decorated parlor. Behind that, a large back room contained a bare floor with tables and chairs arranged around the perimeter for an intimate audience. In one corner sat a battered upright piano, and the open floor remained uncluttered for performers both hired by Hines and spontaneously egged on by his patrons. If a well-known performer like Bert Williams or Ernest Hogan came in for the night, the crowd had a good chance of catching an impromptu song or cakewalk—Hines's joint was beloved among New York's black entertainers and sportsmen. It was also one of the few Tenderloin spaces that regularly hosted white patrons, often couples, James Weldon Johnson noted, "out sight-seeing or slumming," or "variety performers . . . who came to get their imitations first-hand from the Negro entertainers they saw there." Hines had a buffet in a closet off the main room, where he kept the food hot throughout the night. Unlike most Tenderloin clubs, Hines's Professional Club did not serve alcohol, but guests could easily smuggle in their own. Johnson remembered that Hines allowed no gambling and that the "conduct of the place was surprisingly orderly."[34]

Like the ragtime performers who played there, Hines's club displayed African American history, even as it anticipated the future of black cultural possibilities. Photographs of famous, infamous, and forgotten African Americans covered the walls, presenting an archive of the nineteenth century. A portrait of Frederick Douglass hung near a picture of the prizefighter Peter Jackson, alongside images of dozens of other boxers and jockeys, vaudevillians and singers. During an era in which whites excluded blacks from American history, Hines's testament to successful black women and men who, in Johnson's words, had "made it," reminded his patrons and performers that black culture and history mattered.[35] Like the ragtime performers who concocted new forms of entertainment from the cultural expressions of previous generations, Hines recognized the importance of the black past even as he created a modern establishment. It would be clubs like Hines's—offering a mix of sophistication and enthusiastic revelry—that would instigate the cultural world of Harlem decades later.

Ike Hines originally established his club in a rathskeller in Greenwich Village in 1880, and by 1883 had established it as one of the "hot spots" in Manhattan. He named it a "Professional Club" in 1884, perhaps as a way to distinguish it from other hangouts along the West Side.[36] If Hines's was one of Manhattan's most popular black-owned nightclubs, it was not particularly representative. But the club initiated a trend. Throughout the 1890s, honky-tonks, gambling clubs, cabarets, saloons, and bordellos proliferated in the Tenderloin. The musician Perry Bradford remembered that many attempted to follow Hines's example, but few maintained the sophistication of the Professional Club, opting instead to encourage gambling, drinking, and prostitution. Boxers, especially, seemed to enjoy opening up Tenderloin nightclubs. Sam Moore opened a cabaret at Twenty-sixth Street and Seventh Avenue; William "Kid" Banks had a club at Thirty-seventh and Seventh; Johnnie Johnson opened up the Douglass Club on West Thirty-first Street and catered to popular entertainers, black and white. Of the new batch of Tenderloin clubs, only the Douglass Club and Barron D. Wilkins's Little Savoy seemed to attract as many black Broadway stars and Tin Pan Alley songwriters as Hines's place.[37] Wilkins, along with his brother Leroy, would become a leading nightclub owner in Harlem throughout the 1910s and 1920s. During the first decade of the twentieth century, though, the Wilkins brothers were just beginning to capitalize on black commercial spaces that trafficked in licentious consumptions of alcohol, prostitution, gambling, and interracial liaisons.

Ragtime song and dance was always linked to sex and other vices, and the Tenderloin's ragtime clubs, gambling houses, and brothels helped make the district one of Manhattan's centers for commercial leisure. While scholars are just beginning to examine the interconnections between race, commerce, and sex work in New York City during the 1920s, it is clear that African American women traded sex for money in many Tenderloin leisure spaces years before, often in ragtime nightclubs. Most likely, in fact, prostitution and gambling accompanied ragtime music and musicians so thoroughly that most Tenderloin residents would not have strictly distinguished ragtime clubs from gambling saloons or brothels. Writing about New York in the 1920s, the historian Kevin Mumford identifies three types of commercial spaces that offered sex for sale: a "standard speakeasy" (where prostitutes congregated "to make necessary contacts"); a speakeasy where prostitutes worked as servers (and could be hired by patrons); and the "Speak-easy House of Prostitution."[38] Prostitution formed an important part of the Tenderloin's marketplace, both fueling and drawing from the commercial transactions taking place in ragtime nightclubs. While the pianist James P. Johnson recalled that most ragtime musicians who worked in the South and Midwest were "big-time pimps" who "managed girls on the side," this did not hold true for most New York City ragtimers. "The [piano] ticklers and their gals couldn't work in New York right away because there were a lot of hustlers there already who had protection."[39] While sex and music markets in the Tenderloin overlapped, there seemed to be fewer instances of male musicians actually working in the sex trade than in other locales.

Another source of Tenderloin commercialism, gambling, offers a lens into just how fluid one's wealth and social status could be—they could change at the drop of the dice. In James Weldon Johnson's *The Autobiography of an Ex-Coloured Man*, the unnamed narrator learned how fickle not only his winnings and losses could be as he gambled in the Tenderloin but also the social status that came with it. During his first night of throwing dice, as he was winning big, the narrator noted the he "had gained the attention and respect of everybody in the room. In less than three minutes," he recalled, "I had won more than two hundred dollars." But the narrator's winnings on his first night were "a sum which afterwards cost me dearly"—foreshadowing the troubles he would encounter as he got deeper into dice games. As he would soon find out, gamblers in the Tenderloin often found themselves wrapped in "linen dusters" because they had "lost all the money and jewelry they possessed," even gambling away "all their outer clothing and even their shoes." Johnson's narrator would find himself passing "through all the states and conditions that a gambler is heir to. Some days found me able to peel ten- and twenty-dollar bills from a roll, and others found me clad in a linen duster and carpet slippers."[40] While gambling losses give a rather extreme example of the flexibility of wealth in the Tenderloin, Johnson's depiction offers a snapshot of the ways Tenderloin residents' status could quickly climb or fall. Johnson's narration also emphasizes that Tenderloin clubs were spaces where class negotiations took place, where social status was earned and lost—a state quite familiar to the African American sportsmen who liked to live it up in the Tenderloin after big wins.

Alongside the ragtime musicians, black jockeys, boxers, and other sportsmen made for important fixtures in Tenderloin clubs, and their presence further complicates notions of social status among black New Yorkers. Jockeys were some of the first black professional sportsmen in the United States. Most came from the South, where American horse racing began and where African Americans worked as stable boys, trainers, and jockeys for wealthy white landowners. Thirteen of the fourteen jockeys in the first Kentucky Derby in 1875 were black, and Willie Simms, who won the Derby in 1897 and 1898, was the first American jockey to "shorten his stirrups and ride the monkey-on-a-stick (monkey crouch) style" that quickly became the standard.[41] After big wins, jockeys enjoyed celebrating in the Tenderloin, often buying drinks for the whole house. One reporter remembered that a certain jockey earned twelve thousand dollars a year, but spent "about thirty times that rate." After victories, it was "his custom to fete the crowd . . . with champagne at the cost of five dollars a quart!"[42] Winning jockeys who flaunted their enormous, if fleeting, wealth were the biggest spenders on any given night in the Tenderloin. Although they may have attracted attention and a bit of prestige in their communities, African American jockeys, like ragtime musicians, did not rise up into the Talented Tenth. Those who had grown up as servants for southern white horse owners, however, would have undoubtedly celebrated their climb into new levels of social status in ways that categories like "working" and "middle class" do not identify. Likewise, African American boxers' presence in Tenderloin nightclubs reveals other layers to the social dynamics that informed New Yorkers' ragtime identities.

Recalling the prestige boxers held in American culture more generally, Eubie Blake noted that "it's hard for young people of the later twentieth century to understand the importance society granted to boxing idols."[43] Fighters like Jack Johnson, George Dixon, Joe Wolcott, and Joe Gans drew the largest crowds in Tenderloin nightclubs—and they spent the most money. Many boxers even opened up their own nightclubs in the 1890s and early 1900s to capitalize on black New Yorker nightlife. Because most Tenderloin sports stars grew up poor in rural areas, Tenderloin nightlife offered ways for them to claim new levels of social esteem in an exciting urban community. Displays of extravagant spending symbolized their success, even if their lives as sportsmen would be tragically short. As boxers, jockeys, and baseball players, these men helped develop professional sports in the United States, and they participated in Tenderloin nightlife, both shaping and following the contours of new forms of black cultural identities.[44] Boxers were notoriously sharp dressers, and their style certainly shaped the fashion of many in the Tenderloin, indicating the ways that clothing helped develop social status.[45] Perhaps the biggest influence on personal style were the most successful black stage performers of the era, Bert Williams and George Walker, who regularly frequented Tenderloin cabarets when in town.

New York's leading black performers set high standards for high fashion, showing their social status through their beautiful and expensive attire. The duo's promotional shots, song sheet covers, and newspaper ads most often presented them in formal dress, not the blackface and "African" costumes they wore on stage. The two seemed to live in three-piece suits, top hats, spats, full-length overcoats, bowties, and ascots. Walker told the *Toledo Courier* that he had his clothes made at the "best tailors in New York

City" and would stand for "two or three hours . . . for the fitting of the suit, so that when it was finished it would fit perfectly."[46] Both Williams and Walker conspicuously sported diamonds, incorporating them into everything from cuff links to cigarette cases.[47] Their clothing and fame made waves every time they entered a black nightclub. Although their diamonds may have distinguished them from most other patrons, the men's professional status and fashionable attire reveal an important dimension of the ragtime identities finding form in the Tenderloin. During the early Jim Crow era, the duo's public performances of conspicuous consumption proved transgressive indeed. Rather than simply indicating individual choices in personal style, clothing and fashion exemplified how ragtime identities found public expression in New York's commercial marketplaces—in this case, tailors and department stores augmented the self-conscious presentation of black modernity in Tenderloin nightclubs.

Williams and Walker used their public appearances to distance themselves from the tragicomic minstrel types they performed on stage, making sure to distinguish the artist from the caricatures performed. Walker discovered this to be a full-time job, especially when his fashionable style created confusion for white New Yorkers. One day on a streetcar, Walker overheard two white men trying to figure out who he was to be dressed so elegantly. "Who is that swell darky?" Walker remembered hearing. Initially confusing him for the fashionable boxer Joe Gans or a "race horse coon," one of the men approached Walker inquiring, "May I ask why you wear such flashy clothes and that large diamond ring?" Walker told them that "in many cases white people would not believe I was George Walker if I did not wear them. The general public expects to see me as a flashy sort of a darky and I do not disappoint them as far as appearance goes."[48] Walker's assessment indicates how he performed his star status every day through his attire, while also showing that New Yorkers, black and white, understood the direct connection between personal style and profession. Differences existed between black and white assessments, to be sure. Given that most African Americans in the Tenderloin would recognize Walker, the white men's assumptions—and racist impertinence of address—illustrate their quickness to stereotype a well-dressed black man. Yet their appraisal of Walker's style may not have been as disrespectful as it seems. Besides ragtime entertainers, the two types of professions they guessed—boxer and horse jockey—represented the most notable and recognizable professional African Americans in New York.

In New York's Tenderloin, thousands of African Americans with backgrounds similar to Willie "the Lion" Smith and Eubie Blake found themselves in frequent contact with African Americans raised with considerable means and access to education and musical training. This diversity stimulated the development of ragtime identities. Rosamond and James Weldon Johnson, for example, famously enjoyed leisuring in the Tenderloin, and their excursions into the district demonstrate one way that so-called middle-class African Americans experienced and even shaped supposedly working-class spaces. Clearly based on his own intimate engagement with Tenderloin nightlife, James Weldon Johnson's *The Autobiography of an Ex-Colored Man* reads like a tour guide of the various heterogeneous leisure and work spaces he discovered during his early years in the city. Similarly, when Rosamond Johnson or his partner Bob Cole walked into Barron Wilkins's Little Savoy or Ike Hines's Professional Club, patrons swooned, hoping to get a quick performance of one of the biggest hits on Broadway, "Under a Bamboo Tree" or "The Maiden with the Dreamy Eyes," perhaps. These tunes were also imminently popular among Tenderloin musicians and audiences, so even when they were not physically present, the trio's refined syncopated love songs influenced the sounds of Tenderloin rags.

In the 1920s, the Johnsons would fit the profile of elite poets and highbrow slave spiritual arrangers that Alain Locke hoped to coalesce into his ideal of the New Negro. For generations of scholars, the brothers symbolized the classism and elitism of the Harlem Renaissance. Yet the Johnson brothers' presence in the Tenderloin showcases the diversity of the neighborhood before World War I, and their participation in black New York nightlife complicates the often static categories implicit in studies of black elitism. During an era that rarely allowed African Americans a place in concert halls, college educations and conservatory training most often led to vaudeville stages and black-dominated leisure spaces—places where the influence of the Talented Tenth might overlap with that of the working poor, and where strategies for ragging uplift helped shape the sight and sound of Black Manhattan.

RAGTIME PROFESSIONALISM AND THE NEW YORK SOUND

Tenderloin nightclubs presented both metaphorical and literal stages for African Americans to perform modernity. Ragtime music provided the sound track, but this does not suggest that music was merely background. Like a movie's film score, music proved integral to African Americans' creation of black-owned commercial spaces. Black musicians' popular and increasingly professional status opened the door for nightclub owners' to enter into the Manhattan musical marketplace and to shape it—to a degree—in their own mold. In response, Tenderloin nightclubs opened the stage curtain for the arrival of new classes of black professional musicians. And while the Hotel Marshall community had arrived on Broadway and made their professions along Tin Pan Alley, many more black performers became full-time professionals by working long shifts in the Tenderloin. The Talented Tenth may have rejected ragtime nightclubs as spaces where respectable black culture could thrive, but commercial avenues like the ones budding in the Tenderloin laid the groundwork for twentieth-century representations of black people and culture.

In Tenderloin nightclubs, competition for regular work increased the cultural value of black musical professionalism—it propelled good players to become excellent. Competition fostered innovation and pushed musicians to create a recognizable "New York" sound. Because so many musicians hustled for work in the Tenderloin, steady gigs quickly came and went. Even established players rarely rested easy, because up-and-comers could always threaten their piano bench. Club owners demanded that pianists perform most of the night and take few breaks. Taking a break, even for a moment, could threaten job security. As Willie "the Lion" Smith recalled, "you'd rather piss your pants than leave the piano when a rival was in the house. That was the best way to lose your gig."[49] Traveling musicians who made their living touring vaudeville circuits frequently came into town looking for pickup work, and many could vanquish hired players on any given night.[50] Competition was tough, but even regular players needed to take periodic breaks, and younger players did find opportunities to play. The vaudevillian Tom Fletcher remembered that nearly "all saloons had back rooms with pianos and anyone . . . could plunk on them as long as he wished [until] the regular piano player . . . came on [and] practice was over."[51]

That black ragtimers oversupplied the local demand for music meant nightclub owners wielded considerable power in the Tenderloin marketplace, another example of African Americans' rare opportunity to capitalize in America's growing industrial economy. Analyzing the economics of black clubs, Smith noted that for "all night-club bosses, the money was a one-way chute—everything coming in, nothing going out."[52] Owners rarely promised wages to musicians, but they expected performers to play long hours and to live off tips—something Tenderloin musicians seemed able to do. A top-notch piano tickler sometimes received a regular salary, but it was never enough to live on—the goal was to keep the pianist there and to induce tips so that the bar owner would not have to pay a living wage.

James P. Johnson recalled receiving a salary of ten to twelve dollars a week to play twelve hours a night, seven nights a week. Tips could double or triple his take-home though.[53] Smith recalled that his bosses "paid you off in uppercuts. That was a saying we got up in those days; it meant you were allowed to keep your tips, but you got no salary." He remembered sometimes getting promised a small amount, maybe twenty dollars—"that was known as a left hook"—but Smith's professional wages in New York reflect a marked increase from the one-dollar-a-day he started with in Newark as a teenager (though even then, his tips amounted to three or four dollars a day, more than the average unskilled black laborer in the city, who averaged three dollars per day).[54] Making things even more difficult, club owners usually split tips equally between all the performers, servers, bartenders, and dancers. This arrangement made ragtime musicians—and pianists especially—fight for work in the best clubs with the best tippers. It also pushed players to become excellent musicians, unmatched at their instruments. Pianists like Blake and Smith, for example, fought their way to the top and worked relentlessly to maintain their positions.

Pushed by economic realities, competition and the cultivation of individual styles among ragtime entertainers drove musical innovation and added to the energy of Tenderloin clubs. The preeminent ragtime composer and performer Scott Joplin may have famously lamented that amateurs and professionals alike played his ragtime compositions too fast.[55] But in the Tenderloin, blistering improvisations and quick tempos often separated the talented players from the exceptional. Speed, coordination, and energy wowed paying crowds, kept bartenders busy, and club owners happy. Charles "Luckey" Roberts was considered the fastest of the Tenderloin players. Pianists marveled at his "lightning fast chromatic runs" that, James P. Johnson remembered, "no one else seemed able to copy." Johnson himself made a strong impression on Blake when, as a teenager, he sat at Blake's piano and played one of Blake's most difficult compositions, "faster than he himself could."[56] But the high bar of ragtime professionalism did not depend only on tempo and flash.

Among themselves, Tenderloin pianists emphasized musical inventiveness, which referred to a musicians' ability to improvise new harmonic tensions and rhythmic syncopations—to play songs differently every time. Blake remembered that if Paul Seminole "played a tune twenty thousand times, it was twenty thousand times different." Duke Ellington offered a similar recollection about "the Lion" Smith's ability to accompany a singer who "used to sing twenty or thirty choruses" while making "each one different." Smith himself remembered "One-Leg" Willie Joseph

Willie "the Lion" Smith. Music Division, New York Public Library for the Performing Arts, Astor, Lenox, and Tilden Foundations.

who played at Barron Wilkins's Little Savoy as "one of the best of the old time ragtime players." Joseph "had original ideas and never played the same number the same way twice; the melody would stay the same, but he would always vary the harmony."[57] Even as they wowed crowds with their sonic innovations, well-known Tenderloin players like Smith, Blake, and James P. Johnson—all cited by Duke Ellington and other leading figures of 1920s jazz piano as important influences—themselves referenced scores of pianists forgotten by the historical record.[58]

Musical innovation and technical virtuosity, not simply speed, made players like Joseph, Seminole, Jack "the Bear," Fred Bryant, and William Turk stand out. Bryant, for example, was notable because he had a "velvet touch" that distinguished his style from the raucous and fast players. Although he never recorded, piano ticklers remembered Sam Gordon as a "great technician who played in an arabesque style that Art Tatum made famous later. He played swift runs in sixths and thirds, broken chords, one-note tremolandos, and had a good left hand."[59] William Turk, who was not musically trained and "didn't even know what key he was in," blew the minds of musicians and audiences because he could play "one key in one hand and one in the other, and the chords still jelled."[60] Luckey Roberts "had massive hands that could stretch a fourteenth on the keyboard," which allowed him to stretch his fingers past the octave and to the next third scale tone, so he "played tenths as easy as others played octaves." Even more spectacularly, Roberts's "tremolo was terrific, and he could drum on one note with two or three fingers in either hand."[61] While his technique set Roberts apart from others, bass runs in tenths and tremolo shimmers created musical results that impressed local musicians and influenced the sound of New York ragtime. Inventive improvisations, and, of course, ingenious rhythmic syncopations determined the leading pianists in the Tenderloin. Ragtime musicians created new musical vocabularies, intellectual and artistic expressions—they did not simply play fast and wild.

As they cultivated individual musical voices to make a name for both themselves and the bars that employed them, Tenderloin pianists concocted signature musical "tricks" that set them apart from one another. James P. Johnson remembered that he practiced "double glissandos straight and backhand, glissandos in sixths and double tremolos"—showy techniques that would "run other ticklers out of the place." Johnson was "born with absolute pitch," which gave him an advantage in hearing, and borrowing, others' tricks. "I'd steal their breaks and style and practice them until I had them letter perfected," he recalled. Pianists may have referred to them as "tricks," but they were not simply stunts to impress audiences. Their innovations developed from musicians' desires, as well as the professional imperatives, to create unique and recognizable musical voices.

Musicians' abilities to copy each other's trademark play pushed them to create new types of performance practices, as well as musical technique. Luckey Roberts, who Johnson remembered as "the outstanding pianist in New York," invented a "style in making breaks . . . like a drummer's: he'd flail his hands in and out," raising his hands off the keyboard and "lifting them high," proving to Johnson and many others in the crowd that he was a "very spectacular pianist."[62] And Johnson himself recalled composing a tune that incorporated "Dixie," performed "in the right hand," with the Star-Spangled Banner "in the left. (It wasn't the national anthem then.)"[63] Tenderloin nightlife culture forced skilled and driven ragtime musicians to master their musical crafts to unprecedented degrees, often ending careers more readily than making them. Their skillful innovations also helped musicians codify their approaches and capitalize in the Manhattan musical marketplace in ways that made New York City a nexus of American musical creativity, especially among African Americans, for generations to come.

Years before World War I or the Harlem Renaissance, Tenderloin pianists' performance techniques coalesced into a recognizable New York sound, one quite distinct from Southern and Midwestern approaches. Even as Tenderloin players often traveled back and forth between Manhattan and Atlantic City (and other notable New Jersey towns along the Hudson), the Manhattan marketplace, and especially New York's vibrant musical theater industry, drove ragtime players to distinguish themselves from pianists from other regions. James P. Johnson recalled that the "other sections of the country never developed the piano as far as the New York boys did." He easily discerned New Yorkers' piano harmonies from the "other boys from the South and West" who played smaller chords based on thirds "played in unison." "We wouldn't dare do that," because New York audiences were "used to better playing." Tenderloin pianists developed the "orchestral piano," characterized by "round, big, widespread chords and tenths," in an attempt to recreate the sound of Broadway orchestras. Scott Joplin incorporated "octaves and chords" into his playing, "but he didn't attempt the big hand stretches. Abba Labba, Luckey Roberts, and others did that." Johnson understood that New York piano "developed by the European method, system and style" and that because New York theatergoers understood "good piano," ragtime players had to "live up to that standard. They had to get orchestral effects, sound harmonies, chords, and all the techniques of European concert pianists who were playing . . . all over the city."[64]

Besides the advanced harmony they learned from Broadway show tunes—many of them written by Hotel Marshall stalwarts—Johnson thought that New York players incorporated better dynamics into their music. Dynamics refer to subtle shifts in volume and the physical energy musicians bring to their instruments. Similar to ragtime's associations with up-tempo fast playing, most ragtime musicians would generally play as loud as they could, either simply to be heard over a crowd or because high volumes seemed the best way to create ragtime energy. Johnson, however, noted that he learned how to play dynamically as another component of New York's "concert effects." As a young man, he studied for a short time with a formally trained singer named Bruto Gianinni, and though Johnson quickly "got tired of the dull exercises," he learned "a lot of concert effects." Sometimes while ragging a "heavy stomp," he would "soften it right down—then I'd make an abrupt change [in volume] like I heard Beethoven do in a sonata." In another example, Johnson recalled "using pianissimo [very quiet] effects in the groove," bringing his piano volume down so low that "the dancers' feet [could] be heard scraping on the floor."[65] When considering the dynamic and harmonically expansive approach to ragtime by Johnson and Smith, the jazz pianist Billy Taylor remarked, "piano, in their hands, was an orchestra."[66] The final ingredient to Tenderloin ragtimers' New York sound was, of course, rhythmic groove.

As in the Hotel Marshall, and the Manhattan musical marketplace more generally, the defining characteristic of Tenderloin ragtime was rhythmic syncopation. If a player could not groove, he (and, in some cases, she) would not find work. Syncopation occurred through a combination of a consistent bass rhythm, as usually played by a pianist's left hand, and the quick, irregular rhythms in the higher registers, which if performed by a solo pianist would occur in the melodic right hand. Violins, flutes, clarinets, or most other instruments that accompanied pianos would most often play a song's melody in the higher registers, leaving the bass, or "bottom," to the piano. Even when ragtime pianists played with a string bass or tuba, the piano still determined the groove—setting the rhythmic foundation from which all other syncopations followed.

Although ragtime's syncopated melodies seemed so obvious a characteristic of ragtime that Tenderloin musicians rarely commented on it, they regularly distinguished players who had powerful left hands—which laid down the bass line—from those who did not. Blake recalled that William Turk had a "left hand like God," highlighting the importance of a strong bass groove.[67] For Willie "the Lion" Smith, who's own outrageous braggadocio was, according to friends and rivals alike, backed up by his musical prowess, a pianist's bass playing made for the most fundamental marker of a skillful professional. Smith often teased pianists about their weak left hand, asking them, "What's the matter, are you a cripple?" or "When did you break your left arm?"[68] New Orleans–born Jelly Roll Morton may have been one of the finest ragtime musicians in America at the time—he himself thought so, telling musicians and critics all his life that he had invented jazz.[69] Yet even though Smith liked Morton and respected his piano playing, he teasingly called Morton "Mr. One Hand" whenever the two met. Calling attention to Morton's fantastic right-hand flourishes and delicate syncopations, Smith needled Morton for not having a powerful enough left hand to be a New York ragtimer. "I was the only one [Morton] would stand and listen to and . . . [not] open his mouth," Smith recalled in his autobiography.[70]

In many ways, competitive styles reflected a social phenomenon of friendly—and not so friendly—one-upmanship. Egos often clashed, and some players developed bad reputations, if not caustic personalities. Blake remembered that Huey Wolford alienated many of his peers by interrupting their performances, telling them to "Get up, get up! You're ruining the people's music" or "You don't know what you're doing," before taking over their piano benches.[71] But often, this type of talk formed part of the show. Playing to customers and club owners alike, Willie "the Lion" Smith excelled in the competitive environment—having to maintain his place on top pushed his musicality, and also his personality. But Tenderloin competition also fostered partnerships and lifelong friendships. When a teenage Duke Ellington met Willie Smith for the first time, "the Lion" extended his hand and said, "Glad to meet you, kid," and then, looking over his shoulder, continued, "Sit in there for me for a couple of numbers. D-flat. As one of those Western piano plonkers just fell in, I want him to take the stool so I can crush him later."[72] Smith introduced Ellington into the competitive world of ragtime performance, establishing a bond that would last throughout their lives.

Smith's provocations indicate that, alongside ragtimers' musical virtuosity, there existed extramusical presentations of style, showmanship, and personality, what Smith and James P. Johnson both called "attitude." "You had to have an attitude, a style of behaving that was your personal, professional trade-mark," Johnson remembered.[73] Musicians' attitude and professional charisma set the tone of a Tenderloin nightclub. Johnson recalled that he and Smith "studied, practiced, and developed" their demeanor "just like it was a complicated piano piece." "When Willie Smith walked into a place," Johnson recollected, "his every move was a picture." Johnson described in detail the "three-way play" at work whenever a pianist walked into a club.[74] A pianist hoping to "take charge" of the room had to move slowly and confidently; he was never in a rush. The player might take his coat off "with a fancy flourish" and lay it on top of the piano "with the expensive lining turned outward for all to see." Smith recalled that when Jelly Roll Morton visited a Tenderloin club, "he would come in smiling so everyone would get a glance at his diamond-studded tooth."[75] Each piano tickler fashioned his own gesture while removing a hat, for, as Johnson recalled, "that was part of his attitude, too."

Accomplished pianists always began their set with a "signature chord"—something that introduced them to the crowd "like a signal." Even then, the show had not yet begun, as pianists would play some scales or warm-up arpeggios "very offhand, as if there was nothing to it," just to let the crowd simmer down. After playing some background music as he looked over his shoulder or chatted with some friends, a player would, "without stopping the smart talk or turning back to the piano . . . attack without any warning, smashing right into the regular beat of the piece. That would knock them dead." "It took a lot of practice to play this way, while talking and with your head and body turned," Johnson remembered, emphasizing how much time and refinement he and other Tenderloin ticklers put into their ragtime attitude. Finally, at the end of a performance, a pianist would "always finish up with a hot rag and then stand up quickly, so that everybody in the place would be able to see who knocked it out."[76] In Tenderloin leisure spaces, musicality and attitude blended together to reflect the personality of individual ragtime musicians, as well as that of the club owners, workers, and their patrons.

As Johnson's musical and extramusical presentations of ragtime professionalism illustrate, Tenderloin musicians' labors and social relations also displayed gendered ideals. In the competitive environment of Tenderloin nightclubs, the quest for social capital, respect, and regular work depended on musicians' investment in presenting not only their social status but also their masculinity. Black men in the Tenderloin undermined normative representations of black masculinity during an era that seemed fundamentally invested in denying black manliness.

MASCULINITY IN THE PRODUCTION
OF RAGTIME IDENTITIES

During the early years of Jim Crow, representations of black men conformed to narrow caricatures circulating throughout the United States. Images of black men were rooted in racist stereotypes, which worked as both cause and explanation for the reformation of white supremacy. Loafing "Sambos" and displaced urban dandies—the "Zip Coon"—from the minstrel stage informed popular representations of black masculinity, but other tropes worked in more explicitly political ways. As the literary theorist Riché Richardson documents, black men were cast as "inferior and undesirable models of black masculinity": the aging, "innocuous and neutered" Uncle Tom and its opposite, the "sexually pathological . . . lustful and primitive" black rapist of white women.[77] This latter trope, which took on so much ideological power in the late nineteenth century that scholars refer to it as the "black rapist myth," bore the burden of explaining white southerners' embrace of lynching culture, an act that killed more than 3,220 African Americans between 1882 and 1930 and set the violent, repressive tone of white supremacy in the South.[78] Ultimately, white policy makers and culture producers presented black men as incapable of participating as citizens in a democratic society. "In the eyes of white men," the historian Stephen Kantrowitz explains, "black men were inherently unfit for citizenship."[79]

Yet white Americans were not the only group policing black masculinity. African American leaders, social reformers, and many who spoke for the Talented Tenth had their own ideas about the proper representation of black manliness. The men of the Talented Tenth cultivated their own sense of themselves in direct opposition to the male members of the black masses. If ragtime culture threatened to undermine the sense of representative black culture as imagined by James Monroe Trotter and W. E. B. Du Bois, the ragtime musicians who made it challenged the Talented Tenth's clear articulations of gender relations and black masculinity. Alongside etiquette, manners, and chaste morality, modes of dress constituted important markers of African Americans' respectable comportment.[80]

Indeed, clothing and personal style ranked among the Talented Tenth's most obsessive interests, a fact indicated by student catalogs at America's most prestigious black colleges, Howard University and Fisk University. At Fisk in 1904–1905, for example, educators stressed that "the clothing of students must be becoming, plain, and substantial"—rather abstract adjectives until contrasted with the list of unadvisable traits: "unsuitable, extravagant, or unnecessary."[81] As the historian Martin Summers argues, Fisk University officials understood that "dress code was both a reflection, and facilitator, of its students' good character." "Modest dress," Summers notes, "was one of the hallmarks of Victorian manliness."[82] Male ragtime musicians in the Tenderloin may have tried to undermine Victorian standards as they displayed "extravagant" styles of fashion dress. More likely, however, they simply dressed as professional musicians in a competitive marketplace.

Above all, musicians' fashionable clothing helped them present themselves as professional men and New York culture workers—it was an important facet of musicians' "attitude." As Willie Smith understood it, the "guys that dressed to kill always got the good jobs."[83] Smith noticed the importance of ragtime style at a young age. "It behooved us to look spectacular, not only to get and hold a gal, but to make a good impression all around," he wrote. At a time when a black man's masculinity made him the target of white violence, envy, and caricature, Tenderloin entertainers represented authoritative professionals and fashionable, artistic men in ways that undermined popular stereotypes. They were also paid to be personable and showy, earning their living by aggressively advertising their professional skills and decorated bodies. While millions of sharecropping black men could never imagine owning a tailored suit, Tenderloin musicians recognized their rare capacity to construct themselves as urban and cosmopolitan men. For Smith, fashionable style did not suffice—he displayed his professional masculinity in abundance.

The most established Tenderloin ragtimers emphasized their place at the top of the market by indicating their ability to consume conspicuously. Smith recalled that it was "customary for entertainers to have at least twenty-five suits," because "you couldn't wear the same suits too often." Besides the "regular blues, browns, and grays," Tenderloin entertainers displayed "fancy tailoring" of "oxford gray or pepper, brown pinstripes, [and] crocodile black and whites." Smith wore his pants "tight with long, peg-topped fourteen-inch cuffs" and preferred single-breasted suit jackets to "show off" his "gold watch fob and chain." He paid "around a hundred dollars" to have his suits made at Bromberger's near Sheridan Square in the West Village, and for "an added touch," he would order a pair of spats from the suit material. Those spats covered patent leather shoes—with "pointed toes or turnips"—that cost twelve dollars a pair. Piano ticklers had to have "at least fifteen pair on hand." Smith paid ten to twenty-five dollars for his silk and cotton shirts and needed "to own about twenty-five colored shirts to have one ready for all occasions." "The Lion" liked soft blues and candy-colored pinks. He also enjoyed matching his $150 overcoats with his suits, usually selecting plaid linings, shoulder pads, and full, boxlike shapes made from melton fabric cut so thick that "the coat would stand straight up by itself." Smith remembered pianists wearing "military-type coats, coachman's coats" and "Inverness capes with skirts," as well as different kinds of "fancy headwear—Homburgs with buttons on the side and gray Fultons"—anything to make the musicians stand out.[84] James P. Johnson remembered that Fred Tunstall wore a coat with "eighty-two pleats in the back," and when he sat down to play, "he'd slump a little in a half hunch, and those pleats would fan out real pretty."[85] Many musicians carried canes, and most wore diamonds. Smith remembered one pianist who "had a diamond set in his bulldog's teeth," always bringing the dog to gigs and leashing it to his piano bench.[86]

Stylized and expensive clothing helped ragtime musicians enact their social status as Tenderloin professionals in transgressive ways. James P. Johnson thought that ragtime fashion was "copied from the styles of the rich whites," but he emphasized that he and his peers "made improvements."[87] Willie Smith had been raised in Newark by a mother who laundered for mostly Jewish families and a stepfather who drove a wagon during the midnight shift for a meat-packing plant. As he dressed his success as a

Eubie Blake. Photographs and Prints Division,
Schomburg Center for Research in Black Culture, New York Public
Library, Astor, Lenox, and Tilden Foundations.

ragtime musician, he did not dress like his father. Yet his penchant for candy-colored pinks and blues neither reflected the somber tones of the Talented Tenth. Through his clothing, Smith distanced himself from the wageworking conditions of his father, while demonstrating his distinction from the respectable dress of "middle-class" African Americans. In an era in which African American preachers and teachers most often paralleled middle-class and elite whites' sense of functional and unassuming cloth- ing, musicians like Johnson and Smith made their own improvements, challenging white Americans' racist representations of black masculin- ity as they commented on Talented Tenth pretensions. If Smith's cho- sen profession upset black preachers, educators, and the ladies at his mother's church, his clothing also disrupted their sense of proper racial presentation.

A professional musician intent on taking charge of the room, Smith was much more self-conscious about his style than members of the Talented Tenth might guess, however. Most contemporary commentators urging restraint seemed to think that extravagant style was an accident, or the reflection of poor taste, as did Julius N. Avendorph, a member of Chicago's black society, when he complained that black men overdressed. Writing in the *Chicago Defender*, he recommended that "unless you can appear in correct style, stay at home," and advised against "diamonds, rubies, emer- ald or gold studs," noting that "diamonds are beautiful to wear and valua- ble to have, but they have no place at all when it comes to evening dress."[88] Smith, and many others who played music in the Tenderloin, disagreed. But the disagreement was less about the clothing itself than what it meant to those who wore it. Like Avendorph, Smith hoped to present himself as a modern American, a citizen participating in the political discourse of the day and a consumer helping bankroll America's transformation into an industrial economy. Living in Chicago and New York, two of the coun- try's most influential and quickly changing cities in the early twentieth century, both men aimed not only to be included in America's industrial economy but also wanted to form a part of the changing consumer land- scape. Yet whereas Avendorph became one of Chicago's leading arbiters of black society in the 1910s (but mostly forgotten during the New Negro era), Smith helped instigate the sound, meaning, and attitude of American popular music for generations to come.[89]

The Prince Hall Freemasons' dress codes exemplify the investment made by a leading black institution of black society in presentations of black masculinity. Members of Brooklyn's Carthaginian Lodge No. 47 (established in 1904), for example, adhered to strict guidelines for proper attire—"formal and semiformal dark suits, white leather or lambskin aprons, medallions, white gloves"—and took pride being the first lodge to "to make the white gloves compulsory." In some ways, Freemasons' black-and-white formal dress differed significantly from ragtime musicians' colorful attire. But both groups aimed to present themselves as successful, professional black men. One of the country's most elite black periodicals, Boston's *Colored American Magazine*, celebrated the Carthaginian's elaborate inaugural ceremony by noting that "new societies usually commence operations with their paraphernalia incomplete in some respect, but Carthaginian enters the field with a very handsome outfit, complete in every particular."[90] In this case, sartorial excess—its ceremonial robes cost more than nine hundred dollars—seemed to denote professional status and respectability, even as the dapper hats and tailored suits of Willie Smith and James P. Johnson merely symbolized excess.

TENDERLOIN NIGHTCLUBS PROMOTED new racial identities among mixed-class black New Yorkers, creating a sense of cultural belonging among entrepreneurs, entertainers, and wageworking African American patrons. Ragtime music and Tenderloin spaces fostered an environment in which many blacks came to understand themselves as cultural innovators living and working in the nation's capital of commercial entertainment. Even Tenderloin residents who could not sing or dance but who frequented the leisure spaces in their neighborhood, participated in their local economy, contributing to the production of ragtime innovations with their hard-earned dollars. As members of a burgeoning black community, poor and working African Americans had access to community spaces generating black cultural modernity. They too helped produce and circulate ragtime identities. In the Tenderloin, musicians' fresh styles of speech, what Tom Fletcher has called "viper language," not only separated the hip from the square but defined a new sense of collective identity among a heterogeneous group of blacks.[91]

The emergence of ragtime around 1900 testifies to the significance of commercial music forms to black communities and demonstrates some of the ways in which diverse African Americans in the urban North began to understand themselves as members of a racial community.[92] Where the conceptual frameworks of middle/working class and high/low bifurcate black cultural expressions, a study of commercial music opens up new possibilities of analysis, ones in which African Americans of various backgrounds, livelihoods, and imaginations become central historical actors as producers and consumers of American popular culture. Manhattan's

Tenderloin offered blacks a range of seemingly contradictory subject positions, even as both the neighborhood and its leisure spaces created the conditions within which many would cultivate their ragtime identities. African Americans who had access to new styles of black commercial culture before the Harlem Renaissance acted as primary participants in black culture's production, circulation, and in its symbolic and social meanings. As such, the African Americans who worked and played in Tenderloin nightclubs between 1900 and 1915 proved central players in the formation and distribution of both black ragtime identities and Manhattan modernity.

Ragtime musicians and Tenderloin spaces made blackness a symbol of New York City modernity and American culture in ways neither homogenous nor essential. In the Tenderloin, there was no single, authentic way to enact a ragtime identity. Race, class, gender, and space offered a set of resources with which African Americans could constitute themselves as black New Yorkers and modern American citizens. Even though Tenderloin musicians had less influence on the overall cultural and professional values of their crafts, they benefited from the ways Hotel Marshall entertainers raised black musical value. And rather than only responding to others' work in the Manhattan musical marketplace, Tenderloin musicians, their employers, and their audiences played important roles in perpetuating a transformation in the value of black culture and the commercial spaces where one might find it.

During the 1910s and 1920s, increasing numbers of white New Yorkers came to understand African Americans as excellent performers and cultural innovators. Whites' conception of black musical genius often reinforced their racialized preconceptions of black difference—that blacks were highly rhythmic, emotional, and naturally gifted performers—and they might not have respected black entertainers as equals. But in the decades to follow, white New Yorkers more readily shared their public and private spaces with blacks, if only to take part in black culture and its power to signal modernity. In the next chapter, I will turn to a corollary of the ragtime-era Tenderloin: Times Square lobster palaces. While Tenderloin commercial spaces and popular culture anticipated the rise of black Harlem after World War I, they had a more immediate influence on the late-night hotels, restaurants, and cabarets popping up along Broadway Avenue to cater to the theater crowd—white New Yorkers and tourists who wanted to conspicuously consume rich food, expensive drinks, and Manhattan modernity. More than anything, however, Times Square revelers wanted to dance ragtime as performed by black musicians.

TO PROMOTE GREATER EFFICIENCY
AMONG ITS MEMBERS

Ragtime in Times Square and the Clef Club Inc.

In 1903, a twenty-three-year-old African American musician named James Reese Europe moved from his home in Washington, D.C., to New York City to live with his older brother, John. The Black Manhattan that Europe discovered on his arrival contrasted sharply from the one that had greeted James Weldon Johnson two years earlier. Although both Europe and Johnson came from southern families of relative means, and both joined their musician brothers in Manhattan, their immediate impressions of the city differed quite markedly. Rosamond Johnson had studied at the New England Conservatory in Boston, traveled the country with vaudeville troupes, and established himself as a popular songwriter garnering royalties from hit show tunes. But Europe's brother struggled to keep his job playing ragtime piano in a Tenderloin nightclub, where he was fortunate to have steady work.[1] Regular jobs were hard to find in the Tenderloin. Few opportunities existed for African Americans in chamber ensembles or symphonies, and most white dining rooms did not hire black musicians.

Immediately after arriving, James Europe followed his brother's lead and began looking for gigs. He traversed Manhattan with a violin in hand and the skills to work a piano if given a chance. He first attempted to secure work in upper-crust dining rooms along Fifth Avenue, hoping for opportunities commensurate with his musical education. In D.C., Europe had studied with John Philip Sousa's assistant director, Enrico Hurlei, as well as with Frederick Douglass's grandson, Joseph H. Douglass, whom many considered the best black violinist in Washington.[2] Europe soon realized, however, that for a newly arrived black migrant, syncopated melodies and stomping piano made an easier buck than European "classical" music. After six weeks of looking for work as a violinist, he traded in his bow for a mandolin pick and began accompanying his brother at Barron Wilkins's Little Savoy in the Tenderloin. Quick, ragged strums on the eight-string mandolin—tuned like a violin, with each string doubled—seemed a more pragmatic approach to entering the Manhattan musical marketplace in 1903. But even retaining a gig as a ragtimer proved difficult, and Europe continued to expand his search.

Only recently, new restaurant and hotel dining rooms had begun opening along Broadway Avenue. These grand, ostentatious dining spaces, which a reporter for *Everybody's Magazine* named "lobster palaces," catered to a young set of affluent white New Yorkers looking for late-night leisure and entertainment away from the Waldorf Astoria and their parents' homes along Fifth Avenue.[3] Broadway restaurants promised rich food, expensive drinks, late-night dancing, and unparalleled opportunities to consume conspicuously. Through their locales, their prices, and their prickly maître d's, lobster palaces attempted to secure a selective clientele. But, as in the Tenderloin, "class" was a fluid category in Midtown Manhattan.

Located near Broadway theaters, lobster palaces had a constant flux of entertainers who brought "star" status and mischievous energy to the dining spaces. Some entertainers, coming from poor or working-class backgrounds themselves, complicated any simple demonstration of class in Midtown dining rooms; their chosen vocations emphasized the performance aspect to all lobster palace patrons' social status. Between the opening of the *New York Times'* headquarters at Forty-second Street and Broadway on New Year's Eve 1904 and the beginning of World War I, Manhattan's Times Square, as it became known, flourished alongside the new style of restaurant dining rooms. Gilded, over-the-top garden and fountain displays mixed with electric lights, outsized dance floors, and ragtime string bands to produce the city's most deliberately modern leisure spaces.

Lobster palaces capitalized on the fresh and exciting sounds of ragtime entertainments making a splash in Broadway musicals and off-Broadway vaudeville. Featuring dance music by African Americans until early in the morning, lobster palaces used the syncopated sounds to denote their modernity. Working blacks' presence in these spaces also called attention to patrons' whiteness and class privilege. Besides the modernity and racial distinction black bodies seemed to evoke, restaurant managers also liked black musicians because they did not have to pay them to play. Blacks were already in lobster palaces in large numbers. They worked hourly shifts for wages as servers, bartenders, busboys, dishwashers, doormen, bellhops, elevator operators, and laundry workers. After their shifts, musically inclined workers would trade in their dishes for a guitar or mandolin and play dance music for tips, earning a dollar or two per night. During his first year in New York, James Europe found work as a musician in a few lobster palaces.[4]

Early on, he also met the black entertainers working out of the Hotel Marshall, where he quickly gained access to new professional opportunities and established himself as one of the city's leading musicians. In just a few years, he leapfrogged ahead of many of the working black musicians in the Tenderloin—including his older brother—and made both social and professional ties with New York's most established black theater performers.[5]

Europe instigated a revolution in both the professional and cultural values of black musicians in New York. The Clef Club Inc., New York's first labor union and booking agency for black ragtime musicians, represented Europe's efforts to raise the value of African American entertainers and their arts. Building on the work of the Hotel Marshall community before him, Europe transformed the professional and cultural value of his musicians and, by extension, that of working black performers throughout the greater New York area. As in previous chapters, "professional value" indicates the concrete changes the Clef Club brought to black musicians' working conditions: high wages, set hours, or fixed expectations about their duties. Prior to the Clef Club, black musicians who played ragtime often did so after working long hours as menial laborers; Europe's union organized hundreds of men, finding power in numbers, as well as the ability to shape their own professionalism. "Cultural value" in the case of the Clef Club speaks to Europe's deliberate attempts to raise the social status of, and respect for, black ragtime musicians among New Yorkers black and white. As we have seen, the professional and cultural values of black music were intimately entwined with one another, and nothing indicates their connections more clearly than Europe's Clef Club. As the Clef Club ensured high wages and standardized performances, it reshaped the cultural value of black musicians. Likewise, as Europe worked to uplift popular representations of what he called "Negro music," he increased the overall fiscal worth of his musicians. The processes raising the Clef Club's professional value grew from its increasing cultural value—even to the extent that the Clef Club garnered a performance at Carnegie Hall, a milestone that greatly advanced Europe's agenda.

Tracing Europe's arrival to the lobster palace scene continues an investigation into three distinct classes of black ragtime musician in New York in the early twentieth century: Broadway stars and Tin Pan Alley songwriters working out of the Hotel Marshall; full-time entertainers working in black-owned Tenderloin nightclubs, and wage laborers playing for tips in Times Square. These classes were not mutually exclusive, and many sought to cross boundaries as they moved up the hierarchies of black performance. The classes of black musicians, and the spaces where they performed, indicate the heterogeneity of black cultural life in New York City. As in the Hotel Marshall, "ragtime" in the early twentieth century denoted a variety of styles, genres, practices, symbols, and social meanings. There was no single or essential "Negro music," even if musicians like Will Marion Cook or Bert Williams claimed otherwise. African Americans' music styles expressed the diversity and heterogeneity of black life, not black cultural homogeneity.

Evidence of the plurality of black musical expression becomes especially clear when we study the different connotations ragtime had in its various distinct settings. The Hotel Marshall, for instance, resounded with African Americans' expectations for a better position in the cultural, economic, and political life of the United States. Tenderloin nightclubs reverberated with ragtime in ways that called attention to black New Yorkers' cross-class desires to see themselves as modern black Americans participating in the development of mass consumer culture. Lobster palaces, in contrast, largely relegated black musicians to the side of the dance floors. Even as Midtown restaurants used black ragtime to indicate their modernity, they starkly revealed the uneven terrain of consumer capitalism and the instability of racial markers, especially as indicated by white and black consumers' different understanding of ragtime song and dance. Much of the complications swirled around black and white Americans' different conceptions of "modernity" itself.

A study of Europe's Clef Club demonstrates that, no matter how deliberately black entertainers in New York presented modern cultural expressions through their ragtime innovations, white audiences could only understand ragtime as a symbol of African American primitivism. Even as Europe lifted black musicians' professional and cultural value, he could do little to affect white Americans' sense of racial superiority. Even more confounding to African Americans like Europe were the ways their representations of black modernity, social advancement, and artistic ingenuity ultimately reinforced whites' preconceptions of blacks' premodernity and racial inferiority. Europe entered Times Square a new black migrant from the nation's capital just seven years after the U.S. Supreme Court made racial segregation the law of the land. It took him less time to make connections and set to work on shifting the sounds and meanings of black music in the Manhattan musical marketplace. An early example for the thousands of African American performers who would follow, his successes and failures would reverberate throughout the twentieth century.

FROM WASHINGTON, D.C., TO BLACK BOHEMIA

James Reese Europe was born in the South during an era that historians still consider "the nadir" of African American history.[6] The third child of a free woman and a former slave, James was born to Lorraine Saxon Europe and Henry J. Europe on February 22, 1880, in Mobile, Alabama. After the Civil War, Henry Europe worked with the Mobile Post Office. Once James was born, he took a job offer from the National Postal Service in Washington, D.C., and moved his family into a modest brick house at 308 B Street S.E., a middle-class neighborhood just a few blocks to the southeast of the nation's capitol.[7] In many ways, James Reese Europe's move to New York at the dawn of the twentieth century typified African Americans' urban migrations before World War I. Yet he had unlikely opportunities as a young black boy growing up in the 1880s and 1890s.

While not raised in economic abundance, Europe grew up in a black middle-class community honoring racial pride, a strong work ethic, and education. Like Will Marion Cook, Europe was raised to become a member of the Talented Tenth, and early on it seemed music would serve as his primary tool for uplift. He attended M Street High—a crown jewel of the Reconstruction-era Freedmen's Bureau and the first public school for blacks in America.[8] Established in 1870, the Preparatory High School for Colored Youth, as it was originally named, built its reputation by offering first-class instruction on everything from the classics to science, music to mathematics. The school became a beacon for the future of African American education. Fortuitously, within months of the Europes' arrival in the nation's capital, John Philip Sousa, America's premier composer and performer of marches, moved onto their block.[9] Sousa had led the U.S. Marine Corps Band since 1880, making it the most popular band in America. His patriotic tunes had engrained the sound of brass horns and snare drums into the ears of much of the nation, both anticipating and influencing the exciting, swinging brass band music stewing up in New Orleans and many other American cities between the Atlantic coast and the Mississippi. Soon after Sousa became their neighbor, James Europe began studying piano and violin with Sousa's assistant director, Enrico Hurlei. But James, like his siblings, owed the strongest facet of his character to his mother and her love for music.

Fond of music as an integral element of the Baptist Church, Lorraine Europe shared her musical interests with her four children. She played piano and knew enough music theory to give them their first lessons. After learning from their mother, all four Europe children continued on with piano lessons, and three of them eventually became professional pianists (though James would only perform on the piano as a way to make ends meet before his success as a composer and bandleader). Henry Europe also played, having taught himself several instruments, and his enjoyment of less-studied performance practices augmented his wife's more austere approach. In junior high, James Europe began taking violin lessons with Joseph H. Douglass, a friend of Will Marion Cook's, and as a high school student, he studied theory and instrumentation with both Hans Hanke of the Leipzig Conservatory of Music and Harry T. Burleigh, another of Cook's friends and Dvořák's favorite pupil.[10] Lorraine Europe's introduction of piano to her children and her initiative to seek lessons show that she wanted more than simply to occupy her offspring's time—she had high aspirations for her kids.

By insisting on music lessons, Lorraine Europe followed James Monroe Trotter and other African American music educators' directives toward racial uplift. Europe opened doorways to "culture" in Du Bois's sense of the word. She introduced her children to avenues that might enable a professional escape from Jim Crow–era labor inequalities and perhaps, eventually, challenge America's most ubiquitous representations of black culture. Lorraine Europe trained her children to succeed in a society designed to make them fail. James Reese Europe's early access to music education inculcated him at an early age with the Talented Tenth's politics of representation, a frame of reference that would fuel his artistic ingenuity and labor organizing throughout his life. And although Europe would follow Will Cook's footsteps into commercial music—choosing to engage in ragging uplift rather than sticking to Du Bois's and his mother's sense of respectable cultural representation—Europe negotiated the imperatives of uplift ideology, the politics of racial representation, and even the Manhattan musical marketplace in ways far more savvy and complex. Every bit the black nationalist that Cook was, Europe maneuvered white audiences' expectations to introduce ragtime to Carnegie Hall and to become a leading critic of black music in the white press. When Europe moved to New York in 1903, shortly after the death of his father, he started on a path toward ragging uplift his own way.

As Europe roamed New York City looking for work, he quickly gained access to the elite black musician community at the Hotel Marshall. Proficient at piano, violin, and mandolin, Europe could sight-read music notation and arrange music for a wide variety of ensembles, from string bands to symphony orchestras. He was soon immersed in a music scene surpassing any he had known in the nation's capital. Entertainers like Cook, Bob Cole, and the Johnson brothers had come from striving households not dissimilar from Europe's, and it must have been a wonder for the young arrival to meet talented and trained musicians not only debating African American music history but playing leading roles in promoting black music as a resource for the presentation of modern African American culture and citizenship. The Hotel Marshall opened unimagined possibilities for James Europe. He spent the rest of the decade catching up with his surroundings and eventually staked his own claims of artistic ingenuity and racial representation in the Manhattan musical marketplace.

In 1905, Ernest Hogan asked Europe to take part in his landmark performances with the Memphis Students, a series of music concerts quite removed from minstrelsy, vaudeville, or even black musical theater. Employing unusual combinations of European symphonic and American "folk" instruments, but highlighting black singing voices, the Memphis Students made for an extraordinary ensemble. Violins and cellos mixed with mandolins and banjos; the brassy sounds of horns married with a single, reedy saxophone, all of which were threatened by the overwhelming volume of one of the first trap-drum kits ever put together. The Hotel Marshall helped instigate the first concert. Reportedly, Hogan had concocted the idea after walking through the Marshall's basement one day during lunch. When he heard the cacophony of string, wind, and percussive instruments being tuned, played, and banged, he decided to combine them for a new sound, one similar to the small European-style orchestras that Broadway musicals used, but different too.[11] When Europe found out that Cook was helping direct the band, he leapt at the chance to work with the producers of *Clorindy; or, the Origin of the Cakewalk*, and become a violinist in one of the very first "syncopated band" concerts in American history. In his foundational text, *The Negro and His Music*, Alain Locke, called Hogan's unorthodox ensemble, the "first truly genuine Negro playing unit," an example of "jazz . . . in the making."[12]

While it is difficult to know what the Memphis Students sounded like, the music historian Eileen Southern has called Hogan's performance the "first public concert of syncopated music."[13] Writing in 1930, as jazz was just becoming the most popular music in America, James Weldon Johnson heard the Memphis Students as "pioneers," and as the "beginners of several things that still persist as jazz-band features." Most influential, Johnson recalled, were Will Dixon's conducting style and Charles "Buddy"

*The Memphis Students, featuring Ernest Hogan (center) and
James Reese Europe (standing directly to Hogan's left, just below).*

Gilmore's tricky trap-kit drumming. The Memphis Students "introduced
the dancing conductor," Dixon, who cued the band with his bodily movements and performed "an easy shuffle . . . across the whole front of the
band." The Memphis Students may also have introduced the first trap-
drum set. Gilmore, who would excite thousands of dancing audiences
across America in James Reese Europe's Society Orchestra a decade later,
dazzled onlookers by beating out syncopated rhythms on a makeshift
kit composed of an oversized marching-band bass drum, a snare drum,
two crash cymbals, a hi-hat, and a vast assortment of bells, horns, and
whistles—this was an early prototype for jazz drum sets, wrought from
the pieces of a marching band and noisemakers of the vaudeville stage.
The tricky, joking, circus-like manner in which Gilmore played his instrument enthralled his reviewers. But his clowning routine belied his talent
and creativity. Gilmore's revolutionary approach to percussion informed
jazz and swing drumming practices throughout New York in the following
decades.[14]

Just as remarkable as the unusual instrumentation, however, was
that everyone in the orchestra sang, most in a different register than the
instrument they played. "These fellows," Cook recollected, "could play one
part and at the same time sing an entirely different one."[15] The ensemble's

ability to sing while playing their parts astonished critics and concertgoers alike. The *World* reported that the "musical oddity involved was that each player sang a different part from that which the instruments called for."[16] James Weldon Johnson remembered, "the whole band, with the exception, of course, of the players on wind-instruments, was a singing band; and it seems safe to say that they introduced the singing band—that is, a band singing in four part harmony and playing at the same time."[17] The Memphis Students' show, *The Birth of the Minstrel*, opened on August 10 at Hammerstein's Victoria Theatre on Broadway and played fifty-three concerts before closing a month later. A financial success, the Memphis Students received accolades throughout the city before being picked up by white producers, Hurtig and Seamon, and sent on a two-month tour of Europe.

Ernest Hogan (the "Unbleached American," as he presented himself in vaudeville) knew how to strategically employ racial authenticity and racist stereotype in American entertainment markets. In calling his band the Memphis Students, he referenced the South and student groups such as the Fisk Jubilee Singers, who were still identified with their formal concerts of slave spirituals, as well as the dozens of "student" troupes who had burlesqued and caricatured the spirituals on minstrel and vaudeville stages ever since. Even though none of Hogan's performers hailed from Memphis, the band name referred to Dixie to capitalize on its associations with a rural pastoral and black folk music. Equally fictitious was the "students" part of the name. Yet because the Memphis Students presented a music concert, rather than a vaudeville stage show, they mirrored more closely the music concerts of slave spirituals in the 1870s and 1880s than other types of black stage performance. The name Hogan chose for his 1905 ensemble indicates how few precedents existed for his concert. He promoted his group by alluding to both the romantic South and student concerts, but he could not anticipate that James Weldon Johnson would call the Memphis Students the "first modern jazz band ever heard on a New York stage."[18]

The Memphis Students concerts reflect a significant departure from the vaudeville stage on which Hotel Marshall musicians had won renown. Although it was a lively affair, the Memphis Students presented a music concert and not a piece of minstrel-inspired theater—it was one of the first ragtime concerts in American history. Rather than backing up comedians, dancers, or other acts, the musicians performed on stage and constituted the entire entertainment for the night. Additionally, the Memphis Students made for a remarkably idiosyncratic band. Hogan and Cook experimented with new instrument arrangements and orchestrations to create new sonic possibilities. Hogan's emphasis on diversity in arrangement, instrumentation, and program would deeply influence James Reese Europe. In the years to come, Europe borrowed from Hogan's approach as he crafted new styles of both orchestral and commercial music. Hogan's ragtime orchestra not only anticipated the big bands of the jazz era but, also, Europe's symphonic approach to ragtime.

After taking part in the Memphis Students concerts, Europe further embedded himself into the Hotel Marshall scene, composing and directing alongside New York's leading black entertainers. He published songs with Tin Pan Ally publishers, often cowriting them with Bob Cole and R. C. McPherson. He also worked as a musical director, first for a comedy called *Trip to Africa* in 1904, and then for full-scale musicals by Cole and the Johnson brothers, *The Shoo-Fly Regiment* and *The Red Moon* in 1906 and 1908, respectively.[19] Attempting to capitalize on the fervor of American nationalism still resonating years after the Spanish-American War, *The Shoo-Fly Regiment* depicted patriotic black soldiers as their lead characters and explored the themes of black education and uplift.[20] *The Red Moon* dealt with interracial romance and the cultural connections between African Americans and Native Americans. Cook's wife, Abbie Mitchell, played the female lead, and Aida Overton Walker joined the cast during the musical's second season. As they translated their racially progressive agenda to musical theater, the racial politics of Cole and the Johnsons seemed to threaten the New York theatrical establishment. The *New York Age* editor Lester Walton claimed that the Shubert Theatre publicity department convinced New York newspapers not to review *The Red Moon* because it "did not contain enough 'niggerism.'"[21] Ultimately, neither musical made a national hit, but Europe soon found other opportunities.

Alongside his work with Hotel Marshall musicians, Europe spent his first years in New York playing music on both sides of the color line. Within his first year in the city, he had a chance encounter with John W. Love, an acquaintance from D.C. who worked as a secretary for the Philadelphia department store magnate John Wanamaker. Love recommended that Europe perform for a Wanamaker birthday party, and he proved such a hit that the family began hiring him to organize small dance orchestras for all their family engagements. "From that day until his tragic death," Love recalled, "he played at every celebration of the Wanamaker family."[22] Soon after, Europe began receiving requests from other wealthy white families to play their private parties.

Europe's relationship with the Wanamakers began Europe's success at building a new audience for black music, and it also created the conditions for Europe's Clef Club labor union. As early as 1904, Europe acted as a vanguard promoter of ragtime song and dance among elite whites in the greater New York area. As the Clef Club musician Noble Sissle wrote in his unpublished memoir, Europe's partnership with the Wanamakers was the "beginning of his becoming the society favorite of Music producer in the drawing-rooms of New York's Four Hundred."[23]

But Europe did not recruit the musicians for his Wanamaker gigs from the Hotel Marshall or from the Tenderloin nightclubs. Instead, he went to Times Square. Sensitive to the types of music, and racial representation, he wanted for his Wanamaker gigs, Europe enlisted dozens of black musicians out of Midtown Manhattan lobster palaces. He standardized their work, wages, and contracts, and greatly increased their salaries. The seven years between 1904 and 1910 witnessed an explosion of interest in ragtime in New York, as well as in much of the United States, and lobster palaces were just the beginning. Before establishing the Clef Club, when Europe was haphazardly hiring dance bands composed of five or six men, he would take just a few dozen out of their day jobs by promising full-time work as musicians. By 1910, having stolen hundreds of men from lobster palace dining rooms by offering them work as professional musicians who no longer had to wait tables or scrub dishes, Europe would hire these men back to the lobster palaces at ten and twenty times their old wages. And lobster palaces were eager to get Europe's musicians into their spaces. As affluent whites increasingly hired Europe's bands for their private soirées and Times Square restaurants hired the best musicians he could offer, Europe could not keep up with the demand. His mounting popularity encouraged him to organize his working groups of musicians into a more solid booking agency for his high-society gigs. Before turning to the Clef Club, however, an investigation into lobster palace nightlife will highlight the contradictions Europe negotiated as he sold black music to white audiences.

RAGTIME IN TIMES SQUARE

At the dawn of the twentieth century, New York City—its industrial innovations, cultural symbolisms, expanding industrial mass markets, developing commercial spaces, and cosmopolitan heterogeneity—seemed to epitomize Americans' sense of the modern. While this held true for many Americans who lived far from the bustling metropolis, New York

City became a preeminent symbol of American modernity especially for those who lived there. New Yorkers understood themselves to represent the height of American progress and development—their urban, technological, and international environment seemed to hold the promise of America's future. Fundamental to New Yorkers' sense of themselves and their city was Manhattan's growing popular entertainment marketplace. As Broadway Avenue defined American theater and Tin Pan Alley dominated U.S. music production, local phonograph recording companies stood on the cusp of making music recording a viable industry. Ragtime music, theater, and dance, as we have seen, helped make Manhattan the capital of American commercial music culture. Ragtime rhythms were becoming the sound of the city and, consequently, the sound of American modernity.

Replete with ideological associations that even Hotel Marshall musicians could never fully grasp, ragtime song and dance introduced a host of racial assumptions into Times Square dining rooms. When black musicians performed ragtime in white-dominated spaces, they aimed to promote new expressions of black modernity—to translate the power of black performance from the Broadway stage to Times Square restaurants and to transmit their racial representations of modern black culture to white patrons. It seemed like a promising working relationship. African American performers, intent on presenting themselves as modern Americans and quintessential U.S. entertainers, found paying audiences who seemed equally invested in promoting their own modernity as white New Yorkers. But ideas and cultural representations do not flow unmediated from producers to consumers. Manhattan culture markets nullified any direct transmission of cultural representation from one race to another: blacks' presentations of black modernity would not resonate as such to white moderns, and, in fact, the sounds of rhythmic ragtime appeared to white patrons as black primitivism. Innovative black sounds reverberated through whites' racial imaginations as caricature, fulfilling their assumptions of racial difference and natural black musicality. Moreover, white New Yorkers had their own agenda of self-representation. They too were caught up in their own project of defining themselves as modern. But rather than accept African Americans' presentations of modernity, whites enacted their own modernity in direct contrast to their perception of blacks' supposed premodern primitivism.[24]

Even as lobster palaces created complex conditions for African Americans, they opened their doors to many more types of white people than had previously had access to elite spaces in Manhattan. Whereas prosperous executives, barons, and bankers had dominated the Fifth Avenue oyster bars and hotel grills, and wealthy families had dined together at the Waldorf Astoria, lobster palaces catered to growing numbers of white women and men who wanted to take part in the new consumer culture as conspicuously as possible. Looking for fresh and exciting places to leisure, the children of New York's "Four Hundred" wealthiest families sought out new establishments and financed a transformation in New York's nightlife. Lobster palaces like Churchill's, Rector's, Knickerbocker's, and Murray's Roman Gardens offered dynamic new spaces for a younger set of privileged New Yorkers. After Broadway shows let out, patrons raced there to engage in their own performances of class and modernity. Actors, chorus girls, musicians from Broadway—along with their playwrights, managers, and friends—mingled in Midtown dining rooms with the wealthiest young people in New York, as well as with some adventurous members of their parents' generation: wealthy stockbrokers and businessmen, rich "men, seeking escape from the stifling formality of the exclusive circles."[25] Lobster and champagne became the required midnight snack among those who could afford it. Rector's even boasted a pool of live lobster, designed so that diners could choose the exact crustacean to boil for their dinner.[26] Lobster palace dining rooms put an onus on spectacle.

One way these dining rooms demonstrated their modernity (and distinguished themselves from Fifth Avenue restaurants) was through extravagant architecture and decoration. The first two stories of Murray's Roman Gardens on Forty-second Street, for example, attempted to replicate the Hôtel de Rohan in Paris and featured reproductions of "classic masterpieces from the museums of the old world, such as the Louvre, Vatican, and other art centers." The "magnificent" interior court that gave the restaurant its name used dozens of statues of Ramses, Antony, and Cleopatra to create a faux Roman garden. The garden's centerpiece was a thirty-foot fountain surrounded by a "graceful temple" to simulate a Roman barge. Vines, flowers, and foliage ran along the interior walls and combined with immense plate-glass mirrors to give the effect of quadrupling "everything in the court."[27] The Café de l'Opera matched the Roman Gardens' opulence as it attempted to attract New York socialites. The café's color scheme was bright blue and gold, "with black marble columns surmounted by golden capitals representing bulls' heads—or," one critic was left asking, "are they calves of gold?"[28] An immense black marble staircase rose along the back of the main lower dining room, where only those in evening dress were able to sit and order. Those without black ties and properly cut evening attire were ushered upstairs to another large dining room or to the Japanese tearoom. The third and fourth floors offered private dining rooms, banquet rooms, and "bachelor apartments."[29] Architects, designers, and restaurant owners hoped that the excess and luxury on display in the new lobster palaces would attract New York's wealthiest customers, or, at least, their heirs.

As on Broadway marquees and Times Square advertisements, electric signs and colored bulbs helped entice patrons and mark lobster palaces as uniquely modern spaces. From the "buildings hung great living letters," one contemporary remarked; "some of these winked out and flashed up again at regular intervals. Others of them spelled bulletins in sentences that flared automatically . . . the hunt was always for something new, something different, something that caught the eye by its super-ingenuity, its hyper-phosphorescence among all the other radiances." Outside Rector's hung a large, glowing green-and-white dragon.[30] Lobster palaces also used electricity and other types of technology indoors to create the allure of modernity. To make Murray's Roman Gardens seem out of doors, designers installed light bulbs to produce a "deep blue eastern sky," complete with twinkling "electric stars." This arrangement mixed ancient Roman opulence with modernity: electric lights sat beneath the dining tables, generating a "pink glow" through the tablecloth.[31] Changes in Midtown dining rooms marked, for one restaurant owner, "the ending of the old-time restaurants with their quiet atmosphere and subdued lighting."[32] Lobster palaces traded serenity for lavish display, electric lights, and ragtime in hopes of appearing modern.

In the early 1900s, wealthy white urbanites in the Northeast just began embracing dancing in public as an acceptable form of entertainment, and New York City was an early mecca for young people looking to experiment with new types of leisure, physical exertion, and potentially intimate contact with strangers. As ragtime supplanted marching band music as the most popular music style in the urban North, the two-step dances that accompanied the oom-pah feel of marching bands simplified into the one-step, where dancers simply walked one step to each beat. This freed dancers from strict ballroom steps and opened opportunities for wide variations. The new one-step dances, known as "ragtime dances" or "animal dances," moved partners closer together and perfectly complemented the quick tempos and seductive allure of African American ragtime.[33]

The popularity of ragtime song and dance on the Broadway stage ushered in a transformation of Manhattan dining spaces. By 1902, Bert Williams and George Walker ended their musicals with enormous, one hundred–person cakewalks with such celebration that thousands of patrons left the shows wanting to emulate what they had just seen on stage. Times Square establishments provided the space to do so, offering huge dining rooms able to serve more than one thousand diners a night. Lobster palaces underwent a transformation after the dinner hour as Broadway theaters let out: hundreds of tables were swept away to make room for the dance floor. Lobster palaces supplied small dance bands and large dance floors, sometimes including entire dance orchestras based on the standard "eleven plus piano" in Broadway orchestra pits. After refashioning his elegant and cozy dining room into an enormous 1,500–person one, George Rector bemoaned, "There was a time when the old patrons of Rector's had dined to the digestive lubrication of soft string music, but in the new Rector's we had no . . . strains from the strings of the harp and the cello." Now, the "laughing trombone struggled for honours with the muttering tuba, while the clattering cymbals beat time for the trap drummers and the snares."[34] Rector was not the only New Yorker anxious about the transformation occurring along Broadway. In an article entitled, "Music Misplaced," one commentator expressed his "irritation" with ragtime played "by operators on doubtful pianos and more doubtful 'fiddles' when [he] dine[d] in public places."[35] The author's annoyance may have simply mirrored his feeling about popular music in the dining rooms, but his reaction—and Rector's as well—seems to reflect racial concern.

As the Williams and Walker Company introduced ragtime to Broadway, Times Square establishments catered to growing white audiences for black entertainment. Rather than the piano-dominated ragtime strains in the Tenderloin, small bands performed ragtime in the lobster palaces. Since the late nineteenth century, fine dining in Manhattan had often included classical string trios, and it sometimes featured opera singers. For a dash of the exotic, restaurants might have hired "Gypsy" bands of guitars, mandolins, and violins to set the mood.[36] But by the time James Reese Europe arrived in New York in 1903, black musicians had begun to infiltrate lobster palaces. The black menial laborers employed in the dining rooms were neither accomplished nor lucky enough to play music for a living in Tenderloin nightclubs, though they did appreciate a chance to perform after their shifts to make some extra tips. That lobster palace managers refused to pay black musicians and seemed to expect their wageworking servers, bartenders, and dishwashers to play for tips after their long shifts did not deter African Americans from filling the dining rooms with the sound of ragtime.

Throughout the first decade of the twentieth century, Times Square dining rooms became the place for the young and vibrant members of

New York high society to dance in public. Many restaurant owners and older patrons lamented that, in the words of a *Harper's Weekly* writer, "eating is a mere pretext for dancing."[37] "The class of people who patronized the last [final] Rector's," wrote Rector himself, "was absolutely different from anything I had ever met. All they wanted to do was dance."[38] When noting the "class" of his customers, Rector was not only talking about those engaged in social dancing. Lobster palaces catered to a "fast set" of young elites who enjoyed rich food and drink, as well as the company of actors and chorus girls—a much wider swath of the American public than was allowed into Fifth Avenue establishments. As Rector pointed out, "Rector's not only attracted the Four Hundred but also most of O. Henry's Four Million."[39] Lobster palaces resonated as modern spaces not only because of their decor and ragtime entertainment but also because of the relative flexibility they offered in the enactment of class and social standing (for certain white Americans).

Like actors performing on the Broadway stage, New Yorkers exhibited their social status by leisuring amid the luxury of lobster palaces. The magnificent rooms, immense mirrors, spiraling staircases, and expensive menus allowed those who could afford it to feel and act like aristocracy. Many lobster palace patrons did have money, of course, but not all. Times Square spaces offered a stage on which old wealth, new wealth, and working entertainers from Broadway could mingle and commune. Alongside leisure and amusement, this was what diners hoped to buy and consume. Increasingly in the American city, "class" (as performance and symbol) took shape through the cultural transactions and social interactions of commercial leisure spaces.

In lobster palaces, affluent patrons acted out their privilege and performed their class as they had been raised to do, while others gained access by virtue of their abilities to act and perform. In this way, the new lobster palaces presented a stage as reliant on performance as that of a Broadway musical. One restaurant critic noted this phenomenon, writing that dining at Murray's "is like dining on a stage set for the second act of a musical comedy."[40] Another wrote, "Show girls are starred at Rector's." The critic seemed especially taken with the starlets who, he noted, took their stage performance with them to the lobster palace; they seemed to use their acting skills to perform a "class" not truly theirs. "Poor, funny, pretty, dressed-up, painted girls," he wrote; "What wonder that they want to try the game in earnest? Have they not their ideals of luxury, as you and I have ours?"[41] Broadway performers from poor and working families could excite and impress their affluent audience members up close and in person. While the players in the lobster palace game knew it was a one-night act, their interactions called attention to the ways class was enacted in urban American leisure spaces. Wealthy Midtown diners may have understood themselves as central players in the creation of American modernity simply by gaining entry into New York's newest dining establishments and consuming enjoyment in unprecedented ways. But working people—actors and chorus girls alike—also played fundamental roles in producing Manhattan modernity by revealing class to be as much of a performance as an inherited social status or profession. Many who leisured in lobster palaces understood themselves as partaking in, and perhaps embodying, their changing times. Times Square nightlife, like the "Great White Way" itself, seemed to shimmer in electric modernity.

The fluid flexibility of social class on display made restaurant owners and managers want to stabilize their restaurants' connotations of exclusivity. How to maintain a sense of elite social status if "most of O. Henry's Four Million" could leisure alongside the "Four Hundred"? Dining rooms were orchestrated to allow everyone involved—diners, workers, entertainers, and managers—to perform varying degrees of social standing. Restaurant managers maintained an ordered hierarchy, from maître d's and captains to waiters and busboys, to make their patrons feel secure in their social status as consumers. Restaurants also hired black and immigrant labor to create visual differences between patrons and workers. In lobster palaces, whiteness—or, more specifically, perceived "Anglo-Saxonness"— marked the privileged status of all diners, regardless of their income or backgrounds. One maître d' recalled that restaurants "obtained their help from Europe" because they were "polished, subservient, and of handsome appearance." Contrasting immigrant labor with "American boys," because the latter thought themselves "as good as the guests," he appealed to physical and visual differences in race and ethnicity to define the subservient from the guests.[42]

African Americans made good restaurant workers for the same reasons: they knew their place—acquiescent servers and, once finished with the dishes, low-paid entertainers. In lobster palaces, class status developed alongside perceptions of ethnic difference as much as performative social interactions. The color of one's eyes, hair, and skin helped reinforce class distinctions and Anglo privilege. The New York socialite E. Berry Wall understood what united him with other lobster palace patrons: "A similarity in birth and breeding, in race and idea, knit us into the same social fabric."[43] Restaurant managers' overt distinction between their employees and their patrons sought to stabilize the thoroughly unstable class relations taking shape in lobster palaces. Times Square establishments' elitism and investment in racial difference also reveal complications in understanding white New Yorkers' perceptions of ragtime music and the African Americans who performed it for them.

Initially hired as wageworkers to serve white patrons, black musicians had only narrow margins within which to perform in lobster palaces. Whites able to consume lobster and champagne into the early morning hours had access to black sounds and their racy qualities because of their ability to purchase them. The uneven exchanges between consuming whites and wageworking blacks resolutely affected the cultural, social, and economic reverberations of ragtime in Times Square. Diners experienced ragtime as something performed by the same people, literally, who had just deferentially served them. Once a waiter ended his hourly shift and traded in his dishes for a guitar, a patron might well recognize the musician supplying her dance music as an attendant who had been filling her champagne glass mere hours before. Like the food and drink that black workers cooked, served, and cleaned, their ragtime was a commercial product consumed by affluent white customers. Unlike the expensive food and drink, however, diners did not have to pay for the music. They could tip a few coins, maybe a dollar, but only if they wanted to. By consuming lobster until early in the morning and buying bottles of champagne for chorus girls, lobster palace patrons performed their class. Likewise, by listening and dancing to ragtime performed by black laborers, patrons enacted their whiteness. Ragtime music—and the black musicians performing it—helped a heterogeneous assortment of New Yorkers enact new iterations of their social class and their whiteness by marking clearly the sound and look of blackness.

Unlike performers in the Tenderloin, black musicians possessed limited cultural authority in Midtown dining rooms and had but little effect on what Willie "the Lion" Smith called the "attitude" of the spaces. The string-band restaurant ragtime resonated quite differently in sound and symbolic significance than the piano-led groups in black-owned nightclubs. Ragtime certainly played an important role in lobster palace dining rooms, but the individual musicians providing it did not. They performed away from the dining tables, removed to the side of massive dance floors, sometimes even hidden behind palm trees or obscured by screens and other decorations.[44] Sonically, lobster palace musicians presented ragtime very differently than did those playing in the Tenderloin. They played quieter, performed mostly the hit songs of the day, and called less attention to themselves through improvisation. Black musicians carefully balanced pretty melodies and soothing string tones with aggressive rhythmic accents and strummed guitars and banjos to appeal to patrons' sensibilities and, barely, to expand whites' tastes.[45] Even if Smith could have gotten through the door of a lobster palace in his candy-pink shirt and spats, he would not have lasted a single chorus as a musician with his showy performance. His attitude was all wrong. Midtown musicians had to be less assertive in their demeanor. Black musicians were there to be heard and perhaps seen (as on the Broadway stage, black bodies brought an air of authenticity to Midtown), but not to socialize. In the dining rooms of lobster palaces, as in the greater contours of the markets of U.S. capitalism, African Americans' ragtime expressions always harbored a double edge, one that black entertainers might recognize, but never fully controlled.

No matter how deliberately black musicians presented their ragtime innovations as modern black music, whites could only hear black folk primitivism, for two interconnected reasons. First, as with the Hotel Marshall community's approach to black musical theater, the attributes of ragtime culture that seemed so fresh and ingenious also evoked older stereotypes. The ragged rhythms, banjos and guitars, the one-step dances, and even the segregated spaces of lobster palaces struck white consumers as not so different from the music of the antebellum minstrel stage. The long history of black musical difference—and its associations of folk authenticity and racial inferiority—was too deeply rooted in the white American imagination for whites to recognize African Americans' innovations as new and modern. Second, white New Yorkers had no interest in black modernity. Instead, they were deeply invested in enacting their own modernity, itself an ethereal ideal rather than any concrete category. The notion of "modernity" reveals a historical process, one that white Americans at the turn of the twentieth century hoped to embody and produce.[46]

Like that of "class," white New Yorkers' sense of modernity indicated a series of performances and social interactions, rather than any demonstrative object. To understand themselves as modern, whites needed examples of the premodern—something from which to distinguish themselves and their own modern values. As they had throughout much of the nineteenth century, African Americans continued to symbolize some romantic vision of premodernity at the dawn of the twentieth. Black culture seemed to evoke the primitive and uncivilized—tools whites needed to fully evoke the opposite. Black primitivism became a constitutive element of white New Yorker modernity, even as African Americans intended to fashion themselves into modern American culture workers, a reality that Will

Marion Cook recognized in 1903, when he wrote "Swing Along" for the second-year opening of *In Dahomey*:

Come along Mandy, come along Sue,
White folks watchin' and seein' what you do,
White folks jealous when you'se walkin' two by two,
So swing along, chillun, swing along![47]

While the song mostly emphasizes black pride, Cook's lyrics show that he understood the ways in which white consumers were "watchin' and seein'" the development of black cultural expression, tracking new trends in song and dance for their own pleasure and uses.

The idea that blacks played primitive styles of music, which only became modern when whites bought it, presented a certain logic to white New Yorkers who ate in segregated spaces, bought tickets to segregated theaters, and knew few—if any—blacks as anything other than laborers and "help." As in nineteenth-century minstrelsy, white interest in—and even fascination with—black ragtime grew primarily because it seemed to prove the existence of natural and essential differences between the races. The difference was part of the draw, and one of the reasons white people paid good money to consume black cultural expression. As in the heyday of minstrelsy, white audiences came to understand themselves *as white audiences* through their purchase and enjoyment of black entertainment.[48] James Weldon Johnson noticed the ways white consumers enjoyed black dance, writing years later: "I have been amazed and amused watching white people dancing to a Negro band . . . attempting to throw off the crusts and layers of inhibitions laid on by sophisticated civilization . . . seeking to recapture a taste of primitive joy in life and living; trying to work their way back into that jungle which was the original Garden of Eden; in a word, doing their best to pass for colored."[49]

Johnson recognized the commercial power of the notion of "black authenticity," the promise of a premodern experience of life as an elixir for the ills of an urbanizing, industrializing, and increasingly bureaucratic America. For many white dancers, the more primitive the dance steps, the better—the more real their experience of physical and psychological abandon. As one school recreation inspector understood it: "These dances came to us from the Barbary Coast, the Apaches of Paris and similar untutored sources."[50] It hardly mattered where exactly "these dances" originated, so long as they were "untutored" and sprang from exotic sources.

Formally trained black musicians like James Reese Europe were not hired to play in lobster palaces for a reason. The majority of white

New Yorkers had little interest in recognizing that blacks could master formalized European music—that fact did not fit their worldview. Exciting, evocative, and expressive black rhythms, though, did so perfectly. Like Broadway musicals and coon songs—but different too because of the spaces, performers, and audiences—lobster palaces connected new conceptions of black New Yorkers as gifted musicians with older racial stereotypes of black expressivity and naturalness. Thus even as white diners accepted ragtime as a sign of their own modernity, they distinguished themselves from the black producers of modern American music. Ragtime reflected the modernity of the white people who enjoyed it, not the modernity of the African Americans who invented and developed it.

In Times Square leisure spaces, black music played a powerful role in evoking the urban and cosmopolitan modernity that restaurant owners and managers hoped to cultivate. But as lobster palace managers put black wage earners to work after their shifts, they undermined African Americans' efforts to change popular representations of black culture during the early years of Jim Crow. Racial segregation and exploitation, as well as white moderns' explicit rejection of African Americans' own fundamental roles in creating modern American popular culture, defined Midtown Manhattan spaces as thoroughly as did the electric lights and garish decor. Although lobster palaces offered a wide swath of white Americans new opportunities to take part in New York nightlife and to perform their own cosmopolitan modernity, they offered few outlets for black professionalism or artistic creativity. Even more problematically, they helped recreate the social order of white supremacy that African Americans fought to transcend. Race relations in lobster palaces wrought long-lasting legacies. More than half a century after he had worked in a Times Square restaurant, the renowned African American ragtime pianist Eubie Blake stopped a white friend from entering one specific site, telling him that, "If we go in there, they'll piss in my soup."[51] When James Reese Europe arrived in New York in 1903, he aimed to change the professional and cultural value of black ragtime. Shortly after his arrival, Europe saw in the Times Square lobster palace a modern institution and commercial opportunity ripe for change.

JAMES REESE EUROPE'S CLEF CLUB INC.

Due to Europe's success at organizing what he called "society" dance bands for the Wanamaker family since 1904, and also with networking and booking bands among dozens of the Wanamakers' friends, by 1910

Europe found that he alone could no longer fulfill white elites' demand for ragtime dance bands. Europe had hired wageworkers away from their jobs in Times Square and gotten them good work as professional musicians in white elites' private dining rooms. But it was not enough. Black musicians in New York had few spaces to convene or receive calls for jobs. Europe knew them all, and also knew that most Tenderloin nightclubs did not cultivate the types of ragtime professionalism he sought to demonstrate. In an era before private telephone lines, few New York households had a phone, and almost no black businesses had access to the new technology. The musician Noble Sissle remembered that the lack of booking agencies for ragtime musicians seemed particularly galling to Europe because he had so many high-paying gigs and many more patrons keen to recommend him. "But," Sissle recalled, "the embarrassing part would come, after having made such a wonderful impression, to have to give the address of some café or saloon, because there were many people of that set that would not like to be calling up those kind of places."[52] The Hotel Marshall was one of Europe's only options.

Although the stars of the black musical stage back of 1902 no longer lived there, Jim Marshall maintained his popular space in Black Bohemia, even as the black migration to Harlem began in earnest (with many Marshall musicians operating as vanguard home owners uptown). Musicians still convened in the basement bar and leisured, debated, and played music together. In 1906, Cole and Johnson had written the entire script to *The Shoo-Fly Regiment* between meals at the Marshall before selecting Europe as their music director. Europe, too, relaxed at the Marshall, but he increasingly used the hotel as a meeting place for the musicians in his society dance bands. Musicians often came by looking for Europe after they had finished their day jobs to see if he had any work for them. Tom Fletcher, who had been in Ernest Hogan's Memphis Students with Europe, remembered that one day Marshall came down to the basement and approached the group of men playing cards around one of the larger dinner tables and "dropped a hint that maybe the fellows ought to be getting a place of their own to hang out." Realizing both that he had become a nuisance and that he needed his own meeting space, Europe decided to organize a booking agency and to establish a professional space for ragtime musicians. In early April 1910, over a succulent dinner of fresh possum in the basement of the Hotel Marshall, a small group of musicians elected Europe the first president of the Clef Club of New York City Inc.[53]

By establishing the Clef Club, Europe distanced himself from cabaret life and advanced a new image of himself—and of his union members—as established professionals. Combining the attributes of a craft labor union with that of a booking agency, the Clef Club was New York City's first labor union for black musicians specializing in popular music. For five years, Europe had been a member of the New Amsterdam Musical Association (NAMA), which had attempted to organize black classical performers since 1900. But NAMA had little interest in working with ragtime musicians, and rarely did membership help them.[54] Black New Yorkers, too, had applied to the Local 310 of the American Federation of Musicians since the 1890s, but were always rejected because of the union's segregation policies.[55]

Europe's Clef Club forged new labor relations between black musicians and white clients—whether restaurant managers or private hosts—and introduced a new type of black professional musician to New York City. Within its first month, the Clef Club secured a building across the street from the Marshall, installed a telephone, and enlisted 135 members. Membership grew to more than 200 by 1912, but the initial size of the roster illustrates how eager musicians were to join.[56] The Clef Club boasted that its central location could "furnish a dance orchestra from three to thirty men upon request at any time, day or night."[57] Most of the musicians Europe recruited were the bellboys, redcaps, janitors, elevator operators, dishwashers, and waiters who serviced Times Square lobster palaces. Many had no formal musical training, and few of them worked as full-time professionals. But others, like Joe Jordan, Daniel Kildare, and Ford Dabney, were well-established performers, and the Clef Club quickly gained a reputation as an organization of highly skilled musicians.[58]

The Clef Club guaranteed fixed wages and other amenities for its musicians and set labor standards that separated its members from the wage labor often associated with them. Europe stipulated in his contracts that his musicians' duties involved "nothing but playing music and entertaining," carefully delineating that his musicians were not hired by wealthy white families as "help."[59] At a time when ragtime performers might earn just one dollar a night in tips, Europe ensured that Clef Club musicians received fixed wages, sometimes as much as thirty-five dollars per performer for the night, and negotiated for transportation, room, and board for traveling gigs.[60] Tom Fletcher remembered that soon after incorporation, the Clef Club received so many calls that members would simply show up at the Fifty-third Street clubhouse, "where the phone would ring soon, bringing a call from one of the hotels or restaurants." This must have been the case even early on, because Europe established a specific dress code for those jobs considered pickup gigs, rather than the ones booked in advance. Europe specified that a "dark or blue suit with a white shirt and a black bow tie" would prove acceptable for pickup jobs, suggesting that the Clef Club phone rang frequently enough that musicians could swing by the office and get a gig even in the early days of the union.[61] Europe demanded strict adherence to a dress code, requiring members to arrive to gigs dressed in black tuxedos or suits with matching socks and polished shoes. He presented Clef Club bands in fashionable and austere clothing that created an air of dignity and reinforced their professionalism. By separating his musicians from their labors as waiters, busboys, and dishwashers, Europe transformed the professional value of black musicians' labor.

The contracts, fixed wages, and dress code also reinforced one of Europe's central selling points: a Clef Club band brought dignified, modern, and only slightly exotic entertainments to clients' parties. But the Clef Club's attention to style and decorum also created expectations for his clients. By presenting his members well, Europe set a standard for the respect of African American musicians, even among the white elites who hired his bands. Within its first year, the Clef Club supplied dance music for the Vanderbilts, Astors, Goulds, Rhinelanders, Cabots, and other notable families who the pianist Eubie Blake called "blue bloods" and who more than one musician remembered as "millionaires."[62] And in the following years, Europe would send Clef Club bands up and down the Atlantic coast, from Florida to Maine, and as far west as Chicago.[63] Europe's deliberate representation of professional respectability illustrated his musicians' merits and justified their presence at high-society functions throughout much of America, as well as their growing wages. The Clef Club's work for America's most elite families greatly shifted the professional and cultural value of black musicians and their music.

The ways that Europe established and promoted the Clef Club brand illustrate the challenges black musicians faced as they negotiated the racialized expectations of black performance. Europe deliberately selected which battles to fight and which to leave for another day. His marketing strategies indicate a remarkable ability to both resist and reinforce the racial stereotypes of the day in ways that ultimately allowed his club's unprecedented success. Depending on his audience and its expectations, Europe presented different images of various Clef Club ensembles. At root, Europe sold the Clef Club as an organization composed of the best black musicians in the city. For black audiences, the best often meant formally trained or "legitimate" musicians, musicians seeking to raise the cultural value of black music and, by extension, of black people; for whites, the best connoted the most naturally talented musicians, an assessment that fit into white patrons' expectations of racial difference. Even though playing for wealthy whites' private parties could put Clef Club musicians in untenable situations and incur stark reminders of American racism, Europe played to both sides of the color line and fulfilled many of the expectations of his patrons regardless of their race.

From the start, Europe presented the Clef Club as an organization devoted to promoting a new type of black musician: an accomplished professional and symbol of modern African America. He aimed at New Yorkers black and white who supported his attempts to legitimize and make respectable black entertainment through institutional affiliation. The preamble of the Clef Club's constitution echoed that of the Frogs, the Hotel Marshall fraternal organization that Bert Williams and George Walker had initiated and which Europe had joined in 1908. The Clef Club stated as its purpose to "promote greater efficiency among its members in art, technique, and execution of vocal and instrumental music, and to promote good fellowship and social intercourse." While Clef Club uplift ideals correlated with the image of professional and trained musicians Europe promoted, the group was not as exclusive as it purported. Many Clef Club members were trained musicians when they joined, but many more were not—nor could all Clef Clubbers read music.[64] The Clef Club, and Europe's savvy, often inconsistent promotion of it, exemplified Europe's own approach to ragging uplift.

Clef Clubber Eubie Blake's experience indicates that many members learned how to read music through their involvement with the organization. Blake had composed complicated rags for more than a decade before learning to read and write music. He explained that he had composed "Charleston Rag" in 1899, but did not consider that he "wrote it" until he put it to paper in 1915, the year he joined the Clef Club. It was Blake's membership in the club that spurred him to learn to read music. Europe organized musicians in New York who had various levels of training. But as members of the Clef Club, many non-trained players took advantage of their close ties with trained musicians to gain a musical education. Since their livelihood depended on getting gigs, it was in the best interest of all union members to better their musicianship and advance musical literacy.[65]

From its earliest years, the Clef Club garnered a high level of respect among the city's black entertainers. Before Blake joined, he knew of the group's reputation. Making reference to club members' ability to sight-read sheet music, he remembered them as "reading sharks." Blake claimed that

A Clef Club Society Orchestra. Photographs and Prints Division,
Schomburg Center for Research in Black Culture, New York Public Library,
Astor, Lenox, and Tilden Foundations.

the cornetist Russell Smith could read so well that if a "fly landed on the music, he'd *play* it." James P. Johnson called Clef Club musicians "glamorous characters," noting that "the club was a place to go to study" how a ragtime musician's "attitude" and "style of behaving" could be a "professional trade-mark." Although Johnson joined the Clef Club during World War I, he never got to direct his own band because the "older men there vetoed it."[66] Willie "the Lion" Smith also remembered Clef Clubbers as "mostly legitimate men who read the popular music of the day." Smith may have been referring to Clef Clubbers' ability to sight-read when he called them "legitimate," but his recollection also alludes to their higher social status—or, in other words, their cultural value—as black musicians who no longer played ragtime in all-black spaces. While most Clef Club players lived and socialized in the Tenderloin, their reputation as the "society favorite" in the "drawing rooms of New York's Four Hundred" solidified their representations of black musical professionalism, even if many of the men were not trained musicians. This is an image Europe crafted, marketed, and sold.[67] But playing to both sides of the color line could prove vexing.

Eubie Blake recalled the complications Europe navigated as he capitalized on audience expectations. Blake remembered that when playing for white parties, Clef Club musicians "weren't supposed to read music!" Europe demanded that his musicians reinforce white assumptions about blacks' natural musicianship by faking a capacity to play exquisite dance music together, immediately and improvisationally. No sheet music was allowed when playing for white audiences, as it disrupted the act. While some Clef Club members were untrained performers, by the time Blake joined in 1915, most had excellent sight-reading abilities. But Europe made all of them perform a counterfeit innate musicality. Blake remembered that he and the others would "get all the latest Broadway music from the publisher" and "learn the tunes and rehearse 'em until we had 'em all down pat." They would memorize their parts and arrive to gigs able to fake their ability to play naturally and spontaneously—even the newest hit songs, as if black musicians could simply intuit the complexities of ragtime harmony and syncopation, not to mention the difficult demands of improvising with an ensemble. Years later, Blake still recalled the depth of the racial stereotype: "All the high-toned, big time folks would say, 'Isn't it wonderful how these untrained, primitive musicians can pick up all the latest songs instantly without being able to read music?'"[68]

As Europe sold this false—though resonant—image to his audiences, he traded on centuries-old notions of black natural talent, even though his musicians learned the hits of the day the same way most working players did: by reading the sheet music. Playing into popular conceptions of natural black musicianship, Europe transformed his white clients' racial expectations into the Clef Club's financial rewards.

When Europe employed specific images of black natural talent, he walked another fine line. On the one hand, the Clef Club promoted itself as a respectable and highly skilled organization primarily entertaining upper-crust whites. This strategy had two effects—it opened up black music markets to affluent whites unlikely to gain appreciation for black music (professional value) and upheld black middle-class ideals of respectability, countering stereotypes of ragtime as the music of saloons, gambling clubs, and bawdy houses (cultural value). On the other hand, Europe emphasized the exotic qualities he knew white audiences desired of exciting, rhythmic black music. Europe balanced white expectations of black exoticism while also distinguishing Clef Club musicians from other players, a move that raised the cultural value of the Clef Club among whites even as it reinforced their stereotypes of black difference. By trading on both respectability and black essentialism, Europe gave his customers what they wanted. If wealthy customers expected natural musicians who could "just play" anything they heard, Europe fulfilled their desire. But working for white people could prove more difficult than living up to their racialized expectations. Band members faced unconcealed discrimination too.

As the Clef Club supplied the most popular entertainments for New York's wealthiest families, its members regularly encountered stark reminders of their place in a racist society. As they entered the most elite private spaces in New York, for example, they never used the front door. Blake remembered that "we didn't use the Steinway [piano] either. It was locked up and covered with velvet and flowers that said, 'Keep off the grass!' There would always be a rented piano" for the Clef Club.[69] On one occasion, Blake directed a band at a wealthy man's party for his granddaughter, where all the guests were to bring a birthday gift "wrapped in a five cent red handkerchief." During the course of the night, a long hallway table was covered in identical-looking gifts, and one Clef Club musician could not help but sneak over from time to time to try to peak inside the presents. Blake told him to knock it off, but his colleague would not. Finally, on one of his visits to the table, an undercover Pinkerton detective walked up, handcuffed him, and took him over to Blake. "I've seen you warn this fellow to stay away from the table," he said, "I could take him downtown right now for attempted theft, but I won't if you'll keep him away from there." He then explained that by the end of the night there could be "thirty thousand dollars worth of jewelry" on the table and, turning to the man he had handcuffed, warned: "And you'd better pray to God that nothing comes up missing!"[70] It was a harsh reminder of a black band's place in Jim Crow New York.

For some Clef Club musicians, their high wages, and perhaps simply their presence in rich people's homes, created unrealistic assumptions of mutual respect. Blake recalled leading a band for a "big party on Fifth Avenue" in a mansion that "belonged to a millionaire lumber man, and . . . looked like something out of the movies." The hostess had not yet presented herself to the party when one of Blake's men climbed up a second-floor landing to play a large gilded harp. Blake tried to stop him, but only got a taunting response: "Aw, you scared of white folks? I was born up North," said the man as he began to play the harp. Soon after he finished, Blake recalled, "the hostess appeared, dressed like a queen and making her grand entrance." She touched the harp on her way down the wide, curved staircase and walked right over to Blake. "You're from Mr. Europe, aren't you?" she asked, not waiting for an answer—"Which one of you plays the harp?" As the musicians pointed him out, she strolled over, telling him, "Well, keep your goddamn black hands off my harp. And all of you get out of here!" Luckily for Blake, "some of her friends persuaded her to allow [the band] to stay." In another instance, Europe himself was conducting a band on cruise from Atlantic City to Maine. "The yacht was like a dream," Blake remembered, until a Clef Club singer named Carl Cook began his Bert Williams interpretation. "The audience was really enjoying the act when suddenly, midway through his shuffling and singing, he reached over, pulled an expensive panama hat off one of the men's heads, and put it on his own." Cook ended the act by putting the hat back on the owner's head, breaking a strict taboo of the color line. "The crowd was silent and the hat's owner, without a word, removed his hat and threw it into the water." "After an awkward moment," Blake recalled, "everyone applauded, and the man . . . even gave Cook some money" for his performance. Nonetheless, Europe "was furious" with Cook for crossing a racial barrier, one that Europe had created the Clef Club specifically to stealthily navigate, not ignore.[71]

These incidents indicate the limits of Europe's efforts to change black musicians' cultural value. He could make his bands the most respected in the greater New York area, and get paid well; he could get black musicians into elite spaces to an unprecedented degree, and he could even expand white New Yorkers' interest in and admiration for blacks' cultural innovations. But he could not transform American racial norms. Even though Europe perceived that white audiences enjoyed black music for reasons quite different than African Americans, as a historical actor locked in his moment, he could not conceive the ways that white modernity depended on notions of black primitivism. Part of the secret to the Clef Club's success was its ability to reinforce white people's stereotypes, rather than overturning them. Europe worked within narrow margins, and it is important to underscore how and where he did widen them.

Before the Clef Club, black culture implied blackface vaudeville and coon-song stereotypes, even in New York City. By 1914 or so, Europe's Clef Club enjoyed renown along the Atlantic coast and was known as a leading dance band across much of America. He significantly raised the professional value of hundreds of his dance band musicians and reshaped the levels of social prestige of black music enough to gain access to previously unobtainable public and private spaces. Yet the Clef Club could not transcend the white supremacy that operated as the foundation of American race relations during the Jim Crow era.

ON OCTOBER 1, 1910, Bob Cole collapsed on stage at Keith's Fifth Avenue Theater in New York. Throughout the following year, news sources gave sporadic and sometimes contradictory evidence that Cole was healing from a mental breakdown, and those closest to him thought he was recovering. In July 1911, Cole was released from the Amityville Sanitarium on Long Island to a retreat in the Catskill Mountains. Within a week he had drowned while swimming in shallow waters.[72] George Walker had died early in 1910, also collapsing on stage during the *Bandanna Land* tour in 1909, forcing his wife, Aida Overton Walker, to perform in drag and take up his hit songs for the remainder of the tour. On May 20, 1909, Ernest Hogan, "The Unbleached American" had died from tuberculosis.[73] For the black entertainers living and working out of the Hotel Marshall, Cole's death closed the book on the first wave of black musical theater on Broadway—large-scale, all-black shows would not return until Eubie Blake and Noble Sissle's *Shuffle Along* in 1921.

The deaths of Cole, Walker, and Hogan in fact, signaled a shift in the New York theatrical scene, and their partners and companies never recovered from the losses. The deaths of these three leading figures in African American popular music did more than symbolize the end of a creative era—with these men gone, their partners and businesses could not survive. Alongside Black Patti's Troubadours and the Williams and Walker Company, Cole and Johnson's songwriting and performing partnership and Hogan's Smart Set had comprised the backbone of the largest and most influential black theater companies in the United States. Without these central figures, some thought, the golden age of black musical theater over, and in many ways, the historical record concurs. James Weldon Johnson called the years between Cole's death in 1911 and 1921 "a term of exile," and historians often follow suit, ending their studies of black musical theater between 1910 and 1915.[74]

James Reese Europe's Clef Club and his subsequent accomplishments, however, demonstrate that this assessment is not entirely correct. Europe's creative, professional, and public life as a leading authority on black music was just beginning in 1910.[75] It may have been the gap left that allowed for his emergence as a central musician and organizer in the city. After 1910, Europe's black musical performances no longer relied on vaudeville theaters or Broadway stages, nor did they use black dialect, minstrel stereotypes, or coon comedy. As he seized on opportunities to become a dance band leader and labor organizer, Europe increasingly utilized the most exciting and essential sonic signifier of blackness—syncopated rhythm—to instigate new formations of black popular music, the dissemination of social dance, and a continuation of America's love affair with black popular culture.

Europe's confidence in ragtime rhythms led to further innovations and growing professional and cultural value for his musicians. Yet without the heterogeneity Cole, Walker, and Hogan brought to black entertainments in New York, African Americans' music increasingly took on uniform and standardized associations. Rather than the diversity of entertainment commodities forged in the Manhattan musical marketplace, ragtime song and dance came to symbolize the racially essential and folk primitivist cultural expressions of black Americans. Ragtime rhythms became not only the fundamental characteristic of Negro music but also a powerful marker of racial difference in Jim Crow America.

CHAPTER SIX

RHYTHM IS SOMETHING
THAT IS BORN IN THE NEGRO

The Clef Club Orchestra and the

Consolidation of Negro Music

Two years before James Reese Europe desegregated Carnegie Hall with his 125-man Clef Club Symphony Orchestra, he established a concert series at the Manhattan Casino in the burgeoning black neighborhood of Harlem to demonstrate his progressive vision for the future of black music. On a Friday night in late May 1910, Europe conducted the Clef Club Orchestra, which, with one hundred musicians and only ten pianos, was a slightly smaller affair than the Carnegie concert. The orchestra captivated nearly one thousand African American ticket holders with the "Clef Club March" and a concert program combining European art music with dance numbers and ragtime orchestrations.

The "musical melange and dancefest," advertised weeks in advance in the *New York Age*, also consisted of an eccentric mix of vaudeville and variety performances, stand-up comedy, and a boxing match. Clef Club members Joseph "Frenchy" Wetherly sang and danced, George Walker Jr. gave imitations, and a banjo duo played "plantation melodies." James Europe's brother, John, organized the Marshall Trio—named after James Marshall and his Hotel Marshall—for the event and performed a "potpourri" of tunes. Between music sets, the boxers Henry Creamer and Billy Farrell knocked each other unconscious during a two-round match. Neither man "was awarded the decision," the *Age* reported, "as both contestants were unable to rise at the count of ten at the end of the second round."[1] It was Europe's introduction of his ragtime symphony orchestra, however, that made the night particularly unique.

After the bout, one hundred members of the Clef Club Orchestra took their places above, under, and around the Manhattan Casino stage to begin the second set of the concert. Because there were too many musicians to fit on the stage, most of the orchestra set up in a semicircle at the end of the casino's dance floor. There were mandolins, guitars, and "double-necked harp guitars" that looked as cumbersome as their name; banjos of the four-string variety, not finger-picked in a bluegrass style but quickly strummed with a plastic plectrum or "pick"; bowed violins, cellos, and basses; the makings of multiple trap-drum kits, early prototypes of jazz kits wrought from the drum pieces of a marching band but

The Clef Club Symphony Orchestra. Photographs and Prints Division,
Schomburg Center for Research in Black Culture, New York Public Library,
Astor, Lenox, and Tilden Foundations.

with tympani; a single harp amid ten upright pianos set back to back in
five separate pillars spread along the sides and back of the stage: this was
James Reese Europe's decidedly un-European orchestra.[2]

While Europe based his orchestra on a European symphony, he
arranged the concert selections in ways that highlighted his unusual
amalgam of "folk" instruments and their distinctive rhythmic pulses.
Undermining any strict distinction between "formal" and "folk" culture,
or "art" and "commercial" music, Europe emphasized the unmistakably
hybrid nature of his conception of Negro music. Standing over six-feet
tall, the barrel-chested Europe presented an imposing figure even though

his conducting stand also rested on the dance floor amid the hodgepodge of musicians and audience members. His sharp tuxedo, cut with tails, and his round, wire-rimmed glasses formed a portrait of calculated authority and ragtime attitude. Europe expertly led his orchestra through a multihued program of dance tunes, rags, waltzes, ballads, marches, and "light classical" pieces like Paul Lincke's, "Beautiful Spring," to the audience's robust applause.[3] Europe's orchestra advanced popular linkages of blackness with syncopated, ragtime rhythms. But by performing selections from diverse music genres, Europe also demonstrated that African Americans could master a wide array of forms.[4] Although the *New York Age* reported that the audience "lustily applauded each number," the one thousand music lovers who came to see the Clef Club's first concert must have left wondering exactly what it was they had witnessed.[5]

Europe understood that the Manhattan Casino would be the "first opportunity for the colored people to see or hear" the Clef Club, and he selected his concert program to both better black audience members' conceptions of ragtime and to disrupt their assumptions.[6] Because the Clef Club supplied dance music almost exclusively for wealthy whites' private parties and Times Square's lobster palaces, few black New Yorkers knew of Europe's musical innovations, his labor organizing, or his interventions into black musical value. As he demonstrated his musicians' mastery of established European styles, James Europe introduced to open-minded blacks his creative and deliberately uplifting forms of Negro music. He also got many of them dancing. Black patrons at the Manhattan Casino sat politely and clapped appropriately during the concert. But once the main event was over, Europe's orchestra gave way to a Clef Club dance band, and many in the audience danced to ragtime long into the night. Europe's success as an orchestra conductor and dance band leader at the Manhattan Casino indicates that some "middle-class" African Americans were interested in ragtime song and dance, an insight that muddles scholarly distinctions between middle-class uplifters and working-class ragtime revelers. While some may have left directly after the formal concert, many danced through the Harlem night, years before the Great Migration arrived to 155th Street.

The Clef Club concerts in the Manhattan Casino introduced Europe's ragtime ensembles and his unique approach to racial uplift and the politics of representation to Black Manhattan. But it was the Clef Club's desegregation of Carnegie Hall in May 1912 that concretized Europe's transformation of the professional and cultural value of black musicians and their music among many more New Yorkers, black and white. By introducing his orchestra, his booking agency and labor union, and his idiosyncratic fusion of popular music with European classical forms to the Carnegie Hall crowd, Europe demonstrated that black ragtime had gained new levels of cultural currency, a shift that quickly garnered increasing wages for black musicians. As he crafted inventive ragtime sounds, Europe enticed new audiences and mounted a challenge to popular representations of African Americans. He shaped the Manhattan musical marketplace according to his own designs and helped black musicians maintain their central positions in it. After establishing the Clef Club, Europe had two parallel agendas: first, to continue improving black musicians' wages, working conditions, and symbolic capital; second, to promote new representations of black people and black culture in ways that challenged Americans' racial assumptions of white supremacy and black inferiority. Breaking down the color barrier at Carnegie Hall greatly aided Europe in his aims. As he opened up professional opportunities for his musicians, Europe substantiated and circulated new popular representations of African Americans as creative, professional, and enterprising American citizens.

Even as Europe developed new representations of Negro music and black citizenship, however, he fell into the same ideological traps that his friends Bert Williams, Will Marion Cook, and Rosamond Johnson wrestled to escape: the racial essentialism that undergirded Jim Crow America. In many ways, Europe's ragtime orchestras symbolized the immense heterogeneity of black culture in New York. Like the varied sonic expressions of black modernity that circulated out of the Hotel Marshall between 1896 and 1909, Europe imprinted black ragtime with his unique stamp through his Clef Club orchestras. Combining his musical vision with a grander desire to legitimate Negro music among American art critics and patrons, Europe added to the swirling cauldron of creativity that had been brewing at the Hotel Marshall ever since Williams and Walker had opened their doors to the black theatrical community in 1896. Yet by 1912, in large part due to the Hotel Marshall community's success on Broadway and along Tin Pan Alley, the Clef Club also represented the codification and standardization of African Americans' music along specifically racial contours.

Ironically, rather than illustrating the open-ended, fluid, sonically boundless potential of "modern Negro music," Europe's surprising and innovative orchestra represented, instead, a closing off of black musical diversity and a turn to understanding any music composed or performed by African Americans as primarily racially derived, an essentially "black" form of music. The process turning American ragtime commodities into the distinct expressions of the black race had been under way since before Ernest Hogan published his first hit coon song in 1896. But more than any single player in New York after 1909, Europe shaped the commodification of black music and set new standards for the racialized receptions of blues and jazz during and after World War I. Europe's Clef Club prefigured the rise of "race records" in the 1920s and, in fact, laid the groundwork for the acute segregation of American popular music throughout the twentieth century.

This chapter examines Europe's role in producing and selling his music ensembles, labor union, and rhythmic black music more generally in New York City between 1910 and 1912. The first three sections focus on the Clef Club Orchestra concerts, the spaces it performed, and the meanings those spaces held. These sections also demonstrate the ways Europe's successes helped narrow the meaning of black ragtime, turning it from a commercially produced American cultural commodity into the exclusive cultural expression of African Americans. The fourth section documents Europe's status as a leading spokesman for black music and positions his ideas about black authenticity and American music within the context of his promotion of the Clef Club.

MUSICAL UPLIFT IN HARLEM'S MANHATTAN CASINO

Europe danced along a thin line as he attempted to raise the professional and cultural values of black popular music among black and white New Yorkers. And it was not just the color line segregating black from white. Europe's tightrope dangled over class distinctions, aesthetic judgments, cultural Eurocentrism, and American market forces—the very foundations of professional and cultural value that he sought to upend. The Manhattan Casino concerts demonstrate Europe's early attempts to uplift the cultural value of black popular musicians among middle-class black New Yorkers, much as he already had done among wealthy whites. Yet besides catering to an exclusive set of African Americans who could afford admission, the concerts reflect Europe's wider strategies to situate his musicians, his labor union, and his dance bands in the center of the Manhattan musical marketplace.

Europe's Clef Club Orchestra struck many at the first Manhattan Casino concert as an audacious experiment in fusing European art music with African American folk instruments and performance practices. As in the Carnegie Hall concerts two years later, Europe's audience may not have known what to expect. They were surely dazzled, if not shaken, by what the Clef Club member Noble Sissle remembered as the orchestra's "pleasingly strange chords and weird crashes."[7] Europe's was an amalgamation of instruments, sounds, styles, and musical forms unlike any ever heard in New York—if, indeed, anywhere. His innovations in orchestration, arranging, and composition illuminate one way a black artist might respond to the transitory tastes of shifting commercial music markets. His orchestra manifested a mixture of musical approaches. It was a symphony in the European model, yet included dozens of folk string instruments that called to mind the minstrel stage. While the music was highly syncopated and full of ragtime rhythmic effects, the orchestra highlighted black singing voices. Even though there were not yet any horns in the orchestra, Europe's interest in marching band music shone through with the opening number, "Clef Club March." By incorporating every style of music he could imagine, Europe capitalized on the varieties of music then made and sold in New York.

While a vaudeville stage brimming with comedians, banjo trios, and boxers may seem an odd place for the introduction of a black symphony orchestra, there were few precedents for Europe's ensemble, and fewer outlets for its performances. Due to racial segregation policies on the city's leading concert stages and in its dance halls, the Clef Club Orchestra had limited options. That the orchestra performed on the floor of an immense, four-thousand-person-capacity dance hall and split the bill with variety acts reflects some of the restrictions Europe faced as he organized a deliberately highbrow, uplift-oriented orchestra. That May evening, the Manhattan Casino presented a new and self-consciously modern expression of African American culture and professional artistry, even as it revealed the roots of a long history of black stage performance and racialized second-class citizenship in America.

It was this long history that Europe hoped to transcend. By continuing to shape and reshape the professional and cultural values of Negro music—by setting, that is, new expectations for black musicians' salaries and symbolic capital—Europe turned the page on a cultural economy rooted in minstrelsy and racialized vaudeville. He inaugurated new artistic styles, musical forms, paid wages, and social resonances of African American musicians. It was not a simple task, and Europe's revolution did not happen overnight. It began, in fact, years before he established the Clef Club, as he was just starting to organize dance bands for the Wanamakers in 1904. But the Manhattan Casino concerts, and the Carnegie Hall performances later, mark watershed moments in the history of black musical value in the United States.

Europe could have arranged his Clef Club members into any variety of performing ensemble, but he stressed to the press, black and white, that his was a symphony orchestra, just an augmented one. "Although we have first violins," Europe told the *Evening Post*, "the place of the second violins with us is taken by mandolins and banjos."[8] Likewise, Europe conducted a concert where the orchestra was the centerpiece of the show, rather than an accompaniment for musical theater and vaudeville comedy. Like Hogan's Memphis Students performances in 1905, Europe's Clef Club Orchestra "above all" performed music. Even though Europe's biannual Manhattan Casino concerts between 1910 and 1912 interspersed orchestral performances with other variety acts, the Clef Club was always the main event; and it relied on neither blackface comedy nor black dialect in its performances (though other acts during the Manhattan Casino concerts did use both). Marking an even wider transformation in black music performance, the three Clef Club concerts in Carnegie Hall between 1912 and 1914 eschewed vaudeville conventions entirely and presented only music. By 1912, Europe had jettisoned any reliance on African American caricature as he fashioned a concert worthy of Carnegie Hall. Europe combined his individual musical vision with both his professional goals as the president of the Clef Club and his grander desire to legitimate Negro music among American art critics and patrons, black and white.

As he arranged his musicians into a symphony orchestra and performed music concerts, Europe emphasized his connections to European art music and its connotations of respectable culture and formal training. He brought sophistication and technical mastery to the Manhattan Casino. The *New York Age* culture editor (and member of the Frogs) Lester Walton expressed enthusiasm for the fact that many in the orchestra were trained musicians. "Never has such a large and efficient body of colored musicians," Walton wrote in 1910, "appeared together in New York City in a concert."[9] As a youth, Europe had experienced firsthand the cultural and class divides ragtime provoked. Like Will Marion Cook and many other ragtimers, Europe had disappointed his own mother and sister (a classical performer and lifelong music teacher) by choosing to play ragtime after he had left home and moved to New York.[10] Yet even as he recognized the limits that American racial expectations and Manhattan music markets imposed, Europe aimed to uplift the image of ragtime among blacks and whites.

Europe's Clef Club Orchestra marked a milestone for many black New Yorkers invested in changing popular representations of African Americans. Like the Hotel Marshall community, Europe balanced Talented

Tenth imperatives for racial uplift with wider marketplace demands and his own artistic impulses. Building from Will Cook and Rosamond Johnson's efforts to incorporate the advanced harmony, musical form, and instrument-arranging of European art music into their ragtime, Europe sought to "legitimize" Negro music. His desire to combine European musical practices with ragtime rhythms and instruments indicates one of the ways he engaged in ragging uplift. He did not invent the technique. His upbringing and education in Washington, D.C., had inculcated Europe with the ideas of racial uplift; yet, at the same time, he could reject neither the commercial strains of ragtime, nor its unprecedented power to represent African Americans as modern American culture producers. Like the community he found in Black Bohemia, Europe hoped to transcend Talented Tenth distinctions between high and low, formal and folk, art and commercial. But he did so without losing sight of music educators' and race leaders' strategies to challenge white supremacy with cultural uplift and racial representation.

Through the Clef Club Orchestra, Europe honored his roots in Washington, home to both James Monroe Trotter and the *Negro Music Journal*'s uplift-through-music agenda. The Clef Club celebrated black musical education and black talent, cultural "development" as well as the creativity of the black "masses." The name Europe chose for the Clef Club itself demonstrated his debt to black Washington—he borrowed it from the Treble Clef Club, an exclusive black women's choral society established in 1897.[11] Like many black artists and critics who came of age after Reconstruction, Europe invested heavily in black music's ability to sway popular opinion about African Americans' intellectual capacities and suitability for American citizenship. Unlike African American educators such as Trotter, who expected their students to master only European performance and composition techniques, however, Europe believed that building from both European and African American influences would transform America's racist representations of black America. Rather than rejecting the power of ragtime rhythms, Europe embraced them and worked to transform their cultural and professional values. Europe's goals for racial uplift also explain his utilization of the Manhattan Casino.

In its early years, the Manhattan Casino symbolized specific notions of class and culture, abstract notions made seemingly concrete through the relatively high prices the casino charged for admission. One of the first large-scale events held there was the first annual "Frolic of the Frogs" in 1908. Promoted as a fund-raiser for the Hotel Marshall community's exclusive fraternal society, the Frogs charged fifty cents for general admission and up to two dollars for box seats. By charging such prices, the Frogs not only hoped to raise money but also aimed to attract a certain class of black New Yorker. Dressed in formal attire—large hobble skirts, tuxedos, and intricate costumes—hundreds of well-groomed patrons came to the Frogs' late-night cabaret performances and public dances, marking the organization as one of New York's premier, and elite, fraternal societies.[12] The Frogs' first frolic established the Manhattan Casino as an exclusive Harlem space. The annual event became, as the historian Karen Sotiropoulos notes, "central to black middle-class life" in the years prior to World War I.[13] But to call Manhattan Casino patrons "middle-class" obscures a more complex set of class and cultural identities swirling throughout black New York.

African Americans who could pay a dollar or two for a night of leisure most often did not enjoy black cabaret. Neither did they dance ragtime. According to most histories of the black middle class during the era, ragtime cabaret was the antithesis of middle-class African American culture. Du Bois and the Talented Tenth celebrated the slave spirituals and their future development along formal (European) lines, not blacks' involvement in popular music. Yet thousands of black New Yorkers paid high prices to partake in the Frogs' frolics and Clef Club dance expositions. As in Tenderloin nightclubs, black consumers of Manhattan Casino engagements also found fissures in class alignments—they disrupted the Talented Tenth's designs as much as they complicate scholars' assumptions about so-called middle-class African Americans' conceptions of respectable culture and racial representation. Certainly, James Europe's expressions of blacks' mastery of European forms uplifted the race in the eyes of many; that Europe slyly advanced ragtime rhythms into his orchestrations most likely stretched the tastes of his audience. Yet Europe's biannual successes at the Manhattan Casino also indicate a class of relatively affluent African Americans who could accept ragtime. Two years after the Frogs' first fundraiser, the Clef Club charged five dollars for the coveted balcony boxes. During the early years of the Clef Club, so-called middle-class blacks continued to appreciate ragtime culture in New York, and the high prices they paid show that the Clef Club had become a preeminent African American association in New York.[14]

As Europe increased the cultural value of black ragtime among black New Yorkers, he did little to raise its twin component: the professional value of increased musicians' wages and fiscal worth. By and large, blacks could not afford Clef Club prices (and there is no indication that those who could would have hired Europe's ragtime bands). Therefore,

Europe's strategies to improve black musicians' professional value aimed primarily at white lobster palace managers and affluent families like the Wanamakers and Vanderbilts. Nonetheless, the ways the Clef Club expanded black salaries did reinforce its standing as an important social and political organization among African Americans in the city. Black professionals took notice and increasingly approved of Europe's endeavors. They understood the ways Europe worked to raise black music's cultural and professional value—black doctors, lawyers, teachers, and preachers were doing the same for their professions throughout America, as they proved themselves fit for their positions and deserving of appropriate salaries for their work. Many may have been surprised by what they heard that first night in 1910. Few, if any, could have expected the Clef Club Orchestra to be the radically hybrid ragtime symphony that it was. But Europe won them over. His biannual concerts kept a varied demographic of black New Yorkers enthralled with the Clef Club's prospects.

Europe understood that, because his black and white audiences held different expectations for his ensembles, he must approach the ways he transformed Negro music's cultural value differently for both audiences. Over the course of a few years, the Manhattan Casino concerts began to draw white New Yorkers' attention, as well as that of the white press. But Europe's creation of the Clef Club Orchestra, its variety of musical styles from classical to popular, and its early concerts at the Manhattan Casino indicate Europe's interest in pleasing middle-class black New Yorkers too. He deliberately sought to boost the cultural value of black ragtime musicians in the eyes of those African Americans who associated ragtime song and dance with blackface vaudeville, lowdown saloon and juke joint culture, and working-class leisure. His Clef Club convinced growing numbers of black New Yorkers that popular strains of "modern Negro music" could properly represent the race.

NEGRO MUSIC: FROM COMMERCIAL PRODUCT
TO RACIAL EXPRESSION

James Reese Europe's Clef Club concerts mark a historical moment when the heterogeneity of Negro music in New York began to calcify into a racially determined, single iteration of black popular music—when blacks' music became "black music." Building from the demands of the Manhattan musical marketplace to codify and commodify black ragtime song, dance, and theater, the Clef Club began to set new standards for black musical performance in ways that would resonate throughout the twentieth century. This was not deliberate. Like Cook, Cole, and Williams, Europe sought to create a unique artistic voice that would expand and uplift Americans' conceptions of African Americans and their music. None of the Hotel Marshall artists worked to stymie the plurality of black culture or black identity. Even when a musician like Cook seemed to suggest that he knew the difference between real, authentic black music and the counterfeit variety, he did not reject efforts by Cole and the Johnsons. He just thought his were better, perhaps more representative of his own ideal of blackness. Nonetheless, after the deaths of Hogan, Cole, and Walker between 1908 and 1911, "Negro music" in New York increasingly came to signify racially essentialized, homogenous black styles. Part of this transition can be explained by the Clef Club concerts in Harlem's Manhattan Casino and, especially, by Europe's sonic and representative emphasis on syncopated, ragtime rhythms.

On first listen, it could not be the myriad, incongruous, genre-melding sounds of the Clef Club Orchestra that signaled the uniformity of Negro music. The Clef Club Orchestra's Manhattan Casino concerts were musical phenomena, startling as many as they pleased. When the *Age's* Walton noted that a small group of white audience members at the second casino concert "appear[ed] very much surprised, with eyes, mouths, and ears wide open," he could have made a similar case for many African American audience members.[15] As Europe mixed European instruments with American folk ones, he undermined any simple dichotomy. His orchestra called attention to the dialectical and mutually informing relationships that black and white identities held for each other—the ways white Americans (and Europeans too) understood their culture to be "theirs" in contrast to their perception of blacks' culture.. Europe dissembled and recombined the racial connotations of white cultural expressions with black ones, illustrating that African Americans could interpret and incorporate any musical form, style, or genre into their own artistry. The Clef Club Orchestra was a mongrel, hodgepodge, and truly American symphony orchestra, one presented in a form Du Bois or Dvořák might have agreed represented the future of U.S. culture and society. Yet even as he concocted an "American" orchestra, Europe's emphasis on ragtime rhythms marked his ensemble and its music as essentially African American.

More than anything, the Clef Club Orchestra utilized its instruments and performance pieces in the service of creating new worlds of ragtime syncopation. The ensemble incorporated intense rhythms to every piece it performed; the driving beats came not from the trap-drums, but from the dozens of guitars, mandolins, and banjos seated behind the violin section. Although there are no recordings of the performance, it is easy to imagine the energy, excitement, and sheer volume that such a "second violin" section would create.[16] The sound of thirty strummed mandolins and banjos must have sounded like machine-gun bursts in this preamplified performance setting. The sound of the mandolins and banjos, Europe explained to an interviewer, "gives that peculiar steady strumming accompaniment to our music, which all people comment on."[17] Europe was able to control the cacophony, conducting his orchestra's strong rhythms with unparalleled agility and rhythmic nuance. A contemporary of Europe's, the critic Gilbert Seldes, remembered Europe as an excellent conductor, recalling that his ensembles emphasized "contrast; it was out of the contracting stresses of a regular beat and a divergent [one] that he created his effects. The band kept perfect time, and his right knee, with a sharp and subtle little motion, stressed the acceleration or retard of the syncope [rhythm]. His dynamics were beautiful because he knew the value of noise and how to produce it and how to make it effective."[18]

Through the Clef Club Orchestra, and his consistent self-promotions in the black and white press, Europe propelled blacks' sense of racial ownership over ragtime rhythms. When Europe discussed ragtime syncopations, he appealed to blacks' "natural" rhythms. "Rhythm is something that is born in the negro," he told the *Tribune*.[19] Likewise, he told the *Evening Post* that "the negro plays ragtime as if it was a second nature to him—as it is."[20] Even when discussing what he noted was a "modern" music, Europe appealed to blacks' essential and natural character: "The art of playing the modern syncopated music," Europe asserted in the *Age*, "is to him a natural gift."[21] Europe's suggestion hardly differs from the opinions of the Hotel Marshall community. Yet even more than Cook and Rosamond Johnson, Europe championed blacks' rhythmic music and its racial resonances. By 1910, the other markers of Negro music that the Hotel Marshall community had generated—dialect verse, expressive singing practices, comedic racial stereotypes—had grown less thrilling, indeed less lucrative, as ragtime songs and black vaudeville gave way to increased interest in social dancing. This turn may have come about because of the deaths of Hogan, Cole, and Walker and the subsequent demise of their theater companies between 1908 and 1911. Certainly, black musical theater lost its place on Broadway and throughout America's leading vaudeville circuits after these three entrepreneurs passed on. But Europe had been promoting social dance in the greater New York area for years, and lobster palace managers, patrons, and workers had taken note. Europe seized on this break in Manhattan's commercial culture landscape and turned his attention toward dance orchestras and rhythmic, primarily instrumental, music.

Even considering the mayhem of mélange on stage, some non-musical attributes of the Clef Club concerts set the foundations for later, narrower and racially specific, music styles in New York and across America. Significantly, the concert took place in Harlem. By 1910, the "advance guard of the Great Migration" out of the South had begun its move northward.[22] Between 1910 and 1914, black New Yorkers made their own move north too, following the trend up western Manhattan, from Greenwich Village to the Tenderloin, from Black Bohemia to San Juan Hill; in 1914, there were 49,555 blacks in Harlem. By the end of World War I, Harlem was home to 73,000 African Americans—fully two-thirds of Manhattan blacks—and the Dutch-named neighborhood was becoming known, as one resident put it in 1920, as "the Mecca of the colored people of New York."[23] In 1910, the Manhattan Casino's location at 280 West 155th Street was far north by anyone's standards. Yet census records indicate that by 1930, there were 327,706 African Americans in New York, most of whom had been born in the South and now lived in Harlem, which stretched from the top of Central Park at 110th Street to 160th, and from Ninth Avenue to the eastside Harlem River.[24] By the time the Manhattan Casino became the Rockland Palace in 1928, it was in the center of the social, economic, and cultural capital of African America.

In 1910, the Clef Club concerts and the Manhattan Casino itself anticipated the future. The casino's central feature was its massive dance floor. Long and relatively narrow, it dwarfed even the great dance halls in Midtown Manhattan's lobster palaces. By some reports, six thousand dancers could fit in the hall.[25] The dance floor featured dozens of white columns along the outside, separating the dance space from the outside ring that could be covered in tables and chairs for patrons more interested in watching dancers than participating themselves or, in the case of many a late-night dance, pushed away to make more room for dancing. The columns also buttressed the second-floor balcony that circled the entire length of the dance floor. The ceiling was high and convex, so that the building seemed to grow taller down the middle of the dance floor. Electric light bulbs hung from underneath the balcony and encircled the square-bound stage at the far end of the floor.[26] In its size and design, in its use of electricity and light, and in its centering of the dance floor, the Manhattan Casino was African Americans' answer to the lobster palace. Except for the black laborers who sometimes played ragtime for a dollar or two, the Times Square leisure spaces were as segregated as a New

Orleans streetcar. The Manhattan Casino offered black New Yorkers a space to dance, socialize, and express their own modernity. In 1910, it was the only leisure space of its kind in New York. Small, intimate, and primarily black Tenderloin nightclubs may have presaged the smoke-filled and licentious Harlem cabaret of the 1920s, but the Manhattan Casino offers the missing link between the white-dominated lobster palaces of the early twentieth century and the grand ballrooms of Jazz Age Harlem like the Savoy, Small's, and the Radium.

When viewed through this lens—with the Manhattan Casino reflecting a type of "black lobster palace"—Europe's Clef Club Orchestra was not only a black classical music ensemble; it was a big band. African Americans came to Clef Club concerts to take part in modernity and to support black musicians' innovative endeavors. Many came to witness the uplift of black music and to applaud Clef Club interpretations of light classical numbers, understanding the music Europe conducted as a far cry from coon songs and the lowdown rags. But many also came to dance. After the orchestra finished its program, Clef Club dance bands lit up the dance floor for hundreds of African Americans dancing the cakewalk, the one-step, and a host of dances lost to the historical record.[27] These dances became the Charleston and lindy hop. Even as Europe conducted his idiosyncratic iterations of Negro music, the performance spaces where he played combined with his audience's investment in social dancing to shape increasingly standardized conceptions of black musical expression.

Europe's emphasis on ragtime rhythm, therefore, took on new social resonances far beyond his ability to control. His use of rhythmic string instruments, percussion, and syncopated arrangements signaled what he understood as the unique racial character of his orchestra. As he did with his dance bands, which had supplied music for affluent whites since 1904, Europe highlighted his symphony orchestra's use of syncopated rhythms that he understood as the essential characteristic of modern black music. The popularity of the Clef Club orchestras and dance bands throughout New York City, Europe's success as a labor organizer, and his accomplishments as a bandleader document the historical process making syncopation the essential ingredient of African American music.

This process did not, of course, occur simply because of James Europe. But his Clef Club was at the center of a timely and influential community of African Americans who participated in the promotion of black music as racially derived, who created new rhythmic styles and sold them in the marketplace, and who capitalized on the social currents during the early Jim Crow era that sought to recreate a racialized social order in the United

States. By 1910, ragtime songs remained the most popular style of music in America, but New York audiences continued to want newer, fresher, and more exciting types of music and dance. Europe was well situated and well prepared to deliver. Additionally, as a composer, arranger, conductor, and band leader, he was ideally suited to anticipate—and follow the surge of—rhythmic dance music.

THE CLEF CLUB TAKES CARNEGIE HALL

When the Clef Club desegregated Carnegie Hall in 1912, it signaled the fulfillment of a one of Europe's lifelong goals. He had long understood the importance his parents and their peers in black Washington had placed on racial representation. In foundational, familial ways, Europe hoped to represent well the black community from which he came. His first concert at Carnegie brought all this to bear. Yet it also inaugurated much wider social ramifications for African Americans throughout New York City, Washington, D.C., and across the country. The concert at one of the nation's most prestigious concert halls announced the arrival of African Americans in the American arts and set a precedent for generations of black artistry. Carnegie represented another step forward for Europe's designs to symbolize both black American distinction and American national culture through music.

The Clef Club earned the privilege because of its increasing reputation among white cultural elites in New York. In 1911, David Mannes, a prominent white composer—and the son-in-law of the notable German American conductor Walter Damrosch—established the Music School Settlement for Colored People in Harlem in honor of his African American violin teacher, John Douglas. After organizing a board of wealthy, white patrons, Mannes invited black members to join the board, among them Du Bois and Harry T. Burleigh. Mannes also contacted James Europe in hopes of hiring capable instructors from the Clef Club. Immediately enthusiastic about the school settlement, Europe provided the names of his most accomplished instrumentalists and singers and offered his aid in the future. Europe also recommended that Harlem blacks should assume control of the school as soon as possible and, to help raise money and awareness, he and Mannes decided to hold a fund-raiser at Carnegie Hall. Realizing that the young school settlement students would not be prepared to perform such a concert until the following year, Europe suggested that the Clef Club headline the event.[28] Even though, as Europe's biographer notes, Mannes had to convince his mostly white board members that the

Clef Club could "demonstrate their capacity to produce a suitably digni-fied concert," Europe got the billing and began rehearsing his men for the momentous performance.[29]

While preparing for the Carnegie concert, the Clef Club sparked class anxieties, stirring the pot of respectable representation with ragtime rhythms. After initially accepting an invitation to perform, the St. Philips Church choir tried to withdraw because some members felt they might become "sinners" if they shared a stage with ragtime musicians. Europe gently reminded the choir that he and many of his musicians were church-going men and noted that for his musicians "to make a living we have to sing and play what the public wants and will pay for."[30] Yet again, Europe maneuvered between uplift ideology and market demands. Europe also pointed out that the Clef Club knew all the music St. Phillips was to per-form, and that they would sing the spirituals themselves, without the church represented on the momentous occasion, if necessary. The choir stuck it out and performed. But even Will Cook felt upset about the Carn-egie concert, especially that Europe would conduct. Noble Sissle recalled that Cook "raved all over town about Jim not knowing anything about conducting and what right did he have going to Carnegie Hall with his inexperience." In one of Cook's more public "ravings," he feared that "Jim would set the Negro race back fifty years."[31] It was exactly the opposite of what Europe intended. In the weeks preceding the concert, even Mannes expressed concern. Although familiar with Europe's unusual orchestra, and the fact that he could only rehearse the Clef Club in sections due to space constraints, Mannes still "wondered if this scattered and disorderly rehearsal attendance could produce anything but chaos."[32] The Clef Club concert at Carnegie held auspicious implications.

On May 1, the day before the concert, it was still not clear whether Europe would pull it off. The Clef Club's inaugural performance at Carne-gie Hall looked to be an admirable failure due to lack of ticket sales. Fully two-thirds of Carnegie's three thousand ticketed seats remained unsold, and most of the reserved seats were box seats that had been reserved for settlement school patrons. Then, that evening, the *New York Evening Journal* published an anonymous editorial presenting the Music School Settlement for Colored People as a benefit for the "90,000 colored men and women" in the city. "Very little is done for them," the *Journal* asserted, "and very little for their children. In all directions they are denied, repressed and kept back." Urging New Yorkers to support the school by attending the concert or sending donations, the *Journal* called African American music the "only music of our own that is American—national, original and real." By late afternoon, there was a run on the box office, and by the following evening, Carnegie was completely sold out. Mannes remembered that when he arrived at the concert, Carnegie was "packed from floor to ceiling, thousands being turned away for the lack of even standing room."[33] Europe himself almost arrived late to the show, and was surprised to see such a crowd. Sissle remembered that Europe appeared frantic as he ascended the stage. But he was shocked when he looked at his orchestra. Europe "could hardly bring his arms down after he raised them to start . . . when he looked and saw Will Marion Cook sitting in the violin section with a violin in his hand ready to play."[34]

Whether or not Cook had truly vowed, in the mid-1890s, never to play violin again after being pigeonholed as the "world's greatest Negro violinist," he no longer considered himself a violinist, and he was skeptical about participating in Europe's concert. After weeks of entreating, Europe had finally convinced Cook to conduct the three choral pieces to be sung by the Clef Club Chorus, including Cook's own "Swing Along"—a hit song from *In Dahomey*. Cook agreed, under the stipulation that he would not be introduced to the audience. As he agreed to conduct, Cook reiterated to Europe that he would not perform in the orchestra. But just hours before the concert, Sissle recalled, as "such a crowd had gathered . . . [Cook] went home and got his violin, and walked right up into the orchestra determined to be in on the success."[35] Quickly, Europe got over his surprise and counted off "The Clef Club March" and began his intervention into one of the elite cultural institutions of the United States.

As he fashioned the evening's program, Europe highlighted African American composers, performing only three of his own pieces. Europe followed his march with compositions by the celebrated Afro-British composer Samuel Coleridge-Taylor and by four members of the Hotel Marshall community: the baritone Harry T. Burleigh, Will Cook, Rosamond Johnson, and Europe's assistant conductor, William H. Tyers. The concert featured performances by the Clef Club Male Chorus, the choir from St. Philip's Church, the Royal Poinriana Quartet, the Versatile Entertainers Quintette, and two performances by the revered contralto Elizabeth Payne. The vocal groups performed a variety of musical styles from slave spirituals and work songs to banjo tunes and popular songs of the day. Europe ended his concert with two of his own compositions, "Lorraine Waltzes" (named for his mother) and a new march, "Strength of the Nation," which he "dedicated to the proposed Colored Regiment," an African American unit of the New York National Guard that the New York legislature had recently counseled (and that, within four years, would sign up James Europe as one of its first recruits).[36]

Many in the audience that night regarded Cook's "Swing Along" the highlight of the night. When Cook finished conducting, the Carnegie audience rose to a standing ovation and demanded two encores, forcing Europe to break his promise. Sissle noted that Europe "introduced [Cook] to the audience as our greatest composer and musician."[37] "When [Europe] walked over to the chair in which Will was sitting," Tom Fletcher recalled, "and introduced Will Marion Cook, the applause, cheers and calls for 'speech' grew so loud and lasted so long that Will Cook was overcome. He began to weep tears of joy and when he tried to speak he couldn't say a word. All he could do was just bow."[38] Writing in the 1920s, Sissle asserted that "never in the history of Carnegie Hall was there ever such a riotous ovation that greeted the [Clef] club's rendition of Cook's 'Swing Along,' 'Exhortation,' and the 'Rain Song.'"[39]

The Carnegie concert marked a watershed moment for black musicians' cultural value in New York. When Mannes remembered years later that "a wedge in opening the public halls and theatres to colored performers had been made," he noted the reality of physical racial segregation in New York theaters while celebrating the explosion in blacks' cultural value. The folklorist Natalie Curtis-Burlin, writing in 1919, called the concert an "ear-opener" and suggested that it was the moment "colored musicians became professional." In his review of the concert, Walton stated that it was "extremely unfortunate . . . that color prejudice . . . is running riotously rampant in this country." "So," he continued, "when a golden opportunity is afforded us to show that we are no different from other human beings . . . it is a source of great pleasure to take advantage of such a chance as given Thursday evening at Carnegie Hall."[40]

The concert also reflected Europe's goals in raising the professional value of black musicians. Europe and Mannes raised $5,000 and immediately decided to produce another concert in a year's time. Noting the interplay between black musicians' cultural and professional values, Clef Clubber Fletcher recalled that "as a result of the added prestige stemming from their orchestra's appearance at Carnegie Hall, the members of the Clef Club were engaged to play for nearly all of the best functions, not only in America but in London and Paris . . . and on private yachts cruising all over the world."[41] The Carnegie concert animated Europe's agenda to raise the cultural and professional values of his organization and of black New Yorkers more generally. It also catapulted Europe to the spotlight on New York media, where he became a leading spokesperson and promoter of black music. His words and ideas, while frequently contradictory and laudably open-minded, also worked to homogenize black and white New Yorkers' conceptions of Negro music.

CIRCULATING THE DISCOURSE OF BLACK AUTHENTICITY

After the Carnegie concerts, Europe became a leading public authority on Negro music.[42] Europe had two primary goals as a music critic: to argue for the racial distinctiveness of ragtime and to promote his Clef Club ensembles. Both goals reflect Europe's commercial strategies, as well as his growing sense of himself as a spokesman for black Americans. "Music breathes the spirit of a race," Europe told the *Evening Post* in 1914, "and, strictly speaking, it is a part only of the race which creates it."[43] In his interviews with the white press, Europe distilled the various attitudes and promotional strategies he had found at the Hotel Marshall. Like Cook, he championed a cultural nationalism; like Aida Overton Walker, he counseled pride in blackness; and like Rosamond Johnson, Europe pushed for new developments in black music. And he promoted his orchestra as the culmination of Cook's and Johnson's goals a decade earlier: to utilize the technical practices of European art music to concoct new styles of modern Negro music. He stressed that his was a new type of American ensemble, one that could not be evaluated by traditional European standards. Europe rejected, in fact, evaluations of Clef Club performances that did not grant his uniquely racial ingenuity.

The third Clef Club performance at Carnegie Hall, on March 11, 1914, sparked a debate about the merits of black music. In his review, a white critic for *Musical America* took Europe to task for conflating "serious music" with "popular music." The concert, "though more creditable than the two previous," the critic charged, "fell short once more of the serious purpose to which these talents might be directed." Europe's "National Negro March" "proved to be a regulation march *á la* Sousa, devoid of even a single negro characteristic," he asserted, while Burleigh, "after distinguishing himself by singing his spirituals, spoiled his contribution to the musical excellence of the program by singing the popular, 'Why Adam Sinned.'" Like the white critics of Williams and Walker a decade earlier, *Musical America* leveled contradictory criticism: on the one hand, the concert was not black enough; on the other, it failed to live up to the standards of serious music. There was no middle road, no room for Europe's sonic hybridity or racial cross-pollination. Ultimately, the critic advised the Clef Club to include "a movement or two of a Haydn symphony . . . in its next concert" and suggested that "if the composers . . . will write short movements for orchestra, basing them on classical models, next year's concert will inaugurate a new era for the Negro musician in New York and will aid him in being appraised at his full value and in being taken seriously."[44]

This criticism marks an early instance of a white critic assessing African Americans' music (of the nonspiritual variety) by traditional European standards. If the critic did not completely accept the Clef Club by those standards, he legitimated Europe's performance—to a degree—by acknowledging Europe's intentions. Reflecting a racial double standard, the instruction to create works in the style of Haydn was inconsistent. It acknowledged Europe's distance from formal music and, implicitly, African Americans' own distance from white Americans and Europeans' civilized culture. At the same time, it granted a potential. James Europe, the critic implied, *could* create in Haydn's image. The suggestion that African Americans had the intellectual and creative capacities to learn, master, and perform Haydn indicates a significant development since Trotter's writings in the 1870s. The Clef Club concert at Carnegie Hall illustrated that African Americans could indeed create music of the highest order. That musicians like Europe continued to compose ragtime came increasingly to be understood as a choice, a black aesthetic evaluation of sound and meaning.

Europe responded to the *Musical America* by highlighting what he saw as the Clef Club's racially distinct performance practices and rejecting traditional Eurocentric evaluations of it.[45] Pointing out that some of the "melodies we played Wednesday [at Carnegie] were made up by the slaves of the old days, and others were handed down from the days before we left Africa," Europe underscored the difference between his orchestra and the European standard, while alluding to white contempt for that difference: "[Some] would doubtless laugh at the way our Negro Symphony is organized, the distribution of the pieces, and our methods of organization." Europe refuted critics who would only evaluate his music by European aesthetic values: "We have developed a kind of symphony music that no matter what else you think, is different and distinctive, and lends itself to the playing of the peculiar compositions of our race."[46] Europe wanted the respect of white art critics and artists, but he did not align himself strictly with that tradition. He believed he offered new approaches to African American composition, performance, and orchestration. His was the sound of modern blackness.

Europe's public stance as a spokesperson for Negro music combined an artful mix of race consciousness, savvy self-promotion, and an ability to tell white Americans what they wanted to hear. Europe explained his success by highlighting that he stuck to "the music of my own people." "You see," Europe told the *Evening Post*, "we colored people have our own music that is part of us. . . . It's us, it's the product of our souls: it's been created by the sufferings and miseries of our race."[47] In this instance, Europe seemed to imply that social conditions helped shape the sound of black music. As the Fisk Jubilee Singers and their supporters had maintained in the 1870s and 1880s, post-emancipation styles of black music derived from the foundational experience of slavery, a perception Europe agreed with. Likening African Americans' music to other peoples' folk music, Europe told the *Tribune* that the "negro's songs are the expression of the hopes and joys and fears of his race." Prior to the Civil War, Europe explained, slave songs were "the only method he possessed of answering back his boss. Into his songs he poured his heart, and, while the boss did not understand, the negro's soul was calmed."[48] Slave music not only expressed the striving souls of a folk; it also acted functionally, as slave communication and soul-calming catharsis. Yet Europe's conception of Negro music sometimes took on more rigid trappings than these historical and social explanations.

On at least one occasion, Europe appealed to biology to explain African Americans' musical predilections. The "mouth of a negro," he hypothesized to the *Evening Post*, "is so shaped that it is exceedingly difficult to make him more than a passable player of the French horn."[49] This assertion seems to suggest Europe had partially internalized American racial ideologies that taught of the inherent, biological differences between blacks and whites. In some ways, Europe's reliance on biological determinism reflects the logical outgrowth of the Hotel Marshall community's own strategic racialism. The musicians of Black Bohemia spent the first decade of the twentieth century laying claim to Negro music and demonstrating its essential racial and rhythmic underpinnings. To a degree, therefore, Europe was telling his white interviewers what they already took as common sense. Like Bert Williams's blackface routine and Ernest Hogan's coon songs, Europe selectively reinforced aspects of white Americans' racialism to call attention to other items on his agenda. Speaking to New York's white print media, he had a booking agency full of black musicians to promote.

Using his growing authority in the New York press, Europe advocated for the Clef Club as much as he articulated ideas of black musical distinction and racial pride. "All of my men are ambitious," he told the *Evening Post*; "they take to symphonic work with enthusiasm. To give an idea of this, let me say that every member of the orchestra that played at Carnegie Hall the other night had been playing throughout the city, and after the concert was over every man was obliged to hurry back to take up the work of accompanying the tango dancers again." Making it clear how well established Clef Club musicians were, Europe advertised that the "members of the orchestra are all members of my staff of dance musicians who play at the principal hotels and at private dances in this city and out of town," and he pointed out that he furnished the "dance music for the resorts at Aiken [Georgia], Palm Beach, and other places."[50] He told the *Tribune*, "I supply at present a majority of the orchestras which play in the various cafes of the city and also at the private dances. Our negro musicians have nearly cleared the field of the so-called gypsy orchestras."[51]

Europe's strategies to promote the Clef Club often overlapped with his considerations of race and cultural authenticity. It seems as though whenever he had the outlet, Europe made his case for why his bands dominated New York's social dance circuits. "Our people," he suggested, "have a monopoly on this kind of work, for the simple reason that the negro has an inimitable ear for time in dancing."[52] He showcased that African Americans orchestrated the Manhattan musical marketplace in ways that further reinforced the fact that his bands were the best in New York. But Europe's claims of racial ownership of Negro music were not all self-promotion either. Much like Williams and Walker wrestled the mantle of black authenticity away from white blackface minstrels, Europe maintained strict distinctions between the types of music black and white Americans could play.

Further invoking the logic of Jim Crow, Europe emphasized the double edge that belief in natural and inherent racial distinction wrought. He explained his success as a band leader and conductor by highlighting that his symphony orchestra "never tries to play white folks' music." Europe doubled down on the idea that race and racial music could not mix. "I know of no white man who has written Negro music that rings true," he claimed. "Indeed, how could such a thing be possible?" "There is a great deal of alleged Negro music by white composers but it is not real," Europe argued. "Even the Negro ragtime music of white composers falls far short of the genuine dance compositions of Negro musicians." Europe allowed that whites had their own cultural legacies and seemingly innate, racial artistic predilections. Yet he seemed to do so to claim his own racial ownership over ragtime in ways that denied it to whites. "I know that my musicians could not begin to rival white men at interpreting the creations of white composers. . . . It is not in us. . . . And in the same way, what white orchestra could render the music of Will Marion Cook or Rosamond Johnson or the old plantation and spiritual melodies?" That is why, in "playing symphonic music we are careful to play only the work of our own composers."[53] Ragtime belonged to blacks, along with the economic earnings and social prestige that developed with it. Whites could not play ragtime. They could not authentically participate in the performance of America's most popular music style, nor garner its fiscal rewards. Like Cook, Europe saw stark and readily apparent differences between racial approaches to music making. When Europe voiced this type of strategic racial essentialism, however, he sometimes reinforced the racial assumptions of the white press.

In the introduction of the *Evening Post* piece, an interviewer celebrated Europe's ability to perform both symphonic music and popular music. "In some ways," he began, "James Reese Europe is one of the most remarkable men, not only of his race, but in the music world of this country. A composer of some note . . . he is the head of an organization which practically controls the furnishing of music for the new dances, and at the same time, he is able [to] expend considerable energy upon the development of the Negro Symphony Orchestra." "Unaided," the critic proclaimed, Europe "has been able to accomplish what white musicians said was impossible: the adaptation of negro music and musicians to symphonic purposes." This certainly made for excellent press for the Clef Club. But Europe also left the reporter with an impression of racial stability that he—and many other black musicians—in fact hoped to undermine.

His rhetorical strategy reinforced the interviewer's assumptions of the fixed and inherent nature of racial difference. Europe's "attitude," the reporter summed up, "is that in his own musical field the negro is safe from all competition, so why should he go to the useless task of attempting to interpret music that is foreign to all the elements in his character?"[54] As Europe himself had stated clearly, black music was the exclusive province of black people; white music, as whites' own cultural expression, could only ever be "foreign" to African Americans. This did not mean that Europe was ready to forego African Americans' central role in the production of cultural pluralism in the United States, though. Europe sought to intervene in turn-of-the-twentieth century debates about the sound, shape, and meaning of American national culture.

In the second decade of the 1900s, black New Yorkers continued to discuss African Americans' foundational influence on American music. Lester Walton began his first *New York Age* column of 1914 with an article entitled simply, "Negro Music." Walton reported on Will Marion Cook and

Harry T. Burleigh's new Negro Choral Society and used the occasion to argue for African Americans' central place in the development of American music, even suggesting that African Americans would announce the cultural awakening of the United States to the world. "It would not be surprising," he wrote, "if in the days to be[,] America gained a high place in the musical world through Negro music." Noting American political and cultural elites' anxieties over the lack of "American culture" in the early twentieth century, Walton contrasted the United States against European countries' cultural nationalisms: "To-day this country has little to exult over as a worthy contributor to musical literature. When we attend the opera we sit and listen to the works of Germans, Italians, or French writers; and our most ambitious attempt to produce an American grand opera—'the Girl from the Golden West'—the music of which was written by a foreigner, cannot be classed as an unquestioned success. Maybe David Mannes, Kurt Schindler and other white musicians of high standing possess the same perspective as Harry Burleigh, Will Marion Cook and a few other colored musicians, and sincerely believe that some day Negro music will come into its own and make agreeable history for the race for America."[55] Black music, Walton believed, represented the key to national growth and the development of a more pluralistic United States. Europe agreed, and his successes in New York granted him outlets to voice his convictions.

Europe was invested in being an active player in the circulation of a national American music. Echoing Dvořák two decades earlier, Europe suggested to the *Tribune* that "the negro's songs . . . are the only folk music America possesses, and, folk music being the basis of so much that is most beautiful in the world, there is indeed hope for the art product of our race."[56] In 1915, Europe told the *Age* that "perhaps it is fair to say that the Negro has contributed to American music whatever distinctive quality it possesses."[57] But like Cook, Rosamond Johnson, and Dvořák, Europe thought that African Americans must continue to develop their musical approaches and composition skills before truly being able to represent the American nation.

Europe emphasized the need for black musicians to develop their musicality in the service of developing a "new school of music" in the United States. "I firmly believe that there is a big field for the development of negro music in America. . . . What the negro needs is technical education, and this he is handicapped in acquiring. . . . I believe it is in the creation of an entirely new school of music, a school developed from the basic negro rhythm and melodies."[58] But this development would not be easy.

Besides the lack of public funding and interest in blacks' musical development, African Americans themselves sometimes seemed, to Europe, ill prepared for the task. He explained to one interviewer how he scoured the globe in search of excellent black musicians to add to his orchestra. He claimed to have recruited two French horn players from South Africa (where "prolonged training" had produced "satisfactory players") and an oboe player from Sudan (where British regimental bands trained African recruits "rigorously" from young ages): "That is the only way to fit a negro for orchestral work," Europe maintained. "Our people are not naturally painstaking. . . . It takes a lot of training to develop a sense of time and delicate harmony."[59] In this case, "time" meant rhythmic timekeeping. Europe might have often appealed to blacks' natural rhythms, but that did not mean they could naturally master any type of rhythmic practice. They had to practice to play European symphonic rhythms. Nonetheless, Europe gave examples of black mastery of European practices. "I have at least two violinists and a cellist who, I venture to say, are equal to any in town," he told the *Post*. Europe presented Clef Club musicians as both "instinctively good" and "well trained," while confirming that his two hundred–plus players hoped to be involved in the development of African American—and by extension, American—music. "Every man is proud of his part," Europe asserted, "in building up a representative school of real negro music that is worth while." Ultimately, Europe echoed Cook's sense of black cultural nationalism: "We must strike out for ourselves, we must develop our own ideas, and conceive an orchestration adapted to our own abilities."[60]

IT IS A TESTAMENT to the powers of commodification that African Americans' multifarious cultural forms at the turn of the twentieth century could become known as a singular black culture. It is also, of course, an indication of the narrow limits within which American culture industries and consumers understood black Americans. Like the diversity of black cultural commodities themselves, African Americans had been yoked to a racial essentialism that necessitated all blacks being fundamentally "the same": necessarily segregated, disenfranchised, and discriminated against. After the Clef Club concerts, popular conceptions of Negro music, among black and white New Yorkers, increasingly denoted not the ragtime commodities of song sheets, cakewalk steps, and blackface musical theater—commodities forged through new American culture industries and sold in expanding marketplaces across the country and reflective of U.S. national commercial culture—but the innate and natural cultural expressions of black people. Instead of a product produced and sold primarily to make money, ragtime culture was becoming the exclusive property of African Americans. "Authentic Negro music" indicated an essential racial form, rather than myriad musical stylings. Because Europe emphasized ragtime rhythms so thoroughly in his orchestra—indeed, as he discussed the racial character of both his orchestra and ragtime more generally in the white press—his Clef Club Orchestra concerts facilitated the historical process turning Negro music from a varied aggregation of sound, style, and meaning into a racially specific style of music.

Europe's emergence as a major player in the Manhattan musical marketplace underlines important developments occurring in the city. After the passing of Cole, Walker, and Hogan, African American culture became less represented on the theater stage than on the dance floor and in the concert hall. This did not result solely from Europe's influence—indeed, he could not have anticipated the deaths of leading Hotel Marshall players or those of their theater companies, nor the effect their deaths would have on blacks' place in American culture industries. But Europe capitalized on opportunities to break into social dance markets more than anyone else in America before World War I. Although never completely divorced from minstrel performance and its cultural legacies, Europe's music, uplift agenda, and professionalism challenged normative representations of African Americans throughout New York and the United States more broadly. As Europe both reinforced and challenged stereotypical understandings of black culture, he continued to seduce white cultural elites by fulfilling their assumptions about the natural and inherent racial difference. Simultaneously, Europe promoted ideas about what he saw as racial authenticity and the unique musical attributes of his race. Even as he incorporated the pulsating rhythmic sounds of banjos, guitars, and mandolins into his symphony orchestra and created a hybrid amalgamation of American music, he understood the Clef Club as a black ensemble, and he sold the idea of essential Negro music in a marketplace already thriving on notions of racial difference.

Europe's Clef Club Symphony Orchestra calls attention to black musicians' interactions in commercial markets. The market was where black music was sold, but it was also where the meanings of black music took form. Market demands and racial expectations informed black musicians' creativity as much as the musicians themselves fueled the marketplaces' ability to buy, sell, distribute, and commodify new black sounds. The Clef Club concerts and their aftermath in the press indicate some of the ways Europe took advantage of black music's growing popularity in the city and throughout America. The concerts also demonstrate how Manhattan music markets both circumscribed and influenced his artistic visions. Mass consumer markets opened up unprecedented opportunities to advance new artistic stylings and racially progressive representations of black America, even as they followed the contours of a Jim Crow society. In the years after the Carnegie concerts, Europe continued to build on his early successes. Forging a partnership with New York's leading promoters of social dance, he introduced growing numbers of white New Yorkers to the sounds of ragtime and raised the social status of black musicians as he continued to increase their fiscal worth.

CHAPTER SEVEN

A NEW TYPE OF NEGRO

MUSICIAN

Social Dance and Black Musical Value

in Prewar America

In the fall of 1915, a white musician wrote what James Weldon Johnson called a "pitiful wail" to the editor of the *Globe*, asking, "Sir—why does society prefer the Negro musician?"[1] Eugene De Bueris spoke for many as he expressed his dismay, comparing a "Negro 'so-called' musician, who hasn't the slightest conception of music" to the "Caucasian musician, who has spent well nigh a fortune—aside from numerous years of painstaking study." Without mentioning the performers by name, De Bueris asked why the popular and white social dancers, Irene and Vernon Castle, relied exclusively on James Reese Europe's African American society orchestras for their musical accompaniment. "Why," De Bueris asked, "should a famous dancing couple prefer a Negro orchestra for their dancing exhibitions?"[2]

In 1915, white musicians specializing in ragtime dance music grew anxious about the rising popularity of black musicians in New York City and surrounding areas. De Bueris's letter reflects how assumptions of studied skill, natural talent, and professional status developed through the prism of race during the ragtime era. It also demonstrates that many white musicians conceived of themselves as better than black musicians due to their environment and heredity, their training, and their sense of racial entitlement. De Bueris could not imagine that African Americans too had "painstakingly stud[ied]" music and developed a systematic "conception of music." Like many of the black musicians against whom he competed in the Manhattan musical marketplace, De Bueris believed that

African Americans' music derived from natural, innate talent. Yet unlike black musicians, he could not understand why ragtime consumers would choose black over white. Arguing against the common sensibility that black musicians played ragtime better than whites, De Bueris wrote that "surely it isn't because of the oft-refuted contention that ragtime music demands the Negro musician, for the white musician has proven time and time again that he can render a ragtime selection better than the Negro."[3] Having noted De Bueris's letter to the *Globe*, the *New York Age* responded with the ire and irony of James Weldon Johnson and, a week later, of James Reese Europe himself.

A veteran of Tin Pan Alley songwriting and the brother of Rosamond Johnson, still a leading black composer in New York, Johnson leapt into the debate using racial rhetoric like a fist. Historicizing the popular dances of the 1910s as approximations of older, black dance styles, Johnson argued that African Americans were better at performing ragtime song and dance because they originated it. The "dance steps debutantes are now learning," Johnson told De Bueris, "have been known among Negroes for years." It is "only natural," Johnson asserted, "that when it comes to making music for modern dancing, the Negro musician should be the real thing." Because African Americans originated the new styles, Johnson suggested, only they had an authentic claim to ragtime culture, and this authenticity made blacks better performers and innovators.

As he argued for the historical and racial validity of black performance practices, Johnson also acknowledged the ways that ragtime music and dance increasingly symbolized modernity to American producers and consumers of ragtime. "Not only is modern American music a Negro creation," Johnson wrote, "but the modern dances are also."[4] By emphasizing the modernity of African Americans' cultural expressions, Johnson undermined common conceptions of black culture as a folk or primitive art form. Similarly, as Johnson outlined the "Negro" qualities of ragtime—origin, authenticity, mastery of performance practices—he affirmed that ragtime was modern American music. Johnson used the occasion of De Bueris's disgruntled letter to argue that African Americans were the essential producers of modern American popular music—a claim that would become a common trope among musicians and critics throughout the twentieth century, but that, in 1915, still proved quite controversial. Europe agreed.

In his response the following week, Europe seconded Johnson's assertions as he celebrated the arrival of a "new type of Negro musician" in America. Europe stated his case in a five-point list, four of the points demonstrating the Hotel Marshall community's influence: blacks were "natural musician[s]" with a "superior sense of rhythm." "The art of playing the modern syncopated music," Europe suggested, echoing exactly his own phrasing in the *Evening Post* eighteen months earlier, "is to him a natural gift." Fourth, blacks excelled "in the use of guitar, banjo, and mandolin, instruments which are now being generally adopted by orchestras playing dance music to obtain the 'thrum-thrum' effect, and the eccentric, accentuated beat, so desirable in dance music." Yet after reiterating the ideas, commercial strategies, and racial stereotypes that Will Marion Cook, Bob Cole, and George Walker had worked so hard to solidify through ragtime performance and promotion, Europe countered De Bueris's assumption that only whites worked to hone their craft, and this is what distinguished, for Europe, "modern" black musicians from earlier performers: "The modern Negro musician is well trained in his art. He reads readily, memorizes marvelously well, interprets naturally, and not only understands the principles of technique in the use of his instrument, but is remarkably skillful in execution—as is to be expected when one considers that the Negro possess a rare facility for arts requiring physical skill."[5]

Even as Europe essentialized black musicianship, he highlighted African Americans' musical development and called attention to the training, practice, and musical literacy black musicians were internalizing as they became modern entertainers. Europe also reminded De Bueris that in "this occupation, as in all other desirable ones here in America, the Negro's color is a handicap; and wherever he achieves success, he does so in face of doubly severe competition." As De Bueris grumbled over an unfair disadvantage due to his race, Europe reminded him that it was only recently that African Americans had had access to mainstream music markets. "In the last few years," Europe wrote, "a new type of Negro musician has appeared . . . due to the widespread popularity of the so-called modern dances, and the consequent demand for dance music of which the distinguishing characteristic is an eccentric tempo."[6] To understand how Johnson and Europe evaluated questions of race, rhythm, and modernity in 1915, we need to continue our investigation into Europe's unparalleled position in the Manhattan musical marketplace by introducing the white dancers who became Europe's partners.

Working within a field of commercial production where music, theater, and dance had dominated entertainment markets for more than a decade, Europe and his dancing collaborators, Irene and Vernon Castle, entered the New York scene in 1913 by promoting new styles of popular song and social dance. Since at least the 1890s, growing interest in public dancing drove the production and popularity of new syncopated music styles. By 1913, as new groups of wealthy New Yorkers began to dance in commercial leisure spaces, opportunities for musicians and musical innovation increased. By inventing new cultural products to sell to affluent New Yorkers, Europe and the Castles created new strategies for utilizing commercial markets. They also challenged established standards of cultural authority and artistic propriety within American entertainment industries. As their partnership grew, Europe and the Castles redefined how to advertise and sell both cultural commodities and Jim Crow–era racial ideologies to growing audiences throughout the United States.

The Castles popularized social dancing among elite New Yorkers by introducing what they called "refined" dance steps. Taking advantage of racialized, gendered, and class-based assumptions about public dancing, the Castles sold themselves as authorities on the proper way to learn the dance styles that African Americans, immigrants, and even young Anglos had been dancing in the city for years. In many ways, the Castles embodied a privileged position as middle-class whites in New York's burgeoning entertainment marketplace: they borrowed black dance steps and introduced them as their own innovations, something they could only do because they had access to audiences, performance spaces, and financial backing that talented African Americans did not.[7] The Castles' real innovation, therefore, might be one of mediation. They, like Europe before, during, and after his partnership with the Castles, translated working-class black cultural expressions for new Manhattan audiences— wealthy and influential white consumers mostly unaware of the origins of the Castles' modern dances.

The Castles also advanced Europe's agenda of transforming the professional and cultural values of African American musicians and their popular music, opening up unprecedented avenues for his Society Orchestra dance bands and drawing the acclaim of New York and New England elites. Because of their access to exclusive private and public spaces and their agenda to uplift social dance—and too because of the outrageously high prices they charged—the Castles strengthened Europe's position in Manhattan music markets and helped him continue to raise the economic and cultural capital of black music.

As the Castles' exclusive band leader between 1913 and 1915, Europe crafted new hybrid sounds of syncopated dance music and sold them as representative of a distinct African American culture. Even as he sold music commodities in America's nationalizing culture markets, and even though, by 1913, Europe played almost exclusively for affluent whites, Europe continued to utilize a language of racial authenticity, describing his musical styles as "real Negro" sounds.[8] As New York's leading black band leader and one of the most successful popular culture icons in America, Europe reinforced the power of black musical authenticity. What had begun as Bert Williams's and other blackface vaudevillians' commercial strategies to reclaim the name and symbolic meaning of Negro music from white minstrels was becoming a stark delineation of the musical character of a race. And whereas Hogan, Williams, and Cook relied on blackface stage performances and popular songs about stereotypical black caricatures in dialect, Europe aligned a racial sense of black musicality with an approach to rhythmic syncopation toned down enough for an austere white dancing couple and their audiences. Europe relied on, and perpetuated, common conceptions among both blacks and whites that syncopated rhythms were the essential marker of authentic black music.

As a leading promoter of the idea of black cultural authenticity, Europe's partnership with the Castles presents a paradox. Europe wielded the cultural authority to perform, and promote, new, market-derived notions of black musical distinction. Yet by 1913, he accompanied white dancers who emphasized their whiteness to distance themselves and their dance commodities from African American culture. Europe and the Castles' partnership complicates notions of a singular or essential cultural expression of a discrete race and shows how ideas of racial authenticity developed through cross-racial and interracial practices. The trope of "black music" took shape within a marketplace trading on racial distinction and the mystique of African Americans' authenticity, an idea growing in the minds of black and white Americans alike. The idea of black authenticity as a marker of American popular music during the 1910s reflects an instance of interracial cultural production paradoxically founded on conventional ideas of natural and inherent differences between the races.

Europe's partnership with the Castles animated Americans' interest in the popular music coming out of New York City in the second decade of the twentieth century. It also reinforced African American musicians' incomparable status within the nationalizing commercial markets growing out of Manhattan. As such, the notions of black musical authenticity that Hotel Marshall musicians had constructed, debated, and promoted since the late nineteenth century, circulated out of Manhattan entertainment markets and across the United States during the years prior to World War I. The ways that African Americans like Europe used America's burgeoning mass consumer markets to both sell the idea of black musical exceptionalism and promote ideas of authentic Negro music set the stage for the arrival of jazz music from New Orleans and Chicago, as well as for the arrival of "race records" during the war years and the 1920s.

SOCIAL DANCE IN NEW YORK CITY

In the second week of 1914, the *New York Age* entertainment columnist Lester Walton described an unprecedented event. "Last Monday afternoon," Walton wrote, "for the first time in the history of New York, theatre-goers witnessed the unusual spectacle of a colored orchestra playing in the pit of a first class theatre for white artists." Walton explained that this unorthodox occurrence happened not once, but twice in a single afternoon. At both Hammerstein's Victoria Theatre and the Palace Theatre, white audiences listened to a black band as it accompanied white dancers. "Such an unusual condition was due to the insistence of Mr. and Mrs. Vernon Castle, known in the Four Hundred as society dancers, that James Reese Europe's Society Orchestra play their dance music."[9] The Castles surely demanded Europe's dance orchestra because they admired its innovative sounds and Europe's skill as a conductor. Yet by 1913, Europe and his various iterations of African American music ensembles had been playing for affluent white New Yorkers for more than a decade. Through his organizing of New York musicians, his self-promotion and branding of the Clef Club, and his artistic ingenuity, Europe had become one of New York's leading musicians. His position at the top of the Manhattan musical marketplace surely caught the attention of the Castles who themselves banked on the popularity of social dancing in New York as they sought to establish new careers for themselves.

By partnering with the Castles, Europe continued to expand his musicians' professional and cultural values as he advanced progressive representations of black music throughout the city and, increasingly, the United States as well. In 1914, Europe's Society Dance Orchestra toured from Boston to Portland, Oregon, as the Castles' exclusive accompaniment and recorded four phonographs (eight songs) for the Victor Talking Machine Company, becoming the first black band in the studio. (Previous African Americans who recorded did so as vocal groups and small instrumental duos and trios.[10]) Europe's unique position as the exclusive musical director for the nation's premier social dancers offered him new possibilities as both a professional entertainer and an

196   *Social Dance and Black Musical Value in Prewar America*

authority on the meanings of modern African American music styles. The partnership also continued to shift popular representations of black music toward Europe's image, one that paralleled the Castles' agenda to elevate the public perception of social dancing. Until Vernon Castle returned to his native England to serve as a fighter pilot in early 1916, Europe's Society Orchestra would accompany the Castles on a multi-pronged intervention into American popular entertainment markets.

The emergence of James Reese Europe and the Castles as leading proponents of social dancing paralleled the growth of commercial markets for ragtime song and dance during the 1910s in New York and other northeastern urban areas. By 1910, there were more than five hundred dance halls, nightclubs, and saloons throughout New York City, and between 1912 and 1914, New York dancers engaged in more than one hundred new styles of dance, most of them based on the simple one-step, which only required dancers to walk one step to each beat of the music, creating a bouncing, trotting effect. So simple was the footwork that the one-step quickly evolved into an entire range of dances wherein arms, torsos, necks, and heads could move in any variety of ways, giving birth to "tough dancing" and the "animal dances." These new dances—the Turkey Trot, Bunny Hug, Grizzly Bear, and Camel Walk—moved dancing partners closer together, provoking bodily contact and gyrating, as they starkly reflected white perceptions of primitive and animalistic imagery.[11] Tom Fletcher remembered that the newly popular dances among Manhattan whites came from southern and western African Americans. "Dances that had hitherto been performed mainly in honky-tonks, dancehalls on the levee, and in the tenderloin districts," he recalled, "began to be seen regularly in New York," an assertion substantiated by Irene Castle herself.[12] She told a reporter that "we get our new dances from the Barbary Coast. Of course, they reach New York in a very primitive condition, and have to be considerably toned down before they can be used in the drawing room."[13] There is little evidence suggesting that New York City dancers—professional or amateur—did little more than interpret black dance styles that had been around for years, if not generations.

Rather than only dancing in strict, regulated steps, the one-step allowed dancers to spontaneously incorporate ragtime syncopations into their movements, a process that transformed social dance in the United States. Because the one-step dances only required couples to walk in time—a single step to every downbeat—all other bodily movements could become effortlessly syncopated, rhythmically expressive, and fun. As the new dances emphasized exhilarating body movements and put an onus on pleasure, the expression of the body—and the enjoyment of such expression—became more important to dancers than simply doing the correct steps. Like ragtime music itself, which contrasted regular downbeats in the bass register with the irregular rhythms of the melody lines, dancers could join in by keeping time with their steps and wiggling, bumping, and shaking their bodies irregularly to heighten the exotic thrill of syncopated rhythms. Unsurprisingly, this evolution in American dance steps caught the attention of social reformers fearful of changing social mores at the turn of the twentieth century.[14]

Throughout the 1890s, as the waltz and ragtime-inflected cakewalk gained popularity, social reformers, preachers, and music critics regularly denounced the growth of public dancing. T. A. Faulkner's *From the Ballroom to Hell* of 1894 and *The Lure of the Dance* of 1916 sold well across America based on Faulkner's claim to be a "Former Dance Master" who renounced his profession after the death of his sister who, he wrote, "died a victim of one of these human vultures infesting the dancing schools and ballrooms of our land." Faulkner's diatribe connecting public dancing with sexual promiscuity and disease exemplified growing anxiety about changing leisure activities throughout American cities. Faulkner compared a young woman's first dance to a "sexual awakening" that quickly devolved into a "love feast," resulting in her inevitable loss of "virtue and purity"—an analysis Faulkner made in 1894 regarding the growing popularity of the Viennese waltz among middle-class Anglos. By the time the one-step made a hit in the urban Northeast, Faulkner had gained mainstream support. In 1913, the *New York Tribune* music editor H. E. Krehbiel wrote that ragtime dances "threatened to force grace, decorum, and decency out of the ball-rooms of America," and the *New York Sun* proclaimed that the new dances were "rhythmically attractive degenerator[s] which . . . hypnotize us unto vulgar foot-tapping acquiescence." The *American* reported that "New York and Newport society are just at present manifesting a craze for the disgusting and indecent dance know as the Turkey Trot."[15] Irene and Vernon Castle one-stepped their way into this cultural environment and conspired to translate the fun and enthusiasm of ragtime dances, while eschewing the bodily contact, to sell them to Manhattan's most elite families along Fifth Avenue.

The Castles entered the dance marketplace as entrepreneurs intent on raising the cultural and professional values of their art. They emphasized their class, their married status, and their whiteness in a calculated response to a public criticism of social dancing. Born in 1893, Irene Foote grew up in New Rochelle, a middle-class suburb of New York City. Sixteen years later, while Irene was working as a chorus girl in the city, she met Vernon Blythe of Norwich, England. Blythe had immigrated to the United States in 1906 to begin a career in vaudeville, where he took the name Castle and garnered good reviews as a comic, most likely due to his unusual height and thinness. The two married in May 1911, once Irene had turned eighteen, and moved to France. Although their early venture into Parisian theater flopped, the duo gained notoriety by dancing variations of the cakewalk and other common steps from African American vaudeville. On their return stateside, the Castles found themselves at an opportune moment and began pushing social dancing into the realms of legitimacy for middle- and upper-class curiosity seekers. In 1913, the pair introduced what they advertised in the local press as "modern" and "refined" versions of the one-step to wealthy white New Yorkers.[16] They were not the only ones working to modernize and refine social dance, however.

As interest in social dance grew between 1910 and World War I, a small batch of professional entertainers transitioned into dance instruction. Recognizing the expanding clientele for dance lessons, stage performers began to hire themselves out for small private parties, as Aida Overton Walker had a decade earlier when New York high society became enamored with her cakewalk. Dance historians have documented the urge toward "refinement" among dance professionals and their patrons, noting that the ways wealthy Anglo-Americans distinguished themselves from immigrants, blacks, and working peoples shaped racial, gendered, and class-based distinctions throughout the urban Northeast. The historian Danielle Robinson, for example, explores the contradictory ways dance partners Florence Walton and Maurice Mouvet, and Joan Sawyer and Wallace McCutcheon, sought to refine ragtime dance while also claiming that their "modern social dance" was nothing like it. The origin myths some instructors attributed to American dances attempted both to jettison the influence of black dances like the cakewalk (by claiming non-black and even non-American genealogies) and simultaneously to refine black ragtime practices (starkly calling attention to white dancers' own cross-racial borrowing and appropriation).[17] New York–born Mouvet played up his Parisian upbringing to cash in on the exotic allure of his versions of Argentinean tangos, waltzes, and one-steps, dances he told the *New York Times* in 1911 were "all my own ideas—they came out of here," as he tapped his head. After admitting he had picked up the cakewalk from dancers in Paris, Mouvet claimed the rest were all his own invention: "From [Paris] I went to Vienna and created the Apache dance for the Viennese, just as I had created the Mattchiche . . . I should have come right over here to America to show the Americans what the real Apache dance is."[18] Even if the origins of modern social dance were mixed up in self-promotion, transnational culture markets, and cross-race borrowing, all of its purveyors sought to change the social meanings of dancing for fun and leisure. By 1913, the Castles had become America's leading spokespersons and progenitors of social dance—and the most effective at raising its cultural value, which in turn, multiplied their professional value and salaries.

The Castles combated criticism of social dancing by evoking so-called middle-class values and deflected social reformers' concerns that social dancing promoted promiscuity and licentiousness, especially among young women. They constructed their dance styles and their public image in direct contrast to the "tough dancing" of New York's working-class dance halls through a rhetoric of modernity and refinement. By substituting graceful gestures, ballroom-inspired steps, infrequent bodily contact, and fashionable clothing styles for the bouncing and gyrating "animal dances," the historians Jean and Marshall Stearns write, "dancing became much safer with the Castles."[19] Yet refinement was only one way the Castles defined their challenge to social reformers.

The other was through a discourse of health, which they used to combat the appraisals of ragtime dance as being a sickness or a "craze."[20] In 1914, the Castles published a dancing guide titled *Modern Dancing* and wrote in their foreword, "Our aim is to uplift dancing, purify it, and place it before a public in its proper light. When this has been done, we feel convinced that no objection can possibly be urged against it on the grounds of impropriety, but rather that social reformers will join with the medical profession in the view that dancing is not only a rejuvenator of good health and spirits, but a means of preserving youth, prolonging life, and acquiring grace, elegance, and beauty."[21] *Modern Dancing* immediately sold out across the U.S. The *New York Book Review* noted that it was "almost superfluous to add that the tidal wave of advance orders exhausted the supply before the day of publication last week, and that the second edition is already about exhausted."[22] Many in the New York press supported the Castles' attempts and often reinforced the Castles' language of self-promotion. "As scarletine is to scarlet fever," one newspaper reported, "as vaccination is to smallpox, so is Castle House to the ordinary restaurant cabaret."[23] While the Castles sold themselves as exemplars of modernity, refinement, and health to undermine reformers' criticisms, their strategy also helped them capitalize on the increasing popularity of social dancing in the most lucrative way possible: by selling their dances to the wealthiest New Yorkers, the parents of the young lobster palace set who had not yet enjoyed the new, lively dances. The Castles marketed themselves to Fifth Avenue, both expanding and exploiting New York's dancing marketplace.

As the Castles introduced their versions of the one-step to New York society, they distanced their dance styles from the working-class, immigrant, and African American groups from whom they borrowed. The Castles found their commercial niche in denouncing the animal dances and their working-class roots as "vulgar," offering their own refined versions. "Vulgar people," Vernon Castle told an interviewer in 1913, "will make any dance vulgar."[24] In her biography, Irene Castle remembered that "both sides [those for and against social dancing] regarded us as their champions. We were clean-cut; we were married and when we danced there was nothing suggestive about it."[25] When asked by an interviewer how the Castles discriminate their possible patrons at Castle House—their posh dancing school on Madison Avenue—"How do you separate the sheep and the goats without offense?" Vernon seemed unconcerned with offending anyone. "I don't dance with the latter class," he answered. "Nor I," added Irene, "I have a list of brilliant excuses." In case her excuses did not work, however, Fridays and Saturdays at Castle House were designated "society days," wherein the price of admission rose from two dollars a person to three dollars.[26] In their *Modern Dancing*, the Castles end with a final coda of advice: a list of "Castle House suggestions for correct dancing":

Do not wriggle the shoulders
Do not shake the hips
Do not twist the body . . .
Do not hop—glide instead.

The last line of the book's coda told readers to "drop the Turkey Trot, the Grizzly Bear, the Bunny Hug etc. These dances are ugly, ungraceful, and out of fashion."[27] The Castles' instructions to avoid wriggling, shaking, and bouncing registered as clear distinctions from African Americans' dances.

The Castles may have been distinguishing themselves from a whole host of immigrant and working-class leisure activities, but they predominantly emphasized their whiteness—and the perceived whiteness of their dance steps—in contrast to the black styles of ragtime dance they appropriated. As Irene Castle told a local reporter about her new steps, "There is a new one just arrived now—it is still very, very crude—it is called 'Shakin' the Shimmy.' It's a nigger dance of course . . . [our] teachers may try and make something out of it."[28] Considering that the Castles made their name— and lucrative incomes—from promoting themselves as innovators and creators of new styles of dance, this is a rare acknowledgment that she and Vernon frequently borrowed their dances from others. As the Castles attempted to raise the cultural value of ragtime dance by refining it, selling it as healthy, and popularizing it among affluent middle-aged New Yorkers, they increased their own professional value. Soon after opening Castle House, they began charging one dollar per minute for their lessons and jump-started a new industry revolving around dance instruction in New York City.[29] Unlike the African American and immigrant dancers from whom the Castles appropriated, the black musicians they employed benefited significantly from these adjustments in commercial value.

BLACK SOCIETY ORCHESTRAS AND WHITE DANCE STEPS

Through his partnership with the Castles, James Europe continued to embed himself—and hundreds of black musicians who made up revolving ensembles of "James Reese Europe Society Orchestra" dance bands—within new Manhattan music markets and old elite families' homes. In 1914, the *New York Tribune* introduced Europe has having "all but secured complete control of the cabaret and dance field in the city."[30] Remembering Europe's performances after partnering with the Castles, Noble Sissle recalled playing in "parlors, drawing rooms, yachts, private railroad cars," among the "exclusive millionaires' clubs, swanky hotels, and fashionable resorts" throughout the Northeast. Fondly reflecting, Sissle added, "I think we boys who came to New York and were in the music profession at that time lived through the happiest and most interesting time in the development of American music. We were snatched from all walks of life, from all environments, and suddenly found ourselves playing and singing at the homes of the Vanderbilts, the Goulds, the Wanamakers."[31] Eubie Blake, Clef Clubber and partner of Sissle from 1915 through the 1970s, remembered that he "learned to live in tuxedos and swallowtail coats."[32] Sissle also remembered Europe's partnership with the Castles as the "beginning of the Negro taking over New York music and establishing our rhythms." In an interview with the *New York Age* from the 1940s, Sissle recalled that at the turn of the century, gypsy bands were "the rage" at elite New Yorkers' parties, where patrons waltzed to small string orchestras made up of violins, mandolins, cellos, and guitars. Once Europe and the Castles entered the scene with their "lively music—none of this one-two-three stuff, with no in-between steps," white elites flocked to hire the mixed-race entertainment troupe. "The Clef Club," Sissle remembered, "used to go on after the gypsy band finished playing, and whatever the

James Reese Europe's Society Orchestra. Photographs and Prints Division, Schomburg Center for Research in Black Culture, New York Public Library, Astor, Lenox, and Tilden Foundations.

last waltz the gypsy band played, the Clef Club would start off by playing it in ragtime. All of a sudden, people commenced getting up and trying to dance to it."[33]

In the years after the Clef Club performances at Carnegie, Europe codified his dance bands' dance music, instrumentation, and style. His earliest dance bands for the Wannamaker engagements in 1904 and 1905 had featured small string ensembles, and early Clef Club groups most often simply fulfilled customers' requests for groups with specific instrumentation, like more brass or strings, for instance. But by 1913, Europe sent ten-to-fifteen-person bands equipped with trumpets, clarinets, flutes, and trap-kit drum sets along with the standard string-band instrumentation of violins, cellos, guitars, banjos, and mandolins. Europe's bands continued to incorporate popular hits of the day with the dance songs he had written especially for the Castles. These had the twin effect of further propagating the Castles' dance steps as well as aligning the Clef Club brand along with that of the most popular white dancing couple in the city. As New Yorkers learned the hottest new dance steps—the Castle Walk, Hesitation Waltz, or the Fox Trot—they associated the steps with Europe's unique musical accompaniment.[34] Indeed, Europe's dance orchestras received far too many "gigs"—a term Eubie Blake claimed Europe invented—than Europe could possibly attend himself.[35] Ford Dabney, a founding member of the Clef Club and a longtime friend of Europe from the Hotel Marshall days, often worked as a band leader and comanager for the Castle performances. But even the two of them could not fully supply the demand for Europe's music.

As the Castles' exclusive music director, Europe offered his idiosyncratic approach to dance music in ways that augmented the Castles' professional strategies. Like the Castles, Europe worked to legitimize and, in some ways, "refine" ragtime. But he did so less by sanitizing established popular styles than by creating new combinations of musical form, instrumentation, and performance approaches. Europe's Society Orchestra recordings of 1913 and 1914 reflect a sharp, concise, practiced, and highly organized dance band. Compared to the recordings of Prince's Band, a well-regarded and all-white Victor Talking Machine Company recording artist, Europe's band plays faster, with more precision, and includes more subtle dynamic and volume shifts.[36] Europe's instrumentation is more eclectic, and parallels his approach to the Clef Club Orchestra: to use all the musicians he could gather—and their myriad instruments—to his advantage. Where the Prince's Band recording of the tune "Too Much Mustard" is dominated by flutes and a heavy, oom-pah bass line by the sousaphones, Europe's version presents the melody with an unlikely trio of clarinet, violin, and banjo. Adding to the song's rhythmic percussion, the banjo lead lines are trilled in quick sixteenth-note plucks with a plectrum that makes the banjo sound like a marimba. While perhaps reflecting the influence of Russian or "Gypsy" string bands, this approach to the banjo sounded unique in a ragtime ensemble. Most groups that recorded during the 1910s were brass bands (which recorded well due to horns' volume and clarity) or string ensembles (either folk groups with banjos, mandolins, and guitars, or classical trios and quartets using violins, cellos, and violas). Europe combined instruments from both into a new type of dance orchestra.[37]

The well-rehearsed and crisp sound of Europe's bands perfectly complemented the Castles' emphasis on refinement, as did Europe's unique approach to the defining characteristic of ragtime: rhythmic syncopation. Compared to the heavy brass used by Europe's contemporaries, Europe's band sounds light and airy; yet his group emphasized syncopation more than most of the recorded music of the era, and it offered a more driving pulse. Europe's bands included early drum-set innovators, the most notable of whom was Charles "Buddy" Gilmore. Outside of the Victor studio, Gilmore dazzled audiences with his physical dexterity, intensely syncopated timekeeping, and vaudevillian comedic flourishes. (Gilmore also became close with Vernon Castle, giving him drum lessons and performing cacophonous, dueling "drum battles" with him at the close of many of the Castles' dance performances.) Gilmore's contributions to the Victor recordings are unmistakable, adding fire to the band's dance groove and always building to climatic endings with additional syncopations and percussive volume.[38]

At the same time, the Victor recordings reflect Europe's attempts to blend nineteenth-century European marching band rhythms with ragtime syncopation. Even with Gilmore's syncopated dance rhythms, the music does not "swing," nor does it groove much like jazz or blues. The present-day ragtime conductor Rick Benjamin notes that the music of Europe's era has a "squareness" that denotes the "Germanic" influence of marching and polka bands on American ragtime. Unlike the early jazz of the late 1910s and 1920s, which began to emphasize triplet rhythmic figures and other syncopations flowing over bar lines to create the elusive "swing feel," Benjamin suggests that ragtime rhythms reflect a late "remnant of the Victorian era" where "order and place were highly valued."[39] In this context, Europe's precision and attention to strict—and not blurred—rhythmic articulations fits into the presentation of a sophisticated ragtime dance band perfect for accompanying the Castles' own rigid iterations of social dance styles.

Even as Europe concocted his own approaches to African American music, his dance music sounded very different from the music gestating in black-dominated ragtime saloons and nightclubs throughout the Tenderloin and Harlem. Compared to Willie "the Lion" Smith and James P. Johnson, Europe's music sounded rather tame, at least as Manhattan's leading ragtime pianists heard it. The Lion remembered Europe's Clef Club musicians as "legitimate" players, contrasting them with himself by emphasizing that a Clef Club band played at the high-class Libya restaurant—the "dictyest of the dicty"—and "were not allowed to rag or to beautify the melody using their own ideas—they had to read those fly spots [music notation] closely and truly."[40] While respectful of Europe's groups, Smith considered the ability to improvise and "beautify" differently every night a hallmark of black piano ragtime, what by the World War I era was called "stride." In most cases, Europe asked his players not to improvise and to instead keep to his written scores, though he acknowledged that his players did not always follow his instructions. "You would laugh at some of our rehearsals when, in a moment of inadvertence," Europe told the *Evening Post*, "the players begin to transpose their parts into ragtime. We get undesignedly funny effects that way."[41] In his compositions, Europe emphasized ragtime syncopations like ragtime pianists in the Tenderloin did. But he integrated them into songs that included sections without heightened rhythm. As with his genre-fusing Clef Club Symphony Orchestra, Europe incorporated European classical and marching band styles into his dance numbers in ways that helped define his music as distinct in the Manhattan musical marketplace. To black ragtime musicians like the Lion, Europe's music may have sounded as refined as the Castles' iterations of popular dancing styles.

As a composer intent on publishing his songs, Europe capitalized on the Castle brand by naming his new tunes after his partners. Nearly a dozen in all, Europe composed and published "The Castle House Rag," "The Castle Walk," "The Castle Half and Half," "The Castle Lame Duck Waltz," "The Castles in Europe," and the "Castle Perfect Trot."[42] Sissle remembered that Europe's partnership with the Castles allowed him to experiment with new time signatures and tempos. The "Castle Half and Half," for example, utilized a rare five-four rhythm—really one bar of waltz time, three-four, combined with one of ragtime two-four. Likewise, the Castles often mentioned that Europe instigated the famous "Fox Trot rhythm," which they popularized through W. C. Handy's "Memphis Blues," a new song published in 1912 and one interpreted by Europe and the Castles at an inventively slow—nearly halftime—tempo. As Sissle wrote in the *New York Age* in 1948, Europe "broke [the one-step rhythm] down to the dance tempo that he personally suggested to Mr. And Mrs. Vernon Castle, the four-four time that has become the world-wide favorite that we know as the Fox Trot."[43] (Significantly, the musician and scholar Peter Muir suggests that the foxtrot may be the missing link between the

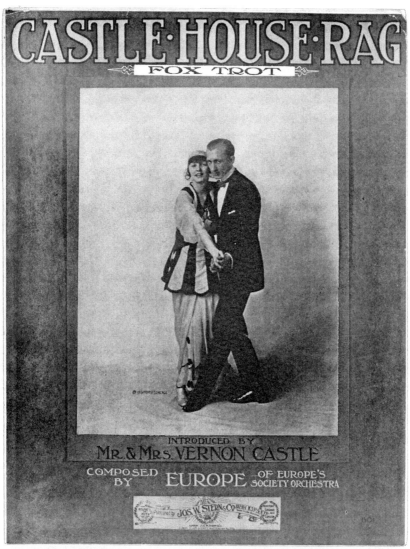

"The Castle House Rag" (1914). Music Division, New York Public Library for the Performing Arts, Astor, Lenox, and Tilden Foundations.

ragtime dances of the 1910s and the slow-drag blues dances—and urban blues musicians' musical feel—of the 1920s.[44]) Although none of Europe's sheet music sold particularly well, the Castles promoted his music as their own, and it was through their name that Europe became the first African American band leader to record a phonograph in 1913 and 1914. Gaining access to the Victor Talking Machine Company, then becoming the leading music recording company in the country, was no easy feat for any New York musician, much less an African American one.

As Europe's partnership with the Castles flourished, he set ever higher prices on black musicians' artistry. Because the Castles were both in demand and expensive, Europe could follow suit—of course it helped that they played almost exclusively for those who could afford their prices. By the time Europe and the Castles were performing their "Castles in the Air" dance concerts in late 1914 and 1915, Europe guaranteed his seventeen-member bands $35 apiece. Even the theater mogul Lee Shubert could not haggle with the band leader. "I have seventeen (17) musicians at work for you at your 'Castles in the Air,'" Europe wrote Shubert, "and the necessity of seventeen musicians in this place I'm sure is evident to you now. Mr. Castle thinks as I do, that it's impossible to get along with any less." When Shubert asked for only fourteen, Europe replied: "It is impossible to take three (3) men out of the orchestra, 'Castle's in the Air,' and still do the work required, aside from the fact that I cannot play Mr. Castle's dances with fewer men, there is the Club to be considered . . . if the three (3) men were taken out of the orchestra, the Club feature would have to be eliminated, and it is absolutely impossible for me to reduce the price of this orchestra."[45] While suggesting Vernon Castle's authority, Europe invoked his own club's standards and insisted on not bending the rules for anyone. As Europe knew well, increased wages led to increased cultural capital, which fed demands for more work and higher salaries.

JAMES REESE EUROPE AND THE CASTLES ON BLACK MUSICAL VALUE

During their three-year partnership, James Reese Europe and the Castles adjusted tremendously what each could gain from their professions. As the Castles charged exorbitant prices for their dance lessons, they helped Europe in his quest to alter the professional value of black musicians' music. By 1915, James Weldon Johnson reported that black musicians in New York earned more money on average than white musicians. Responding to Eugene De Bueris's concerns that blacks were taking over social dancing markets, Johnson pointed out that it was not because they were undercutting the competition. "The fact is," Johnson wrote, "colored musicians charge more than white musicians."[46] Years before his partnership with the Castles, Europe had augmented the professional and cultural value of black dance bands in New York City, throughout urban New England, and along the Atlantic coast with his Clef and Tempo

Clubs.[47] But as the partnership opened up even more opportunities for black dance musicians, he and the Castles further transformed the symbolic value and economic worth of African American musicians and their innovations.

Europe and the Castles were able to intervene in the value of their professions so thoroughly because they marketed themselves to stardom. Between 1913 and 1915, the Castles utilized a dizzying array of media, promotion, and business strategies to dominate Manhattan's entertainment industries and become increasingly well known nationally. Over an eighteen-month period, the Castles opened four commercial establishments—all of which featured public dancing and two of which acted as dancing schools—wrote a dance instructional book, filmed themselves dancing and circulated the film to nickelodeon houses nationwide, wrote and acted in their own autobiographic film production, endorsed the phonograph company Victor Talking Machine Company exclusively, and toured thirty-one cities in twenty-eight days along with James Europe's Society Orchestra. In print, film, sound recording, and on tour, the Castles embedded themselves—and James Europe—into every commercial outlet they could find. As the music, recording, and film industries were in their inception, during an age in which the concept of a star performer was just entering the consciousness of Americans, the Castles were early stars in American popular culture.[48]

In 1913, the Castles hired one of New York's early personal managers, who approached the Castles as an experiment in trademarking and promotion. Raised in an elite New York family—one of the city's "Four Hundred," in fact—and versed in the contours of Manhattan theater and culture markets, Elisabeth Marbury ensured that the Castles received popular media coverage in abundance.[49] Irene Castle, especially, became simultaneously a spokesperson and an advertisement for the New Woman, a self-consciously modern ideal of femininity that challenged nineteenth-century assumptions of morality, domesticity, labor, and leisure.[50] Marbury placed Castle in New York's leading magazines as a fashion consultant, model, and expert on social dance and health, where her choices in clothing and leisure spawned articles and photo essays. The dance historian Susan Cook notes that Castle "became one of the most written about and with her enormous photogenic appeal, one of the most photographed women in America." A photo of Castle in *Vanity Fair* from 1914 includes the caption, "*Vanity Fair* began its career by registering a vow to publish a picture of Mrs. Castle in every issue."[51] Due to her seemingly ubiquitous presence in fashion and culture magazines, Castle helped popularize New Woman styles such as the "bob" haircut, the Dutch cap, velvet "headache bands," ankle-length skirts, and—according to some—the girdle-less, "natural" figure.[52] Castle's self-promotion opened new opportunities as a professional dancer and commercial culture icon.

It was Marbury's idea to open up Castle House, the first and most elite of the Castles' establishments, to cater explicitly to affluent New Yorkers. Marbury had an eye for profit, and she dedicated her efforts to securing fruitful commercial ventures. Lunching at the Ritz Carlton, at the corner of Madison Avenue and Forty-sixth Street, one afternoon, Marbury noticed an empty "double house" across the street and "thought of making it into a smart dancing center." She remembered in her autobiography that she "visualized the trade mark 'Castle House'" and quickly rented the space out. Even as she began renovations, Marbury was concerned with the duration of social dance's popularity. "Time was essential as the craze might die out," she wrote. "The cream had to be quickly skimmed from the pail."[53] Her goal was to introduce social dance to one of the few subsets of New Yorkers not yet dancing for fun: the wealthy middle-aged who associated lobster palaces with their children and ragtime with the Tenderloin.

Marbury saw the "fat years ahead" if she could entice her affluent clientele to dance, and she hurried to take advantage of her unique social position and access to entertainers like the Castles. Irene Castle recalled that she would not have invested in a dance school had Marbury not told her that "some society women had suggested that we should think about it. They wanted an exclusive place for dancing, and we were not averse to making money."[54] It was a good idea. In Castle House's first season, the Castles earned two thousand dollars a week, teaching dance lessons and hosting performances. Marbury so successfully cultivated a new audience for social dance that one commentator in the 1930s recalled that, due to the Castles, thousands of "plump middle-aged men and women who had not been on a dance floor since they were boys and girls discovered with enthusiasm that Castle Walking around a room made them feel young again. . . . Today we do not think it in the least strange to see men and women in their fifties and sixties cavorting at the Rainbow Room or the St. Regis; it was the dance craze which dealt one of the heaviest blows to the theory that the dignity of maturity is dependent upon stiff joints."[55] After taking over Fifth Avenue, the Castles' next stop was the rest of America.

In the summer of 1914, the Castles organized a "Whirlwind Tour" to introduce their own dance steps—and James Reese Europe's band—to New England, the Midwest, and the West.[56] The tour was a huge financial success and boosted the popularity and social status of both the Castles and Europe's musicians. The Castles became a national hit whose popularity reached from the distant Northwest to the South, where neither social dancing nor interracial partnerships were accepted. The tour took the troupe as far north as Toronto and Montreal, and as far west as Portland, Oregon. Washington, D.C., was the furthest south the company toured. Much of the tour concentrated on the Midwest, where they played Minneapolis, Milwaukee, St. Louis, Akron, Cincinnati, and Columbus for audiences ranging from the hundreds to three thousand. Over the course of the tour, James Europe introduced his band and unique brand of dance music to tens of thousands of Americans. So expansive was their popularity that a paper in Portland cited Irene Castle's advice for health and beauty: "The woman who dances does not need other beauty aids; beauty will seek her." Even the *Houston Post* excitedly anticipated a future visit, imagining that it "is with a becoming sense of modesty we declare our firm conviction that it will be but a question of a short time until Mr. and Mrs. Vernon Castle, the most important people in the world, will visit Houston." During their national tour, the *Grand Rapids Michigan News* made news with the couple's tour intake—$85,000 or "22,000 a week"—and reported that the Castles "have 'indorsed' everything from a pair of shoes to a family cook stove, for which they have been beautifully remunerated, have been filmed, written a book on dancing, promoted Castle house, a highly exclusive and just as highly expensive restaurant and ballroom, and interested themselves in hundreds of other pastimes that made them money faster than the Philadelphia mint turns it out."[57]

Just as Europe and the Hotel Marshall community had aimed to raise the value of their entertainments, the Castles instigated twin interventions into the professional and cultural values of social dance and popular music. They were uncannily savvy about the ways dollar signs could generate social prestige—and vice-versa—and they were remarkably frank about their business goals. The dancers did not shy away from discussing finances and earnings in public and, in fact, seemed to use their income, accumulated wealth, and ostentatious spending as promotional assets. The Castles' home on Long Island, their multiple automobiles, horses, and Irene's growing accumulation of exotic pets became new ways to interest the public. Newspapers across America regularly commented on the couples' income, rarely agreeing on the daily, weekly, or annual sums.[58] Neatly explaining her interest in increasing both the cultural and professional values of her craft, Irene Castle told a popular magazine that the Castles' early dance lessons at Castle House "spread our fame and increased our earning capacity rapidly."[59] Fame signaled Castle's growing symbolic capital even as it worked dialectically to expand her earning capacity—her professional value. In another interview, Castle boasted about receiving "fifty percent of the gross receipts" from her restaurants in the same breath as she, according to the interviewer, "whispered laughing: They pay the most ridiculous prices at our restaurant, the Sans Souci—a dollar for a glass of whiskey."[60] Castle was onto something: cultural capital could transform into fiscal earnings.

Like Europe's strategies for promoting the Clef Club, the Castles traded on the allure of blackness, even as they distanced themselves from many of its connotations. In some ways, the Castles' decision to use Europe's society dance bands exclusively challenged racial norms in New York, and in the United States too. But there is scant evidence that the Castles saw themselves as revolutionaries. While Irene Castle's memories of interracial camaraderie reflect her sense of herself—and Vernon—as racially progressive, her various printed autobiographies rarely mention Europe or other black musicians.[61] The Castles capitalized on the excitement black ragtime generated while keeping blackness at arm's length, a strategy not that different from Europe's. Considering the inherent complexity of negotiating the color line in the United States, the Castles succeeded remarkably at positioning themselves on a middle ground. But their aesthetic and commercial strategies laid bare contradictions.

Given that much of the Castles renown came from distancing their refined iterations of ragtime dance from African Americans' versions, why did they insist on working exclusively with a black band? It seems counterintuitive: the Castles used black musicians in their effort to disassociate themselves from styles generally associated with African Americans. Like the lobster palaces in Times Square a decade earlier, the Castles presented ragtime dances toned down for wealthy white New Yorkers. But they did so precisely by working with black musicians. Even if Europe's Clef Club guidelines that demanded tuxedos and refined, nearly orchestral sounds helped the Castles' appearance, this does not explain why they did not hire well-groomed white musicians to play the latest "light" ragtime.

Perhaps the Castles used Europe's society orchestras because, as Vernon often claimed, they thought Europe furnished the best dance bands in America. The Castles certainly thought highly of the conductor and his ensembles, and they advertised the fact in print, on dance floors, and through their endorsements for Victor phonographs. For years, the success of Europe's Clef Club had put him on top of Manhattan music markets. Before partnering with the Castles, Europe's annual Clef Club

Symphony Orchestra concerts at Carnegie Hall had extended Europe's reach among New York's most affluent and garnered new levels of professional and cultural value throughout much of the Northeast and Atlantic region. By 1913, Europe had successfully promoted his ensembles as the best in the city, an evaluation that many in the white press affirmed. As the *Musical Leader* noted on viewing Europe perform with the Castles: "The orchestra, composed of colored men, is not made up of mandolin, guitar, and banjo, but of regular orchestral instruments, and the quality of tone which these men produce is something indescribable. Just as the negro singer has a peculiarly individual tone which vibrates with emotion and which is unique in quality, so the tone of the orchestra has the same thrill, the same vibration, and in serious music this proves very moving."[62]

If Europe's bands seem an odd complement to the Castles' attempts to legitimize ragtime music and dance, their partnership made good business sense. Before the Castles came to New York, Europe had already worked for a decade at establishing himself, his unique sounds, and his Clef Club brand so that his commercial products had become synonymous with black musical talent and the exciting, new, and modern dances. Having already done much of the heavy lifting, Europe was a perfect match for opportunistic dancing partners. On the flipside, Europe's partnership with the Castles continued to expand his reach into New York high society, opening unprecedented opportunities for black musicians to earn more money and climb new echelons of social prestige. By 1914, Europe and hundreds of his African American musicians had performed for elite family occasions like those of the Wanamakers, revolutionized Negro music's presence in Times Square lobster palaces, performed spectacularly at both the Manhattan Casino and Carnegie Hall, and furnished the exclusive bands at Castle House on Madison Avenue. Europe may not have relied on the Castles to enable his ascent into New York City's most elite classes, but the partnership helped him continue his interventions in shifting black musical value.

Although potentially problematic for both parties, the racial facets of the partnership directly affected the entertainers' professional and cultural values. The Castles legitimated Europe—and his club's musicians— in the eyes of wealthy and influential white New Yorkers, marking them both worthy of entering elite white homes and leisure spaces and worth their high wages. At the same time, it was Europe's blackness and racial authenticity that made the Castles stand out in a crowded cultural marketplace. The blackness of Europe's skin and the perceived blackness of his rhythmic music stamped the Castles with a racial authenticity few others could claim. In the case of Europe's work with the Castles, the color line allowed this interracial partnership to swell the value of black popular music, dance, and performance.

By the time Vernon Castle left the United States to volunteer for the British Air Force in early 1916, Europe had transformed the professional and cultural values of black musicians' labor. In March 1914, just three months after Europe began working with the Castles, the *Age's* Lester Walton wrote a column titled "An Economic Question." He reported that an "invitation has been extended to the colored musicians of Greater New York" to join the American Federation of Musicians (AFM).[63] Almost four years after Europe had established the Clef Club as an alternative to the discriminatory AFM, New York's Musical Mutual Protective Union Local No. 310 ended its racist practices and invited African Americans to join. Prior to this invitation, black musicians, vaudevillians, and other types of performers had regularly applied for admittance into the union and always been rejected. But by early 1914, the success of the Clef Club, as well as black musicians' increasingly dominant position as the city's leading performers of ragtime music, had irrevocably altered the Manhattan musical marketplace. Although Walton did not mention Europe by name, the lone image that accompanied his article in the black newspaper was a promotional photograph of Irene and Vernon Castle.

Both James Europe's Clef Club and his work with the Castles surely influenced the Local 310's amended policy, but not simply because the club's popularity and Europe's interracial partnership changed hearts and minds. As Walton indicated by astutely titling his column "An Economic Question," Europe had transformed the monetary value of black musicians' labor. "Never before in the history of New York have colored musicians been in such demand," Walton wrote, "and the prediction is made that owing to the present dance craze this demand will increase."[64] James Europe's Clef Club, his symphony concerts, dance bands, and partnership with the Castles revolutionized the earning potential and commercial viability of African American culture workers in New York to such a degree that the American Federation of Musicians could no longer remain competitive as an all-white union. As black progressives, boycotters, and freedom fighters would learn over the course of the twentieth century, racial progress in the United States more often came with economic pressure than with moral or political will. Walton may not have mentioned James Europe by name. But, writing in the 1970s, the president of the New Amsterdam Musical Association underscored Walton's report, concluding in his history of New York musicians' labor unions that "James Reese Europe was responsible for the [Local 310's] sudden change in policy."[65]

BY 1914, JAMES REESE Europe's partnership with the Castles had two significant effects. First, the partnership changed the meaning, value, and signification of blackness as a commercial entertainment commodity. Europe's Clef Club had organized black ragtime musicians and codified the black dance orchestra in the greater New York area by 1910, and his partnership with the Castles continued to raise the professional and cultural values of black music. More than the plays of Williams and Walker on Broadway, and more than Europe's desegregation of Carnegie Hall, social dancing changed the color and sound of popular entertainment in New York. Second, Europe and the Castles initiated a process whereby increasing numbers of Americans living outside of New York City became consuming audiences of ragtime commodities crafted in Manhattan. Europe's sonic, discursive, and racial conceptions of ragtime began to circulate nationally from the United States' largest commercial center to the rest of the country.

Ultimately, there is no clear barometer with which to evaluate the partnership between Europe and the Castles. Like the ways other African Americans challenged U.S. culture industry standards in the early twentieth century, Europe succeeded remarkably in some ways, while remaining mired in a history and society far too strong for any single individual, or performing partnership, to revolutionize. Europe's and the Castles' roles in popularizing social dance in Manhattan prove instructive, though. The trio expanded popular tastes among a wealthy and powerful urban elite and allowed for an entrance of African American laborers into their private spaces, as well as into New York's competitive commercial markets. Working and touring together, the interracial trio challenged aspects of Americans' racial assumptions and prejudice. Black music and dance, for example, appealed to growing numbers of Americans, especially those invested—or at least interested—in embracing a new phase of U.S. culture.

Yet as African Americans like Europe intervened within the Manhattan musical marketplace, they advanced ideologies of natural and inherent differences between the races and promoted simplified, essentialist ideas of black people and black culture. Rhythmic, syncopated, and electrifying dance music became the primary type of Negro music in the United States. For African Americans of the early Jim Crow era, ideas like "Negro music," "black rhythm," and "black authenticity" hearkened back to notions of folk primitivism, often doing more harm that good for American race relations. These ideas put African Americans in a box. Even as innovators like Europe, Cook, and Rosamond Johnson did everything they could to create heterogeneous, sophisticated, and modern representations of African

Americans through their studied and inventive musical approaches, they still ended up constructing conscribing and racially determined cultural commodities. Having a racial delineation for a type of music is no great evil in and of itself. But in the United States, in the first two decades of the twentieth century, black music became a trap from which its originators would never escape.

Nonetheless, professionally and artistically speaking, Europe's and the Castles' endeavors represent progressive, even positive, developments on many accounts. By the prewar era, African American musicians had largely disassociated their art from blackface minstrelsy, coon songs, coon humor, and degrading aspect of vaudeville and musical theater; hundreds, perhaps even thousands, had become professional entertainers during the period between 1910 and 1921, when African Americans troupes no longer appeared in large-scale musical theater like those on Broadway. African Americans' music continued to increase in popularity even as black entertainers shifted the social meanings and cultural value of their art products. Black entertainers stood on the cusp of bringing the "Jazz Age" to Harlem, to New York City, and to the United States.

EPILOGUE

From Ragtime Identities to the New Negro

On September 21, 1948, the former Clef Club member Noble Sissle introduced a new weekly column in the *New York Age*. Entitled "Show Business," Sissle excavated the history of black entertainment in the city to remind readers of African Americans' struggles to enter the Manhattan musical marketplace before the 1920s. He began his first column by writing: "At last I am able . . . to publicly pay tribute to the great array of artists and musicians who have played such important roles in the development of American Negro idioms, folklore, rhythms, and original harmonies that today enjoy the distinction of being the very foundation of all modern expressions in music [and] the dance." And he expressed surprise that what he called both the "Golden Era of Jazz" and "The Lost Decade of Jazz" between 1909 and 1919 "has been so overlooked by writers and would-be historians." Sissle ended the column by announcing that he would dedicate his "first series of articles" to the forgotten "heroes" of the era.[1]

One week later, Sissle began his second column with a headline— "Lt. 'Jim' Europe The Jazz King Is Dead"—and spent the next ten articles unearthing the memories of Europe's Clef Club.[2] Only months after returning home from fighting on French battlefields in World War I, Europe was killed backstage at one of his own performances. More tragically, the killer was one of Europe's own musicians, a man who had served with Europe in the 369th Infantry and was a featured drummer in Europe's triumphant marching band tour across the United States. Upset with Europe for reprimanding him during a set break at Boston's Mechanic's Hall on May 9, 1919, Herbert Wright jumped over a table and stuck a penknife in Europe's neck, slicing a major artery and killing him. Clef Club member

Eubie Blake celebrated Europe all his life, telling a biographer, "People don't realize yet today what we lost when we lost Jim Europe. He was the savior of Negro musicians. He was in a class with Booker T. Washington and Martin Luther King. I met all three of them. Before Europe, Negro musicians were just like wandering minstrels. Play in a saloon and pass the hat and that's it. Before Jim, they weren't even supposed to be human beings. Jim Europe changed all that. He made a profession for us out of music. All of that we owe to Jim. If only people would realize it."[3] Likening Europe to John Philip Sousa, Noble Sissle wrote that Europe was "one of two individuals who, with their military bands, did more to popularize American music than any other musicians in the history of America." "Europe," Sissle continued, "was a great organizer and leader of men" and he wanted readers to learn of Europe's role in instigating the "beginning of this most revolutionary dance renaissance in modern civilization."[4]

When Sissle eulogized Europe, he emphasized not the man's musical innovations but his role in producing new audiences for black music, for gaining access to elite white leisure spaces, and for expanding the professionalization of African Americans musicians. "I want you to know Jim Europe as he was known by every society matron and scion of New York's '400,'" he told his readers. "I want to take you right smack into the parlors, drawing rooms, yachts, private railroad cars, exclusive millionaires' clubs, swanky hotels, and fashionable resorts from the Everglades Club in Palm Beach to Green-Brier Hotel in White Sulphur Springs, the Metropolitan Club in New York and Newport's finest."[5] Sissle wrote his memories of Europe in the late 1940s, and doubtless many New Yorkers read them. Still, nearly a century after Europe's untimely death, neither his story nor what it shows us about wider themes of U.S. history have received the attention they deserve.

It is telling that Sissle attempted to revive Europe's story and that of the entire "lost decade of jazz" in the 1940s, for already both Europe and pre-1920s black musical history had ceased to resonate in cultural memory. Music fans, critics, scholars, and many musicians themselves had forgotten about Europe, largely because of the remarkable artistic and technological innovations that took place after 1919—transformations in American music industries that so radically altered popular perceptions of black music that Europe no longer counted as a leading progenitor. The phonograph recording business that Europe helped instigate in 1913 did not become a powerful industry until 1920 (and this was primarily due to black artists and consumers demonstrating the commercial viability of phonograph recordings).[6] As recording became a lucrative entrepreneurial pursuit, diverse and pioneering styles of blacks' music caught the public's ear and disseminated even newer sounds than the ones Europe had concocted before World War I: those of female-led urban blues bands in New York and Chicago; acoustic blues, folk, and "country blues" from Appalachia, Texas, and the Mississippi Delta; and jazz music in every American city. Sonically, these new styles built on earlier ones—echoes of ragtime, dance music, and marching bands resounded. But overwhelmingly, consuming audiences heard novel styles of blues and jazz as fresh, exciting, and "original" variations on the older forms, which already sounded outdated in the quickly shifting world of pop. As a result, consumers quickly expressed ambivalence about yesterday's products. After Bessie Smith, Blind Lemon Jefferson, and Duke Ellington made their marks on the recording industry in the 1920s, Clef Club Society Orchestras no longer reverberated with the inventiveness they once had.

But it was not only musical development that obfuscated prewar music in New York. In their zeal to narrate a single, teleological "jazz tradition," early black music critics and most historians ever since have understood the development of black popular music along certain contours: birth, development, and ideal form (usually, the 1940s jazz style, bebop).[7] Jazz music, most critics today in the twenty-first century still contend, is a music based on specific discernable qualities (improv, swing, group play) and instrumentation (horns, piano, string bass, and drums, most regularly). Ragtime, in this telling, is a precursor to later, more developed styles. While many see ragtime as a necessary ingredient of jazz—like the blues—jazz writers rarely take it on its own merits, much less on its own historical circumstances. All of which opens up another quandary for researchers of the ragtime era: the fact that so many historians of black history more generally still overlook the political, social, and economic work black musicians in New York advanced.

Although hundreds of books on black intellectual and cultural history of 1920s New York begin with W. E. B. Du Bois, most scholars leap from his early twentieth-century writings to his work during World War I and the 1920s. Very much like the scholarly constructed "jazz tradition," Du Bois's *The Souls of Black Folk* resounds as an ur-text of black thought, with little regard for historical context. Historians of the Harlem Renaissance and the New Negro Movement most often search for the roots of their interests, find them in Du Bois, and then rush to the postwar era, as if Du Bois's thoughts in 1903 resonated in 1923 unmediated by the debates and cultural creations of the meantime. Scholarship rarely explores the ways Du Bois's early thought resonated with black culture workers reading Du

Bois as he wrote—popular entertainers who felt inspired by Du Bois and his empowering interpretation of the slave spirituals and their political significations of the future development of African American culture and citizenship.

Even scholars of 1920s black music, many of whom are quite clear about filling in gaps in the scholarship, tend to focus on the transition from slave spirituals to black "classical" composition, overlooking African Americans' unparalleled roles in producing popular music. James Reese Europe rarely finds mention in these studies, even though his orchestra was one of the first and most well-known of its era. Will Marion Cook, too, gets scant attention, while studies of Rosamond Johnson's formal arrangements of the spirituals almost universally elide his own critical involvement in popular music—as if his and Bob Cole's struggles over incorporating the spirituals into one of their biggest hit songs on Broadway is somehow irrelevant. Hopefully, this study of Will Cook and George Walker, James Europe and Ernest Hogan, Bert Williams and Rosamond Johnson demonstrates that these musicians were very much influenced by the writings and debates of black critics like Du Bois. Hopefully too, I have properly shown that these musicians cultivated their own readings of black politics and culture, influenced by but not beholden to the racial politics of their day. They were ragging uplift, creating their own considerations of black culture and political advancement, and, with these, the popular sound of modern America.

In this sense, Sissle correctly labeled the years prior to World War I a lost decade of jazz. In another sense, however, Europe and the Hotel Marshall community continued to resonate in American cultural history through the advance of the New Negro, the rise of the Harlem Renaissance, and the popularity of jazz and blues. A bridge figure between the prewar and postwar eras, as well as a leading player in what he called "Black Manhattan," James Weldon Johnson in his writings of the 1920s pointed to the continual influence of ragtime-era black New Yorkers. Until his death in 1938, Johnson promoted American cultural pluralism, an idea he had honed since moving into the Marshall in 1901. Neither essentializing black people nor reifying blacks' culture through a static, race-based lens, Johnson continued to write multidimensional and fluid cultural criticism as he celebrated African Americans' achievements in the United States, promoted blacks' qualifications for full citizenship, and bound these two central themes—culture and politics—together. I will conclude this study by briefly exploring, first, how James Europe engaged in the transnational circulation of black music during World War I and, second, how James Weldon Johnson translated the Hotel Marshall community's political and cultural agendas into his writings of the 1920s. Both examples open up new interpretations of African American history during the Harlem Renaissance and beyond.

"Jazz" was not a word that most African American entertainers used when Europe set off to fight for his country in 1917. After he volunteered to be a soldier in the newly christened Fifteenth Infantry Regiment (Colored) of the New York National Guard, Europe's regiment was transferred to a French battalion soon after arriving in France on New Year's Day, 1918. According to U.S. General George Pershing and his American Expeditionary Forces, African American soldiers were to see no combat. They were there as menial labors: to dig, build, cook, and clean for white soldiers fighting to make Woodrow Wilson's world—the Jim Crow South where the president grew up—"safe for democracy." The Fifteenth's commander, the white Colonel Hayward, did not agree with Pershing. He arranged to have his troops don French uniforms, carry French rifles, and compose the 369th Division of the French Fourth Army. Nicknamed the Harlem Hell Fighters, the members of the 369th were the first Allied soldiers to reach the Rhine River and the most decorated U.S. force in the war, receiving 171 Croix de Guerre, France's highest military honor.[8] A lieutenant for a machine-gun battalion, James Europe fought for the Allies, even while also directing a sixty-man marching band and introducing ragtime-inflected brass band music to English and French soldiers and civilians.

While abroad, Europe made ragtime, blues, and jazz symbols of the modern American nation, becoming an early twentieth-century transnational cultural figure. Soon after the Fifteenth arrived in France, American officers recognized the Hell Fighters Marching Band's potential to represent the United States to European audiences. After a performance for the U.S. General Francis Joseph Kernan, Kernan thanked the Hell Fighters and, Captain Arthur Little recalled, "prophesied that the tour [of France] would be a great success. . . . But he appealed to the men to remember their duty throughout the tour was not merely to consist of playing music." Kernan told the African American soldiers that where they were going, "no American soldiers had as yet been," and reminded the band that "they were not merely musicians and soldiers of the American Army but . . . representatives of the American nation." "The eyes of France would be upon them," the general asserted, "and through the eyes of France, the eyes of the world." Always aware of how he presented himself, Europe utilized many of the strategies he had honed with the Clef Club: he did what was asked of him, demanded strict discipline from his band members, and performed his music at an extraordinarily high level. In his history of the regiment, the white Captain Little proclaimed: "As I watched the faces of the crowd . . . I knew that in so far as the eyes of France might be centered upon the spirit of America, through the representation of Jim Europe and his colored band, that the *entente cordiale* between our two countries was safe."[9] As the Hell Fighters Marching Band introduced W. C. Handy's early blues hits to France, their "Negro music" reverberated as modern American culture across war-torn Western Europe.[10]

In August 1918, after they had performed for much of the French countryside, Colonel Hayward sent the Hell Fighters to Paris for a single concert for the esteemed guests of the Allied Conference at the Théâtre des Champs-Elysées. James Europe recalled that before his band played "two numbers the audience went wild." They had "conquered Paris." The concert turned into an eight-week engagement during which the band performed for thousands of French, from those recuperating in hospitals to the military elite. At the Tuileries Gardens, Europe's band captured the attention of a crowd of fifty thousand people there to hear the famed British Grenadiers, the Royal Italian Band, and the French Garde Républicaine. "My band," Europe told the *New York Tribune*, "of course could not compare to any of these, yet the crowd, and it was such a crowd as I never saw anywhere else in the world, deserted them for us." After the concert, the Garde Républicaine's conductor asked Europe for one of his scores, which Europe gladly gave him. But the next day, he returned, telling Europe that he could not reproduce the music. Europe went to the next rehearsal, recalling that, "the great band played the composition superbly, but he was right; the jazz effects were missing." Europe took up a horn and showed the band his musicians' techniques, but some of the French players still believed that the Hell Fighters used "special instruments." "Indeed," Europe remembered, "some of them, afterward attending one of my rehearsals, did not believe what I had said until after they had examined the instruments used by my men."[11]

By war's end, Noble Sissle, who also played drums and sang in the Hell Fighters, thought that the music he helped introduce to a war-torn French countryside would soon set the sound track for the entire world. Everywhere the band played during their eight-week engagement in Paris, French musicians eagerly asked the musicians how to "play ragtime."[12] From amateurs to virtuosos, French musicians wanted to know how to produce offbeat syncopations and make "peculiar" sounds with their horns. Sissle wrote home that while they played the "Army Blues" in a small town in northern France, an "old lady about sixty years of age . . . started doing a dance that resembled 'Walking the Dog.'" A French dancer's spontaneous response to the Hell Fighters' ragged rhythms impressed on Sissle the idea that "American music would some day be the world's music."[13] As the Hell Fighters liberated small French towns and Europe's band performed for the Parisian elite, African American musicians staked a claim in representing the U.S. nation in ways that set the stage for further cultural development after the war.

As an editor for the *New York Age*, an early secretary for the NAACP, and a principal writer and historian of the Harlem Renaissance, James Weldon Johnson charted many of these developments through his prose. A participant in the Manhattan musical marketplace years before James Europe arrived in town, Johnson understood the significance of the Hell Fighters' accomplishments. He spent the 1920s and 1930s both celebrating and theorizing African Americans' cultural influence on the United States. In 1917, Johnson gave a paper at the Intercollegiate Socialist Society at Belleport, Long Island, where he argued for a reappraisal of blacks' contribution to American culture. Reminiscing about the paper and its enthusiastic reception in his 1933 autobiography, Johnson repeated "the statement that provoked the greatest interest": "The only things artistic in America that have sprung from American soil, permeated American life, and been universally acknowledged as distinctly American, had been the creations of the American Negro."[14]

Five years later, when he published a fuller treatment of the piece in the introduction to his edited collection, *The Book of American Negro Poetry*, Johnson gave four examples of blacks' contributions to American culture: Joel Chandler Harris's "Uncle Remus" stories (which were largely based, in Johnson's appraisal, on slave folklore), spirituals, ragtime music, and the cakewalk. He argued that these cultural contributions proved blacks' fitness for American citizenship. "The final measure of the greatness of all peoples," Johnson wrote, "is the amount and standard of the literature and art they have produced. . . . No people that has produced great literature and art has ever been looked upon by the world as distinctly inferior." Echoing Du Bois, Johnson imagined that "nothing will do more to change the mental attitude [of white Americans] and raise [blacks'] status than a demonstration of intellectual parity by the Negro through the production of literature and art."[15] *The Book of American Negro Poetry*, and its introduction, became a landmark articulation of African Americans' cultural contributions to the United States. In 1925, Johnson worked with his brother Rosamond and

Lawrence Brown to arrange sixty-one spirituals for *The Book of American Negro Spirituals* (the first of its kind to be published by African Americans). On his own, he published *God's Trombones: Seven Negro Sermons in Verse*, a collection of poetry that established Johnson as a leading light of the Harlem Renaissance.

As a Harlem Renaissance author and cultural critic of the New Negro era, Johnson celebrated the heterogeneity of African Americans' experiences, often emphasizing the historical and changing nature of racial identity in America. For Johnson, race was an idea, not a skin color. He did not reify black identity into a single type, but embraced difference and celebrated the plurality of black experiences. "The Negro problem," Johnson wrote in 1928, "is not a problem in a sense of being a fixed proposition." A social manifestation founded in power relations and circulated through science, culture, and law, the idea of race was unstable, often needing science, culture, and law to find its shape. "It is not a static condition; rather, it is and always has been a series of shifting interracial situations, never precisely the same in any two generations."[16] A result of Americans' post–Civil War social order, race was both constitutive and reflective of the times. As a hit songwriter for Tin Pan Alley, Johnson knew well the interconnections between culture and race. He had helped create some of them.

As he discussed African Americans' contributions to U.S. culture, and as he anticipated the political empowerment blacks might gain from the development of "Negro" culture, Johnson acknowledged that black popular entertainment could never completely overthrow American racial norms. In "The Dilemma of the Negro Author" of 1928, Johnson emphasized a problem that affected all African Americans, whether culture producers or consumers: white Americans' inability to see African Americans as complex human beings, undefined by racial stereotype. "White America has some firm opinions as to what the Negro is, and consequently some pretty well fixed ideas as to what should be written about him, and how," he wrote, before asking, "What is the Negro in the artistic conception of white America?" Johnson suggested two answers, both contrived in stereotype: "In the brighter light, he is a simple, indolent, docile, improvident peasant; a singing, dancing, laughing, weeping child . . . a pathetic and pitiable figure. In a darker light, he is an impulsive, irrational, passionate savage, reluctantly wearing a thin coat of culture, sullenly hating the white man, but holding an innate and unescapable belief in the white man's superiority." Even as Johnson's generation had created the conditions for white Americans to understand black Americans as a diverse, cosmopolitan, culturally expansive, and modern population, whites retained simplistic racial imaginations, more beholden to minstrel caricature of "the folk" than reality. In the white mind, blacks could only ever be one of these two tropes: "stencils," in Johnson's words, that "the Negro author finds . . . inadequate for the portrayal and interpretation of Negro life today."[17] The stencils of minstrel conventions had given Williams and Walker, Cook and Hogan, Cole and the Johnson brothers the material with which to produce new popular representations of black art and new forms of American commercial culture. Writing in the 1920s, Johnson still grappled with the limits and opportunities an increased black presence in U.S. culture industries allowed in the early twentieth century.

CONCLUSION

Scholarly work on African American political and cultural history of the 1920s is vast. New interpretations about the New Negro, the Harlem Renaissance, the Garvey movement, and the Jazz Age (as well as of the development of jazz, blues, and gospel music) continue to take shape in interdisciplinary academic departments, just as the era still fuels the popular American imagination. In *The Product of Our Souls*, I have historicized the period leading up to the 1920s, focusing on black popular entertainers and their commercial settings to expand the parameters within which we understand African Americans' creative impulses and their strategies to represent themselves as modern U.S. citizens.

I highlight three central findings. First, blacks' cultural achievements did not arise in a vacuum. Rather, African Americans' inventive creations were fashioned in a marketplace and were shaped by both commercial demands and Americans' racial imperatives during the early years of Jim Crow. Second, while quite aware of Americans' (black and white) considerations of high and low culture, black performers in New York did not adhere to these distinctions and regularly crossed them, calling attention to the socially constructed nature of Americans' notions of culture, aesthetics, and class. Third, commercial music presents an important lens for conceptualizing American history. We cannot understand many of the seminal events of the Jim Crow era without highlighting the power of popular music and the people who invented it. Not only does the history of the New Negro and the Harlem Renaissance look different after an in-depth distillation of ragtime but so, too, do the histories of the Talented Tenth, the reformation of white supremacy after emancipation, and the rise of American consumer culture. Most significantly, a study of black music indicates some of the fundamental ways African Americans have fought to become American citizens. Even as black entertainers debated the best ways to fashion new cultural commodities, they always aimed both to promote African American political power and to advance a pluralistic approach to representative democracy in the United States, one that might someday live up to the nation's own ideals.

In his influential study of the Harlem Renaissance, *When Harlem Was in Vogue*, and his introduction to *The Portable Harlem Renaissance Reader*, the historian David Levering Lewis marks three distinct epochs of the movement. The first, beginning roughly around 1917 and ending in 1922, is notable for white "bohemians'" roles in introducing black authors and artists to commercial publishers and popular outlets in New York. The second transpired as members of the Talented Tenth began using black art in the service of their political organizations (such as the NAACP and the National Urban League) between 1922 and 1924. And a third centered on young black writers and their New Negro voices until the Harlem Riot of 1935.[18] In some ways, *The Product of Our Souls* demonstrates a need to revisit these stages or, at least, to recognize an earlier era of black political and cultural exchange in New York.

A clear understanding of the social forces that shaped African Americans' production of ragtime culture between 1896 and 1919 opens up new ways to think about the political and cultural moments of the New Negro; it also sheds new light on the interconnections between culture and politics throughout U.S. history. Ragtime entertainers' commercial invention and discursive interventions not only anticipated the Harlem Renaissance and the New Negro Movement. They laid the groundwork for these social movements. In New York's Black Bohemia and Tenderloin communities, ragtime musicians negotiated the politics of respectable representation and bent uplift ideology to their own designs. They produced new strains of American commercial culture while keeping their eye on political advancement, and they celebrated the folk and popular music of the black masses without romanticizing a black past. African American musicians created modern American music as it would reverberate throughout the world for much of the twentieth century.

Additionally, a study of black ragtime suggests a series of important questions for the history of American popular music well into the twenty-first century. Explorations of categories such as racial representation, commercial exploitation, segregation, black masculinities, and class status between "bourgeois blacks" and "the masses" resonate throughout the rise of jazz, rock and roll, soul, hip-hop, and many other genres. My approach to the ragtime era is deeply informed by scholarship about jazz, soul, and hip-hop, and I could never have articulated my questions about black authenticity, racial representation, and the hegemonic influence of the marketplace without researching and considering post–World War II popular music. Yet I hope that my exploration of African Americans' early interventions into U.S. culture industries also reveals new ways to think about these later styles of black popular music, culture, and politics. While I have gone out of my way not to frame my analysis through the lens of the New Negro movements, the black freedom struggle of the 1950s, 1960s, and 1970s, and the post–civil rights era, I hope that this study's approach to key themes in African American and U.S. history resonates across the generations and will, perhaps, initiate a series of call-and-responses between scholarly inquiries into later forms of black culture. It is my understanding that we cannot truly outline the complex reverberations of jazz, soul, and hip-hop without grounding our analysis in history, a history that I believe began in the Jim Crow era. The legacy of racialized music resonates today, through our segregated consumption and racially derived leisures, even if many culture consumers (and, perhaps, some culture producers) seem not to realize it. Racial segregation remains as one of the most deeply rooted truths of post-emancipation American society, and popular culture has played a role in producing and reinventing the perceived differences and distances between the races.

One of the most profound lessons to be learned from a study of black activism during the ragtime era is the double edge that popular culture provides for producers and consumers alike. It shows us that, no matter African Americans' deliberate attempts to portray themselves as modern citizens, white Americans often heard black modernity as black primitivism—due, mostly, to the ways that whites wanted to hear black culture. A study of the ways black entertainers created new cultural and political discourses, contextualized in a historical period of both great transformation and racial reconstruction, shows us that, often, the tools of our resistance to established power structures work as the tools of our oppression. There simply is no clean line demarcating progressive social advancement from retrograde retreats into the comfort of the known and of accepted ways of life. In many ways, the story of ragtime culture workers is one of self-determination and the voluminous expressions of new types of black subjectivity. It offers a tale about blacks' transcendence of their slave past and their rejection of reconstructed black caricatures, of

African Americans' formation of various New Negro identities and the rise of black political empowerment. But that story is too neat, and history is never so tidy. Unbeknownst to themselves—and against all indications of their own self-conscious desires—ragtime-era African Americans' successes created some of the most pernicious and ubiquitous markers of racial difference of the protracted Jim Crow era, a period that stretched long into the twentieth century if, indeed, one may say that the basic contours of life during Jim Crow have shifted at all.

African American culture workers have so often shaped the conditions of their own oppression not because they were too blind or too gullible to see the true magnitude of white supremacy in the United States, but because the American power relations that govern our social order simply work at a level too subtle and fluid, too masked and nebulous, for any historical subject to ever fully grasp. Ragtime entertainers' failures were not their own. They reflect all Americans' wider failings to secure the proper legal protections, economic adjustments, and mutual respect that a right and ordered society needs to function for the good of everyone. True, as I have argued, the segregating of American music occurred to some degree because of black musicians' own claims about racial authenticity and the modern sound of black rhythms. Black ragtimers' marketing ploy worked too well—it boxed them into the same racial categories U.S. lawmakers and American custom dictated as they reconstructed white supremacy in the decades after emancipation. But it was the wider historical period and its exigencies—neither the artists nor their products themselves—that dictated the social and cultural reverberations of black ragtime.

Although the leading players in *The Product of Our Souls* could only negotiate aspects of white Americans' racial status quo, they all tried to circumvent derogatory stereotypes and disabuse white supremacy of its power. Few succeeded. Yet these entertainers imagined an American democracy that included them, just as they anticipated the future development of cultural pluralism in the United States. Few of the Hotel Marshall community claimed to speak wholly for the race, even as they hoped masses of African Americans might choose them as representative ambassadors. Rarely did Will Marion Cook, Bert Williams, or James Reese Europe essentialize blackness or the so-called "race problem." When they articulated fundamental or innate attributes to blacks, they understood the adaptable and improvisational nature of African Americans' arts and entertainments. James Weldon Johnson spent the 1920s and 1930s trying to translate turn-of-the-century Hotel Marshall debates into useful propositions and pithy editorials by, for, and about African Americans. Ultimately, like all historical processes wedded to the industrial marketplace, the varied and contested notions of race, identity, and culture calcified into a singular proposal: a reified, essential notion of "black music." Yet as they worked to amplify the symbolic power of both race and U.S. commercial culture, as they attempted to expand American democracy to include African Americans, black ragtimers opened the door for artists of future generations.

Notes

ABBREVIATIONS

HAJ   Helen Armstead Johnson Miscellaneous Theater Collection, Schomburg
Center for Research in Black Culture, New York Public Library

JWJ   James Weldon Johnson Manuscript Collection, Beinecke Library,
Yale University

NYA   *New York Age*

RLC   Robinson Locke Collection, Billy Rose Theater Collection, Library for the
Performing Arts, New York Public Library

SCRBC   Schomburg Center for Research in Black Culture, New York Public Library

INTRODUCTION

1. Sissle, "Memoirs," 17–23; Mannes, *Music Is My Faith*, 218.

2. Sissle, "Memoirs," 17.

3. Ibid., 18–23; Curtis-Burlin, "Black Singers and Players," 503. See also, Carnegie Hall Program, May 2, 1912, Carnegie Hall Archives; *NYA*, May 9, 1912; Badger, *A Life in Ragtime*, 60–65.

4. Curtis-Burlin, "Black Singers and Players," 501.

5. On uplift ideology, see Gaines, *Uplifting the Race*, and Wolcott, *Remaking Respectability*. In Wolcott's exploration of "racial uplift ideology," her analysis differs from that of Gaines in her emphasis on uplift being a process negotiated by African Americans of different classes, rather than a primarily top-down account of the problems and complexities black elites faced as they attempted to re-present modern black citizenship. Both ideas influence the shape of this study, and I hope that my analysis draws out the similarities and differences these two authors have outlined.

6. The trope of "primitivism" in this work is both similar to and distinct from the ways scholars have used the term to describe the culture, art, and literature of the Harlem Renaissance and New Negro eras of the 1920s and 1930s. When the notion of primitivism is used as a critical lens into the ways blacks' art resonated in white consumers' already racialized imaginations in the twenties and thirties, the category reveals similar insights into the ragtime era—black culture registered in many unintended ways as the work of a supposedly "folk" and "primitive" people. But scholars also document the ways black artists in the 1920s and 1930s often deployed such primitivism deliberately and self-consciously, hoping to capture the "African" elements of their past, or to communicate an aesthetic "realism" about African American life. It is important to emphasize for this study that ragtime entertainers, even as they succumbed to the

tropes of minstrel humor and racialized sensibilities of syncopated rhythm, most often believed they were creating specifically modern forms of culture. Ragtime song, dance, and theater, I argue, were not intended to represent black primitivism, but its opposite. On primitivism, see Huggins, *Harlem Renaissance*; Anderson, *This Was Harlem*; Kelley, "Notes on Deconstructing the 'Folk'"; Gates, "The Trope of a New Negro and the Reconstruction of the Image of the Black"; Hutchinson, *The Harlem Renaissance in Black and White*; Anderson, *Deep River*; Lemke, *Primitivist Modernism;* de Jongh, *Vicious Modernism*; Vogel, *Scenes of Harlem Cabaret*.

7. My conception of professional and cultural value is indebted to Pierre Bourdieu's distinctions between various types of capital: social, cultural, and symbolic. My use of "cultural value" especially relates to Boudieu's concept of "cultural capital" and builds from his insight that capital is not only a product of economic transactions; it finds expression within a network of social relations and modes of cultural production. In differentiating between the ways James Europe shaped the fiscal and symbolic meanings of black music, I want to use the adjectives "professional" and "cultural" to describe a consistent noun—in this case, "value." I could have more clearly invoked Bourdieu's language, but because he too distinguishes between fiscal and economic capital, I hope to articulate fresh parameters on what I see as black music's "professional" value in a racialized political economy. See, Bourdieu, "The Forms of Capital"; *Distinction*; and Bourdieu and Wacquant, *An Invitation to Reflexive Sociology*.

8. Lhamon, *Raising Cain*; Smith, "Blacks and Irish on the Riverine Frontiers."

9. Lhamon, *Raising Cain*, 15.

10. For histories of minstrelsy, see Huggins, *Harlem Renaissance*; Toll, *Blacking Up*; Saxton, *The Rise and Fall of the White Republic*; Roediger, *The Wages of Whiteness*; Lott, *Love and Theft*.

11. Johnson, *Black Manhattan*, 93. Brenda Dixon-Gottschild makes a similar point, arguing that minstrelsy "set the precedent" for the entrance of blacks into entertainment markets, in *Waltzing in the Dark*, 8.

12. For an analysis of vaudeville and variety theater, see Abbott and Seroff, *Out of Sight*.

13. David Krasner analyzes black entertainers' embrace of racial authenticity, looking at many of the same figures this book covers. Because Krasner contextualizes the rise of "black authenticity" in the American industrial revolution and the subsequent nostalgia for premodern, "authentic" experience, rather than uncovering the specific historical precedents linking blackness with cultural authenticity, our analyses are quite different. See Krasner, "The Real Thing." For more scholarship on black minstrelsy, see Woll, *Black Musical Theatre*; Riis, *Just before Jazz*; Krasner, *Resistance, Parody, and Double Consciousness in African American Theatre, 1895–1910*; Sotiropoulos, *Staging Race*; Brooks, *Bodies in Dissent*; Chude-Sokei, *The Last Darkey*; Forbes, *Introducing Bert Williams*.

14. Miller, *Segregating Sound*, 98–99.

15. Walker, "The Real 'Coon' on the American Stage."

16. For a critical analysis of black authenticity as a historical process, see Miller, *Segregating Sound*; Cruz, *Culture on the Margins*; Radano, *Lying Up a Nation*; Favor, *Authentic Blackness*.

17. Recent scholarship has convincingly demonstrated that Williams and Walker subverted racial stereotypes and used the tools of blackface vaudeville both to critique white supremacy and to enact new forms of black cultural expression. Yet even as they expanded the contours of black stage performance, they but barely updated minstrel caricatures of the uneducated and hapless Sambo figure and the urbanized bumpkin, Zip Coon. And when they experimented too far afield of minstrel caricature, white critics rejected their shows as being "too white" and not stereotypically "Negro" enough. By analyzing shifts in black entertainers' cultural and professional values, this study contextualizes Williams and Walker's myriad accomplishments in a racist marketplace to indicate the ways black cultural innovation was often circumscribed by the commercial and ideological demands of the day.

18. Much of this discourse grew out of white interest in slave spirituals between the 1870s and 1910s. For an excellent collection of primary sources, see Koenig, *Jazz in Print (1856-1929)*. A leading critic both celebrating and essentializing black music was the longtime *New York Tribune* critic Henry Krehbiel. Besides his many *Tribune* editorials, see his influential *Afro-American Folksongs*. For scholarly work on spirituals and white audiences, see Cruz, *Culture on the Margins*; Anderson, *Deep River*; Radano, *Lying Up a Nation*.

19. Southern, *The Music of Black Americans*; Floyd, *The Power of Black Music*; Brothers, *Louis Armstrong's New Orleans*.

20. Radano, *Lying Up a Nation*, 164–229; and Cruz, *Culture on the Margins*.

21. Ronald Radano has outlined the basic contours of this historical process, and the central arguments of this book build on his analysis. Because Radano ends his study with the arrival of what he terms "black rhythm" in the 1890s, I have narrated a specific story about the further musical and ideological development of ragtime. See Radano, *Lying Up a Nation*, 230–77.

22. On black modernity, see Lewis, *When Harlem Was In Vogue*; Baker, *Blues, Ideology, and Afro-American Literature* and *Modernism and the Harlem Renaissance*; Gates, "The Trope of a New Negro and the Reconstruction of the Image of the Black"; Kelley, "Notes on Deconstructing 'The Folk,'"; Gilroy, *The Black Atlantic*; Sundquist, "Red, White, Black, and Blue"; Radano, "Hot Fantasies"; Weheliye, *Phonographies*; Baldwin, *Chicago's New Negroes*; Brown, *Babylon Girls*.

On civilization, see Moses, *The Golden Age of Black Nationalism, 1850–1925*; Gatewood, *Aristocrats of Color*; Gaines, *Uplifting the Race*; Anderson, *Deep River*; Allen, "Du Boisian Double Consciousness"; Summers, *Manliness and Its Discontents*.

23. Du Bois, *The Souls of Black Folk*, 100–101.

24. Gaines, *Uplifting the Race*.

25. Higginbotham, *Righteous Discontent*, 185–230; Sotiropoulos, *Staging Race*, 163–96; Gaines, *Uplifting the Race*, 67–99; Wolcott, *Remaking Respectability*.

26. Scholars of black uplift most often offer dynamic and nuanced studies, and this study offers not so much a critique of the scholarship as a widening of the terrain. Popular ragtime musicians, I demonstrate, offer insight into the ways African Americans negotiated class-based expectations and various political strategies during a contentious era. Some of the best work includes Gaines, *Uplifting the Race*; Higginbotham, *Righteous Discontent*; Gilmore, *Gender and Jim Crow*; Shaw, *What a Woman Ought to*

Be and to Do; Moore, *Leading the Race*; Wolcott, *Remaking Respectability*; Summers, *Manliness and Its Discontents*; Baldwin, *Chicago's New Negroes*.

27. On elite African Americans' Eurocentrism, see Moses, *The Golden Age of Black Nationalism, 1850-1925*; Allen, "Du Boisian Double Consciousness."

28. Hurston, "The Characteristics of Negro Expression," 59.

29. Johnson, *Along This Way*, 171–73.

30. Washington, *A New Negro for a New Century*.

31. Logan, *The Negro in American Life and Thought*, 52.

32. Franklin, *From Slavery to Freedom*; Fredrickson, *The Black Image in the White Mind*; Morgan, *American Slavery, American Freedom*; Morgan, *Slave Counterpoint*; Berlin, *Many Thousands Gone*; Hale, *Making Whiteness*; Bay, *The White Image in the Black Mind*; Radano, *Lying Up a Nation*.

33. Hartman, *Scenes of Subjection*, 29. On the post-emancipation racial order, see Bay, *The White Image in the Black Mind*; Gilmore, *Gender and Jim Crow*; Hale, *Making Whiteness*; Radano, *Lying Up a Nation*.

34. Suisman, *Selling Sounds*; Berlin, *Ragtime*.

35. This sensibility, like Americans' conceptions of modernity itself, developed alongside new ideas about the American—and African American—folk. The historian Karl Miller has argued that late nineteenth-century interest in the folk dramatically reshaped the ways Americans heard race and music during the twentieth century. Due to the work of folklore societies, academics, and music producers, Miller argues, a "folkloric paradigm" began to replace a "minstrel paradigm" of racial listening. Whereas white minstrels and their nineteenth-century audiences had allowed that "authentic" black music could be something learned and performed by anyone, regardless of race, the folkloric paradigm bound racial music to racial bodies, so that only blacks could perform black music, and whites, white music. Miller notes that this paradigmatic shift shaped the rise of Jim Crow segregation. This study bolsters and complicates Miller's claims, for a new folkloric ideology was not the lone cause for new understandings of racial music. The segregating of American music—and especially the racial assumptions that produced the idea of a single, essential black authenticity—also occurred due to black musicians' own claims about the modern sound of black rhythms. See Miller, *Segregating Sound*, and Kelley, "Notes on Deconstructing 'The Folk.'"

36. Hale, *Making Whiteness*; Dubin, "Symbolic Slavery"; Cronon, *Nature's Metropolis*; William Leach, *Land of Desire*; Brown, "Reification, Reanimation, and the American Uncanny."

37. Grosz and Spivak, "Criticism, Feminism, and the Institution," 184. See also Hall, "What Is This 'Black' in Black Popular Culture?"

38. Hale, *Making Whiteness*, 8.

CHAPTER 1

1. Cook, "Clorindy, the Origin of the Cakewalk," 64.

2. Ibid.

3. Dunbar and Cook, "Who Dat Say Chicken in Dis Crowd?"

4. Cook, "Clorindy, the Origin of the Cakewalk," 65.

5. Ibid.

6. For a short history of "culture," a word that Raymond Williams calls "one of the two or three most complicated words in the English language," see Williams, *Keywords*, 87–93.

7. *Negro Music Journal* 1, no. 1 (September 1902): 9.

8. Higginbotham, *Righteous Discontent*, 185–230; Sotiropoulos, *Staging Race*, 163–96; Gaines, *Uplifting the Race*, 67–99.

9. I take as my inspiration for placing Cook in Manhattan, Michel de Certeau's essay, "Walking in the City," in *The Practice of Everyday Life*, 91–110.

10. Leach, *Land of Desire*, 48. For an excellent analysis of color, light, and electricity, see 39–70.

11. Shorpy Historical Photo Archive, http://www.shorpy.com/node/7504?size=_ original, accessed on October 11, 2012.

12. Hughes, *The Real New York*, 91. See also Van Dyke, *The New New York*.

13. Leach, *Land of Desire*, 42.

14. Ibid., 48.

15. On Gypsy string bands in this era, see Noble Sissle, *NYA*, September 24, 1948.

16. Joplin's first ragtime hit was "Maple Leaf Rag" in 1899. See Berlin, *King of Ragtime*.

17. On song-pluggers, see Ewen, *The Story of George Gershwin*, 37–41; and Suisman, *Selling Sounds*, 56–89.

18. Although it was unclear exactly what reporter Monroe H. Rosenfeld meant when he dubbed Twenty-eighth "Tin Pan Alley," legends have accrued concerning whether the name referred to the song publisher Harry Von Tilzer's practice of "preparing" his songwriters' pianos by sliding strips of newspaper into the piano strings to accentuate their percussive rhythms, or whether Rosenfeld was speaking of the general cacophony of noise and sound emanating along Twenty-eighth Street. See Goldberg, *Tin Pan Alley*, 173–74; and Suisman, *Selling Sounds*.

19. James Weldon Johnson named black New York "Black Manhattan" in his seminal study by the same name, encompassing Harlem and many other pre-Harlem black neighborhoods. See Johnson, *Black Manhattan*.

20. Anderson, *This Was Harlem*, 8–16; Ottley and Weatherby, *The Negro in New York*, 145–64.

21. Cook, "Clorindy, the Origin of the Cakewalk."

22. Suisman, *Selling Sounds*, 22–23.

23. Pre-1910 song sales are notoriously difficult to gauge, so it is hard to chart Tin Pan Alley's early growth. Piano production in the United States, however, offers an indication—the sale of pianos increased tenfold, from 32,000 to 374,000, between 1890 and 1904, and hundreds of piano companies prospered throughout the country. Leach, *Land of Desire*, 16–17.

24. Suisman, *Selling Sounds*, 30. For an excellent discussion of the transformation of the music industry by Tin Pan Alley publishers, see Suisman, *Selling Sounds*, 18–65.

25. For overviews of ragtime, see Schuller, *Early Jazz*; Berlin, *Ragtime* and *King of Ragtime*; Jasen and Jones, *Black Bottom Stomp*; Gioia, *The History of Jazz*; Magee, "Ragtime and Early Jazz"; Abbott and Seroff, *Out of Sight*.

26. "Presenting the World's Oldest Ragtime Pianist (and Black Philosopher)," undated, Eubie Blake folder, HAJ.

27. *NYA*, April 3, 1913.

28. Magee, "Ragtime and Early Jazz," 389. For more on the commodification of ragtime, see Berlin, *Ragtime*; and Abbott and Seroff, *Out of Sight*.

29. "Pickaninny" was a term to describe black children actors; although derogatory, black entertainers often used the term to describe themselves and other youngsters. *Variety*, December 15, 1906. On Hogan, see Undated article, Ernest Hogan folder, HAJ. See also, *Indianapolis Freeman* April 20, 1901; Abbott and Seroff, *Out of Sight*, 433–37.

30. Hogan, "La Pas Ma La."

31. Untitled article, Ernest Hogan folder, HAJ.

32. Hogan, "All Coons Look Alike To Me."

33. Hale, *Making Whiteness*; Daily, *The Age of Jim Crow*.

34. Fletcher, *One Years of the Negro in Show Business*, 138.

35. For a discussion of the etymology of the term "coon," see Roediger, *Wages of Whiteness*, 98–100 which follows the term from a 1840s Democratic Party slur against the Whig Party in "coongress" to the Zip Coon, an urbanized dandy character from the minstrel stage.

36. Dormon, "Shaping the Popular Image of Post-Reconstruction American Blacks." On whites' invented fears of black sexuality, see Gilmore, *Gender and Jim Crow*; Bay, *To Tell the Truth Freely*; Hale, *Making Whiteness*.

37. On coon songs, see Sotiropoulos, *Staging Race*, 81–122; Magee, "Ragtime and Early Jazz." On white women "coon shouters," see Miller, *Segregating Sound*, 41–50.

38. Karen Sotiropoulos argues that the black-passing-for-white Ben Harney's "Mister Johnson Turn Me Loose" from 1896 paralleled Hogan's instigation of coon song popularity, and James Dorman notes various uses of "coon" in song sheets as early as 1883. See Sotiropoulos, *Staging Race*, 89–94, and Dorman, "Shaping the Popular Image of Post-Reconstruction American Blacks," 452.

39. See Berlin, *Ragtime* and *King of Ragtime*; Jasen and Jones, *Black Bottom Stomp*.

40. For Hogan, see *Variety*, December 15, 1906; for Johnson, see *NYA*, December 24, 1908. As early as the 1910s, New York pianists like Willie "the Lion" Smith and James P. Johnson called their highly technical approach to ragtime "stride piano" to distinguish the virtuosi professional musicians who "knew all the progressions and can move them around" to any key or tempo from popular ragtime songs. Stride, for these musicians, differed from "ragtime" because the latter implied popular songs—often mass-produced and formulaic tunes from Tin Pan Alley—or, simply, "messin' around" on the piano. See, *Willie the Lion*.

41. Dormon, "Shaping the Popular Image of Post-Reconstruction American Blacks," 453. For an analysis of pre-1910 sales as well as the changes in Tin Pan Alley production techniques beginning in the mid-1890s, see Suisman, *Selling Sounds*.

42. Suisman, *Selling Sounds*, 37, 54. Although Suisman expertly proves his claims with extensive evidence, he does not incorporate the significance of black performance styles into his analysis. While presenting an excellent chapter on the black-owned Black Swan recording company of the 1920s, Suisman rarely centers on black performers or

their role in popularizing ragtime in his analysis on the expansion of Tin Pan Alley in the 1890s.

43. Fletcher, *One Hundred Years of the Negro in Show Business*, 141.

44. Neither Hogan's claim, nor my argument, means to imply that African American music only began to be identified as rhythmic in 1896—commenters on black music frequently noted rhythmic complexity, syncopation, and polyrhythms since the earliest days of slavery. And evidence suggests that there were continuations of African music practices and traditions in places like New Orleans' so-called Congo Square and other southern plantations, as well as various Atlantic seaports, which influenced the sound of early blackface minstrelsy. Yet the following chapters will chart how black music became increasingly considered an essentially rhythmic music in the late nineteenth century and the early twentieth in ways that marked a transition in Americans' ideological assumptions about black music.

45. Carter, *Swing Along*, 12.

46. Star, "Oberlin's Ragtimer."

47. Masur, *An Example for All the Land*, 259–60; Green, *The Secret City*, 131.

48. Gaines, *Uplifting the Race*; McGinty, "Gifted Minds and Pure Hearts" and "'That You Came So Far to See Us.'"

49. On black civilization, see Moses, *The Golden Age of Black Nationalism, 1850–1925*; Anderson, *Deep River*; Gaines, *Uplifting the Race*; Gatewood, *Aristocrats of Color*; Allen, "Du Boisian Double Consciousness."

50. On training, see Trotter, *Music and Some Highly Musical People*, 55–65. John Aveni analyzes Trotter's agenda in the first chapter of his dissertation, "Such as Benefits the New Order of Things," 23–80.

51. Trotter, *Music and Some Highly Musical People*, 4.

52. Ibid., 8.

53. Ibid., 65–105.

54. Ibid., 268.

55. Ibid., 269.

56. Broad historical changes at the end of the nineteenth century, of course, also shaped the changing evaluations of the spirituals. Included are debates about modernity and its corollary, the folk. For scholarly work on this transitional era, see Miller, *Segregating Sound*; Cruz, *Culture on the Margins*; Radano, *Lying Up a Nation*; Lears, *No Place of Grace*.

57. *New York Herald*, May 21, 1893.

58. Recently there has been a bit of controversy over whether or not Dvořák truly penned the "Dvořák Statement." Regardless of whose words showed up in the series of interviews and articles in the *Herald* under Dvořák's name, the composer endorsed both the words and the spirit of the piece, so it strikes me as rather unproblematic. For a well-researched analysis of the controversy, see Beckerman, *New Worlds of Dvořák*. For more on Dvořák in the United States, see Snyder, "A Great and Noble School of Music"; Hamm, "Dvořák in America"; Floyd, "The Invisibility and Fame of Harry T. Burleigh"; Peress, *Dvořák to Duke Ellington*.

59. Du Bois, *The Souls of Black Folk*, 186, 192.

60. Du Bois was a notoriously fluid thinker whose ideas changed much over his long life, and I do not want to read his 1926 essay "Criteria of Negro Art"—wherein

he asserted that "all Art is propaganda and ever must be"—back to his *Souls* of 1903. It is clear, however, that much of *Souls*, no matter how beautiful and evocative the prose, was first and foremost a political piece; it was designed to convince. My analysis has been informed by Reed, *W. E. B. Du Bois and American Political Thought*; Singh, *Black Is a Country*; Gooding-Williams, "Du Bois, Politics, Aesthetics"; Anderson, *Deep River*; Radano, *Lying Up a Nation*; Allen, "Du Boisian Double Consciousness." Du Bois's "Criteria of Negro Art" appeared in the *Crisis*, October 1926, 290–97.

61. Du Bois, *Souls of Black Folk*, 39.

62. Washington, *A New Negro for a New Century*. My conception of folk and modernity here builds on Levine, *Black Culture and Black Consciousness*; Lewis, *When Harlem Was in Vogue*; Baker, *Modernism and the Harlem Renaissance*; Gates, "The Trope of a New Negro and the Reconstruction of the Image of the Black"; Gilroy, *The Black Atlantic*; Radano, *Lying Up a Nation*; Anderson, *Deep River*.

63. This is a central theme in Trotter, *Music and Some Highly Musical People*. For more analysis, see Aveni, "Such as Benefits the New Order of Things," 53–58.

64. *Negro Music Journal* 1, no. 1 (September 1902): 10.

65. *Negro Music Journal* 1, no. 5 (January, 1903): 69.

66. *Negro Music Journal* 1, no. 5 (January 1903): 69.

67. *Negro Music Journal* 1, no. 9 (May 1903): 173.

68. Ibid., 183.

69. *Negro Music Journal* 1, no. 7 (March 1903): 120.

70. For Cook on "real Negro melodies," see Carter, *Swing Along*, 10; for "modern Negro music," see "The Negro on the Stage," *Theatre Magazine* 3 (1903): 96–97, 97.

71. Carter, *Swing Along*, 29–35.

72. Cook, "From 'Clorindy' to the 'Red Moon' and Beyond," African American Theater Papers, HAJ; Cook, "Clorindy, the Origin of the Cakewalk"; Star, "Oberlin's Ragtimer"; Carter, *Swing Along*, 10.

73. Cook, "Clorindy, the Origin of the Cakewalk."

74. Lewis, "Wm. Marion Cook Champion of Folk Lore Song," *Chicago Defender*, May 1, 1915, 6.

75. Cook, "Clorindy, the Origin of the Cakewalk."

76. Abbie Mitchell's excerpts in Cook, "From 'Clorindy' to the 'Red Moon' and Beyond."

77. Johnson, *Along This Way*, 172.

78. Lewis, "Wm. Marion Cook Champion of Folk Lore Song."

79. "The Negro on the Stage," 97.

80. Lewis, "Wm. Marion Cook Champion of Folk Lore Song."

CHAPTER 2

1. Johnson, *The Autobiography of an Ex-Coloured Man*, 98–99.

2. Johnson, *Along This Way*, 172.

3. Ibid.

4. Ibid.

5. Williams, Walker, and Cook even created their own publishing company for a short time. For an analysis of Gotham-Attucks, see Shirley, "The House of Melody."

6. This notion of black authenticity was new to the extent that black entertainers self-consciously invoked and advertised the trope. Yet performers recognized that the idea of racial authenticity had a long history rooted in racial difference.

7. For scholarship on the ways Hotel Marshall entertainers attempted to transform black cultural representation, see Woll, *Black Musical Theatre*; Riis, *Just before Jazz*; Krasner, *Resistance, Parody, and Double Consciousness in African American Theatre, 1895-1910*; Sotiropoulos, *Staging Race*; Brooks, *Bodies in Dissent*; Chude-Sokei, *The Last Darkey*; Seniors, *Beyond Lift Every Voice and Sing*.

8. Johnson, *Along This Way*, 177.

9. Untitled article, Ernest Hogan folder, HAJ.

10. Walker, "The Real 'Coon' on the American Stage," 14.

11. For information on the Hotel Marshall, see various issues of *NYA, Indianapolis Freemen*, 1897-1902; Walker, "The Real 'Coon' on the American Stage"; Fletcher, *One Hundred Years of the Negro in Show Business;* Johnson, *Along This Way;* Badger, *A Life in Ragtime*; Sotiropoulos, *Staging Race*; Fronc, *New York Undercover*.

12. Woll, *Black Musical Theatre*; Riis, *Just before Jazz*; Sotiropoulos, *Staging Race*.

13. James Weldon Johnson notes many of the Broadway stylings Hotel Marshall entertainers established in his *Along This Way* and *Black Manhattan*. For scholarly analyses, see Woll, *Black Musical Theatre*, and Riis, *Just before Jazz*.

14. Fletcher, *One Hundred Years of the Negro in Show Business*, 108. On the origins on the cakewalk, see Gottschild, *Digging the Africanist Presence in American Performance*, 114–22; Stearns, *Jazz Dance*, 122–23.

15. Walker, "The Real 'Coon' on the American Stage."

16. "Cakewalk in Society," *New York Times*, March 29, 1903, Williams and Walker clipping folder, RLC; Fletcher, *One Hundred Years of the Negro in Show Business*, 108. *America Dances! 1897-1948* offers captivating footage of black performers dancing the cakewalk, as well as hundreds of young whites running around in the pretense of cakewalking along a beach as remarkable evidence of the phenomenon in the early twentieth century.

17. Thomas Riis notes that Bert Williams "was not inclined towards syncopated rhythms" because his slow, humorous "parlando-rubato style of performance was inimical to the rhythmic strictness required for ragtime." Williams's non-ragtime songs distinguished his act from the otherwise thoroughly ragtime-inflected Williams and Walker Co. scores and songs, as produced by Will Cook, George Walker, and their various songwriting partners (and which Riis, a musicologist, explores in detail). See Riis, *Just before Jazz*, 114.

18. *Chicago Examiner*, November 1, 1906, and unnamed Milwaukee paper, December 10, 1906, Williams and Walker folder, RLC.

19. Abbott and Seroff, *Ragged but Right*, 64.

20. Much of the recent scholarship on Williams and Walker emphasizes the comedians' agency and celebrates their ability to navigate the complexities of performing racial stereotypes in commercial theater. This is important analysis, one that I build on as I highlight the challenges the pair faced as they entered U.S. entertainment markets.

For recent studies, see Krasner, *Resistance, Parody, and Double Consciousness in African American Theatre, 1895–1910*; Sotiropoulos, *Staging Race*; Brooks, *Bodies in Dissent*; Chude-Sokei, *The Last Darkey*.

21. Alex Rogers, "I'm a Jonah Man," in Woll, *Black Musical Theatre*, 36.

22. Undated newspaper, Williams and Walker folder, RLC—reprinted as "Says Negro on the Stage Can Not Be Serious," *Indianapolis Freeman*, January 12, 1908, 5.

23. *Majestic Theatre* 2 (May 1908), Williams and Walker folder, RLC.

24. *Variety*, December 14, 1907, reprinted in Sampson, *Ghost Walks*, 421.

25. Undated, unnamed clippings in clippings files in "Abyssinia" and "Williams and Walker" folders, RLC. There are many indications of the white press calling *Abyssinia* "too white." Sotiropoulos explores this in *Staging Race*, 158–62.

26. "Says Negro on the Stage Can Not Be Serious."

27. Johnson, *Along This Way*, 159.

28. Ibid., 160.

29. Krasner, *Resistance, Parody, and Double Consciousness in African American Theatre, 1895–1910*, 9.

30. Stuart Hall discusses this type of strategic racial essentialism in "What Is This 'Black' in Black Popular Culture?" Mia Bay has also described the rise of post-Reconstruction essentialism as the locus of white supremacist ideologies shifted from science to politics and culture. "Ironically," Bay writes, "just as the white scientific establishment was finally beginning to dismantle the racial edifice built by nineteenth-century science, racial essentialism was achieving unprecedented popularity in some quarters of the American black community" (Bay, *The White Image in the Black Mind*, 189). Wilson Jeremiah Moses makes similar arguments concerning the political efficacy of racial essentialism among black intellectuals in *The Golden Age of Black Nationalism, 1850–1925*.

31. Walker, "The Real 'Coon' on the American Stage."

32. *Majestic Theatre* 2 (May 1908).

33. Krasner, "The Real Thing." See also, Lott, *Love and Theft*, and Huggins, *Harlem Renaissance*.

34. All these names were taken at random from various *Indianapolis Freeman* entertainment pages between 1895 and 1901.

35. For more on the formation of vaudeville circuits, see Woll, *Black Musical Theater*, and Abbott and Seroff, *Out of Sight*.

36. "The Passing of the Minstrel," *Theatre* 6, no. 61 (March, 1906).

37. *NYA*, January 12, 1911. On wages, see Henri, *Black Migration*, 32–55.

38. Hogan, "The Negro in Vaudeville," *Variety*, December 15, 1906.

39. *NYA*, June 4, 1908.

40. *NYA*, January 24, 1908.

41. *NYA*, June 4, 1908.

42. *NYA*, January 12, 1911.

43. Riis, "'Bob' Cole."

44. *Indianapolis Freeman*, August 16, 1902, 5.

45. Riis, *Just before Jazz*, 28. Other historians emphasizing *Coontown* as a break from variety include Johnson, *Black Manhattan*, 102; Woll, *Black Musical Theater*, 5–12.

46. *Indianapolis Freeman*, October 20, 1900, and December 30, 1900.

47. *Indianapolis Freeman*, May 31, 1902, and April 11 1903; Riis, *Just before Jazz*, 84;

48. *Clipper*, August 27, 1898, reprinted in Sampson, *Ghost Walks*, 157.

49. *Indianapolis Freeman*, May 31, 1902; Riis, "'Bob' Cole," 138.

50. Johnson, *Along This Way*, 177–78.

51. Ibid., 179–82, 191.

52. *Colored American Magazine* 8, no. 4 (April 1905): 195.

53. Johnson, *Along This Way*; Riis, *Just before Jazz*, 54.

54. Hogan, "The Negro in Vaudeville."

55. *Colored American Magazine* 8, no. 4 (April 1905): 194, and 9, no. 5 (November 1905): 638–39.

56. *New York Sun*, undated clipping, James Weldon Johnson scrapbook No. 2, James Weldon Johnson MSS Collection, Beinecke Library, Yale University.

57. Johnson, *Along This Way*, 5–71.

58. Scholars debate whether or not Dvořák literally incorporated the spiritual in his work. For a synopsis, see Jean E. Snyder, "'A Great and Noble School of Music." In general, however, while the music scholar John Tibbetts says there are only "general allusions" to it, the Hotel Marshall musician Harry T. Burleigh—who introduced the song to Dvořák —maintained that Dvořák "used the second and third measures almost note for note, as a comparison will show." To my ear, the second theme of *From the New World* sounds very close, rather than an allusion, though I have not compared scores. See Tibbetts, "The Missing Title Page," 351, and Burleigh, "The Negro and His Song," 188.

59. Southern, *The Music of Black Americans*, 276.

60. Levy, *James Weldon Johnson*, 90.

61. Cole and Johnson, "Under the Bamboo Tree."

62. Radano, *Lying Up a Nation*; Cruz, *Culture on the Margins*.

63. Fredrickson, *The Black Image in the White Mind*, 102–3. On the shifting ideological underpinnings of racialized slavery, see also Franklin, *From Slavery to Freedom*; Morgan, *American Slavery, American Freedom*; Bay, *The White Image in the Black Mind*.

64. Both quotes in Webb, "Authentic Possibilities," 67.

65. On rhythm, see Magee, "Ragtime and Early Jazz," and Radano, "Hot Fantasies: American Modernism and the Idea of Black Rhythm."

66. Fletcher, *Hundred Years of the Negro in Show Business*, 141.

67. Magee, "Ragtime and Early Jazz," 390.

68. *New York Sun*, January 25, 1903, clippings, JWJ.

69. Lomax, *Mr. Jelly Roll*, 62.

70. Goodrich, "Syncopated Rhythm vs. 'Rag-Time.'"

71. *New York Sun*, January 25, 1903, clippings, JWJ.

72. The influence of "Spanish rhythms" in Manhattan music markets would continue well into the 1910s, especially as social dancing became more popular in New York and other U.S. cities between 1910 and 1917. In some ways, Bob Cole's account suggests that Spanish, or Latin, rhythms might have instigated new commercial interventions in popular American music in ways different from ragtime. But Latin

American and Caribbean music was already racialized as black (or "Negro") in U.S. culture markets, from New Orleans to New York. Cuban habaneras, Brazilian maxixe, and Argentinean tangos may have sounded freshly exotic, but their ideological resonances overlapped—and reinforced—the changing sounds of black music. The blues composer W. C. Handy famously included a "tango" section in one of his earliest, and most popular, blues tunes, "St. Louis Blues," in 1914. In his autobiography, Handy notes two reasons he did so: first, "the tango was the vogue" among dancers; second, he understood Cuban habanera and Argentinean tango rhythms to embody a "racial trait" (Handy, *The Father of the Blues*, 96–122). There is much more research to be done on the transnational influences on U.S. popular music in many historical periods, and further study of the ragtime era will surely lead to rich new interpretations of the intersections of Hispanic, Caribbean, and U.S. rhythms. For excellent examples of this kind of scholarship, see Roberts, *Latin Jazz*; Brennan, *Secular Devotion;* Seigel, *Uneven Encounters*; Putnam, *Radical Moves*. Thanks to Fritz Schenker for reminding me of Handy's discussion of the tango.

73. *New York Sun*, undated clipping, James Weldon Johnson scrapbook 2, JWJ.

74. *Ladies' Home Journal*, May 5, June 5, July 5, August 5, 1905. The Johnsons actually wrote six separate songs for their suite, but the magazine only published four of them. For analysis, see Berlin, "Cole and the Johnson Brothers' 'The Evolution of Ragtime.'"

75. Johnson, *Along This Way*, 196.

CHAPTER 3

1. Riis, *Just before Jazz*, 153; Sotiropoulos, *Staging Race*, 125–34.

2. In her excellent analysis, the historian Karen Sotiropoulos explores the ways Hotel Marshall musicians presented themselves as uplifters of the race. "Black popular artists," Sotiropoulos writes, "helped transform stage life and helped lead the way to acceptance of public amusements in [black] middle-class life." She is certainly right. Talented Tenth magazines like Boston's *Colored American Magazine* and Du Bois's *Crisis* regularly praised Williams, Walker, Cole, and Johnson, most often singling them out for providing "clean and legitimate" cultural expressions, in contrast to most black acts. Rather than demonstrating the ways Hotel Marshall entertainers legitimated themselves to the Talented Tenth, however, this chapter shows the ways they critiqued uplift ideology. Never wholly removed from the Talented Tenth's teachings, Marshall musicians interpreted notions of uplift, representation, black nationalism, and even respectability through their own lenses. See Sotiropoulos, *Staging Race*, 163–96.

3. *Musical Observer* 11, no. 1 (September 1914): 15.

4. Reprinted in *Musical Courier*, May 28, 1913, 22–23.

5. In an article titled "Ragtime: A Pernicious Evil and Enemy of True Art," Leo Oehmler began with the *Elson's Music Dictionary* definition of "Syncope," before noting that the practice "is probably as old as the art of music itself and has been used by great composers in all ages." *Musical Observer* 11, no. 1 (September 1914): 14.

6. *Outlook*, February 27, 1918, 345.

7. W. F. Gates, "Ethiopian Syncopation—The Decline of Ragtime," *Musician* (1902), reprinted in Koenig, *Jazz in Print (1859-1929)*, 69.

8. Ronald Radano has shown that criticisms of ragtime often referenced the body, disease, and epidemics, and Edward Berlin has categorized various criticisms of ragtime as musical, social, and commercial force. See Radano, *Lying Up a Nation*, 230-77, and Berlin, *Ragtime*.

9. Radano cites emancipation, segregation, black migration, social Darwinism, and new travelogues and fictions about Africa, as well as the expanding U.S. cultural marketplace. See Radano, *Lying Up a Nation*, 230-77.

10. Ibid., 272. Radano also argues that the common alignment of African American rhythm with African musical practices resulted from this new reformation of black music in the United States. "Increasingly," he writes, "the identification of rhythmic character in song spawned associations with Africa" (272). For more on this conversation, see Agawu, "The Invention of 'African Rhythm'" and *Representing African Music*. Writing about coon songs and their role in both creating and reflecting the transformative era of the turn-of-the-twentieth century, James Dormon makes a similar point, asserting that the "national fascination with coon songs between *circa* 1890 and 1910 underlay a major shift in white perception of blacks; a shift whereby existing stereotypes came to be either confirmed or embellished and indelibly encoded as part of the semiotic system of the period" (Dormon, "Shaping the Popular Image of Post-Reconstruction American Blacks," 450).

11. Both quotes from Krasner, "The Real Thing," 116.

12. Gatewood, *Aristocrats of Color*, 192, 183.

13. Krasner, "The Real Thing," 116.

14. Gaines, *Uplifting the Race*, 67-99.

15. Lester Walton, "The Future of the Negro on the Stage," *Colored American Magazine* 6, no. 6 (May-June 1903): 441.

16. George W. Walker, "Bert and Me and Them," *NYA*, December 24, 1908.

17. *New York Globe and Commercial*, October 27, 1905, Williams and Walker folder, RLC.

18. *Chicago Inter Ocean*, January 17, 1909, Bert Williams clipping file, SCRBC.

19. Riis, *Just before Jazz*, 88.

20. Ibid., 87.

21. Newman, "'The Brightest Star,'" 466.

22. *Indianapolis Freeman*, June 23, July 1, and July 3, 1903, reprinted in Sampson, *Ghost Walks*, 297-98. For evidence from British papers, see other *Freeman* articles reprinted in Sampson (296-309).

23. Walker, "Colored Men and Women on the Stage," 571.

24. Ibid., 571, 575.

25. Ibid., 575.

26. Carter, *Swing Along*, 20.

27. Cook's biographer claims that none of the story's sources were substantiated. Ibid., 111-13.

28. Ellington, *Music Is My Mistress*, 97.

29. Fletcher, *One Hundred Years of the Negro in Show Business*, 259. Sidney Bechet tells the story in *Treat It Gentle*, 125.

30. Tommie Shelby's intellectual history of nationalism, and especially his term "pragmatic nationalism," have helped me untangle Marshall musicians' race consciousness from more ideological and encumbered labels. One of the reasons black nationalism is such a complex subject before World War I (or Marcus Garvey's arrival in New York in 1914), is because self-described black nationalists of the nineteenth century, people like Martin Delaney, harbored such strong Eurocentric considerations of culture and civilization. See Shelby, *We Who Are Dark*; Moses, *The Golden Age of Black Nationalism, 1850–1925*; Allen, "Du Boisian Double Consciousness"; Gatewood, *Aristocrats of Color*.

31. Carter, *Swing Along*, 10.

32. Sotiropoulos, *Staging Race*, 84.

33. Ibid., 150, 51.

34. Ibid., 124.

35. Walker, "The Real 'Coon' on the American Stage."

36. *Indianapolis Freeman*, January 13, 1906.

37. Lewis, "Wm. Marion Cook Champion of Folk Lore Song."

38. Johnson, *Along This Way*, 187.

39. Ibid., 187–88.

40. *Colored American Magazine* 8, no. 4 (April 1905): 195.

41. *Colored American* 9, no. 3 (September 1905).

42. Johnson, "Why They Call American Music Ragtime."

43. *Cleveland Plain Dealer*, n.d., JWJ.

44. Johnson, "Why They Call American Music Ragtime."

45. Undated newspaper, Williams and Walker folder, RLC; reprinted in *Indianapolis Freeman*, January 12, 1908, 5.

46. *Variety*, December 14, 1907.

47. *New York Globe and Commercial*, October 27, 1905, Williams and Walker folder, RLC.

48. *Majestic Theatre* 2 (May 1908), Williams and Walker folder, RLC.

49. W. E. B. Du Bois and James Weldon Johnson had also discussed organizing the "colored musical and theatrical talent in New York, in connection with the Niagara Movement" as Du Bois worked to create the early black political organization in 1905. Referenced in a letter from Johnson to Du Bois dated December 16, 1905, W. E. B. Du Bois papers, SCRBC.

50. *New York Telegraph*, January 25, 1906, clipping file, RLC; *Indianapolis Freeman*, November 13, 1906.

51. *NYA*, July 9, 1908.

52. Armstead-Johnson, "Themes and Values in Afro-American Librettos and Book Musicals."

53. The Frogs sent their official statement to (at least) the *Indianapolis Freeman*, July 18, 1908, and *NYA*, July 9, 1908.

54. *NYA*, July 9, 1908. On Aristophanes, see *NYA*, August 6, 1908.

55. *NYA*, June 10, 1909.

56. *NYA*, July 9, 1908.

57. Sotiropoulos, *Staging Race*, 202.

CHAPTER 4

1. Rose, *Eubie Blake*, 31.

2. Ibid., 39–40.

3. Ellington, *Music Is My Mistress*, 90.

4. Kelley and Lewis, *To Make Our World Anew*, 67.

5. In describing the process of identity formation, I am influenced by Nan Enstad's definition of historical subjectivities. For Enstad, subjectivity denotes the "particular way that an individual becomes a social person, part and product of the corner of world she or he inhabits." She contrasts this from identity, which implies full realization or a state of being "static," by emphasizing that subjectivity implies a "process of becoming that is never completed." Even though I use the term "identity," I invoke Enstad's insight in the ever-shifting, relational processes taking place between formations of self and Tenderloin music, spaces, classes, and gender identities. See Enstad, *Ladies of Labor, Girls of Adventure*, 12–13.

6. Booker T. Washington used the term "New Negro" in the late nineteenth century, so I am not claiming that black New Yorkers' ragtime identities were the first indication of African Americans' attempts to distance themselves from the past by claiming new forms of self-representation. I am, however, arguing that the process of identity-formation taking place in the Tenderloin—and in other locales across America—was a significant precursor to both A. Philip Randolph's politically radical New Negro of the World War I era and Alain Locke's cultural movement of the 1920s. On the New Negro, see Washington, *A New Negro for a New Century*; Locke, *The New Negro*; Lewis, Introduction; Moses, *The Golden Age of Black Nationalism, 1850–1925*; Fink, "A Voice for the People"; Foley, *Spectres of 1919*; Baldwin, *Chicago's New Negroes*.

7. Osofsky, *Harlem*, 14; Anderson, *This Was Harlem*, 11–16.

8. On space, see Certeau, *The Practice of Everyday Life*; Lipsitz, "The Racialization of Space and the Spatialization of Race"; McKittrick, *Demonic Grounds*; Mumford, *Interzones*; Quintana, "The Plantation All in Disorder."

9. On black culture in the Tenderloin, see Bradford, *Born with the Blues*; Ottley and Weatherby, *The Negro in New York*, 145–64; Schneider, *Negro Mecca*; Anderson, *This Was Harlem*.

10. Although the main sources are all based on interviews with Eubie Blake, they are unclear about his siblings. Al Rose writes that a single previous boy had been born before, but only lived two months, while Kimball and Bolcolm note that he "was one of eleven children to reach adulthood; he never knew any of his brothers and sisters." In an interview with Max Morath, Blake told Morath that he had ten siblings, but that "none of them lived to be over three or four months old." Because two concur, it seems as though Rose misunderstood Blake on this point. See Rose, *Eubie Blake*, 5–7; Kimball and Bolcolm, *Reminiscing with Noble Sissle and Eubie Blake*, 36; Morath, "The Ninety-Three Years of Eubie Blake," 58; Rose, *Eubie Blake*, 11.

11. Morath, "The Ninety-Three Years of Eubie Blake," 59.

12. Rose, *Eubie Blake*, 11.

13. Kimball and Bolcolm, *Reminiscing with Noble Sissle and Eubie Blake*, 42.

14. Henri, *Black Migration*, 54.

15. Morath, "The Ninety-Three Years of Eubie Blake," 60. This story is told in both Carter, *Eubie Blake*, 30–31, and Rose, *Eubie Blake*, 25.

16. Rose, *Eubie Blake*, 25–26.

17. The census numbers from 1890 only include blacks living in Manhattan and Brooklyn, whereas the data collected in 1900 and thereafter includes the five boroughs. Gilbert Osofksy also discusses the difficulty in accurately gauging the population of African Americans in New York City between 1890 and 1910. For more, see Osofksy, *Harlem*, 219n2.

18. Overton, "The Negro Home in New York," 2; Du Bois, *The Black North in 1901*, 1–9; Schneider, *Negro Mecca*, 7–10, 221; Osofsky, *Harlem*, 18.

19. Osofsky *Harlem*, 13–16; Overton, "The Negro Home in New York"; Du Bois, *The Black North in 1901*.

20. Overton, "The Negro Home in New York."

21. Du Bois, *The Black North in 1901*, 11–12; Osofsky, *Harlem*, 16.

22. Du Bois, *The Black North in 1901*, 9; Ottley and Weatherby, *The Negro in New York*, 134; Summers, *Masculinity and Its Discontents*, 51–57. On Prince Hall Freemasons, see Kantrowitz, *More than Freedom*.

23. Du Bois, *The Black North in 1901*, 11; Ottley and Weatherby, *The Negro in New York*, 133; Overton, "The Negro Home in New York"; Riis, *Just before Jazz*, 30–32.

24. Wolcott, *Remaking Respectability*, 8.

25. James Weldon Johnson's future father-in-law, John Nail, discusses blacks in Brooklyn, noting how rarely they left their borough, in an article titled, "New York's Rich Negroes," *New York Sun*, January 18, 1903, James Weldon Johnson scrapbook 2, James Weldon Johnson MSS Collection, Beinecke Library, Yale University. See also, Johnson, *Along This Way*, 202; Johnson, *Black Manhattan*, 59; Taylor, *The Black Churches of Brooklyn*.

26. Davin, "Conversations with James P. Johnson," *Jazz Review*, June 1959, 16.

27. Smith with Hoefer, *Music on My Mind*, 91–92.

28. While women did perform as singers in the Tenderloin, in the sources I have found, nearly all description of singers' accompanists were men, though Willie Smith and James P. Johnson both mention the pianist Alberta Simmons in passing (see Smith, *Music on My Mind*, 63, and Davin, "Conversations with James P. Johnson," June 1959, 17). Not only have I been unable to find further evidence of female instrumentalists but I have found exceedingly slim recollections of the women who sang and performed in Tenderloin spaces, which says more about the male pianist sources than it does about women's roles as performers in nightclubs. Still there are not many indications that women engaged in music performance in the Tenderloin to the degree that men did. In her excellent study of female dancers and performers during this era, Jayna Brown offers a few indications of women performing in the Tenderloin, but they too are few. See Brown, *Babylon Girls*, 107, 214.

29. Smith's birth certificate did not match the date he celebrated his birthday, so it is difficult to tell the exact date. See Smith, *Music on My Mind*, 5–6.

30. Ibid., 12.

31. Ibid., 26, 28.

32. Ibid., 28–29.

33. Ibid., 1.

34. Johnson, *Black Manhattan*, 75–77; Fletcher, *One Hundred Years of the Negro in Show Business*, 135.

35. Johnson, *Black Manhattan*, 75–76.

36. For the date of Ike Hines's name change, I cite Bradford, *Born with the Blues*, 164. Bradford was an entertainer of the era and the man who first convinced Okeh Records to record Mamie Smith's "Crazy Blues," thus inaugurating the highly lucrative "race record" recording era of the 1920s. Some details of Bradford's memory of Ike Hines's place contradict the recollections of James Weldon Johnson and others, so I am mostly sticking to Johnson's, Osofsky's, Ottley's, and Weatherby's descriptions of the club. It is also unclear exactly when Hines moved the club to West Twenty-seventh Street, but Tom Fletcher recalled that it was there by 1890.

37. The music historian Edward A. Berlin notes that the Douglass Club was a hotspot, "very much in the style of Ike's [Hines]," and the vaudevillian Tom Fletcher concurs. Certainly, Tenderloin nightclubs offer a ripe area for further study, with both Wilkins's Little Savoy and the Douglass Club leaving a trail of historical sources. See Berlin, *Reflections and Research on Ragtime*, 49–56, and Fletcher, *One Hundred Years of the Negro in Show Business*, 289–90.

38. Mumford, *Interzones*, 96.

39. Davin, "Conversations with James P. Johnson," June 1959, 15.

40. Johnson, *The Autobiography of an Ex-Coloured Man*, 96, 114.

41. Ottley and Weatherby, *The Negro in New York*, 147.

42. Ibid., 146.

43. Rose, *Eubie Blake*, 46.

44. Ottley and Weatherby, *The Negro in New York*, 146–53; Johnson, *Black Manhattan*, 64–74; Anderson, *This Was Harlem*, 15.

45. Jack Johnson's expensive taste in fashion, for both himself and his wives, is well documented. See Theresa Runstedtler, *Jack Johnson, Rebel Sojourner*; Bederman, *Manliness and Civilization*, 8–10; *Ebony*, September 1999, 36.

46. *Toledo Courier*, December 20, 1907, Williams and Walker Clipping File, RLC, BRTC.

47. Bert Williams had his diamond cuff links stolen in Pittsburgh, as reported by the *Morning Telegraph*, January 13, 1907, and Walker's cigarette case is mentioned in an undated article. Both articles are in Williams and Walker Clipping File, RLC.

48. *Toledo Courier*, December 20, 1907, Williams and Walker folder, RLC.

49. Smith, *Music on My Mind*, 91.

50. On black touring shows, see Blesh and Janis, *They All Played Ragtime*; Woll, *Black Musical Theatre*; and Abbott and Seroff, *Out of Sight*.

51. Fletcher, *One Hundred Years of the Negro in Show Business*, 135.

52. Ibid., 92.

53. Davin, "Conversations with James P. Johnson," June 1959.

54. Smith, *Music on My Mind*, 92, 30. Florette Henri charts black wages before, during, and after World War I. Even during the war years, black laborers made only three dollars a day. See Henri, *Black Migration*, 55–138.

55. Berlin, *King of Ragtime*, 154, 179; Ping-Robbins, *Scott Joplin*, 68, 296.

56. Brown, *James P. Johnson*, 73–76; Carter, *Eubie Blake*, 71.

57. Blesh, *They All Played Ragtime*, 196; Ellington, *Music Is My Mistress*, 92; Smith, *Music on My Mind*, 55.

58. James P. Johnson and Willie Smith were stalwarts of 1920s ragtime in Harlem, and in their reminiscing about their early years, it is often unclear if they are talking about Harlem cabarets in the 1920s or Tenderloin nightclubs in the 1910s. While I do recognize that my argument about 1910s Tenderloin spaces puts an onus on being able to distinguish these two spaces, much of what the musicians remember about one space complements the other. Additionally, the continuities between these locales, and the decades of 1910 and 1920, emphasize one of this book's larger arguments: the Harlem Renaissance did not happen in a vacuum and, in fact, developed out of existing social relations, commercial spaces, and cultural innovations. Finally, both Johnson and Smith are clear that they were visiting (and performing in) New York commercial sites at exceedingly young ages—between eleven and thirteen years old—so there is no doubt that both men (though youths at the time) had intimate knowledge of Tenderloin nightclub life.

59. Davin, "Conversations with James P. Johnson," July 1959, 13.

60. Blesh and Janis, *They All Played Ragtime*, 193.

61. Davin, "Conversations with James P. Johnson," July 1959, 13, 12. For more on older pianists, see Smith, *Music on My Mind*; Carter, *Eubie Blake*; Rose, *Eubie Blake*; Brown, *James P. Johnson*.

62. Davin, "Conversations with James P. Johnson," July 1959, 12.

63. Ibid., 13.

64. Davin, "Conversations with James P. Johnson," June 1959, 17. On ragtime harmonies, see Berlin, *Ragtime*; Brown, *James P. Johnson*; Carter, *Eubie Blake*, 83.

65. David, "Conversations with James P. Johnson," July 1959, 12.

66. *Willie "the Lion."*

67. Blesh, *Eight Lives in Jazz*, 195.

68. Ellington, *Music Is My Mistress*, 91–92.

69. Morton's claims have long been contextualized by scholars. See, for example, Jasen and Jones, *Black Bottom Stomp*. For some examples of his own take, see Smith, *Music on My Mind*, 101; Lomax, *Mr. Jelly Roll*.

70. Smith, *Music on My Mind*, 212.

71. Carter, *Eubie Blake*, 68.

72. Ellington, *Music Is My Mistress*, 91–92.

73. Davin, "Conversations with James P. Johnson," August 1959, 15. See also Smith, *Music on My Mind*, 53.

74. Davin, "Conversations with James P. Johnson," August 1959, 13.

75. Smith, *Music on My Mind*, 53.

76. Davin, "Conversations with James P. Johnson," August 1959, 15. In his description, Johnson actually said, "special chord," but Smith called it a "signature chord" in *Music on My Mind*, 53.

77. Richardson, *Black Masculinity and the U.S. South*, 2–4. See also Frederickson, *The Black Image in the White Mind*; Staples, *Black Masculinity*; Summers, *Masculinity and Its Discontents*.

78. Bay, *To Tell the Truth Freely*, 2. On the "black rapist myth," see Kelley, *Freedom Dreams*; Markovitz, *Legacies of Lynching*; Mitchell, *Living with Lynching*; Richardson, *Black Masculinity and the U.S. South*. On lynching as practice, politics, and culture see, Bederman, *Manlinesss and Civilization*, 45–76; Gilmore, *Gender and Jim Crow*; Hale, *Making Whiteness*; Schechter, *Ida B. Wells-Barnett and American Reform, 1880–1930*.

79. Kantrowitz, *Ben Tillman and the Reconstruction of White Supremacy*, 45.

80. On clothing style and racial representation see, Camp, *Closer to Freedom*; Foster, *"New Raiments of Self"*; White and White, *Stylin'*, 222–34; Blackwelder, *Styling Jim Crow*; Alvarez, *The Power of the Zoot*.

81. Summers, *Masculinity and Its Discontents*, 256.

82. Ibid., 257–58.

83. Smith, *Music on My Mind*, 46–47.

84. Ibid., 47–49.

85. Davin, "Conversations with James P. Johnson," August 1959, 14.

86. Smith, *Music on My Mind*, 47–49.

87. Davin, "Conversations with James P. Johnson," August 1959, 15.

88. *Chicago Defender*, December 3, 1910, 2.

89. Avendorph, the "Ward McAllister of the South Side," shows up as a minor historical actor in accounts of black labor organizing and sporting life in turn-of-the-twentieth-century Chicago. See Best, *Passionately Human, No Less Divine*; Gems, "Blocked Shot."

90. Summers, *Manliness and Its Discontents*, 28, 54.

91. Fletcher, *One Hundred Years of the Negro in Show Business*, 61. "The Viper" was slang for reefer and reefer smokers, and there are numerous examples of the term in 1920s and 1930s blues and jazz recordings. Louis Armstrong's 1933 recording of "Sweet Sue, Just You" documents the sound of the "Viper language," as Bud Johnson scats a verse. See Armstrong and His Orchestra (1932–33), *Laughin' Louie*. Thanks to Lynnea Godfriaux and Brad Pregeant for pointing me in the direction of the Viper.

92. I do not mean to generalize that everyone participated in the production and consumption of popular music—many black New Yorkers refused Tenderloin entertainments. Yet by unpacking aesthetic values of high and low from assumed class correspondences, this study seeks more nuanced readings of class and entertainment differences in Manhattan's black community.

CHAPTER 5

1. Sissle, "Memoirs," 12–14; Fletcher, *One Hundred Years of the Negro in Show Business*, 265.

2. Badger, *A Life in Ragtime*, 22.

3. Julian Street, "Lobster Palace Society," *Everybody's Magazine*, May 1910.

4. There is little evidence about how often Europe worked in a lobster palace, but considering that he pooled his two hundred–man labor union in 1910 from them, he had to have known the scene pretty well. The only specific reference to Europe playing in an elite hotel is Tom Fletcher's recollection of seeing him study music theory as he

played an engagement at the famous Brevoort Hotel. See Fletcher, *One Hundred Years of the Negro in Show Business*, 252. Also see Badger, *A Life in Ragtime*, 27.

5. Sissle, "Memoirs," 12–20; *NYA*, April 28, 1910.

6. Logan, *The Negro in American Life and Thought*.

7. Sissle, "Memoirs," 7–8; Badger, *A Life in Ragtime*, 10–15.

8. Sissle, "Memoirs," 7. Europe's sister, Mary, became a music teacher and choir director at M Street in 1903, where she worked until her death in 1947. See her obituary from an unnamed paper, October 22, 1947, Mary Europe clipping file, Washingtonia Collection, Washington, D.C., Public Library. See also, McGinty, "Gifted Minds and Pure Hearts."

9. Badger, *A Life in Ragtime*, 18–20.

10. Cuney-Hare, *Negro Musicians and Their Music*, 137n4; Badger, *A Life in Ragtime*, 19–21.

11. Fletcher, *One Hundred Years of the Negro in Show Business*, 139; Cook, "From 'Clorindy' to 'The Red Moon' and Beyond."

12. Locke, *The Negro and His Music*, 65.

13. Southern, *The Music of Black Americans*, 343–44.

14. Johnson, *Black Manhattan*, 122.

15. Cook, "From 'Clorindy' to 'The Red Moon' and Beyond."

16. *World*, June 20, 1905, reprinted in Sampson, *Ghost Walks*, 344–45. The *World* article was actually reviewing what must have been a test run for *The Birth of the Minstrel*. Although the principle players, Hogan and Abbie Mitchell, led a twenty-five-member cast, the show was called the "Songs of Black Folk" and "came closer to the old-fashioned minstrel show than any of the tinsel and burnt cork productions that have been seen on Broadway in the last ten years." While it is curious that this show referenced minstrelsy more than *The Birth of the Minstrel*—which is historically important precisely because it was a concert and not a minstrel show—the point that all the instrumentalists sang is the one I am after, and it correlates with both Will Cook's and James Weldon Johnson's assessments.

17. Johnson, *Black Manhattan*, 122.

18. Ibid., 120.

19. Badger, *A Life in Ragtime*, 29–33.

20. *Indianapolis Freeman*, February 8, 1908; Seniors, *Beyond Lift Every Voice and Sing*, 39–70.

21. *NYA*, May 13, 1909. The force of the white backlash against Walton's assertion was so great that he was most likely correct. See Walton's reprinting of *Life Magazine*, *The Sun*, and other national papers rebuking him in the *Age*, May 20, 1909.

22. Sissle, "Memoirs," 14.

23. Ibid., 13.

24. White audiences' conception of black culture as primitive is an idea that runs throughout this study. Although I have chosen not to overly emphasize the ways white theater producers and audiences heard musical theater by Williams and Walker, Hogan, and Cook as racial stereotype, the fact that black culture most often reinforced white Americans' racial desires is a point that I have made throughout the text. African Americans' engagement with coon songs and blackface comedy always threatened to

undermine their self-conscious attempts at advancement. What is new in this chapter are the ways wealthy whites themselves incorporated black song and dance into their own sense of modernity—an ideological process that could not accept black modernity, only an imagined black primitivism.

25. Erenberg, *Steppin' Out*, 50. For more on lobster palaces, see Berlin, *Reflections and Research on Ragtime*.

26. Hughes, *The Real New York*, 99.

27. Henry Erkins, "Murray's Roman Gardens," *Architects' and Builders' Magazine*, September 1907.

28. Julian Street, "Lobster Palace Society," *Everybody's Magazine*, May 1910; Golden, *Vernon and Irene Castle's Ragtime Revolution*, 45.

29. Erenberg, *Steppin' Out*, 57.

30. Hughes, *The Real New York*, 91.

31. Erkins, "Murray's Roman Gardens."

32. Rector, *The Girl from Rector's*, 210.

33. I will further analyze the connection between ragtime dance and race in chapter 7. On the one-step, see Cook, "Passionless Dance and Passionate Reform"; Stearns, *Jazz Dance*, 123.

34. Rector, *The Girl from Rector's*, 204–5.

35. "Music Misplaced," *Hotel Monthly*, April 1913.

36. Sissle, "Memoirs," 12–14.

37. Harrison Rhodes, "New York Restaurants," *Harper's Weekly*, November 1, 1913.

38. Rector, *The Girl from Rector's*, 204.

39. *New York Times*, September 2, 1906; Street, "Lobster Palace Society"; Rector, *The Girl from Rector's*, 60. For an excellent cultural analysis of the shifting moral and sexual mores of late nineteenth-century New York as represented by the lobster palaces and social dancing, see Erenberg, *Steppin' Out*.

40. Street, "Lobster Palace Society."

41. Street, *Welcome to Our City*, 84.

42. Erenberg, *Steppin' Out*, 46–47.

43. Wall, *Neither Pest nor Puritan*, 109.

44. Erenberg, *Steppin' Out*, 47; Smith, *Music on My Mind*, 90. Black musicians' space to the side is also evident in photographs of James Reese Europe's Society Orchestra in Castle, *Modern Dancing*, 46, 49.

45. There is little to no historical record about the sound of ragtime in lobster palaces. But considering that James Europe would expand his audiences from New York's wealthiest set, Smith's and others' recollections about the austere sound Europe produced for white dancers helps fill in the gaps. See Smith, *Music on My Mind*, 90; Davin, "Conversations with James P. Johnson," August 1959, 11; September 1959, 27.

46. For scholarly work historicizing black and white modernities, see Baker, *Modernism and the Harlem Renaissance*; Gates, "The Trope of a New Negro and the Reconstruction of the Image of the Black"; Kelley, "Notes on Deconstructing 'The Folk'"; Gilroy, *The Black Atlantic*; Radano, "Hot Fantasies"; Baldwin, *Chicago's New Negroes*; Brown, *Babylon Girls*.

47. Lyrics in Brooks and Spottsman, *Lost Sounds*, 295.

48. Roedgier, *The Wages of Whiteness*; Lott, *Love and Theft*; Lhamon, *Raising Cain*; Miller, *Segregating Sound*.

49. Johnson, *Along This Way*, 328.

50. Mae Halstead quoted in Malnig, "Apaches, Tangos, and Other Indecencies," 81.

51. Max Morath, personal interview, January 24, 2012.

52. Sissle, "Memoirs," 20.

53. Ibid., 19; Fletcher, *One Hundred Years of the Negro in Show Business*, 251–52.

54. Established in 1900, NAMA was not incorporated until 1905. Southern, *The Music of Black Americans*, 302.

55. Prior to 1910, Chicago was the only city in the United States boasting a black AFM union, Local 208.

56. Clef Club roster, James Reese Europe Collection, Manuscripts, Archives and Rare Books Division, Schomburg Center for Research in Black Culture, New York Public Library.

57. *NYA*, April 28, 1910.

58. Smith, *Music on My Mind*, 62; Badger, *A Life in Ragtime*, 54.

59. Fletcher, *One Hundred Years of the Negro in Show Business*, 261–64.

60. Work receipts, "General Correspondence file of Lee Shubert 1910–1926," 1360 A, Shubert Theater Archive; Fletcher, *One Hundred Years of the Negro in Show Business*, 261. James P. Johnson remembered making $18 to $25 per Clef Club job, and he sometimes worked "three jobs a day." Davin, "Conversations with James P. Johnson," September 1959, 27.

61. Fletcher, *One Hundred Years of the Negro in Show Business*, 261.

62. Undated article titled "Eubie," *Penthouse Magazine*, James Reese Europe Collection, SCRBC; *NYA*, September 24, 1948.

63. Carter, *Keys of Life*, 94; Morath, "The Ninety-Three Years of Eubie Blake," 62; *NYA*, September 24, 1948.

64. *NYA*, February 19, 1912, 6.

65. Rose, *Eubie Blake*, 26.

66. Davin, "Conversations with James P. Johnson," August 1959, 11; and September 1959, 27.

67. Rose, *Eubie Blake*, 59; Smith, *Music on My Mind*, 62; Sissle, "Memoirs," 13–15.

68. Rose, *Eubie Blake*, 59. Blake makes this point in a separate interview with a celebrated pianist of the post–World War II era, Max Morath. "Jim [Europe] told us that. All the musicians were told never to let a white man think you can read music. That lessens the money he's going to give you." Morath, "The Ninety-Three Years of Eubie Blake," 62.

69. Blesh, *Eight Lives in Jazz*, 205.

70. Carter, *Keys of Life*, 94.

71. Ibid., 93–96.

72. Johnson, *Along This Way*, 272; *Indianapolis Freeman*, July 23, 1910; *NYA*, August 3 and 10, 1911.

73. *NYA*, January 12, 1911; May 27, 1909.

74. Johnson, *Black Manhattan*, 170. For other examples, see Riis, *Just before Jazz*; Krasner, *Resistance, Parody, and Double Consciousness in African American Theatre, 1895–1910*; Brooks, *Bodies in Dissent*; Chude-Sokei, *The Last Darkey*.

75. Karen Sotiropoulos recognizes James Europe as a transitional figure in American cultural history. I am thankful that she only included one chapter on James Europe and the Clef Club at the end of *Staging Race*.

CHAPTER 6

1. *NYA*, June 2, 1910.

2. A picture from a later Clef Club concert at the Manhattan Casino illustrates that the orchestra performed from the ballroom floor rather than the stage, James Reese Europe Photo Collection, SCRBC.

3. *NYA*, June 2, 1910.

4. Besides combining ragtime and orchestral music, Europe displayed his admiration for the massive orchestral and choral concerts by nineteenth-century American conductors like Theodore Thomas and Patrick S. Gilmore. Most notably, Thomas had organized and conducted a one thousand–person concert as the music director for the Chicago World's Fair in 1893. See Southern, *The Music of Black Americans*, 227; Peress, *Dvořák to Duke Ellington*, 31. On the "mastery of form," see Baker, *Modernism and the Harlem Renaissance*.

5. *NYA*, June 2, 1910.

6. Sissle, "Memoirs," 19.

7. Ibid., 3.

8. "Negro's Place in Music: James Reese Europe Tells of Colored Orchestra," *Evening Post*, March 13, 1914, 7.

9. *NYA*, June 2, 1910.

10. Badger, *A Life in Ragtime*, 50. An accomplished pianist, Mary Europe performed in some of the most revered concerts in the capital in the early twentieth century, including those of the Afro-British composer Samuel Coleridge-Taylor in 1904 and 1906. See McGinty, "Gifted Minds and Pure Hearts" and "'That You Came So Far to See Us.'"

11. Georgia Fraser Goins, "The History of the Treble Clef Club" [lecture presented in 1947], Georgia Fraser Goins Collection, Box 36–15, Moorland-Spingarn Research Center, Howard University. The Treble Clef Club prefigured Washington's much larger, though still exclusive, S. Coleridge-Taylor Society with whom Mary Europe performed. See ibid.

12. *NYA*, May 18, 1911.

13. Sotiropoulos, *Staging Race*, 202. On the "Frolics," see *NYA*, August 20, 1908; December 14, 1911; August 14, 1913.

14. The *Pittsburgh Courier* reported that casino guests danced until four in the morning after one Clef Club concert. See *Pittsburgh Courier*, May 27, 1911, 1.

15. *NYA*, October 27, 1910.

16. Europe referred to his banjo and mandolin sections as a "second violin section" in "A Negro Explains Jazz," *Literary Digest*, April 26, 1919.

17. "Negro's Place in Music."

18. Seldes, *The Seven Lively Arts*, 151.

19. "Negro Composer on Race's Music: James Reese Europe Credits Men of His Blood with Introducing Modern Dances."

20. "Negro's Place in Music."

21. "A New Type of Negro Musician," *NYA*, September 30, 1915.

22. Osofsky, *Harlem*, 17.

23. Ibid., 122–23.

24. Ibid., 128.

25. Wintz and Finkelman, *Encyclopedia of the Harlem Renaissance*, 767. The *Pittsburgh Courier* reported that ten thousand people attended the third Clef Club concert, May 27, 1911, 1.

26. I have found only three photographs of the Manhattan Casino before World War I. Two are group shots of the Clef Club Orchestra, and one is from a Harlem blog website, http://digitalharlemblog.wordpress.com/tag/manhattan-casino/ (accessed March 6, 2013). Besides the photograph presented, another photo of the Clef Club is shown in Curtis-Burlin, "Black Singers and Players," 498.

27. *Pittsburgh Courier*, May 27, 1911, 1.

28. Letter from Elizabeth Walton to W. E. B. Du Bois, Du Bois papers, SCRBC; Mannes, *Music Is My Faith*, 213; Walton et al., "Black-Music Concerts in Carnegie Hall, 1912–1915"; Martin, *The Damrosch Dynasty*, 214; Badger, *A Life in Ragtime*, 61.

29. Badger, *A Life in Ragtime*, 63–64.

30. Fletcher, *One Hundred Years of the Negro in Show Business*, 258.

31. Sissle, "Memoirs," 22–23. Europe thoroughly respected Cook and refers to him and Harry T. Burleigh as "the two foremost" black "composers of great ability," and also calls Cook a "true creative artist" in the article "Negro Composer of Race's Music" in the *New York Tribune*, November 22, 1914.

32. Mannes, *Music Is My Faith*, 218–20.

33. Ibid., 218; the *New York Evening Post* article is reprinted in Martin, *The Damrosch Dynasty*, 212.

34. Sissle, "Memoirs," 23.

35. Ibid.

36. Carnegie Hall Program, May 2, 1912, Carnegie Hall Archives.

37. Sissle, "Memoirs," 23; Curtis-Burlin, "Black Singers and Players."

38. Fletcher, *One Hundred Years of the Negro in Show Business*, 260.

39. Sissle, "Memoirs," 22.

40. Mannes, *Music Is My Faith*, 218–19; Curtis-Burlin, "Black Singers and Players"; *NYA*, May 9, 1912.

41. Fletcher, *One Hundred Years of the Negro in Show Business*, 260–61.

42. Ron Welburn argues that Europe was one of the first public critics of "jazz," emphasizing that Europe elevated jazz "in the minds of his readers and . . . establish[ed] a paradigm for later jazz criticism." I choose to call Europe an authority on "Negro music" because, until World War I, that is what he called his music. I also situate Europe in a historical context with other early black music critics like Will Marion Cook, Rosamond Johnson, James Weldon Johnson, and George Walker, none of whom referred to black music as "jazz" prior to 1915. See Welburn, "James Reese Europe and the Infancy of Jazz Criticism."

43. "Negro's Place in Music."

44. "Negroes Perform Their Own Music," *Musical America*, March 21, 1914. A black musician in Philadelphia also critiqued the Carnegie performance, echoing James

Monroe Trotter's instructions: "If we expect to do anything that is lasting from an artistic stand-point, we, too, must study the classics as a foundation of our work." See *Philadelphia Tribune*, November 21, 1914.

45. There is confusion in the secondary literature about the actual dates of the Carnegie Hall concerts or, at least, about Europe's interview for "Negro's Place in Music," which was published in the *Evening Post* on March 13, 1914. Samuel Charters (*Jazz*, 28–29) simply mistakes the Clef Club's third concert in Carnegie Hall for its premiere performance and therefore cites Europe's response in the *Evening Post* as directly following his first concert there. Eileen Southern—in her classic *The Music of Black Americans* (288–89)—has the wrong dates in her discussion of the *Musical America* article, as well as of Europe's response. In his 1996 article, "The Black-American Composer and the Orchestra in the Twentieth Century," Olly Wilson uses Southern as his only source and therefore follows her incorrect dates.

46. "Negro's Place in Music."

47. Ibid.

48. "Negro Composer on Race's Music: James Rees [sic] Europe Credits Men of His Blood with Introducing Modern Dances."

49. "Negro's Place in Music."

50. Ibid.

51. "Negro Composer on Race's Music." By November 1914, Europe had established another two-hundred–man musicians' organization called the Tempo Club. When speaking to the *Tribune*, Europe was referring to the Tempo Club rather than the Clef Club, although both clubs were quite similar. See the next chapter.

52. "Negro's Place in Music."

53. Ibid.

54. Ibid.

55. *NYA*, January 1, 1914, 6.

56. "Negro Composer on Race's Music."

57. *NYA*, September 30, 1915.

58. "Negro Composer on Race's Music."

59. "Negro's Place in Music."

60. Ibid.

CHAPTER 7

1. In James Weldon Johnson's reprinting of De Bueris's letter in the *New York Age*, it is difficult to tell which *Globe* newspaper De Bueris wrote to. De Bueris's letter was reprinted in dozens of newspapers and became the topic of debate, most notably in the Richmond *Times-Dispatch*. See *NYA*, September 23 and 30, 1915.

2. *NYA*, September 23, 1915.

3. Ibid.

4. Ibid.

5. *NYA*, September 30, 1915.

6. Ibid.

7. I am thinking here of Brenda Dixon Gottschild's use of the term "license" when discussing white elite's appropriation of the cakewalk dance in the late 1890s; her work illustrates that, like minstrelsy, this trend of unequal cultural appropriation set a precedent that would continue throughout the twentieth century. See Gottschild, *Digging the Africanist Presence in American Performance*, 114.

8. *NYA*, September 30, 1915.

9. *NYA*, January 14, 1914.

10. Brooks and Spottsman, *Lost Sounds*, 271.

11. Peiss, *Cheap Amusements*, 88–102; Cook, "Passionless Dance and Passionate Reform"; McBee, *Dance Hall Days*, 51–81; George-Graves, "'Just Like Being at the Zoo'"; Malnig, "Apaches, Tangos, and Other Indecencies."

12. Fletcher, *One Hundred Years of the Negro in Show Business*, 193.

13. Erenberg, *Steppin' Out*, 164. For more on the African American origins of one-step styles, see Stearns, *Jazz Dance*, 96–103, and Stoddard, *Jazz on the Barbary Coast*.

14. Susan Cook, conversation with the author, June 10, 2009. Cook writes about the loosening of dance steps in "Passionless Dance and Passionate Reform" and "Watching Our Step." Others making similar points include, McBee, *Dance Hall Days*, 99–100; Peiss, *Cheap Amusements*, 101–2; Erenberg, *Steppin' Out*, 153; Stearns, *Jazz Dance*, 15, 63.

15. Faulkner, *From the Ballroom to Hell and The Lure of the Dance*, dedication, 8–11; newspaper quotes in Sullivan, *Our Times*, 254. For histories of reformers and dance, see Wagner, *Adversaries of Dance*; and Perry, "'The General Motherhood of the Commonwealth.'"

16. Castle, *Castles in the Air*; "My Memories of Vernon Castle'"; Allen, "When America Learned to Dance"; Cook, "Watching Our Step."

17. Robinson, "The Ugly Duckling"; George-Graves, "'Just Like Being at the Zoo.'"

18. "Dancer from Paris Introduces New Steps to Society," *New York Times*, December 10, 1911.

19. Stearns, *Jazz Dance*, 97.

20. Cook, "Watching Our Step," 194; Ronald Radano has analyzed the relationships between the rhetoric of "hot rhythms," "dance crazes," and turn-of-the-century racial anxiety in "Hot Fantasies."

21. Castle, *Modern Dancing*, foreword.

22. *New York Book Review*, undated, Irene Castle scrapbook, RLC.

23. "Castle House Is Exclusive: Vulgar Mob Not Welcome at New York's Newest Fad," *Rochester Herald*, undated, scrapbook vol. 495, RLC.

24. "Tango According to Castle," *Metropolitan*, June 1913, Irene Castle scrapbook, RLC.

25. Castle, *Castles in the Air*, 86.

26. "How the Castles Built Castle House," *Theatre Magazine*, March 1914.

27. Castle, *Modern Dancing*, coda.

28. Erenberg, *Steppin' Out*, 164.

29. Castle, *Castles in the Air*, 89.

30. *New York Tribune*, November 22, 1914.

31. *NYA*, January 14, 1914, and September 24, 1948.

32. Rose, *Eubie Blake*, 58.

33. *NYA*, September 24, 1948.

34. *NYA*, January 14, 1914, and September 28, 1948; Castle, "Jim Europe—A Reminiscence."

35. "I want that to come out in the record," Blake told Vivian Perlis. "He was the one who invented that word—gig. Now you hear everybody say that." Cited in Badger, *A Life in Ragtime*, 288n37.

36. See James Reese Europe, "Too Much Mustard" and Prince's Band, "Too Much Mustard."

37. On Gypsy string bands, see *NYA*, September 24, 1948. For a comparison, see James Europe's and Prince's Band's recordings of "Too Much Mustard." Other comparative listening could include Europe's "Down Home Rag" with versions by Harry Adams, the Happy Hollow Hoodlums, and Pete Daily and his Chicagoans, all available in the Archives Center, National Museum of American History, Smithsonian Institution.

38. "Castle House Rag" also known as the "Castles in Europe."

39. Rick Benjamin, interview with the author, November 14, 2007.

40. Smith, *Music on My Mind*, 90.

41. "Negro's Place in Music."

42. Thanks to Max Morath for giving me copies of Europe's Castle-era songs published through Jos. W. Stern and Company. Morath has since helped publish an amazing collection of Europe's songs and dance music in *The Music of James Reese Europe: Complete Published Works*.

43. "Negro Composer on Race's Music"; *NYA*, September 28, 1948: 8; Castle, "Jim Europe—A Reminiscence." For an excellent musical analysis of the foxtrot and its transference from Handy, through Europe and the Castles, into the "basis for many subsequent popular dances and the rhythm for many familiar American popular songs," see Badger, *A Life in Ragtime*, 115–16.

44. Muir, *Long Lost Blues*, 56–59.

45. James Reese Europe, correspondence with Lee Shubert, January 2 and March 15, 1915, General Correspondence File of Lee Shubert 1910–1926, 1360 A, Shubert Theater Archive. Thanks to Susan Cook for pointing me in the direction of this source.

46. *NYA*, September 23, 1915.

47. On December 30, 1913, Europe resigned as president of the Clef Club. It is unclear exactly why he did so, but Europe's biographer speculates that he responded to Clef Club members who may have felt that his association with the Castles overshadowed his commitment to the club. I find this reason rather suspect considering Europe's incessant promotion of the club alongside the Castles. Regardless, Europe began a new organization called the Tempo Club almost immediately and took many Clef Club members with him—although it may be that musicians could belong to both clubs simultaneously. Clef Club members continued to perform in Europe's symphony orchestra. Europe continued to support the Clef Club throughout his life and, even as he fought in France in World War I, he kept up with the Clef Club, advising in print that "everyone should rush to build a monument to this wonderful organization" (*Age*, July 28, 1918). By November 1914, the Tempo Club had grown to "about two hundred

members," though there is no evidence that it became an actual rival to the Clef Club. See *NYA* January 1, 1914; *New York Tribune*, November 22, 1914; and Badger, *A Life in Ragtime*, 93, 111–13.

48. Various clippings from Irene Castle scrapbooks, RLC; Victor ads in *The Voice of Victor*, May 1914; undated clipping in James Reese Europe Collection, SCRBC.

49. For more on Marbury, see Golden, *Vernon and Irene Castle's Ragtime Revolution*.

50. On the New Woman, see Peiss, *Cheap Amusements*; Enstad, *Ladies of Labor, Girls of Adventure*; Glenn, *Female Spectacle*.

51. Cook, "Watching Our Step," 180—*Vanity Fair* quoted in 206n5.

52. "Irene Castle, 71, Prefers a Waltz," *New York Tribune*, April 4, 1964; Marisa Berenson, "The Have-It Girls," *Vogue*, February 1976, Irene Castle Clipping File, Jerome Robbins Dance Division, Performing Arts Library, New York Public Library.

53. Marbury, *My Crystal Ball*, 224.

54. "How the Castles Built Castle House," *Theatre Magazine*, March 1914.

55. Allen, "When America Learned to Dance," 17.

56. Castle, *Castles in the Air*, 107–8.

57. Undated, *Portland, Oregonian*, undated *Houston Post*, undated *Grand Rapids Michigan News*, all in Irene Castle scrapbook, RLC; various clippings from Irene Castle scrapbook, RLC.

58. For examples of reports on the Castles' amorphous income see, *NYA* March 26, 1914; *Grand Rapids Michigan News*; "Castles Dance to the Tune of $8000," undated Philadelphia paper; "Castles in the Air—$6000 at Feet of Tango Royalty," undated *Sun* (Baltimore), Irene Castle scrapbook, RLC.

59. Castle, "My Memories of Vernon Castle."

60. *Theatre Magazine Advertiser*, March 1914.

61. A significant exception to this is Irene Castle's article, "Jim Europe—A Reminiscence," wherein she fondly remembered Europe and their 1914 tour together. Additionally, Noble Sissle remembered her campaign in defiance of the Ginger Rogers and Fred Astaire film about her own life, because the 1944 film did not properly reflect the significance of black musicians to her career. In 1948, Sissle commended Castle for her "one-woman fight . . . against injustice." See, *NYA*, September 21, 1948.

62. *Musical Leader*, April 16, 1914.

63. *NYA*, March 26, 1914.

64. Ibid.

65. NAMA quote in Badger, *A Life in Ragtime*, 121.

EPILOGUE

1. *NYA*, September 21, 1948. Sissle did not condemn younger musicians for not knowing New York music history. But in an early column, he printed fellow "Old Timer" Ivan H. Browning's irritation at jazz vibraphonist Lionel Hampton's suggestion that Bing Crosby play Bert Williams in a biopic. Browning's letter seemed to prove to Sissle the need for a column devoted to "trying to let our younger generation know the history of its own race in the development of the American theater." *NYA*, November 6, 1948.

2. Sissle notes that the headline was on the top of "every Hearst Newspaper from coast to coast" the day after Europe's death on May 9, 1919. *NYA*, September 24, 1948.

3. Rose, *Eubie Blake*, 60–61.

4. *NYA*, September 24, 1948.

5. Ibid.

6. Mamie Smith's "Crazy Blues" revolutionized the recording industry, demonstrating both that black artists could sell and that black consumers would buy blues records. See Bradford, *Born with the Blues*.

7. DeVeaux, "Constructing the Jazz Tradition."

8. Little, *From Harlem to the Rhine*, xi; *New York Times*, February 18, 1919, 6. Europe's biographer, Reid Badger, deals extensively with his wartime service. See Badger, *A Life in Ragtime*.

9. Ibid., 128–30.

10. The Hell Fighters performed Handy's "Memphis Blues" and "St. Louis Blues." Handy, the "Father of the Blues," credited James Europe with being the first to ever perform the latter, which became Handy's most famous composition. See, W. C. Handy telegram to James Reese Europe Jr., James Reese Europe Collection, SCRC.

11. "The Negro Explains Jazz," *Literary Digest*, April 26, 1919.

12. Sissle, "Memoirs," 121.

13. *St. Louis Post-Dispatch*, June 10, 1918.

14. Johnson, *Along This Way*, 327.

15. Johnson, Preface, 427.

16. Johnson, "Race Prejudice and the Negro Artist," 344–45.

17. Johnson, "The Dilemma of the Negro Author," 379.

18. Lewis, *When Harlem Was in Vogue* and Introduction.

Bibliography

PRIMARY SOURCES

Manuscript Collections

New Haven, Conn.
    Beinecke Rare Book and Manuscript Library, Yale University
        James Weldon Johnson Manuscript Collection
        James Weldon Johnson Sheet Music Collection
        Irving S. Gilmore Music Library
    Gilmore Music Library, Yale University
        J. Rosamond Johnson Papers
New York, N.Y.
    Billy Rose Theater Division, New York Public Library for the Performing Arts
        Abyssinia Clippings File
        American Place Theatre Company Records
        Bandanna Land Clippings File
        Bert Williams Clippings File
        Bob Cole Clippings File
        Clorindy Clippings File
        Ernest Hogan Clippings File
        In Dahomey Clippings File
        Mr. Load of Koal Clippings File
        The Oyster Man Clippings File
        Red Moon Clippings File
        Robinson Locke Collection
        The Shoo-Fly Regiment Clippings File
        The Southerners Clippings File
        Rufus Rastas Clippings File
        Smart Set Clippings File
        Williams and Walker Clipping File
        Will Marion Cook Clipping File
    Carnegie Hall Archives
        Attraction: Clef Club Orchestra
    Jean Blackwell Hutson Research and Reference Division, Schomburg Center for
            Research in Black Culture, New York Public Library
        Vertical Files
            Clarence C. White
            Emancipation Expo (1913)

Ernest Hogan

Harry T. Burleigh

J. Rosamond Johnson

James Reese Europe

James Weldon Johnson

John E. Bruce

Theater, Pre-1925

Will Marion Cook

Williams and Walker

World War I

Writer's Program (New York, New York) Collection 1936–1941

Jerome Robbins Dance Division, New York Public Library for the
Performing Arts

Aida Overton (Walker) Collection

Irene Castle Clipping File

Irene Castle Scrapbook Collection

Vernon and Irene Castle Collection

Manuscript and Archives Division, New York Public Library

Committee of Fourteen Records, 1905–1932

Manuscripts, Archives, and Rare Books Division, Schomburg Center for Research
in Black Culture, New York Public Library

Bert Williams Joke Books, n.d.

Clarence Cameron White Papers

Eliot Carpenter Papers

Emerson Collection on Vaudeville

Florence Mills Collection

Helen Armstead-Johnson Miscellaneous Theater Collection

James Reese Europe Collection

James Reese Europe Score Collection

James Reese Europe Jr. Papers

Lester Walton Papers

Miscellaneous American Letters and Papers

Opal Cooper Collection

Samuel E. Hayward Papers

Sidney Easton Papers, 1913–1980

W. E. B. Du Bois Papers

Music Division, New York Public Library for the Performing Arts

Cole and Johnson Collection

Kurt Schindler Papers

Rosamond Johnson Collection

New-York State Historical Society

Industrial Trade Publications Collection

Archive of American Folk Song

Shubert Archive

Lee Shubert Papers

Washington, D.C.
> Archive Center, National Museum of American History, Smithsonian Institution
>> Alphabetical Trade Literature Collection
>> Ellington Collection
>> N W Ayer Advertising Agency Collection, 1849–1996
>> Sam DeVincent Collection of Illustrated Sheet Music
>> Smithsonian Institution Libraries Trade Literature Collections
>> Warsaw Collection of Business Americana, ca. 1790–1945
> Manuscript Department, Moorland Spingarn-Research Center, Howard University
>> Andrew F. Hilyer Collection
>> Georgia Fraser Goins Collection
>> Mercer Cook Papers
>> Samuel Coleridge Taylor Choral Society of Washington Vertical File
>> Washington Conservatory of Music Records
> Manuscript Division, Library of Congress
>> Booker T. Washington Papers
> Martin Luther King Jr. Memorial Library
>> Mary Europe Vertical File
>> Washingtoniana Collection

Newspapers and Periodicals

Appleton's Magazine
American Magazine
American Music
American Visions
Amsterdam News
Architect's and Builder's Magazine
Black Music Research Bulletin
The Black Perspective in Music
Brooklyn Daily Times
Chicago Defender
The Colored American
The Colored American Magazine
The Crisis
The Dramatic Mirror
Ebony
Etude
Everybody's Magazine

Harper's Weekly
The Hotel Monthly
Indianapolis Freeman
The Jazz Review
Ladies' Home Journal
Literary Digest
Metropolitan
Mobile Daily Register
Musical Courier
Musical Leader
Musical Observer
Musical Record
The Musician
Negro Music Journal
New York Age
New York Evening Post
New York Sun
New York Tribune
New York Times
New York World
Oberlin Alumni Magazine

Opportunity
The Outlook
Philadelphia Tribune
Pittsburgh Courier
Popular Negro Composers
St. Louis Post-Dispatch
Survey Graphic
Talking Machine World
The Theatre
The Theatre Magazine Advertiser
The Theatre Magazine
The Scrap Book
Theatre Arts
Variety
Vogue
Washington Bee
Washington Post
Wisconsin Weekly Advocate

Sheet Music

Cole and Johnson, "Under the Bamboo Tree." James Weldon Johnson Manuscript Collection, Beinecke Library, Yale University.

Dunbar, Paul Laurence, and Will Marion Cook. "Who Dat Say Chicken in Dis Crowd?" M. Witmark and Sons (1898), Mercer Cook Papers, Box 157–11, Folder 30, Manuscript Division, Moorland-Spingarn Research Center, Howard University.

Europe, James Reese. "Castle House Rag." Jos. W. Sterns and Co, 1914. James Reese Europe Score Collection, Schomburg Center for Research in Black Culture, New York Public Library.

———. *The Music of James Reese Europe: Complete Published Works.* New York: Edward B. Marks Music Company, 2012.

Hogan, Ernest. "All Coons Look Alike To Me." M. Witmark and Sons (1896), Music Division, Library for the Performing Arts, New York Public Library.

———. "La Pas Ma La." J. R. Bell (1895), Music Division, Library for the Performing Arts, New York Public Library.

Music Recordings, Videos, and Websites

America Dances! 1897-1948: A Collector's Edition of Social Dance in Film. Dancetime Publications, 2003.

Armstrong, Louis. "Sweet Sue, Just You." Louis Armstrong and His Orchestra (1932–1933). *Laughin' Louie* [original recording reissued]. BMG/Bluebird.

Dvořák, Antonín. "From the New World (No. 9 in E minor)." Dvořák: Symphony No. 9, "From the New World." Performed by the Chicago Symphony Orchestra. Decca, 1990.

Europe's Society Orchestra. "Amapa-Maxixe Brasilien; Irresistible." Victor 35360. Performing Arts Reading Room, Library of Congress.

———. "Ballin' the Jack." Victor 35405–A. December 29, 1913. Mills Music Library, University of Wisconsin-Madison.

———. "Castle's Lame Duck; Castle House Rag." Victor 35372. Performing Arts Reading Room, Library of Congress.

———. "One-Step or Turkey Trot." Victor 35359. New York Public Library for the Performing Arts. New York Public Library.

———. "Too Much Mustard; Down Home Rag." Victor 35359. Performing Arts Reading Room, Library of Congress.

———. "You're Here and I'm Here; Castle Walk." Victor 17553. Performing Arts Reading Room, Library of Congress.

Lieut. Jim Europe's 369th U.S. Infantry "Hell Fighters" Band. The Complete Recordings. Memphis Archives, 1995.

Paragon Ragtime Orchestra. *Black Manhattan: Theater and Dance Music of James Reese Europe, Will Marion Cook, and Members of the Legendary Clef Club.* Conducted by Rick Benjamin. New World Records, 2003.

Prince's Band. "Too Much Mustard." February 15, 1913. Columbia Phonograph Company.

Steppin' on the Gas: Rags and Jazz, 1913–1927. New World Records NW 269.

Too Much Mustard: The Bands of James Reese Europe and Arthur Pryor, 1907–1919.
Performed by James Reese Europe, W. C. Handy, Cecil Makin, et al. Saydisc, 2007.

Victor Military Band. "Amapa-Maxixe Brasilien." Victor 17528. Performing Arts
Reading Room, Library of Congress.

Willie the Lion: A Musical Biography about Jazz Legend Willie "the Lion" Smith. NJN
Public Television, 2001.

Published Works and Interviews

Bechet, Sidney. *Treat It Gentle: An Autobiography.* [1960] New York: Da Capo Press,
1978. 125.

Benjamin, Rick. Personal interview, November 14, 2007.

Blesh, Rudi. *Eight Lives in Jazz: Combo: U.S.A.* New York: Hayden Book Co., 1971.

———, with Harriet Janis. *They All Played Ragtime.* New York: Oak Publications,
1966.

Bradford, Perry. *Born with the Blues.* New York: Oak Publications, 1965.

Carter, Lawrence T. *Eubie Blake: Keys of Life.* Detroit: Balamp Publishing, 1979.

Castle, Irene. *Castles in the Air.* [1958] New York: Da Capo, 1980.

———. "Jim Europe—A Reminiscence." *Opportunity*, March 1930, 90–91.

———. "My Memories of Vernon Castle." *Everybody's Magazine*, November 1918–
March 1919, 36–41.

Castle, Vernon, and Irene Castle. *Modern Dancing.* New York: Harper and Brothers,
1914.

Cook, Mercer. "From 'Clorindy' to 'The Red Moon' and Beyond." Mercer Cook folder,
Helen Armstead-Johnson Miscellaneous Theater Collection, Schomburg Center
for Research in Black Culture, New York Public Library.

Cook, Will Marion. "Clorindy, the Origin of the Cakewalk." *Theatre Arts*, September,
1947, 61–65.

Cook, Susan. Personal interview, June 10, 2009.

Cuney-Hare, Maud. *Negro Musicians and Their Music.* Washington, D.C.: Associated
Publishers, 1936.

Curtis-Burlin, Natalie. "Black Singers and Players." *Musical Quarterly* 5 (October
1919): 499–504.

Davin, Tom. "Conversations with James P. Johnson." *Jazz Review* (June–Sept. 1959).

Dillon, Philip Robert. "Princely Profits from Single Songs." *Scrap Book* 4 (August
1907): 181–89.

Du Bois, W. E. B. *The Black North in 1901: A Social Study; A Series of Articles
Originally Appearing in The New York Times, November–December 1901.* New
York: Arno Press, 1969.

———. *Black Reconstruction in America, 1860–1880.* [1935] New York: Atheneum,
1962.

———. *The Souls of Black Folk.* [1903]. Edited by David W. Blight and Robert
Gooding-Williams. Boston: Bedford/St. Martin's, 1997.

Ellington, Duke. *Music Is My Mistress*. New York: Doubleday, 1973.

Erkin, Henry. *New York Plaisance: An Illustrated Series of New York Places of Amusement*. New York: New Amsterdam Theater, 1908.

Europe, James Reese. "A Negro Explains Jazz." *Literary Digest*, April 26, 1919, 28–29.

——. "The Negro Musician." *New York Age*, September 30, 1915, 6.

——. "Negro's Place in Music: James Reese Europe Tells of Colored Orchestra." *Evening Post*, March 13, 1914.

Faulkner, T. A. *From the Ballroom to Hell and The Lure of the Dance*. La Crosse, Wis.: The Light, 1922.

Fletcher, Tom. *One Hundred Years of the Negro in Show Business*. New York: Burdge and Company, 1954.

"The 'Fortune' in a Popular Song." *Literary Digest*, July 1, 1916, 30–31.

Goldberg, Isaac. *Tin Pan Alley: A Chronicle of American Popular Music*. [1930] New York: Frederick Ungar, 1961.

Goodrich, A. J. "Syncopated Rhythm vs. 'Rag-Time.'" *Musician 6* (November 1901): 336.

Handy, W. C. *Father of the Blues: The Autobiography of W.C. Handy*. London: Sidgewick and Jackson, 1957.

Hughes, Robert. *The Real New York*. New York: Smart Set Publishing, 1904.

Hurston, Zora Neale. "The Characteristics of Negro Expression." [1934]. In *Sweat*, edited by Cheryl Wall, 55–71. New Brunswick: Rutgers University Press, 1997.

——. "Spirituals and Neo-Spirituals." In *Negro: An Anthology*, edited by Nancy Cunard. [1933] New York: Frederick Ungar, 1970.

Johnson, James Weldon. *Along This Way: The Autobiography of James Weldon Johnson*. [1933] New York: Penguin Books, 1990.

——. *Black Manhattan*. [1930] New York: Atheneum, 1968.

——. "The Dilemma of the Negro Author." [1928]. In *The New Negro: Readings on Race, Representation, and African American Culture, 1892–1938*, edited by Henry Louis Gates Jr. and Gene Andrew Jarrett, 378–82. Princeton, N.J.: Princeton University Press, 2007.

——. *God's Trombones: Seven Negro Sermons in Verse*. [1927] Delaware Water Gap, Pa.: Shawnee Press, 1955.

——. "Preface to *The Book of American Negro Poetry*." [1922]. In *The New Negro: Readings on Race, Representation, and African American Culture, 1892–1938*, edited by Henry Louis Gates Jr. and Gene Andrew Jarrett, 426–43. Princeton, N.J.: Princeton University Press, 2007.

——. "Race Prejudice and the Negro Artist." [1928]. In *The New Negro: Readings on Race, Representation, and African American Culture, 1892–1938*, edited by Henry Louis Gates Jr. and Gene Andrew Jarrett. 343–50. Princeton, N.J.: Princeton University Press, 2007.

Johnson, James Weldon, J. Rosamond Johnson, and Lawrence Brown, eds. *The Book of American Negro Spirituals*. New York: Viking Press, 1925.

Johnson, J. Rosamond. "Why They Call American Music Ragtime." *New York Age*, December 24, 1908, 2.

Krehbiel, Henry E. *Afro-American Folksongs: A Study in Racial and National Music*. [1913] New York: Frederick Ungar, 1962.

"Legitimizing the Music of the Negro." *Current Opinion* 13 (May 1913): 384–85.

Lewis, Carey B. "Wm. Marion Cook Champion of Folk Lore Song." *Chicago Defender,* May 1, 1915, 6.

Little, Arthur West. *From Harlem to the Rhine: The Story of New York's Colored Volunteers.* New York: Covici, Friede, 1936.

Locke, Alain. *The Negro and His Music.* Washington, D.C.: The Associates in Negro Folk Education, 1936.

———. *The New Negro.* [1925] New York: Atheneum, 1992.

Lomax, Alan. *Mr. Jelly Roll: The Fortunes of Jelly Roll Morton, New Orleans Creole, and "Inventor."* Berkeley: University of California Press, 1973.

Mannes, David. *Music Is My Faith: An Autobiography.* New York: W. W. Norton, 1938.

Marbury, Elisabeth. *My Crystal Ball.* New York: Boni and Liveright Publishers, 1923.

Morath, Max. "The Ninety-Three Years of Eubie Blake." *American Heritage* 6 (October 1976): 56–65.

———. Personal interview, January 24, 2012.

"Negro Composer on Race's Music: James Rees [*sic*] Europe Credits Men of His Blood with Introducing Modern Dances." *New York Tribune,* November 22, 1914.

Overton, Mary White. "The Negro Home in New York." *Charities* 15 (October 1905): 25–30.

Prageant, Brad. Personal interview, April 2, 2002.

Rector, George. *The Girl from Rector's.* New York: Doubleday, Page, 1927.

Rose, Al. *Eubie Blake.* New York: Schirmer Books, 1979.

Scott, Emmett J. *Scott's Official History of the American Negro in the World War.* [1919] New York: Arno Press, 1969.

Seldes, Gilbert. *The 7 Lively Arts.* 1924; New York: Sagamore Press, 1957.

Sissle, Noble. "Memoirs." James Reese Europe Collection, SCRC.

Smith, Willie "the Lion," with George Hoefer. *Music on My Mind: The Memoirs of an American Pianist.* New York: Da Capo, 1964.

Street, Julian. *Welcome to Our City.* New York: John Lane, 1913.

Trotter, James Monroe. *Music and Some Highly Musical People* [1878] New York: Johnson Reprint Corporation, 1968.

Van Dyke, John C. *The New New York.* New York: Macmillan Co., 1909.

Walker, Aida Overton. "Colored Men and Women on the Stage." *Colored American Magazine,* October 1905, 571–75.

Walker, George W. "The Negro on the American Stage." *Colored American Magazine,* October 1906, 243–48.

———. "The Real 'Coon' on the American Stage." *Theatre Magazine Advertiser,* August 1906, 78–84. Williams and Walker Folder, Robinson Locke Collection, Billy Rose Theater Collection, Library for the Performing Arts, New York Public Library.

Wall, E. Berry. *Neither Pest nor Puritan: The "Memoirs" of E. Berry Wall.* New York: Dial Press, 1940.

Walton, Lester A., et al. "Black-Music Concerts in Carnegie Hall, 1912–1915." *Black Perspective in Music* 6 (Spring 1978): 71–88.

Washington, Booker T., et al., eds. *A New Negro for a New Century: An Accurate and Up-To-Date Record of the Upward Struggles of the Negro Race*. [1900] New York: Arno Press, 1969.

SECONDARY SOURCES

Books and Articles

Abbott, Lynn, and Doug Seroff, eds. *Out of Sight: The Rise of African American Popular Music, 1889–1895*. Jackson: University of Mississippi Press, 2002.

——. *Ragged but Right: Black Traveling Shows, "Coon Songs," and the Dark Pathway to Blues and Jazz*. Jackson: University of Mississippi Press, 2007.

Agawu, Kofi. "The Invention of 'African Rhythm.'" *Journal of the American Musicological Society* 48, no. 3 (1995): 380–95.

——. *Representing African Music: Postcolonial Notes, Queries, Positions*. New York: Routledge, 2003.

Allen, Ernest, Jr. "Du Boisian Double Consciousness: The Unsustainable Argument." *Massachusetts Review* 43, no. 2 (2002): 217–53.

Alvarez, Luis. *The Power of the Zoot: Youth Culture and Resistance during World War II*. Berkeley: University of California Press, 2009.

Anderson, Jervis. *This Was Harlem: A Cultural Portrait*. New York: Farrar, Straus, Giroux, 1981.

Anderson, Paul Allen. *Deep River: Music and Memory in Harlem Renaissance Thought*. Durham, N.C.: Duke University Press, 2001.

Armstead-Johnson, Helen. "Themes and Values in Afro-American Librettos and Book Musicals." In *Musical Theater in America*, edited by Glenn Loney. Westport, Conn.: Greenwood Press, 1984.

Aveni, John Anthony. "Such Music as Befits the New Order of Things: African American Professional Musicians and the Cultural Identity of a Race, 1880–1920." Ph.D. diss., Rutgers University, 2004.

Badger, Reid. "The Conquest of Europe: The Remarkable Career of James Reese Europe." *Alabama Heritage* 1, no. 1 (1986): 34–49.

——. *A Life in Ragtime: A Biography of James Reese Europe*. New York: Oxford University Press, 1995.

Baldwin, Davarian. *Chicago's New Negroes: Modernity, the Great Migration, and Black Urban Life*. Chapel Hill: University of North Carolina, 2007.

Baker, Houston A., Jr. *Blues, Ideology, and Afro-American Literature: A Vernacular Theory*. Chicago: University of Chicago Press, 1984.

——. *Modernism and the Harlem Renaissance*. Chicago: University of Chicago Press, 1987.

Barlow, William, and Thomas L. Morgan. *From Cakewalks to Concert Halls: An Illustrated History of African American Popular Music from 1895 to 930*. Washington, D.C.: Elliot and Clark, 1992.

Barrett, Joshua. "The Golden Anniversary of the Emancipation Proclamation." *Black Perspectives in Music* 16, no. 1 (1988): 63–80.

Bay, Mia. *To Tell the Truth Freely: The Life of Ida B. Wells*. New York: Hill and Wang, 2009.

———. *The White Image in the Black Mind: African-American Ideas about White People, 1830–1925*. New York: Oxford University Press, 2000.

Beckerman, Michael. *New Worlds of Dvořák: Searching in America for the Composer's Inner Life*. New York: W. W. Norton, 2003.

Beckert, Sven. *The Monied Metropolis: New York City and the Consolidation of the American Bourgeoisie, 1850–1896*. New York: Cambridge University Press, 2001.

Bederman, Gail. *Manliness and Civilization: A Cultural History of Gender and Race in the United States, 1880–1917*. Chicago: University of Chicago Press, 1995.

Berlin, Edward A. "Cole and Johnson Brothers' *The Evolution of 'Ragtime.'*" *Current Musicology* 36 (1983): 21–40.

———. *King of Ragtime: Scott Joplin and His Era*. New York: Oxford University Press, 1994.

———. *Ragtime*. Berkeley: Berkeley University Press, 1980.

———. *Reflections and Research on Ragtime*. New York: Institute for Studies in American Music, 1987.

Berlin, Ira. *Many Thousands Gone: The First Two Centuries of Slavery in North America*. Cambridge, Mass.: Harvard University Press, 1998.

Berresford, Mark. *That's Got 'Em: The Life and Music of Wilbur C. Sweatman*. Jackson: University of Mississippi Press, 2010.

Best, Wallace D. *Passionately Human, No Less Divine: Religion and Culture in Black Chicago, 1915–1952*. Princeton, N.J.: Princeton University Press, 2007.

Blackwelder, Julia Kirk. *Styling Jim Crow: African American Beauty Training during Segregation*. College Station: Texas A&M University Press, 2003.

Bourdieu, Pierre. *Distinction: A Social Critique of the Judgment of Taste*. Translated by Richard Nice. Cambridge, Mass.: Harvard University Press, 1984.

———. *The Field of Cultural Production: Essays on Art and Literature*. Translated by Randal Johnson. Cambridge: Polity, 1993.

———. "The Forms of Capital." In *Handbook of Theory and Research for the Sociology of Education*, edited by J. Richardson, 241–58. New York: Greenwood Press, 1986.

———, and Loïc J. D. Wacquant. *An Invitation to Reflexive Sociology*. Chicago: University of Chicago Press, 1992.

Brennan, Timothy. *Secular Devotion: Afro-Latin Music and Imperial Jazz*. New York: Verso, 2008.

Brooks, Daphne A. *Bodies in Dissent: Spectacular Performances of Race and Freedom, 1850–1910*. Durham, N.C.: Duke University Press, 2006.

Brooks, Tim, and Dick Spottsman. *Lost Sounds: Blacks and the Birth of the Recording Industry, 1890–1919*. Urbana: University of Illinois Press, 2004.

Brothers, Thomas. *Louis Armstrong's New Orleans*. New York: W. W. Norton, 2007.

Brown, Bill. "Reification, Reanimation, and the American Uncanny." *Critical Inquiry*, no. 32 (2006): 175–207.

Brown, Jayna. *Babylon Girls: Black Women Performers and the Shaping of the Modern*. Durham, N.C.: Duke University Press, 2008.

Brown, Scott E. *James P. Johnson: A Case of Mistaken Identity*. Metuchen, N.J.: Scarecrow Press, 1986.

Buckner, Reginald T., and Steven Weilnad, eds. *Jazz in Mind: Essays on the History and Meanings of Jazz*. Detroit: Wayne State University Press, 1991.

Butler, Judith. *Gender Trouble: Feminism and the Subversion of Identity*. New York: Routledge, 1990.

Camp, Stephanie M. H. *Closer to Freedom: Enslaved Women and Everyday Resistance in the Plantation South*. Chapel Hill: University of North Carolina Press, 2004.

Carney, Court. *Cuttin' Up: How Early Jazz Got America's Ear*. Lawrence: University of Kansas Press, 2009.

Carter, Marva Griffin. *Swing Along: The Musical Life of Will Marion Cook*. New York: Oxford University Press, 2008.

Certeau, Michel de. *The Practice of Everyday Life*. Translated by Steven Rendall. Berkeley: University of California Press, 1984.

Charters, Samuel, and Leonard Kunstad. *Jazz: A History of the New York Scene*. New York: Doubleday, 1962.

Chude-Sokei, Louis. *The Last Darkey: Bert Williams, Black-on-Black Minstrelsy, and the African Diaspora*. Durham, N.C.: Duke University Press, 2006.

Cook, Susan. "Passionless Dance and Passionate Reform: Respectability, Modernism, and the Social Dancing of Irene and Vernon Castle." In *The Passion of Music and Dance*, edited by William Washabaugh, 133–50. New York: Berg, 1998.

———. "Watching Our Step: Embodying Research, Telling Stories." In *Audible Traces*, edited by Elain Barkin and Lydia Hamessley, 177–212. Zurich: Cariofoli Verlagshaus, 1999.

Cronon, William. *Nature's Metropolis: Chicago and the Great West*. New York: W. W. Norton, 1991.

Cruz, Jon. *Culture on the Margins: The Black Spiritual and the Rise of American Cultural* Princeton, N.J.: Princeton University Press, 1999.

———. "Nineteenth-Century US Religious Crisis and the Sociology of Music." *Poetics*, no. 30 (2002): 5–18.

De Jongh, James. *Vicious Modernism: Black Harlem and the Literary Imagination*. New York: Cambridge University Press, 2009.

DeVeaux, Scott. "Constructing the Jazz Tradition: Jazz Historiography." *Black American Literature Forum* 25, no. 3 (1991): 525–60.

———. "The Emergence of the Jazz Concert." *American Music* 7, no. 1 (1989): 6–29.

Dodson, Howard, with Christopher Moore and Roberta Yancy. *The Black New Yorkers: The Schomburg Illustrated Chronology; Four Hundred Years of African American History*. New York: John Wiley and Sons, 2000.

Dormon, James H. "Shaping the Popular Image of Post-Reconstruction American Blacks: The 'Coon Song' Phenomenon of the Gilded Age." *American Quarterly* 40, no. 4 (1988): 450–71.

Douglas, Ann. *Terrible Honesty: Mongrel Manhattan in the 1920s*. New York: Noonday Press, 1995.

Dowling, Robert M. "A Marginal Man in Black Bohemia: James Weldon Johnson in the New York Tenderloin." In *Post-Bellum, Pre-Harlem: African American Literature and Culture, 1877–1919*, edited by Barbara McCaskill and Caroline Gebhard, 117–32. New York: New York University Press, 2006.

Dubin, Steven C. "Symbolic Slavery: Black Representations in Popular Culture." *Social Problems* 34, no. 2 (1987): 122–40.

Ellison, Ralph. *Shadow and Act*. New York: Random House, 1964.

———. "What America Would Be Like without Blacks." In *Going to the Territory*. New York: Random House, 1986.

Enstad, Nan. *Ladies of Labor, Girls of Adventure: Working Women, Popular Culture, and Labor Politics at the Turn of the Twentieth Century*. New York: Columbia University Press, 1999.

Erenberg, Lewis A. *Steppin' Out: New York Nightlife and the Transformation of American Culture, 1890–1930*. Chicago: University of Chicago Press, 1981.

Ewen, David. *The Story of George Gershwin*. New York: Henry Holt, 1947.

Favor, J. Martin. *Authentic Blackness: The Folk in the New Negro Renaissance*. Durham, N.C.: Duke University Press, 1999.

Fields, Barbara. "Ideology and Race in American History." In *Region, Race, and Reconstruction: Essays in Honor of C. Vann Woodward*, edited by J. Morgan Kousser and James M. McPherson, 143–77. New York: Oxford University Press, 1992.

Filene, Benjamin. *Romancing the Folk: Public Memory and American Roots Music*. Chapel Hill: University of North Carolina Press, 2000.

Fink, Leon. "A Voice for the People: A. Philip Randolph and the Cult of Leadership." In *Progressive Intellectuals and the Dilemmas of Democratic Commitment*. Cambridge, Mass.: Harvard University Press, 1997.

Floyd, Samuel A. The Invisibility and Fame of Harry T. Burleigh: Retrospect and Prospect." *Black Music Research Journal* 24, no. 2 (2004): 179–94.

———. *The Power of Black Music: Interpreting Its History from Africa to the United States*. New York: Oxford University Press, 1991.

Foley, Barbara. *Spectres of 1919: Class and Nation in the Making of the New Negro*. Chicago: University of Illinois Press, 2003.

Forbes, Camille F. *Introducing Bert Williams: Burnt Cork, Broadway, and the Story of America's First Black Star*. New York: Basic Civitas, 2008.

Foster, Helen Bradley. *"New Raiments of Self": African American Clothing in the Antebellum South*. New York: Berg, 1997.

Franklin, John Hope. *From Slavery to Freedom: A History of Negro Americans*. New York: Alfred A. Knopf, 1947.

Fredrickson, George. *The Black Image in the White Mind*. New York: Harper and Row, 1971.

Freeland, David. *Automats, Taxi Dances, and Vaudeville: Excavating Manhattan's Lost Places of Leisure*. New York: New York University Press, 2009.

Fronc, Jennifer. *New York Undercover: Private Surveillance in the Progressive Era*. Chicago: University of Chicago Press, 2009.

Furia, Philip. *The Poets of Tin Pan Alley: A History of America's Great Lyricists.* New York: Oxford University Press, 1990.

Gaines, Kevin K. "Assimilationist Minstrelsy as Racial Uplift Ideology: James D. Corrother's Literacy Quest for Black Leadership." *American Quarterly* 45, no. 3 (1993): 341–69.

———. *Uplifting the Race: Black Leadership, Politics, and Culture in the Twentieth Century.* Chapel Hill: University of North Carolina Press, 1996.

Garrett, Charles Hiroshi. *Struggling to Define a Nation: American Music and the Twentieth Century.* Berkeley: University of California Press, 2008.

Gates, Henry Louis, Jr. "The Trope of a New Negro and the Reconstruction of the Image of the Black." *Representations,* no. 24 (1988): 129–55.

Gatewood, William B. *Aristocrats of Color: The Black Elite, 1880–1920.* Bloomington: Indiana University Press, 1993.

Gems, Gerald R. "Blocked Shot: The Development of Basketball in the African American Community or Chicago." *Journal of Sports History* 22, no. 2 (1995): 135–48.

George-Graves, Nadine. "'Just Like Being at the Zoo': Primitivity and Ragtime Dance." In *Ballroom, Boogie, Shimmy, Shake: A Social and Popular Dance Reader,* edited by Julie Malnig. Urbana: University of Illinois Press, 2009.

Gilmore, Glenda. *Gender and Jim Crow: Women and the Politics of White Supremacy in North Carolina, 1896–1920.* Chapel Hill: University of North Carolina Press, 1996.

Gilroy, Paul. *The Black Atlantic: Modernity and Double Consciousness.* Cambridge, Mass.: Harvard University Press, 1993.

Gioia, Ted. *The History of Jazz.* New York: Oxford University Press, 1997.

Glasser, Ruth. *Music Is My Flag: Puerto Rican Musicians and Their New York Communities, 1917–1940.* Berkeley: University of California Press, 1995.

Glenn, Susan. *Female Spectacle: The Theatrical Roots of Modern Feminism.* Cambridge, Mass.: Harvard University Press, 2000.

Goines, Leonard, and Mikki Shepard. "James Reese Europe and His Impact on the New York Scene." *Black Music Research Journal* 10, no. 2 (1988): 5–8.

Golden, Eve. *Vernon and Irene Castle's Ragtime Revolution.* Lexington: University of Kentucky Press, 2007.

Gooding-Williams, Robert. "Du Bois, Politics, Aesthetics: An Introduction." *Public Culture* 17 no. 2 (2005): 203–15.

Gottschild, Brenda Dixon. *The Black Dancing Body: A Geography from Coon to Cool.* New York: Palgrave Macmillan, 2003.

———. *Digging the Africanist Presence in American Performance: Dance and Other Contexts.* Westport, Conn.: Greenwood Press, 1996.

———. *Waltzing in the Dark: African American Vaudeville and Race Politics in the Swing Era.* New York: St. Martin's Press, 2000.

Graber, Katie J. "American Dreams: Opera and Immigrants in Nineteenth-Century Chicago." Ph.D. diss., University of Wisconsin–Madison, 2010.

Green, Adam. *Selling the Race: Culture, Community, and Black Chicago, 1940–1955.* Chicago: University of Chicago Press, 2007.

Green, Constance McLaughlin. *The Secret City*. Princeton, N.J.: Princeton University Press, 1967.

Grosz, Elizabeth, and Gayatri Spivak. "Criticism, Feminism, and the Institution: An Interview with Gayatri Chakravorty Spivak." *Thesis Eleven* 10, no. 11 (1984–85): 175–87.

Hale, Grace Elizabeth. *Making Whiteness: The Culture of Segregation in the South, 1890–1940*. New York: Pantheon Books, 1998.

Hall, Stuart. "What Is This 'Black' in Black Popular Culture?" *Social Justice* 20, nos. 1-2 (1993): 104–11.

Hamm, Charles. "Dvořák in America: Nationalism, Racism, and National Race." In *Putting Popular Music in Its Place*, edited by Charles Hamm, 344–50. New York: Cambridge University Press, 1995.

———. "Dvořák, *Stephen Foster, and* American National Song." In *Dvořák in America 1892–1895*, edited by John C. Tibbetts, 149–56. Portland, Ore.: Amadeus Press, 1993.

Harris, Bill. *The Hellfighters of Harlem: African-American Soldiers Who Fought for the Right to Fight for Their Country*. New York: Carrol and Graf Publishers, 2002.

Harris, Jeffrey H. *Making Jazz French: Music and Modern Life in Interwar Paris*. Durham, N.C.: Duke University Press, 2003.

Harris, Stephen L. *Harlem's Hell Fighters: The African-American 369th Infantry in World War I*. Washington, D.C.: Brassey's, 2003.

Hartman, Saidiya V. *Scenes of Subjection: Terror, Slavery, and Self-Making in Nineteenth-Century America*. New York: Oxford University Press, 1997.

Henri, Florette. *Black Migration: Movement North, 1900–1920*. Garden City, N.Y.: Anchor Books, 1976.

Higginbotham, Evelyn Brooks. *Righteous Discontent: The Women's Movement in the Black Baptist Church*. Cambridge, Mass.: Harvard University Press, 1993.

Huggins, Nathan. *Harlem Renaissance*. New York: Oxford University Press, 1971.

Hutchinson, George. *The Harlem Renaissance in Black and White*. Cambridge, Mass.: Harvard University Press, 1995.

Jasen, David A., and Gene Jones. *Black Bottom Stomp: Eight Masters of Ragtime and Early Jazz*. New York: Routledge, 2002.

Jasen, David A., and Trebor Jay Tichenor. *Rags and Ragtime: A Musical History*. New York: Dover Publications, 1978.

Jones, LeRoi. *Blues People*. New York: William Morrow, 1963.

Jones, William P. *The Tribe of Black Ulysses: African American Lumber Workers in the Jim Crow South*. Urbana: Chicago University Press.

Kantrowitz, Stephen. *Ben Tillman and the Reconstruction of White Supremacy*. Chapel Hill: University of North Carolina Press, 2000.

———. *More than Freedom: Fighting for Black Citizenship in a White Republic, 1829–1889*. New York: Penguin Books, 2012.

Kasson, John F. *Amusing the Millions: Coney Island at the Turn of the Century*. New York: Hill and Wang, 1978.

Kelley, Robin D. G. *Freedom Dreams: The Black Radical Imagination*. Boston: Beacon Press, 2003.

———. "Notes on Deconstructing 'The Folk.'" *American Historical Review* 97, no. 5 (1992): 1400–1408.

———. "Without a Song: New York Musicians Strike Out against Technology." In *Three Strikes: Miners, Musicians, Salesgirls, and the Fighting Spirit of Labor's Last Century*, edited by Howard Zinn, Dana Frank, and Robin D. G. Kelley, 119–70. Boston: Beacon Press, 2001.

Kelley, Robin D. G., and Earl Lewis, eds. *To Make Our World Anew*. Vol. 2 of, *A History of African Americans since 1880*. New York: Oxford University Press, 2005.

Kimball, Robert, and William Bolcolm, eds. *Reminiscing with Noble Sissle and Eubie Blake*. New York: Cooper Square Press, 1973.

Kirchner, Bill, ed. *The Oxford Companion to Jazz*. New York: Oxford University Press, 2000.

Koenig, Karl, ed. *Jazz in Print (1859–1929): An Anthology of Early Source Readings in Jazz History*. London: Pendragon Press, 2002.

Kraft, James P. "Artists as Workers: Musicians and Trade Unionism in America, 1880–1917." *The Musical Quarterly* 79, no. 3 (1995): 512–43.

Krasner, David. *Beautiful Pageant: African American Theatre, Drama, and Performance in the Harlem Renaissance, 1910–1927*. New York: Palgrave Macmillan, 2002.

———. "Black Salome: Exoticism, Dance, and Racial Myth." In *African-American Performance and Theater History: A Critical Reader*, edited by Harry J. Elam and David Krasner, 192–211. New York: Oxford University Press, 2001.

———. "The Real Thing." In *Beyond Blackface: African Americans and the Creation of American Popular Culture, 1890–1930*, edited by W. Fitzhugh Brundage, 99–123. Chapel Hill: University of North Carolina Press, 2010.

———. *Resistance, Parody, and Double Consciousness in African American Theatre, 1895–1910*. New York: St. Martin's Press, 1997.

Leach, William. *Land of Desire: Merchants, Power, and the Rise of a New American Culture*. New York: Vintage, 1994.

Lears, T. J. Jackson. "The Concept of Cultural Hegemony: Problems and Possibilities." *American Historical Review* 90, no. 3 (1985): 567–93.

———. "Making Fun of Popular Culture." *American Historical Review* 97, no. 5 (1992): 1417–26.

———. *No Place of Grace: Antimodernism and the Transformation of American Culture, 1880–1920*. New York: Pantheon, 1981.

Lemke, Sieglinde. *Primitivist Modernism: Black Culture and the Origins of Transatlantic Modernism*. New York: Oxford University Press, 1998.

Leonard, Neil. *Jazz and the White Americans: The Acceptance of a New Art Form*. Chicago: University of Chicago Press, 1962.

Levine, Lawrence. *Black Culture and Black Consciousness: Afro-American Folk Thought from Slavery to Freedom*. New York: Oxford University Press, 1977.

———. *Highbrow/Lowbrow: The Emergence of Cultural Hierarchy in America*. Cambridge, Mass.: Harvard University Press, 1988.

Levy, Alan. *Musical Nationalism: American Composers' Search for Identity*. Westport, Conn.: Greenwood Press, 1983.

Levy, Eugene. *James Weldon Johnson: Black Leader, Black Voice.* Chicago: University of Chicago Press, 1976.

Lewis, David Levering. Introduction to *The Portable Harlem Renaissance Reader,* edited by David Levering Lewis, xiii–xli. New York: Viking, 1994.

———. *When Harlem Was in Vogue.* New York: Alfred A. Knopf, 1979.

Lhamon, W. T. *Raising Cain: Blackface Performance from Jim Crow to Hip Hop.* Cambridge, Mass.: Harvard University Press, 1998.

Lipsitz, George. "The Racialization of Space and the Spatialization of Race: Theorizing the Hidden Architecture of Landscape." *Landscape Journal* 26, no. 1 (2007): 10–23.

Logan, Rayford W. *The Negro in American Life and Thought: The Nadir, 1877–1901.* New York: Dial Press, 1954.

Lott, Eric. *Love and Theft: Blackface Minstrelsy and the American Working Class.* New York: Oxford University Press, 1993.

Lutz, Tom. "Curing the Blues: W. E. B. Du Bois, Fashionable Diseases, and Degraded Music." *Black Music Research Journal* 11, no. 2 (1991): 137–56.

Madell, Martha Jane. *Enter the New Negroes: Images and Race in American Culture.* Cambridge, Mass.: Harvard University Press, 2005.

Magee, Jeffrey. "Ragtime and Early Jazz." In *Cambridge History of American Music,* edited by David Nicholls, 388–417. New York: Cambridge University Press, 1998.

———. *The Uncrowned King of Swing: Fletcher Henderson and Big Band Jazz.* New York: Oxford University Press, 2005.

Mahar, William J. *Behind the Burnt Cork Mask: Early Blackface Minstrelsy and Antebellum American Popular Culture.* Urbana: University of Illinois Press, 1998.

Malnig, Julie. "Apaches, Tangos, and Other Indecencies: Women, Dance, and New York Nightlife of the 1910s." In *Ballroom, Boogie, Shimmy, Sham, Shake: A Social and Popular Reader,* edited by Julie Malnig, 72–90. Urbana: University of Illinois Press, 2009.

Marcuse, Maxwell F. *Tin Pan Alley in Gaslight: A Saga of the Songs that Made the Gray Nineties "Gay."* New York: Century House, 1959.

Markovitz, Jonathan. *Legacies of Lynching: Racial Violence and Memory.* Minneapolis: University of Minnesota Press, 2004.

Martin, George. *The Damrosch Dynasty.* Boston: Houghton Mifflin, 1983.

Masur, Kate. *An Example for All the Land: Emancipation and the Struggle over Equality in Washington, D.C.* Chapel Hill: University of North Carolina Press, 2010.

McBee, Randy D. *Dance Hall Days: Intimacy and Leisure among Working-Class Immigrants in the United States.* New York: New York University Press, 2000.

McClary, Susan. *Feminine Endings: Music, Gender, and Sexuality.* Minnesota: University of Minnesota Press, 2002.

McGinty, Doris. "Gifted Minds and Pure Hearts: Mary L. Europe and Estelle Pinckney Webster." *Journal of Negro Education* 51, no. 3 (1982): 266–77.

———. "The Black Presence in the Music of Washington, D.C.: 1843–1904." In *More Than Dancing: Essays on Afro-American Music and Musicians,* edited by Irene V. Jackson, 81–104. Westport, Conn.: Greenwood Press, 1985.

———. "'That You Came So Far to See Us': Coleridge-Taylor in America." *Black Music Research Journal* 21, no. 2 (2001): 197–234.

McKittrick, Katherine. *Demonic Grounds: Black Women and the Cartographies of Struggle*. Minneapolis: University of Minnesota Press, 2006.

Miller, Karl Hagstrom. *Segregating Sound: Inventing Folk and Pop Music in the Age of Jim Crow*. Durham, N.C.: Duke University Press, 2010.

Mitchell, Koritha. *Living with Lynching: African American Lynching Plays, Performance, and Citizenship, 1890–1930*. Urbana: University of Illinois Press, 2011.

Moore, Jacqueline M. *Leading the Race: The Transformation of the Black Elite in the Nation's Capital, 1880–1920*. Charlottesville: University of Virginia Press, 1999.

Morath, Max. "Thinking about the Music." In *The Road to Ragtime*, 134–37. Virginia Beach, Va.: Donning Company, 1999.

Morgan, Edmund S. *American Slavery, American Freedom: The Ordeal of Colonial Virginia*. New York: Norton, 1975.

Morgan, Phillip D. *Slave Counterpoint: Black Culture in the Eighteenth-Century Chesapeake and Lowcountry*. Chapel Hill: University of North Carolina Press, 1998.

Moses, Wilson Jeremiah. *The Golden Age of Black Nationalism, 1850–1925*. New York: Oxford University Press, 1978.

———. "The Lost World of the Negro, 1895–1919: Black Literary and Intellectual Life before the 'Renaissance.'" *Black American Literature Forum* 21, nos. 1–2 (1987): 61–84.

Muir, Peter C. *Long Lost Blues: Popular Blues in America, 1850–1920*. Urbana: University of Illinois Press, 2010.

Mumford, Kevin J. *Interzones: Black/White Sex Districts in Chicago and New York in the Early Twentieth Century*. New York: Columbia University Press, 1997.

Nasaw, David. *Going Out: The Rise and Fall of Public Amusements*. Cambridge, Mass.: Harvard University Press, 1999.

Nelson, Peter N. *A More Unbending Battle: The Harlem Hellfighters' Struggle for Freedom in WWI and Equality at Home*. New York: Basic Civitas Book, 2009.

Newman, Richard. "'The Brightest Star': Aida Overton Walker in the Age of Ragtime and the Cakewalk." *Prospects* 18 (1993): 465–81.

Nowlin, Michael. "James Weldon Johnson's Black Manhattan and the Kingdom of Culture." *African American Review* 39, no. 3 (2005): 315–25.

Ogasapian John, and N. Lee Orr. *Music of the Gilded Age*. Westport, Conn.: Greenwood Press, 2007.

Osofsky, Gilbert. *Harlem: The Making of a Ghetto: Negro New York, 1890–1930*. New York: New York Public Library, 1963.

Ottley, Roi, and William Weatherby. *The Negro in New York*. New York: New York Public Library, 1967.

Patterson, Lindsay, ed. *The Afro-American in Music and Art*. Cornwells Heights, Pa.: Publishers Agency, 1976.

Peiss, Kathy. *Cheap Amusements: Working Women and Leisure in Turn-of-the-Century New York*. Philadelphia: Temple University Press, 1986.

Peress, Maurice. *Dvořák to Duke Ellington: A Conductor Explores America's Music and Its African American Roots*. New York: Oxford University Press, 2004.

Perry, Elisabeth I. "'The General Motherhood of the Commonwealth': Dance Hall Reform in the Progressive Era." *American Quarterly* 37, no. 5 (1985): 719–33.

Perry, Imani. *Prophets of the Hood: Politics and Poetics in Hip Hop*. Durham, N.C.: Duke University Press, 2004.

Perry, Jeffrey Babcock. *Hubert Harrison: The Voice of Harlem Radicalism, 1883–1918*. New York: Columbia University Press, 2008.

Ping-Robbins, Nancy R. *Scott Joplin: A Guide to Research*. New York: Routledge, 1998.

Putnam, Lara. *Radical Moves: Caribbean Migrants and the Politics of Race in the Jazz Age*. Chapel Hill: University of North Carolina Press, 2013.

Quintana, Ryan A. "The Plantation All in Disorder: Black Carolinians' Spatial Practices and the Construction of the Lowcountry Landscape, 1739–1830." Ph.D., diss., University of Wisconsin–Madison, 2010.

Radano, Ronald M. "Hot Fantasies: American Modernism and the Idea of Black Rhythm." In *Music of the Racial Imagination*, edited by Ronald M. Radano and Philip V. Bohlman, 459–80. Chicago: University of Chicago Press, 2000.

———. *Lying Up a Nation: Race and Black Music*. Chicago: University of Chicago Press, 2003.

Reed, Adolph L., Jr. *W. E. B. Du Bois and American Political Thought: Fabianism and the Color Line*. New York: Oxford University Press, 1997.

Richardson, Riché. *Black Masculinity and the U.S. South: From Uncle Tom to Gangsta*. Athens: University of Georgia Press, 2007.

Riis, Jacob A. *How the Other Half Lives: Studies among the Tenements of New York*. Edited and by David Leviatin. Boston: Bedford/St. Martin's, 2011.

Riis, Thomas L. "'Bob' Cole: His Life and His Legacy to Black Musical Theater." *Black Perspective in Music* 13, no. 2 (1985): 135–50.

———. *Just before Jazz: Black Musical Theater in New York, 1890 to 1915*. Washington, D.C.: Smithsonian Institution Press, 1989.

Roberts, John Storm. *Latin Jazz: The First of the Fusions, 1880s to Today*. New York: Schirmer Books, 1999.

Robinson, Danielle. "The Ugly Duckling: The Refinement of Ragtime Dancing and the Mass Production and Marketing of Modern Social Dance." *Dance Research* 28, no. 2 (2010): 179–99.

Roediger, David R. *The Wages of Whiteness: Race and the Making of the American Working Class*. New York: Verso, 1991.

Rogin, Michael. "'Democracy and Burnt Cork': The End of Blackface, the Beginning of Civil Rights." *Representations*, no. 46 (1994): 4–34.

Rose, Tricia. *Black Noise: Rap Music and Black Culture in Contemporary America*. Middletown, Conn.: Wesleyan University Press, 1994.

Runstedtler, Theresa. *Jack Johnson, Rebel Sojourner: Boxing in the Shadow of the Global Color Line*. Berkeley: University of California Press, 2012.

Sampson, Henry T. *Ghost Walks: A Chronological History of Blacks in Show Business, 1865–1910*. Metuchen, N.J.: Scarecrow Press, 1988.

Saxton, Alexander. *The Rise and Fall of the White Republic: Class Politics and Mass Culture in Nineteenth Century America*. New York: Verso, 1990.

Schechter, Patricia A. *Ida B. Wells-Barnett and American Reform, 1880–1930*. Chapel Hill: University of North Carolina Press, 2000.

Scheiber, Andrew J. "The Folk, the School, and the Marketplace: Locations of Culture in the Souls of Black Folk." In *Post-Bellum, Pre-Harlem: African American Literature and Culture, 1877–1919*, edited by Barbara McCaskill and Caroline Gebhard, 250–67. New York: New York University Press, 2006.

Scheiner, Seth. *Negro Mecca: A History of the Negro in New York City, 1865–1920*. New York: New York University Press, 1965.

Schuller, Gunther. *Early Jazz: Its Roots and Musical Development*. New York: Oxford University Press, 1968.

———. *Musings*. New York: Oxford University Press, 1986.

Scott, Joan W. "The Evidence of Experience." *Critical Inquiry* 17 (1991): 773–97.

Seniors, Paula Marie. *Beyond Lift Every Voice and Sing: The Culture of Uplift, Identity, and Politics in Black Musical Theater*. Columbus: Ohio State University Press, 2009.

Seigel, Micol. *Uneven Encounters: Making Race and Nation in Brazil and the United States*. Durham, N.C.: Duke University Press, 2009.

Shack, William A. *Harlem in Montmartre: A Paris Jazz Story between the Great Wars*. Berkeley: University of California Press, 2001.

Shaw, Stephanie J. *What a Woman Ought to Be and to Do: Black Professional Women Workers during the Jim Crow Era*. Chicago: University of Chicago Press, 1996.

Shelby, Tommie. *We Who Are Dark: The Philosophical Foundations of Black Solidarity*. Cambridge, Mass.: Harvard University Press, 2005.

Shirley, Wayne D. "The House of Melody: A List of Publications of the Gotham-Attucks Music Company at the Library of Congress." *Black Perspective in Music* 15, no. 1 (1987): 79–112.

Singh, Nikhil Pal. *Black Is a Country: Race and the Unfinished Struggle for Democracy*. Cambridge, Mass.: Harvard University Press, 2004.

Slotkin, Richard. *Lost Battalions: The Great War and the Crisis of American Nationality*. New York: Henry Holt, 2005.

Snyder, Jean E. "A Great and Noble School of Music: Dvořák, Harry T. Burleigh, and the African American Spiritual." In *Dvořák in America, 1892–1895*, edited by John C. Tibbetts, 123–48. Portland, Ore.: Amadeus Press, 1993.

Sotiropoulos, Karen. *Staging Race: Black Performers in Turn-of-the-Century America*. Cambridge, Mass.: Harvard University Press, 2006.

Southern, Eileen. *The Music of Black Americans: A History*. New York: W. W. Norton, 1971.

———, ed. *Readings in Black American Music*. New York: W. W. Norton, 1971.

Spaeth, Sigmund. *A History of Popular Music in America*. New York: Random House, 1948.

Spencer, Jon Michael. *The New Negroes and Their Music: The Success of the Harlem Renaissance*. Knoxville: University of Tennessee Press, 1997.

Stansell, Christine. *American Moderns: Bohemian New York and the Creation of a New Century*. New York: Metropolitan Books, 2000.

Staples, Robert. *Black Masculinity: The Black Male's Role in American Society*. Sausalito, Calif.: Black Scholar Press, 1982.

Star, S. Frederick . "Oberlin's Ragtimer: Will Marion Cook." *Oberlin Alumni Magazine* 85 (1989): 13–15.

Stearns, Jean, and Marshall Stearns. *Jazz Dance: The Story of American Vernacular Dance*. New York: MacMillan, 1968.

Stoddard, Tom. *Jazz on the Barbary Coast*. Berkeley: Heyday Books, 1982.

Stovall, Tyler. *Paris Noir: African Americans in the City of Light*. Boston: Houghton Mifflin Company, 1996.

Suisman, David. *Selling Sounds: The Commercial Revolution in American Music*. Cambridge, Mass.: Harvard University Press, 2009.

Summers, Martin. *Manliness and Its Discontents: The Black Middle Class and the Transformation of Masculinity, 1900–1930*. Chapel Hill: University of North Carolina Press, 2003.

Sundquist, Eric J. "Red, White, Black, and Blue: The Color of American Modernism." *Transition*, no. 70 (1996): 94–115.

Swiencicki, Mark A. "Consuming Brotherhood: Men's Culture, Style, and Recreation as Consumer Culture, 1880–1930." In *Consumer Society in American History: A Reader*, edited by Lawrence B. Glickman, 207–40. Ithaca, N.Y.: Cornell University Press, 1999.

Tawa, Nicholas E. *The Way to Pin Pan Alley: American Popular Song, 1866–1910*. New York: Schirmer Books, 1990.

Taylor, Clarence. *The Black Churches of Brooklyn*. New York: Columbia University Press, 1996.

Tibbetts, John C. "The Missing Title Page: Dvořák and the American National Song" In *Music and Culture in America, 1861–1918*, edited by Michael Saffle, 343–65. New York: Garland, 1998.

Tischler, Barbara L. *An American Music: The Search for an American Musical Identity*. New York: Oxford University Press, 1986.

Toll, Robert. *Blacking Up: The Minstrel Show in Nineteenth-Century America*. New York: Oxford University Press, 1974.

Tosches, Nick. *Where Dead Voices Gather*. New York: Little, Brown, 2001.

Tucker, Mark. "In Search of Will Vodery." *Black Music Journal* 1, no. 1 (1996): 123–80.

Vogel, Shane. *The Scene of Harlem Cabaret: Race, Sexuality, Performance*. Chicago: University of Chicago Press, 2009.

Von Eschen, Penny. *Satchmo Blows Up the World: Jazz Ambassadors Play the Cold War*. Cambridge, Mass.: Harvard University Press, 2006.

Wagner, Ann. *Adversaries of Dance: From the Puritans to the Present*. Urbana: University of Illinois Press, 1997.

Waldo, Terry. *This Is Ragtime*. New York: Hawthorn Books, 1976.

Webb, Barbara L. "Authentic Possibilities: Plantation Performance in the 1890s." *Theatre Journal* 56, no. 1 (2004): 63–82.

Weems, Robert E. *Desegregating the Dollar: African American Consumerism in the Twentieth Century.* New York: New York University Press, 1998.

Weheliye, Alexander G. *Phonographies: Groove in Sonic Afro-Modernity.* Durham, N.C.: Duke University Press Books, 2005.

Welburn, Ron. "James Reese Europe and the Infancy of Jazz Criticism." *Black Music Research Journal* 7 (1987): 35–44.

White, Shane, and Graham White. *Stylin': African American Expressive Culture, from Its Beginnings to the Zoot Suit.* Ithaca, N.Y.: Cornell University Press, 1998.

Williams, Raymond. *Keywords: A Vocabulary of Culture and Society.* New York: Oxford University Press, 1985.

Wilson, Olly. "The Black-American Composer and the Orchestra in the Twentieth Century." *Black Perspective in Music* 14, no. 1 (1996): 26–34.

Wintz, Cary D., ed. *The Harlem Renaissance, 1920–1940: Emergence of the Harlem Renaissance.* New York: Garland, 1996.

Wintz Cary D., and Paul Finkelman. *Index.* Vol. 2 of *Encyclopedia of the Harlem Renaissance.* New York: Routledge, 2004.

Wolcott, Victoria W. *Remaking Respectability: African American Women in Interwar Detroit.* Chapel Hill: University of North Carolina Press, 2001.

Woll, Allen. *Black Musical Theatre: From Coontown to Dreamgirls.* Baton Rouge: Louisiana State University Press, 1989.

Wondrich, David. *Stomp and Swerve: American Music Gets Hot, 1843–1924.* Chicago: Chicago Review Press, 2003.

Index

Page numbers in italics represent illustrations.

8, 16–17, 37–40, 68, 69; as American music, 3, 9, 15, 38, 92, 174, 187, 188–90; history of (in U.S.), 6–8, 26, 27, 42, 43, 92, 93, 112, 120, 192; commodification of, 6–9, 12–15, 19, 22–31, 63–73, 145–52, 163–67, 173–77, 188–90; and racial essentialism, 6–9, 14, 15, 26, 30–32, 40–43, 56, 57, 70, 87, 88, 150, 155, 158, 167, 175, 182–90, 193, 215, 216; African Americans' debates about, 9–11, 18, 19, 33, 39–52, 68, 79–88; and coon songs, 16, 17, 24, 28–32; and development, 35, 36, 38, 44, 45, 76, 88–97, 171, 187, 188; and Spanish rhythm, 70, 71; white critics of, 77, 78, 182, 183, 198; in lobster palaces, 133, 134, 145–52; and Memphis Students' concerts, 138–40; and James Reese Europe's Society Orchestra, 202–8, 211–13. *See also* Tenderloin

Black Patti Troubadours, 63, 82, 94, 161

Blake, Eubie: on origins of ragtime, 26; in the Tenderloin, 99, 120, 123, *128*; background of, 103–5, 116; and James P. Johnson, 152; and Clef Club, 155–60; on faking sight-reading, 158; and *Shuffle Along*, 161; on Clef Club society orchestras, 202, 204; on James Reese Europe, 218

Bok, Edward, 71, 72

Book of American Negro Poetry, The (1922), 223

Book of American Negro Spirituals, The (1925), 224

Bradford, Perry, 113

Brazilian maxixe, 70

Broadway theaters: and Manhattan modernity, 3, 19–24, 143; as site for transformation in black cultural value, 5, 6, 50; as site for ragging uplift, 11, 74, 75, 80–98; and *Clorindy*, 16, 17; and Tenderloin, 23; and coon songs, 29–31; and Bob Cole's goals, 49; and black commercial strategies,

50, 52; and Williams and Walker musicals, 53, 54, 56; and Cole and the Johnsons, 64, 65, 71; and black rhythms, 64, 79–71; social overlap with Tenderloin, 113; influence on the New York piano sound, 122; and social dance in lobster palaces, 133, 134, 143–48; and the Memphis Students, 140; and loss of major black musical companies, 161; and codification of black music, 167

Brown, Lawrence, 224

Brown, Tom, 95

Bryant, Fred, 120

Brymn, J. T., 52

Burleigh, Harry T.: and studies with Dvořák, 33; and introduction of spirituals to Dvořák, 37; and introduction of Will Marion Cook to Dvořák, 40; and Abbie Mitchell, 43; and James Reese Europe, 137; and Music School Settlement, 178; and songs of performed by Clef Club Symphony Orchestra, 180, 182; and New Choral Society, 187

Café de l'Opera, 144

Cakewalk: and *Clorindy*, 16, 17, 41; origins of, 53; and Aida Overton Walker, 53, 54; in England, 53, 54, 82, 83; and rise of ragtime, 69; and Williams and Walker's influence on lobster palace patrons, 145; at Manhattan Casino, 177; as antecedent to modern dances, 199

"Camptown Races," 25

Cannibal King, The (1901), 61, 75

Carnegie Hall: and Clef Club concerts, 1–3, 134, 137, 178–81; and prestige of, 1, 5, 170

Castle, Irene and Vernon: and arrival in New York markets, 191, 196; and James Reese Europe, 193–96; and popularity of social dance, 197; racial appropriation, 197, 201, 202; and background of, 198, 199; and role in raising cultural value of social dance, 199–201, 204, *207*; on refinement, modernity, and health, 200; and the fox-trot, 206; on increasing black musical value, 208–16; Irene Castle and the New Woman, 209, 210; and "Whirlwind Tour," 210, 211

"Castle Half and Half, The," 206

Castle House, 200, 201, 210

"Castle House Rag, The," 206, *207*

"Castles in Europe, The," 206

"Castle Lame Duck, The," 206

"Castle Perfect Trot," 206

"Castle Walk, The," 206

Champagne Charlie (1901), 64

Charleston (dance), 177

"Charleston Rag," 156

Churchill's, 144

Classical music. *See* Art music

Clef Club: and Clef Club Symphony Orchestra, 1–3, 8, *164–65*; and changes in labor practices and black musical value, 5, 134, 142, 154–60, 184, 185–88; origins of, 134, 141–42, 153; early years of, 154–60; "preamble," 156; and society orchestras, *157*, 202, *203*; and racism, 158–60; and Clef Club Orchestra, 163–78; at Carnegie Hall, 178–81; and the American Federation of Music, 214

"Clef Club March," 2, 163, 169, 180

Clorindy; or, The Origin of the Cakewalk (1898), 16–18, 45, 52, 74, 138; and Broadway audition, 24; and composition of, 41; and Abbie Mitchell, 43

Cole, Bob (Robert Allen Cole Jr.): and Will Marion Cook, 40; and debates with Cook, 48, 49; and the Johnson brothers, 49, 52, *65*; and *A Trip to Coontown*, 52, 63; as Willie Wayside (whiteface stage character), 63; and role in uplifting ragtime, 64; and role in expanding music markets, 64–72; and *The Cannibal King*, 74, 75; and

Black Patti Troubadours, 82, 117, 220; as stage performer, 89, *90*, 91; and "Colored Actor's Declaration of Independence," 94; and the Frogs, *95*, 96; and James Reese Europe, 141, 193; death of, 160, 189

Cole and Johnson (songwriters), 49, 52, 62, *65*, *90*, 97, 117; and role in expanding music markets, 64–72; and *Ladies Home Journal*, 71–72; and *The Cannibal King*, 74, 75; and stage performance, 89, 91; and James Reese Europe, 141, 153. *See also* Cole, Bob; Johnson, J. Rosamond; Johnson, James Weldon

Coleridge-Taylor, Samuel, 180

Colored American Magazine, The: on Cole and Johnson songs, 66; on popular culture and uplift, 80; and Lester Walton, 80, 95; Aida Overton Walker in, 82–84; on Cole and Johnson stage performance, 91, 92; on Prince Hall Freemason attire, 130

"Come Out, Dinah, on the Green," 64

"Congo Love Song, The," 65

Cook, Will Marion: and *Clorindy*, 16, 17, 24, 45, 46; background of, 18, 33, 84, 85, 108; and introduction to popular culture, 18–20, 22; and the Tenderloin, 23; and Dvořák, 33, 40; and Bob Cole, 40; on "real Negro melodies," 40, 41, 44, 85; writing *Clorindy*, 41; on spirituals and black music history, *42*, 43, 67, 87, 135; and Abbie Mitchell, 43; and black nationalism, 43–44, 84, 85; on musical "development," 44, 45, 88, 89; on ragtime, 44, 220; and entrance into music markets, 45, 46; and debates with Bob Cole, 48, 49; and Williams and Walker, 49, 52, 53; and *Abyssinia*, 54, 56, 86; on problems with racial essentialism, 58; and ragging uplift, 74, 75, 79; and commonalities with and influences on James Reese

77, 78; in Tenderloin, 99, 100–103, 108, 123, 124; in lobster palaces, 146, 147, 149–52; in Manhattan Casino, 163–67; and James Reese Europe, 171, 175, 182, 185, 186, 213, 215, 216; and the Castles' promotion of, 202, 215, 216

"Rain Song," 181

Randolph, A. Philip, 76

Reconstruction, 3, 13, 34

Rector's, 144–47

Red Moon, The (1908), 141

Respectability, 10, 19, 34; popular culture alternatives to, 10, 75, 79–88, 91, 92, 96, 118; and fashionable alternatives to, 115, 116, 126–30; and black elites' clothing style, 126, 129, 130

Rhythm. *See* Ragtime rhythms

Rice, Ed, 24

Rice, Thomas D. ("Daddy"), 6, 12

Roberts, Charles "Lucky," 99, 119, 121, 122

Rogers, Alex, 95

Royal Poinriana Quartet, 180

Russell, Sylvester, 63

St. Phillps Church Choir, 179, 180

Sawyer, Joan, 199

Schindler, Kurt, 187

Seldes, Gilbert, 175

Seminole, Paul, 119, 120

Shelton, Aggie, 104

Shipp, Jesse, 52; and the Frogs, *95, 96*

Shoo-Fly Regiment, The (1906), 141, 153

Shubert, Lee, 208

Shuffle Along (1921), 161

Sissle, Noble: on Clef Club Symphony Orchestra, 1; on Clef Club Inc., 142, 153; and *Shuffle Along*, 161; on Clef Club Orchestra, 169, 179–81; on Clef Club society orchestras, 202, 206; and "Show Business" (column), 217–20; on James Reese Europe, 218

Sleeping Beauty and the Beast, The (1901), 64

Smart Set, 97, 161

Smith, Bessie, 219

Smith, Russell, 157

Smith, Willie "the Lion": and piano playing in Tenderloin, 100, 103, 109; background of, 110, 111, 116; on uplift, 111; on musical labor, 118, 119; and piano performance, *120*; as critique of other pianists, 123; attitude and clothing style of, 124–27, 130, 149; on Clef Club, 157, 206

Social dance: in England, 53, 54, 82, 83; and cakewalk, 53, 54, 145, 146; and middle-class whites, 145–47, 151, 152; at Manhattan Casino, 166; and James Weldon Johnson, 192; and white critics of, 198; and working-class whites, 201. *See also* Castle, Irene and Vernon

Society of the Sons of New York, 105

Sons of Ham (1900), 61, 82

Souls of Black Folk, The (1903), 37, 89, 219

Sousa, John Philip: influence on James Reese Europe, 2, 132, 136, 218

Spirituals: as performed by Clef Club orchestras, 2, 3, 163, 179, 180; and popularization of, 8; and racial representation, 19, 172; and debates about, 36–40; and Cole and Johnson, 67, 68; and Rosamond Johnson, 92; James Reese Europe on, 184–87

"Star-Spangled Banner, The," 121

Stereotypes. *See* Racial stereotypes

"Still wie die Nacht," 91

"Strength of the Nation," 180

"Sugar Babe," 66

"Swing Along," 151, 180, 181

"Swing Low, Sweet Chariot," 68

Supper Club (1901), 64

Syncopation. *See* Ragtime rhythms

Talented Tenth: defined by W. E. B. Du Bois, 9; and ragtime, 9, 11, 19, 41–45, 67, 74–80; and uplifting racial representations, 9–11, 18–20, 33–40; and Will Marion Cook, 18–20, 33, 41–45; and James Monroe Trotter,

Tenderloin, 107; fashion of, 115, 116; and cakewalk on Broadway, 145, 146; death of, 161, 189; and Du Bois, 220

Walker, George, Jr., 163

Wall, E. Berry, 148

Walton, Florence, 199

Walton, Lester: on professional value, 62; on popular culture and uplift, 80; and the Frogs, *95*, 96; on *The Red Moon* and racism, 141; on the Clef Club, 170, 174, 181; on Will Marion Cook and Harry T. Burleigh, 186, 187; on the Castles, 196, 214

Wanamaker, John, 141; and family parties, 142, 152, 169, 203

Washington, Booker T., 11–12, 218; invoked by Williams and Walker, 76, 81

Washington, D.C.: and James Reese Europe, 11, 132, 136, 137, 178; and Will Marion Cook, 25, 33, 45; and James Monroe Trotter, 34; and *Negro Music Journal*, 40, 171; and Treble Clef Club, 171

Washington Conservatory of Music, 40

Wetherly, Joseph "Frenchy," 163

White, Clarence, C., 40

White supremacy: reformation of, 3, 13, 14, 31, 34, 78, 177; and slavery, 13, 68, 69; and black masculinity, 125, 126

"Who Dat Say Chicken in Dis Crowd?," 16–17, 41, 79, 80

Wilkins, Barron D., 102, 113

Wilkins, Leroy, 113

Williams, Bert, 7; musicals of, 46, 49, 53, *54*, *55*; and role in selling racial authenticity, 50, 58–61, 185, 228; at the Hotel Marshall, 51, 52, 167; as Jonah Man, 56; and professional value, 62; and uplift, 81; and role in and ragging uplift, 82; on black nationalism and Africa, 86–88; and the Frogs, *95*, 96, 156; and role in commodifying black music, 97; in Tenderloin, 107, 112; fashion of, 115, 116; and cakewalk on Broadway, 145, 146; and Du Bois, 220

Williams and Walker Company, 53, *54*, 56; and racial authenticity, 60; and professional value, 62; and racial uplift, 80–82; and critique of Talented Tenth, 82–88; on black nationalism and Africa, 86–88; and cakewalk on Broadway, 145, 146; demise of, 161, 189

Wilson, Jack "the Bear," 99

Wilson, Woodrow, 221

Wolcott, Joe, 107, 115

Wolford, Huey, 124

World War I, 217, 221–23

Wright, Herbert, 217

CPSIA information can be obtained
at www.ICGtesting.com
Printed in the USA
LVOW12s1803240117
522011LV00005B/410/P